Pearl Harbor Declassified

ALSO BY JAMES M. D'ANGELO

Victory at Midway: The Battle That Changed the Course of World War II (McFarland, 2018)

Pearl Harbor Declassified

The Evidence of American Foreknowledge of the Attack

JAMES M. D'ANGELO

Foreword by William S. Dudley

McFarland & Company, Inc., Publishers
Jefferson, North Carolina

LIBRARY OF CONGRESS CATALOGUING-IN-PUBLICATION DATA

Names: D'Angelo, James M., 1937– author. | Dudley, William S., writer of foreword.
Title: Pearl Harbor declassified : the evidence of American foreknowledge of the attack / James M. D'Angelo ; foreword by William S. Dudley
Description: Jefferson, North Carolina : McFarland & Company, Inc., Publishers, 2021 Includes bibliographical references and index.
Identifiers: LCCN 2021030883 | ISBN 9781476684383 (paperback : acid free paper) ∞
ISBN 9781476642376 (ebook)
Subjects: LCSH: Pearl Harbor (Hawaii), Attack on, 1941. | Roosevelt, Franklin D. (Franklin Delano), 1882-1945. | World War, 1939-1945—Naval operations, American. | Military intelligence—United States—History—20th century. | Strategy—History—20th century. | World War, 1939-1945—United States. | BISAC: HISTORY / Military / World War II
Classification: LCC D767.92 .D36 2021 | DDC 940.54/26693—dc23
LC record available at https://lccn.loc.gov/2021030883

BRITISH LIBRARY CATALOGUING DATA ARE AVAILABLE

ISBN (print) 978-1-4766-8438-3
ISBN (ebook) 978-1-4766-4237-6

© 2021 James M. D'Angelo. All rights reserved

No part of this book may be reproduced or transmitted in any form or by any means, electronic or mechanical, including photocopying or recording, or by any information storage and retrieval system, without permission in writing from the publisher.

Front cover image: Naval photograph of battleships USS *West Virginia* and USS *Tennessee* after the Japanese attack on Pearl Harbor, December 7, 1941 (National Archives and Records Administration)

Printed in the United States of America

McFarland & Company, Inc., Publishers
Box 611, Jefferson, North Carolina 28640
www.mcfarlandpub.com

This book is dedicated to all the men who fought and those who died in the Japanese attack on Pearl Harbor on December 7, 1941, and is devoted to expressing the truth about the U.S. government's foreknowledge of the attack.

Acknowledgments

I would like to express my appreciation and gratitude to my wife, Margaret Christine Sims, for her support and effort in editing this book. Her diligence, literary sense, and commitment greatly contributed to the quality of this work.

I also want to acknowledge the support and suggestions offered by my friend, Dr. William S. Dudley, former director of the Naval Historical Center (now Naval History and Heritage Command) throughout this process. His depth of knowledge as a historian and long experience as an author and editor have been invaluable, and I am grateful for his guidance in those areas.

Another significant contributor to whom I owe a debt of gratitude is Thomas K. Kimmel, Jr., the grandson of Admiral Husband E. Kimmel, commander of the Pacific Fleet at the time of the attack on Pearl Harbor. He is a Pearl Harbor scholar and was a 25-year career FBI agent. Tom is a graduate of the U.S. Naval Academy, served in the U.S. Navy during the Vietnam War, and attended John Marshall Law School prior to joining the FBI. He is the author of many scholarly articles about Pearl Harbor and a frequent guest speaker at many notable occasions both in the United States and throughout the world. I owe a great debt of gratitude to Captain James A. Noone, USNR (Ret.), lawyer, copy editor at the *Scranton Tribune* and *Washington Post*, and longtime member of the National Press Club, for his scrupulous editing of the entire manuscript. I want to especially thank Captain Jack Crawford, USN (Ret.), a Battle of Midway veteran (USS *Yorktown*-CV-5), for his assistance in introducing us to Tom Kimmel. Jack is a longtime supporter of the International Midway Memorial Foundation and a personal friend. Jack was kind enough to review the manuscript before publication and offer helpful suggestions.

I also want to very much thank the NSA Museum of Cryptology, Colonel Bill Williams, USAF, (Ret.), Naval History and Heritage Command's John DeLuca, the National Archives' Nathaniel Patch, National Archives of the United Kingdom, and the FDR Library at Hyde Park for their great assistance in helping me in my research and providing declassified documents and photographs for this book.

Table of Contents

Acknowledgments — vi
Foreword by William S. Dudley — 1
Preface — 5
Introduction — 7

1—Japan Opens Its Doors — 9
2—Room 1649 — 12
3—The Sun Rises in the East — 18
4—All Roads Lead to Pearl Harbor — 25
5—The Jewel of the Pacific — 50
6—Radio Silence Is Broken — 78
7—The Die Is Cast — 104
8—Wake Island's Heroic Defense — 125
9—Southern and Central Pacific Operations — 135
10—The Final Analysis of the Japanese Attack on Pearl Harbor — 154
11—Connecting the Dots — 187
12—Epilogue — 198

Appendix A. General George Marshall's Actions on the Morning of December 7, 1941 — 205
Appendix B. The Pearl Harbor Attack: December 7, 1941 — 206
Chapter Notes — 211
Bibliography — 219
Index — 221

Foreword

by WILLIAM S. DUDLEY

This book by James M. D'Angelo, M.D., noted author of *Victory at Midway*, analyzes the events preceding the dramatic opening of the Pacific War on December 7, 1941. From a distance of 200 miles, a six-carrier Japanese task force launched a surprise attack on U.S. naval and military installations on Oahu, Hawaiian Islands. It resulted in the sinking of several battleships of the U.S. fleet at Pearl Harbor, the destruction of hundreds of land-based aircraft and sea planes at other bases, the killing of about 2,500 sailors, soldiers, and civilians, and the wounding of thousands more.

This account comprises the most recent example of revisionist history as applied to the perennial controversy over whether the Japanese attack on Pearl Harbor was as much a "surprise" to the government leadership in 1941 as it was to all other American citizens. It is worthwhile to consider the meaning of revisionism in history, as it is far from a one-time event. Rather, revisionism is a constant process as historians with new resources and different perspectives try to make sense out of the past. One definition of revisionism is the following: the advocacy of revision of some political theory, religious doctrine, historical or critical interpretation. Nearly all historians resort to a degree of revisionism in the effort to contribute something new to our understanding of the past.

Some view revisionism as an aberration, while others see it as a betrayal of the past as they know it. To many, however, revisionism is a way of gaining new insight on events that might otherwise be unknowable or misunderstood, like turning a kaleidoscope to see new patterns or using a stronger microscope to see more details on a slide. Since 1945 the events leading up to the attack on Pearl Harbor have been examined in more than one hundred historical books and thousands of articles. Historians have tried to understand how it was that the United States was caught off guard by Japan, a nation some 3,800 miles away from the Hawaiian Islands, then a U.S. territory, not a state. The Second World War had begun in Europe in September 1939, and by 1941 it had spread from Germany to Poland, France, Belgium, the Netherlands, Great Britain, Scandinavia, Italy, and the Soviet Union. The United States, at first, had not wished to get involved, but with world-wide financial interests, as well as political and cultural ties to western Europe, Americans were gradually drawn into a war not of their making, but one in which their vital interests were at stake.

In early 1941, Franklin Delano Roosevelt began his third term in office, but even before this he had been struggling with the question of whether, how, and when his administration would enter the war. He had spoken out adamantly to U.S. citizens about avoiding war because a predominant part of the American population opposed involvement in the late 1930s. There were still bitter memories of losses and scarcities during World War I among the public at large. On the other hand, in order to lift the nation out of the Great Depression, the administration supported legislation to strengthen the U.S. fleet, build more tanks and modern military aircraft, and increase employment.

The president called up the National Guard for training in August 1940. One month later Congress heatedly debated the first peacetime Selective Service Act to register all men between ages 21 and 36 for conscription in case of war. It finally passed by just one vote. Early that year, only 35 percent of the population favored entering the war on the side of the British and Free French, but during the Battle of Britain, from July to October 1940, the public mood began to shift.

When it began to look as if Britain could not survive without U.S. assistance, Roosevelt and his advisors devised ways to help them while still remaining neutral. By autumn 1940, the polls showed 52 percent favorable to U.S. assistance. By April 1941, an increasing proportion had shifted toward assisting Britain, if not actually entering the war. The president, however, could still not afford to offend the powerful anti-war isolationists in Congress, and thus he tread cautiously.

In the western Pacific, the island nation of Japan had been building up and modernizing its military forces since the 1850s, anticipating conflicts with the western European nations, China, and the United States. The Japanese victories in the Sino-Japanese war of 1894–1895, the Russians in 1904–1905, and its participation in World War I on the side of the Allies, convinced the Japanese military of their prowess. At the same time, the reach of the U.S. Navy into Far Eastern seas during the Spanish-American War and the takeover of the Philippine Islands and Guam raised Japanese suspicions that the United States intended to limit their ambitions. After accepting the League of Nations' mandate to take over the former German islands of the western Pacific, Japan began to extend its empire to the southeast and to convert these islands into colonies and military bases.

Since the end of World War I, Japan was treated as one of the world's rising naval powers. Our naval attachés in China and Japan carefully observed Japan's attitudes toward the United States and sensed its growing hostility, one of them predicting an inevitable war between the two nations. At the same time, the U.S. Naval War College had begun studying that possibility in theoretical war games that pitted an American "blue" fleet against a Japanese "orange" fleet on an annual basis. American military and naval cryptographers made a constant practice of trying to break Japan's encoded messages; Japanese intelligence likewise attempted to read American secret message traffic. After the outbreak of World War II in Europe, Germany, Japan, and Italy joined in a pact of mutual assistance, the Axis Tripartite (September 1940), committing themselves to enter in war against the United States, if and when that occurred. This was known in the United States and Britain. During the 1940 Battle of Britain, the governments of President Franklin Roosevelt and Prime Minister Winston Churchill became much closer in terms of collaboration and sharing of intelligence information. It was very much in the British interest to persuade the United States to join the war, despite America's declaration of neutrality. Yet, the U.S. armed forces were not prepared for war with Germany, much less with Japan.

In mid–1941, Roosevelt faced the fact that he would need full congressional support if it came to a matter of declaring war. Yet, Congress was unconvinced this was in America's best interest at that time. Thus, it was a waiting game, while the United States built up its forces and negotiated with Japan to restrain its territorial ambitions. The Japanese, on the other hand, had a military-dominated government that was impatient and wanted to move its forces into Southeast Asia before the United States was ready to prevent it. Their impatience had been goaded by American financial sanctions and an embargo placed on exporting oil and aviation fuel to Japan. The U.S. had undertaken this in an effort to convince Japan to continue negotiations, but these measures had the opposite effect of provoking the Japanese government just when it had an urgent need for these commodities. It became clear to both sides that it would take a major incident to bring a clash between the two nations. To Roosevelt and his advisors, it was clear that only if the U.S. did not initiate hostilities would he be able to convince our reluctant Congress to declare war against Japan.

Japanese forces attacked U.S. military and naval installations at Pearl Harbor on December 7, 1941, at great cost to the United States. This indeed brought out the congressional and public support the Roosevelt administration needed for a declaration of war against Japan. But the aftermath of the attack brought many serious questions that have been investigated and debated for over 75 years. The majority of established historians adopted the administration's point of view that it had no specific knowledge that the attack would be aimed at Pearl Harbor, although our on-scene commanders were blamed for failing in their mission to be ready for such an attack.

Over the years, a growing minority of critics—historical revisionists—have taken the opposite view: that President Roosevelt and a handful of senior civilian, naval, and military leaders had at least 10 days foreknowledge that the Japanese fleet was on its way to attack Pearl Harbor but had withheld that intelligence from the commanders on Oahu for fear that Japan would call off the attack if it were not a surprise. In that case, they reasoned, the president would have no precipitating attack to use as a persuasive lever to get Congress to declare war. In other words, the Roosevelt administration was willing to accept a costly blow, a sacrifice in terms of thousands of human lives and millions in damage to ships and aircraft, as the price of entering the war. Many citizens had come to trust President Roosevelt after nine years in office and were unwilling to believe that he and others would betray this trust in order to enter the war. Still, the historical record contains many tantalizing clues that point in the opposite direction, indicating that is exactly what the Roosevelt administration did.

This is where Dr. James D'Angelo brings to bear his specialized historical research. He applies to this historical study a particular cast of mind. He is a medical man, a scientist by training, who analyzes historical events in a disciplined, deliberate way. Readers will also notice that the author is always thinking about the "what ifs" of the past, alternate ways in which events might have, or could have, worked out had a different path been followed by key personalities and institutions, whether they were American or Japanese. Some historians would call this a "counter-factual" approach, which enlivens the reading of this book. He studied both sides of this controversy and considered the major arguments, counter-arguments, and evidence from many sources. In the last thirty years, new evidence has emerged due to the declassification of records previously held close at secret and higher levels of classification in the

National Archives and Records Centers of the United States and the United Kingdom (where some documents have still has not been released). What James D'Angelo has done here, in his own words, is "to connect the dots" so that the readers can decide for themselves where the truth stands.

                              William S. Dudley
                              Former Director of Naval History

William S. Dudley, Ph.D. (Columbia University), was the director of the Naval History and Heritage Command from 1995 to 2004. He served on destroyers during the 1960s, taught history at SMU, and joined the Naval Historical Center in 1977. He was the original editor of The Naval War of 1812: A Documentary History, *4 vols. He is author of* Maritime Maryland: A History, *and co-author, with Scott Harmon, of* The Naval War of 1812: America's Second War of Independence. *He lives in Easton, Maryland.*

Preface

The controversy over whether the United States had foreknowledge of Japan's attack on Pearl Harbor on December 7, 1941, has existed for many years. This mystery has haunted me ever since I was aware of the suspicion in my early adult life that the United States may have had warning of the attack before it occurred. It was greatly important to me to know if our government might have deceived us for political reasons.

Initially, the evidence seemed to indicate that the attack came as a complete surprise to our country's leaders. However, with the publication of David Kahn's *The Code Breakers* in 1967, John Toland's *Infamy* in 1982, Layton, Pineau, and Costello's *And I Was There* in 1985, and Robert B. Stinnett's *Day of Deceit* in 2000, the pendulum began to swing in the opposite direction. The foregoing authors' books provided new evidence that the U.S. government and military were forewarned of the attack on Pearl Harbor.

To further support the idea that the U.S. was aware of the planned Japanese attack on Pearl Harbor, evidence is presented in this book from a number of sources, including:

- The testimony of eye witnesses;
- The Vice Chief of Naval Operations *Vacant Sea* Order that cleared the shipping lanes in the North Pacific, leaving it open for the Japanese task force to sail undetected;
- The fact that General George Marshall, U.S. Army, order to move *Enterprise* and *Lexington* out of Pearl Harbor prior to the attack on Pearl Harbor came from the Army and not from the Navy;
- The decision not to provide *HYPO* with a Purple diplomatic decoding machine;
- The deliberate withholding of vital naval intelligence from Admiral Husband E. Kimmel and General Walter Short;
- The existence of the *Bomb Plot Order*;
- The unusual behavior of General Marshall on the morning of December 7, 1941;
- A copy of a Churchill/Roosevelt conversation on November 26, 1941.

It has been a contention by those who oppose the *conspiracy theory* that the United States could not have detected the Japanese Task Force as it sailed across the North Pacific because Japan maintained complete radio silence on its way to Hawaii. This position has been disproven by Stinnett, who discovered in the records at the

Navy's Radio Direction Finder Station at Dutch Harbor, Alaska, that the station had detected that the Japanese Task Force was sailing across the North Pacific. The records also show that this information was then passed to Robert Ogg, a special investigator for San Francisco's Twelfth Naval District. Ogg plotted the findings on a nautical chart which revealed the course and location of the Japanese warships. This information was subsequently sent to the White House.

Stinnett's investigation not only provided proof that prior to the attack on Pearl Harbor that United States knew the location and course of the Japanese task force, but also that the enemy carriers had broken radio silence by sending 129 messages. These messages were intercepted by U.S. naval monitoring stations between November 15 an December 6, 1941. The intercept rate can be documented from the records of Stations CAST and H.[1]

In addition, in 1979 the National Security Agency (NSA) released 2,413 Japanese Navy messages about Pearl Harbor (intercepted between September 1 and December 4, 1941, but deciphered after the war) and subsequently sent them to the National Archives. A number of these now decoded messages have identified Pearl Harbor as the target of the Japanese fleet. More importantly, in late 1997 the official U.S. Navy position on its capability to read the main Japanese fleet code (JN-25B) was declassified: "By December 1, we had it solved to a readable Extent," National Archives RG 457, SRH-355, page 398, Naval Security Group History World War II by Captain J.S. Holtwick. Until the Navy admitted this truth, they denied they had the ability to do so.

One unresolved area of investigation that needs to be explored is a missing telegram sent by Churchill to FDR on November 26, 1941, at 3:00 a.m. and marked urgent and top secret. There is reason to believe that this telegram contained foreknowledge of the Japanese attack on Pearl Harbor because on that date the Japanese task force left Japan for Hawaii. It is felt that this communication may exist in Churchill's confidential files which are scheduled to be declassified in 2020.

If one looks into the U.S. National Archives for telegrams sent and received on November 26, 1941, one will find that forty telegrams went through U.S. embassy channels between London and Washington. Of importance is that there are two telegrams whose serial numbers are listed in the National Archives but the telegrams are nowhere to be found. They have disappeared. This author intends to try to obtain and review Winston Churchill's confidential files when they are declassified.

In summary, this book presents enough evidence to dispel the objections by those who oppose the "conspiracy theory" and to make the case that the "conspiracy theory" actually has its roots founded in facts.

Introduction

There have been a number of excellent books written about the attack on Pearl Harbor. This book explores the root causes of Japan's assault on the United States and the events leading to that infamous attack. It begins with a brief insight into the early days of Japan's history to give the reader a perspective into its rise to power which occurred over a period of 88 years.

Special attention is given to the events leading up to Japan's surprise attack on Pearl Harbor on December 7, 1941, and more specifically, raising serious questions and supplying answers to whether the United States knew of Japan's intentions to attack Pearl Harbor.

The book proceeds to describe the aftermath of Pearl Harbor, the heroic stand by the U.S. Marines at Wake Island until its fall on December 23, 1941 (Wake date), the fall of the Philippines and U.S. operations into the south and central Pacific in January, February, and March of 1942. This set the stage for the Doolittle Raid and the battles of the Coral Sea and Midway. These latter events have been described in detail in my previous book, *Victory at Midway: The Battle That Changed the Course of World War II*, published in January 2018. Thus, this book is the prequel to *Victory at Midway*.

For more than a hundred years, there has been much mystery surrounding the events that led up to the Japanese attack on Pearl Harbor on December 7, 1941. What follows will unravel this uncertainty by producing evidence that heretofore has not been readily available to the public. Armed with such evidence, the reader will be able to come to his/her own conclusion on this subject.

Chapter 1

Japan Opens Its Doors

"The death of a civilization seldom comes from without; internal decay must weaken a society before external influences or attacks can change its essential structure, or bring it to end."[1]

If one is to consider giving a critical review of a major event in human history, the occurrence cannot be studied in a vacuum, because events in history are linked together with cause and effect. The constant in this analysis is human nature which, by its very essence, will never change. The variable in the equation is time, which is always changing. Therefore, events in history can only be understood and judged by knowing what went before and what came after. It is with this paradigm in mind that one must study Japan's history and the role it played in Japan's declaring war against the United States in World War II. The above concept is best illustrated by studying the history of Japanese society over the past 1500 years. The United States' civilization is not as well-suited to demonstrate this principle, spanning a period of only 237 years. To observe history repeating itself, one must analyze the cyclical rise and fall of a civilization over a significant period of time.

Within this fabric is woven the complex processes that influence decisions made at a given moment in time. We will begin at the beginning, centuries ago, in the year 522 A.D. when Japan was basically uncivilized and lived in a semi-feudal and tribal society. However, in the early to mid-sixth century, Japan, influenced by a high degree of culture from China and Korea, became civilized and began its own era of enlightenment. Buddhism, a pacifist philosophy, began to reign supreme in Japan.[2] In this religious climate and with a stable government, cultural development of the arts, music, painting and literature flourished to a point that from 901 to 922, Japan was in the midst of what historians refer to as its *Golden Era*.[3] During this time, cultural development reached a height never to be seen again in Japanese history.[4] With enlightenment, however, came a loss of individual discipline and the unintended consequences of moral decay, which led to the eventual corruption of the Japan's governing party.[5] The rulers were unable to enforce law and order, and as a result Japan slowly lost its power.[6] The Japanese people enjoyed the pleasures of the day and were disinclined to have any hardships placed on them. This political landscape came to an abrupt end in 1853 when an American fleet led by Commodore Matthew C. Perry arrived in Japan. Over the next 88 years, Japan would utilize every resource available to become a major geopolitical power in the western Pacific, setting in motion a series of events that would put it on a collision course with the United States. Five years after Perry's arrival in Japan, the Japanese government capitulated to virtually every demand put forth by the United States, this time in a treaty negotiated between U.S. Consul Townsend Harris and Japan's chief negotiator, Hotta Masayoshi.[7]

With its capitulation to Perry's demands in 1853, Japan suffered the humiliating defeat of not being able to militarily defend its own government as an alternative to diplomacy. In retaliation, Japanese leaders ended the authority of the Shogunate power and reestablished it with the Emperor—in this case, Meiji Mutsuhito.[8] This turn of events led to the end of the feudal states and the beginning of an industrialized Japan, a transition known as the "Era of Meiji," beginning on January 1, 1868.[9] Japanese leaders now were determined to mimic the West in its institutions and industry, and in so doing eventually became a world class power in the Pacific. By importing supervisors and consultants from western Europe, Japan was able to elevate its industrial, military, political, social, legal, economic, scientific, and cultural levels to those closer to the West.[10]

By December 1898, the Treaty of Paris convened to end the Spanish-American War, and America received ownership of Puerto Rico, Guam, and more importantly the Philippine Islands.[11] This latter acquisition clearly catapulted the United States into becoming a major player in the geopolitical game being played in the Pacific.

The next significant geopolitical event in Japanese history was the Russian-Japanese War of 1904. This conflict provides important lessons to be learned that one can apply to the war in the Pacific decades later, and specifically to Japan's attack on Pearl Harbor. First and foremost is the fact this decisive victory by Japan in the Straits of Tsushima was a turning point in modern history regarding European influence in Asia. The victory not only ended the Russian expansion into Chinese territory, but was the beginning of the end of European rule in the Far East. Second, it clearly placed Japan as a major player at the table with the West in deciding policy in Asia and as a force to be reckoned with in the future. The irony here is that the United States both diplomatically and financially assisted Japan in the winning of its war with Russia. As a result of Japan's victory, all Asia took courage in witnessing a little Oriental island empire defeat the most populous country in Europe. Seeing this, China planned her revolution, India began to think of her freedom and independence, and a series of revolutions took place in Czarist Russia.

With Russia's fading influence, Japan became a major threat to the U.S. foreign policy in the Far East.[12] Japan on its part had become concerned about America's recently acquired possessions, namely Alaska, Hawaii, Midway, Guam, and the Philippines in the Pacific. Strategically, they placed the United States in a position to check any advances by Japan on the Asian continent and the neighboring islands.[13] In response to this threat, Japanese leaders in 1914 decided to join the allied cause in World War I, and declared war on Germany to acquire territories in the Pacific in exchange for their entry into the war. In return for entering the war, Japan was able to retain her control over the Shantung Peninsula and allowed to boldly annex the German controlled Mariana, Caroline, and Marshall islands in the Pacific. These actions were of great concern to the United States since the Philippine Islands would be much more difficult to defend with Japan's control of these island groups.[14] It had become obvious that U.S. diplomacy had failed to influence Japan's geopolitical aggression. Without the threat of force by the United States, the fate of China was in Japan's hands.

In 1919, the worst fears of the United States were realized when the League of

Nations mandated the Marshall, Caroline, and the Mariana islands to Japan. In 1921, a meeting was attended initially by the United States, France, Great Britain, and Japan, whereby all of which agreed to honor the geopolitical situation as it existed in the Pacific and to seek the advice of each other if the security of any one power was in danger (the Four Power Treaty).[15] This treaty replaced the older Anglo-Japanese Alliance of 1902. Later, when Italy joined the conference, it was called the Five Power Treaty, but became better known as the Washington Naval Conference. In this treaty all parties agreed to a moratorium on construction of all capital ships—battleships and heavy cruisers—with an accepted 5–5-3 ratio for capital ships of the United States, Great Britain, and Japan, in that order. All other ships were to be scrapped except for aircraft carriers.[16] The battleship was supreme and naval air power was in its infancy, leading many western naval leaders to use tunnel vision in evaluating the future of air power in a Pacific war. However, Japan's insight was better, as it converted the battleships that were to be scrapped into aircraft carriers.[17] The Washington Naval Conference Treaty signed in 1922 was now called the Nine Power Treaty because four more countries agreed to sign the document, now including the United States, Great Britain, France, Japan, China, Italy, Belgium, Holland, and Portugal. Its intention was to protect China's sovereignty, maintain the *Open Door Policy,* and help create a stable China. A compromise was reached when Japan agreed to return the Shantung Peninsula to China but retained her economic rights in the territory.[18] In return, the West promised not to build new bases or improve existing ones in the Pacific.[19] The goals of the conference, though well intentioned, had no real means of enforcement, permitting Japan eventually to disregard its terms. By signing the Five Power Treaty, however, Japan gained with one stroke of the pen a superior position of naval strength in the western Pacific waters.

With respect to the overall impact of these treaties, two points come to mind. The first is that in the short or long term, diplomacy is only effective if it is backed up by the real threat of military force, no matter how noble the goals may be. The second point concerns the value of intelligence in achieving diplomatic success. It is clear that diplomatic intelligence assured success in obtaining Japan's agreement to the 5–5-3 ratio of capital ships. This conclusion is based on the fact that the United States had foreknowledge of secret information sent in Japanese code to its diplomats in Washington, as we shall see in the next chapter.[20] The secret messages were intercepted and decoded by U.S. intelligence and used to America's advantage. The messages revealed that Japanese diplomats should press for a ratio more favorable to Japan. However, as a last resort, the Japanese government would be willing to accept the ratio proposed by the United States in order not to offend American government.[21] In 1929, the U.S. stock market crashed and represented a harbinger of events to come that would explode on the world scene in the 1930s and set in motion a series of actions that would inevitably lead to the war in the Pacific.

CHAPTER 2

Room 1649

In 1917, Herbert O. Yardley arrived in Washington to serve in the code-breaking unit of Military Intelligence (MI) of the American Expeditionary Force.[1] At age 23, he gave up on his idea to become a lawyer and was hired as a code clerk in the Department of State. He soon discovered that he had an innate ability to quickly decipher codes in short order, and his love of cryptanalysis began.

Shortly after the United States entered World War I in April 1917, Yardley was able to sell the idea of a cryptologic service to the War Department. The organization was entitled Military Intelligence, Section 8 (MI-8). MI-8 grew as new personnel arrived. It soon was able to handle a work load of 50,000 words per week. Its growth required larger and larger quarters. Beginning in the balcony overhanging the library of the National War College at Fort McNair in Washington, it moved to the Colonel, an apartment house on 15th and M streets, and subsequently to a building site on F Street where the famous Capitol Theater would later be built.[2] He passionately felt that America had a desperate need for cryptanalysis, both in war and peace time. MI-8 needed to be rescued.

Therefore, on May 16, 1919, Yardley forwarded a request for a *"permanent organization for code and cipher investigation and attack."*[3] The request was approved three days later by Frank L. Polk, Acting Secretary of State. The plan called for the State and War departments to fund the program. The expenditures over a ten year period would be $33,000 per year, with the State Department contributing two-thirds and the War Department one-third of that amount each year. The State Department's contribution, however, could not legally be expended within the District of Columbia.[4] This obstacle was overcome by moving the cryptanalytic section in October 1919 to New York City.[5] The organization was initially located in the townhouse of a New York society man, T. Suffern Tailer, at 3 East 38th Street.[6] After one year, the unit moved to a four story brownstone at 141 East 37th Street where Yardley's living quarters were on the top floor.[7]

All outside connections with the government were cut. The rent, utilities, and office supplies were paid from secret funds.[8] This building had its drawbacks, as the rooms in which MI-8 worked were only 12 feet wide.[9] However, this inconvenience did not hamper their diligence or their results. This clandestine operation was to become known as the American Black Chamber. (I visited this building on May 22, 2008, and found the four story brownstone building on 37th Street still intact, except for the fading numbers "141" on the transom which could barely be seen. A symbol of a time gone by.)

One of the first assignments for the organization was to solve the codes of Japan.

Yardley's excitement for the project led him to predict that the group would have the problem solved in one year. He soon appreciated the difficulties that the Japanese language presented in the plain text, let alone the coded text.[10]

In the summer of 1921, the Black Chamber intercepted and deciphered Japanese telegram 813, which was sent by the Japanese ambassador in London to officials in Tokyo.[11] It contained hints of the upcoming naval disarmament conference in Washington.[12] To maintain complete secrecy between the Chamber and the State Department, the latter created a daily courier service between New York and Washington which carried the deciphered messages of Japan's diplomats.

Over a period of 12 years (1917–1929), the team is said to have decoded over 45,000 telegrams from more than 20 countries.[13]

Entrance of the brownstone townhouse that housed the Black Chamber in 1920. The house is at 141 East 37th Street in New York (author's photograph).

Then, abruptly, the Black Chamber came to an end. The problem began when the presidents of Western Union Telegraph Company and the Postal Telegraph Company began to balk at turning over the telegrams to the Chamber.[14] The reluctance of the foregoing companies led Yardley to test the political winds. Herbert Hoover had just delivered his first speech as president in 1929, the tone of which was of the highest ethical standards and led Yardley to believe that the end of the Black Chamber was near.[15] This conclusion was verified by the Office of the Secretary of State. Yardley had sent to Secretary Henry L. Stimson a summary of the important messages solved by the Chamber and the role they had played in protecting American security. However, Stimson was outraged at the report and absolutely rejected the idea of spying on countries with whom the United States had peaceful diplomatic relations. His famous statement was "Gentleman do not read each other's mail."[16] Stimson subsequently withdrew all of the State Department's funds for Yardley's group. Since the State Department made up the most of the funding for the Black Chamber, the organization was forced to shut down.[17] An unexpended $6,666.66 and the organization's files were turned over to the Army Signal Corps.[18] On October 31, 1929, the American Black Chamber dissolved and the staff scattered.[19] Of interest is that none of its members went to the Army's Signal Intelligence Service.[20]

In the meantime, and shortly before the State Department withdrew its financial support for the Black Chamber, the Army decided to unite its cryptographic and cryptanalytic sections in the Signal Corps.[21] Cryptologic responsibility fell on the shoulders of its Chief Signal Officer. The Signal Corps then established a Signal Intelligence Service (SIS) in its War and Training Division, with William Friedman as its director.[22] Friedman's background is interesting. He had testified before a congressional committee regarding his reading of some of the messages in the Teapot Dome scandal during President Warren Harding's administration in 1924.[23] A few months later, he was caught up in the craziness of the Roaring Twenties, when he posed as ready to translate any messages coming from Mars as that planet passed very close to the Earth that year. In 1929, he became a recognized world leader in cryptology when the *Encyclopædia Britannica* published his article on "Codes and Ciphers."[24] Friedman's Signal Corps mission was to ensure the cryptographic and cryptanalytic capability of the United States in war time but to limit the SIS's activities to training personnel and doing research in peace time.[25] Friedman hired three junior cryptanalysts and upon this foundation created the cryptologic organization that would later become our present day National Security Agency.[26]

The Navy was slow to develop an interest in having its own cryptologic organization. Initially, during World War I, the service relied on British intelligence for most of its information. However, as the war progressed, the Navy restructured itself with the establishment of a Chief of Naval Operations.[27] The responsibility for cryptography was transferred from the Bureau of Navigation in October 1917 to a new Office of Naval Communications (ONC).[28] Four young assistant communication officers had already been coding and decoding messages in the same State-War-Navy Department building where Yardley worked.[29]

The Navy's participation in World War I was too limited to warrant the development of a fully-fledged organization devoted to cryptology, but interest in the science was stimulated. Near the end of the war, the Secretary of the Navy was finally able to win President Woodrow Wilson's approval for the funding of code-breaking operations.[30] By this time, the Navy fully realized that tight security was of the essence in the code-breaking business. Thus, it felt obliged to set up a secret slush fund for a subsidy it was receiving for the Office of Naval Intelligence (ONI).

By 1920, ciphers and codes were becoming increasingly complicated, demanding greater effort and time from those in the cryptanalytic world. More and more man-hours were required for code-breaking. To those in the field in the early 1920s, it was becoming clear that theft from a foreign government was one method of obtaining secret codes, in this case, from Japan. In the spring of 1920, when the ONI learned that a Japanese officer was impersonating a Japanese vice-consul, it financed a major FBI undercover operation at the Japanese Consulate in New York City.[31, 32] This invasion of Japanese privacy led to the discovery by Yardley's group of the infamous *Red Code*. The code book was then translated from Japanese to English over a four-year period by Dr. Emerson J. Haworth and his wife, both of whom were Japanese linguists.[33] The title *Red Code* was used as a reference to the color of the binding of the two volumes of translations. *Red Code* contained the ciphers and codes of Japan's naval code and thus permitted the ONI to monitor Japan's naval exercises.

In 1922, the Navy's Code and Signal Section was formally made part of the Office of Naval Communications and designated OP-20-G. *Red Code* was subsequently turned over to the Code and Signal Section of ONC, whose function it was to handle and preserve the security of our own codes and ciphers.[34] The Section's mission was to intercept, decrypt, and analyze naval communications from the Japanese, German, and Italian navies. The section also followed the diplomatic messages of many foreign governments; however, the majority of its efforts were directed toward Japan. This focus on Japan led to the Navy's construction of High Frequency Direction Finder (HFDF) sites and the development of intercept stations in the Pacific, as well as on the continental United States in the 1920s and 1930s.

In 1924 the Navy placed an intercept station in Shanghai, its first in China. Over the next ten years, the following additional radio intercept stations were constructed in the Pacific: (1) Station CAST was located at the Cavite Navy Yard on the island of Luzon in the Philippines, but was subsequently moved to Corregidor in Manila Bay when Cavite was captured by Japanese forces in early 1942. With the fall of Corregidor in April 1942, the site was permanently moved to Melbourne, Australia, where the station united with that of the Australians to form the U.S.-Australian Station, FRUMEL (Fleet Radio Unit, Melbourne); (2) Station H in Pearl Harbor, Hawaii; (3) Station BAKER on Guam; (4) Station P in Peking, China, and (5) Station SAIL, the most significant intercept station covering the Pacific from the continental United States, located on Bainbridge Island in Washington State.[35]

The Navy also began the construction of HFDF sites in the continental United States as well as in the Pacific. Some of the HFDFs were located on the same sites as the radio intercept stations at Station H in Pearl Harbor, Hawaii; Station SAIL on Bainbridge Island, Washington; Station ITEM in Imperial Beach, California; Station AE in Sitka, Alaska; Station KING in Dutch Harbor, Alaska; Station CAST on Cavite in the Philippine Islands, and Station BAKER on Guam.[36] All of the foregoing stations reported back to OP-20-G, which was the headquarters of all facets of radio intelligence and was located in the old Navy Department Building in Washington.[37] The code name for OP-20-G was Station Negat. A cryptographic section had been created in Washington by the Navy in late 1923 and early 1924; its function was to analyze our own ciphers and codes and suggest improvements. The section was to work with the code desk but only in an advisory capacity. This concept completely changed after January 1924, when Lieutenant Laurence F. Safford (known as the Father of Naval Cryptography) was designated the head of the new unit whose office was then located in "Main Navy," Room 1649 of the Navy Department Building on the National Mall along Constitution Avenue in Washington, D.C.[38] Room 1649 was the location of the first cryptanalytic unit in Navy history. For security reasons the post was located at the end of the first deck's sixth wing and was one of the most guarded secrets of the U.S. government.[39] It was in this room that Americans looked into the secret thoughts and plans of our enemies by decoding their messages. Room 1649 housed OP-20-G.[40]

Working in Room 1649, a tiny unit of Safford, two typists realized that the *Red Book* offered the possibility of deciphering the Japanese naval code. Accordingly, the potential value of the previously established Pacific network of radio intercept stations became obvious. Now the Office of Naval Communications could not only listen to radio traffic but decipher it as well. It is interesting to note that both the Office of Naval Intelligence and the Office of Naval Communications gave Safford's unit their blessings, with no evidence of the rivalry that was to develop over the next five years.

In 1924, the Navy finally established its first official code-breaking programs for the deciphering of foreign codes. An operation that began as a one-man unit grew into an organization of over 5,000 men and women, dedicated to the task of deciphering codes during World War II.

Another individual who played a fascinating role in the development of American cryptanalytic capability was known as the "First Lady of Cryptography." Agnes Meyer was born in Geneseo, Illinois, and later studied mathematics, statistics, physics, music, and languages at Ohio State University where she received her B.A. degree.[41] In 1914, she became the head of the mathematics department at Amarillo High School in Texas, and four years later she enlisted in the Navy Reserve as a Yeoman in the cryptologic unit.[42] In 1921, Edward Hebern, who had invented the first machine that used the rotor principle to decipher coded messages, published in a Marine magazine what he thought was an unbreakable cipher.[43] To his surprise, Miss Meyer decoded the sample message. Hebern hired her immediately and put her to work as a technical advisor in his private company, the Hebern Electric Code Company.[44] Shortly after she joined the fledgling company, however, it failed.[45] During that period of time, Miss Meyer had married Michael Driscoll, a Washington lawyer.[46] In 1924, she returned to the Office of Naval Communications and enlightened the men of the code-breaking unit as to the finer points of cryptanalysis, including Lieutenant Safford.

Also in the unit were Lieutenant Joseph Rochefort, a major code breaking player in the battles of the Coral Sea and Midway, and Lieutenant Thomas Dyer, leader of the team responsible for the breakthroughs in reading Japanese naval communications prior to those battles. Both played significant roles in the outcomes of these two crucial battles. Their successes were "in large part due to the talent and influence of 'Miss Aggie' as Agnes Meyer was known."[47]

In describing the history of American cryptanalysis, it is fitting that we pay further tribute to Lieutenant Joseph J. Rochefort, who reported for duty in the ONC in 1925 and was assigned to its research desk. Rochefort had entered the Navy during World War I after graduating from Stevens Institute of Technology.[48] Not having graduated from the U.S. Naval Academy, he was considered an outsider by the Academy's graduates. However, he was fully accepted by Safford, who, although an Academy graduate, was considered to be outside the loop himself due to his inattention to detail in his outward appearance.[49] Rochefort's easy-going manner disguised his independent mindset and intense fastidiousness in tackling a problem.[50] In 1926, Safford, fulfilling requirements for promotion in the Navy, was sent back to sea, and Rochefort was left in charge of the cryptographic section.[51] It was under Rochefort's charge that the first *Red Book* Japanese naval code was broken.[52] Ultimate credit here, however, was awarded to Agnes Meyer Driscoll for her efforts in discovering the cipher key that unlocked the Japanese Naval Code. This feat was more amazing because the *Red Book* contained over 100,000 code groups, with as many as three groups assigned to each Japanese word or expression.[53]

It was in this atmosphere, and with the realization that Japanese intelligence had gained access to America's latest changes in War Plan Orange (See Chapter 1), that those in the War Plans Department were feeling very unsettled.[54] In the 1930s, Japanese intelligence was able to decipher most of U.S. coded messages. This situation changed in August 1941 when Army and Navy intelligence created a cipher machine, designated *SIGABA* by the Army. This device was so sophisticated that the coded messages sent through the machine were never deciphered by any of our enemies in World War II. Unlike the German *Enigma* machine which consisted of three rotors, this machine contained 15 rotors. In addition, our intelligence had learned in 1930 that Japan believed that her Navy was capable of defeating the U.S. fleet in any fleet engagement in the Pacific. Japan's Navy also anticipated in their war games their capture of the Philippines and Guam, as well as potential air raids on Tokyo from U.S. carrier-borne aircraft.

During this time, Army Signals Intelligence and OP-20-G had become rivals, competing with each other to provide their intelligence data, code-named "Magic," to those who needed to know. It was not surprising that the rivalry occurred considering the competitive nature that had always existed between the two services. Word came down from high command that the two organizations should cooperate. This was not to be, however, as the rivalry between the two cryptanalytic units would continue and remain a problem right up to December 7, 1941.

Meanwhile, a feud was developing within the Navy Department itself. The Office of Naval Intelligence had turned its *Red Book* asset over to the Office of Naval Communications. This was done with the agreement that ONI would be furnished with information that ONC derived from the *Red Book*.[55] That agreement was not carried out. Thereafter, efforts were made by the ONI to bring Rochefort's cryptographic section to ONI. However, these efforts failed because both the Director of ONC and Chief of Naval Operations were very concerned over security leaks within ONI.[56]

By 1930, ONI was actually being denied information obtained from Japanese fleet exercises because Admiral Charles Hughes, then Chief of Naval Operations, insisted upon maintaining tight security over the cryptographic section's intelligence and not subjecting the information to leaks within the ONI.[57] It was within this framework that the United States' intelligence and cryptanalytic sections would enter the next decade.

CHAPTER 3

The Sun Rises in the East

During the 1920s, America may have appeared to be a step closer to peace with Japan. However, beneath the surface in this Far East country were burning embers that would eventually ignite the conflagration inflicted on Pearl Harbor a little more than a decade later. The years 1906–1931 mark important developments in every aspect of Japanese life. Japan had become a world leader, but its territorial gains occurred at the end of the nineteenth century when imperialism was coming to an end. The country approached parity with the world leaders at a time when military and naval standards were about to change, marked by a call to disarmament after World War I.

Following the end of the Russo-Japanese War in 1905, Japan emerged as the strongest power in Asia. In the next 20 years, its stature increased, and Japan's power rose to the point where she became one of the five Great Powers and maintained a permanent seat on the Council of the League of Nations. Throughout the world, monarchies and empires were imploding; Ottoman Turkey, Germany, Austria-Hungary, Russia, and Imperial China all disintegrated in a little more than a decade (1911–1923).[1]

In North China, the warlords eliminated each other in suicidal battles in 1924 and 1925. In 1926 in South China, the Kuomintang and communist forces united and prepared to launch a *Northern Expedition* from Canton to the Yangtze River. The purpose of the expedition, which was aided by Soviet arms and advisors, was to defeat the warlords in the northern part of China.

When Kuomintang and communist troops arrived in Nanking, anti-foreigners led attacks on non–Chinese people. Japanese Foreign Minister Shidehara Kijuro declined to join the other powers in taking countermeasures. Soon after, when the Kuomintang troops reached Shanghai, Chiang Kai-shek turned on his communist allies in a bloody coup; the left-wing survivors retreated to Wuhan where they too dismissed their Soviet advisors. Meanwhile, Chiang prepared to march north to Peking where he would promote national unification.[2]

Following the World War I expansion of the Japanese economy, a depression set in as Japan returned to the market of international competition. The high rate of inflation made it difficult for Japan to compete in the world market. The government imported rice from Taiwan and Korea to counter the inflationary effects of the economy, but those actions led to the rice riots of 1918, and Japan's farmers were forced to compete with import prices. The Yokohama-Tokyo earthquake on September 1, 1923, worsened the existing downturn of the economy, resulting in fires that raged for 40 hours and led to the loss of 120,000 buildings with an additional 450,000 buildings damaged by fire. There were 40,000 casualties, and over 250,000 people lost their jobs as a result of the damage inflicted on the economy.[3]

The previously described economic depression created political unrest which resulted in many assassinations of Japanese government officials by radical liberal dissidents in Japanese society. Government by assassination crippled the power of the government to act in the crisis. The Army and Navy decided not to intervene in the crisis for fear of complications. As a result, there was little the Japanese government could do. By the early 1930s, the Army of Manchuria now felt confident of its own power and that it was no longer under the control of the civil government.[4]

The conspiracy for the military takeover of Manchuria had better results than the failed Cherry Blossom coup of March 1931. To ensure success of their plot, Colonel Itagaki Seishiro and Lieutenant Colonel Ishiwara Kanji had deployed a significant number of Japanese troops to the area. Colonel Komote Daisaku, who arranged for the murder of Chang Tso-lin near the Manchurian border, was present; he had financed the operation. Kwantung Army officers were in contact with individuals in the Tokyo General Staff who favored the coup but objected to the timing. These members of the staff sent Lieutenant General Tatekawa Yoshitsugu, a member of the General Staff, to the scene to urge caution and delay. Those officers involved in the plot staged a party for him in an attempt to prevent him from arriving on the scene until after the plot had taken place.

A few Japanese soldiers planted dynamite on the railroad tracks of South Manchurian Railroad on the night of September 19, 1931. The explosives were to be set off near the barracks of the 7th Chinese Brigade so as to incriminate the Chinese troops as being the suspects who were trying to destroy the Japanese-owned railroad. Shortly thereafter, the Japanese Kwantung Army set off the explosives and then fired on the unsuspecting men in the Chinese barracks, killing a number of soldiers. A few dead Chinese bodies were then removed from the barracks and planted near the railroad tracks to provide testimony to the diligence of the Kwantung Army guards in protecting the railroad. The incident provided Japan with the political justification for a military takeover of China's Manchurian territory, which it was seeking. The die was cast when, in order to avoid further provocation, the Chinese war lord commander of the Fengtien Army issued orders to his troops not to return fire from Japanese troops. The Kwantung Army of 10,000 defeated a much larger Fengtien Army in a matter of hours. The door was now wide open and, in a series of military victories over a five-month period, the Japanese Army conquered all of Manchuria.

In Manchuria, the Kwantung Army continued to advance rapidly and brought all three provinces under Japanese control. Japan was now in clear violation of the Nine Power Pact and the Kellogg-Briand Pact of Paris. While Japan's diplomats were reassuring foreign governments of Japanese actions, the military was moving relentlessly forward.

The Manchurian aggression was also supported by many of the Japanese people because it provided an economic alternative to the severe depression existing in Japan and throughout the world. Manchuria became a successful industrial base for the Japanese Army and also provided the necessary raw materials (iron, coal, aluminum, gold, industrial salt, and agricultural products) to make Japan self-sufficient. In the eyes of the Japanese people, these results vindicated the Army's decision for the military takeover of this province.

Japanese democracy was teetering on the edge in the early 1930s, and with its people unable to withstand the pressures of a faltering economy, the nation looked for an alternative form of government. The choice that remained for the citizens of Japan was between imperialism and communism. The heated debate between these two factions ended when two top communist leaders in 1933 defected from the communist party and embraced the new nationalistic mood now infecting the Japanese people. This conversion resulted in a groundswell of support for the imperialistic party.[5]

In March 1932, and in the presence of a League of Nations' delegation sent to monitor the situation, the Japanese government annexed Manchuria and declared the territory an independent state, giving the territory a new name: Manchukuo. When the United States and the League of Nations balked at this takeover, Japan precipitously resigned its membership and walked out on the world body on February 24, 1933.[6]

Like Japan, China had also become frustrated with years of European powers using forceful diplomacy to achieve their goals on the Asian mainland. A wave of nationalism was spreading throughout the land. The seeds of this nationalism were planted in 1911 when the decadent Manchu Empire collapsed under the attacks of China's first Nationalistic leader Dr. Sun Yat-sen. The ensuing bloody conflicts between the warlords and Dr. Sun's troops led him to seek assistance from the Soviet Union.[7] With this help, the Chinese republic grew in power, and under the gifted leadership of a young general, Chiang Kai-shek, set out to defeat his warlord opponents. Communism was also on the rise in the country and within Chiang's own ranks. A peasant named Mao Tse-tung now inspired scores of communists to enter the fight against Japanese aggression. The number of recruits grew to the point whereby the Communist Party was now represented by a formidable guerrilla army. Realizing the danger that Mao posed, Generalissimo Chiang outlawed communism in 1927. From that day forward, all three factions fought against each other on one day or sided with one of its foes against the remaining enemy on another day.[8]

On July 5, 1937, a formal Kuomintang-Communist Party agreement was signed and both sides agreed to work together in driving the Japanese out of Peking and North China. Two days later, an incident occurred at an ancient stone bridge (named after the explorer Marco Polo) south of Peking that changed the course of the conflict in China. A Japanese army company was holding night military operations near a very large Chinese unit. As the operation came to an end, bullets were fired from the Chinese lines. When a second Japanese company was sent to the area for reinforcement and to negotiate a truce, a second barrage of bullets were fired into the Japanese companies.[9] While a second truce was being negotiated, firecrackers sounding like machine gun fire were set off, causing a resumption of hostilities. Finally, General Sung Chi-yuen, commander of all Chinese troops in North China, and General Gun Hashimoto, chief of staff of the Japanese North China Garrison, stepped in. Their friendship aided in moving the incident to a peaceful solution. However, Chiang refused to accept the truce and sent orders to reinforce the area. General Sung nevertheless kept his word and continued to withdraw his troops from the area. Japan, being unaware of these movements, demanded that the Chinese stop sending troops into North China. This action outraged Chiang, who proclaimed that China would no longer give up an inch of territory even if war was the outcome. There was fear on both sides that if war prevailed, the winners would be neither Japan nor the republic of China, but the Russians and the Chinese communists.[10] When the Japanese government received news that the truce was being enforced, it cancelled the order to send reinforcements to North China.

Japan assumed Chiang would respect the truce signed by his general. However, on July 25, at the railroad station of Langfang (50 miles from Peking), gunfire between Japanese and Chinese troops again broke out. The exchange of gunfire escalated into a major conflict as Japan sent in heavy reinforcements and bombed the Chinese barracks. Within a few hours the city was in Japanese hands, and the war with China had begun.

Japan's military felt that punitive measures by her military forces in China would bring Chiang around to accepting the truce within three months. So, Japanese bombers attacked three Chinese cities, and its ground forces engaged Chinese forces on the outskirts of Peking. City after the city fell into Japanese hands, and the fever of nationalism in Japan grew to unprecedented heights. The League of Nations condemned Japan's aggression as did the United States, even though Japan, at this time, was not a member of that body.

On November 19, 1937, Japan captured Soochow (50 miles west of Shanghai) and left the path to the city of Nanking wide open. Seizing the opportunity, the Japanese army then proceeded to march on to Nanking. On December 5, Colonel Hashimoto Kingoro (founder of the Cherry Blossom Society) ordered his artillery to open fire on the British gunboat *Ladybird* and seize her.

One week later, on the eve of Nanking's capture by Japanese troops, diplomatic relations between the United States and Japan were almost severed due to the *Panay* incident. The U.S. Navy *Panay* gunboat anchored in the Yangtze River outside Nanking was evacuating Americans from the besieged city when Japanese naval aircraft from the aircraft carrier *Kaga* bombed and sank the gunboat. *Panay* had been built to patrol the Yangtze River in order to protect American lives and property. On that day, its destruction resulted in the death of three sailors, with 43 sailors and five civilians wounded. The United States received a formal apology from the Japanese government on Christmas Eve, stating that Japan accepted full responsibility for the incident but maintained that the attack was unintentional. However, U.S. Navy cryptographers intercepted and deciphered radio traffic from *Kaga* aircraft that clearly indicated that they were under orders to attack the gunboat. This information was not disclosed publicly because of security reasons. Reparations were paid by Japan in the sum of $2,214,007.36 on April 22, 1938, closing the incident.[11]

General Chiang made the decision to withdraw all his forces from Nanking in late November, leaving behind a defenseless city. On December 13, 1937, Japanese forces marched in and occupied a city whose population now stood at 630,000. Over a period of six weeks, the Japanese troops tortured, raped, and murdered almost 300,000 Chinese civilians. Still, there were groups of Americans and Europeans who refused to leave the city and stayed behind in order to create safe haven zones that would ultimately save an estimated 300,000 Chinese from harm.

In March 1938, the Japanese army's proposal for a national mobilization law was accepted by Japan's Diet (the bicameral legislative body of Japan), essentially placing control of the war in the hands of the military and away from civilian control. Japanese military victories continued; Hankow and Canton fell, forcing Chiang inland to

Chungking. By early 1939, Japan was still continuing its military advances into China but was unsuccessful in breaking the will of the Chinese people, resulting in thoughts of a negotiated peace with China. However, news of Japan's armies conquering all of the major cities in eastern China and the establishment of a puppet state in Peking preempted any chance of a successful peace treaty.[12]

Elsewhere, the Battle of Nomonhan between Japan and Russia erupted in the summer of 1938 on the Manchurian-Soviet border, where the Japanese army suffered a devastating defeat. Ten months later, another incident occurred on the Manchurian-Outer Mongolian border near Peking that escalated into a full-blown battle. Once again, Soviet forces shattered Japanese forces, inflicting over 50,000 casualties. This humiliating defeat moved Japan closer to an alliance with Germany and Italy.[13] On August 23, 1939, China and Japan were stunned when Stalin signed a mutual non-aggression pact with Hitler. Ten days later, Germany invaded Poland. Prior to the invasion of Poland, Japan was planning to withdraw most of its troops from China. However, impressed by Germany's military boldness and success, Japan's military entered the 1940s with a sense of inflated military superiority.

Meanwhile, in the United States there were growing concerns about a potential war with Japan. The U.S. continued surveillance of Japan's military and diplomatic radio traffic. U.S. Army and Naval intelligence would find a way to finance their intelligence operations after the State Department withdrew its funding to Yardley's "Black Chamber" in 1929. This expectation was never fulfilled.[14]

To compound the U.S. intelligence disarray, Yardley's *Black Chamber*, published in 1931, made Japan aware of how the United States had decoded their secret cables and now created an incentive for Japan to make a greater effort to decipher America's encoded radio traffic and change its secret codes.[15] Japanese naval code breakers began to pay increasing attention to the U.S. diplomatic traffic that was being sent to the Far East on U.S. naval transmitters. Japanese intelligence officers, realizing that the process was slow and tedious, looked for a way to speed up the process. Japan decided, as America had, that stealing foreign information was a much faster and more productive technique.

Japan, realizing that her diplomatic and naval codes had been violated, proceeded to change them. The American code-breaker Agnes Meyer Driscoll was the first one to notice that a new code had replaced the previously existing *Red Code*. This observation came about when cryptanalyst Lieutenant Tommy Dyer was unable to make any progress on what he thought was the *Red Code* (Japanese naval code) for six months. Dyer, a U.S. Naval Academy graduate, had joined OP-20-G as a trainee to work on the *Red Code*. Mrs. Driscoll then deduced that the Japanese had changed the code because the code that Dyer was working on was a four-kana code system, and the *Red Code* had been a three-kana system.[16] Unlike other countries in the world, Japan used the Katakana system, which contains nearly twice the number of dots and dashes as the Morse code, in its telegraphic transmissions, adding to the complexity of enciphering the code. In spite of this observation, many months of arduous work were required before the code was broken. (Katakana is a Japanese phonetic syllabify—a series of written characters, each one of which is used to represent a single syllable.)

Working over a three-year period, U.S. intelligence eventually broke a complex and multilayered cipher system, solely due to Mrs. Agnes Meyer Driscoll and her co-workers. These cryptanalysts teased away the two-tier layer of protective decipherment and discovered the meaning of a code made up of almost 85,000 basic groups. The code groups were solved one at a time and then entered in the *Blue Book*, named after the color of its binding.[17] Dyer became tired of manually trying to come up with a solution to the myriad possibilities in solving the key to the code. Eventually he discovered a way to use IBM tabulating machines to ease the process. His superior, Lieutenant Joseph Wenger, concurred with the solution, and both men managed to get the Bureau of Engineering to grant them the $5,000 needed to rent IBM equipment and hire two keypunch card operators. The use of the IBM tabulating machines permitted easier access to detecting new systems and keeping track of changing cipher keys. Dyer's innovative work was responsible for the United States overtaking Britain's lead in the cryptologic world. Even with the significant advance that machine technology allowed in traffic analysis, human error (for example, transmitting in the plain text) that occurred in repeated enemy transmissions still provided the fastest breakthroughs in code breaking.[18]

By 1937, the Navy established the Mid–Pacific Strategic Direction Finder Net among those High Frequency Directional Finders in existence. This net not only permitted U.S. intelligence to follow the daily locations of Japanese war ships in the Pacific but provided early warning signs of an impending operation by observing the volume of radio traffic. The combination of these two observations could often provide the location and date of a planned movement.[19] A breakthrough in U.S. Intelligence came in 1939, when William Friedman, chief cryptologist of the SIS, and his team of code-breakers solved Japan's diplomatic enciphered messages and proceeded to construct a number of devices that cryptographically duplicated the Japanese machine. The Signal Corps called the cipher machine Purple, naming after the code it enciphered. In earlier days, U.S. intelligence named the first Japanese diplomatic intercept Orange; subsequent intercepts were also named by color. The most difficult diplomatic code to break was Purple, a diplomatic code that Japan continued to use until the end of the war (1939–1945). Magic was the name given to the deciphered information derived from the Purple machine.

The Purple machine was replicated by Navy technicians at the Washington Navy Yard and passed on to OP-20-G.[20] "It was housed in a drawer-sized box between two big electrically operated Underwood typewriters, which were connected to it by 26 wires plugged into a row of sockets called a plug board. To encipher a message, the cipher clerk would consult the thick Yu Go book of the machine keys, plug in the wire connections according to the key for the day, turn the four disks in the box so the numbers on their edges were those directed by the Yu Go, and type out the plain text, according to David Kahn."[21]

Intelligence was able to duplicate the Purple machine because the messages were sent out electronically, unlike the transmissions of Japan's naval code that utilized radio waves as its medium for transmission.[22] Naval codes were always deciphered by hand before and during the war.[23]

America entered the 1930s in the midst of the greatest depression ever to affect the United States and the world. The Navy was struggling for its existence as funds for defense were minimal in the 1920s with world peace and isolationism being the political themes of the day. This political climate and the depression (1929) resulted in not a single warship being built during the Herbert Hoover administration (1928–1932).

The three existing carriers in the Navy fleet were built between 1922 and 1927, and were *Langley, Lexington* and *Saratoga*. Although there was a controversy in the Navy among the admirals who felt that the battleship was the main offensive weapon in the fleet and the naval aviators who foresaw the aircraft carrier replacing the battleship in this role, many in the Navy favored the latter position. The Naval War College used carriers in the 1921 war games. The early performance of *Langley* prompted an immediate request for the construction of *Saratoga and Lexington*.

In 1923, fleet exercises demonstrated that the Panama Canal could be bombed by carrier aircraft. Rear Admiral W.A. Moffett, the father of naval aviation, had lobbied in Congress for the gradual replacement of the battleship with a carrier, believing that the carrier was the capital ship of the future. However, Navy policy still maintained that the carrier's aircraft be restricted to reconnaissance and self-defense. This tactical concept continued into 1940 when Rear Admiral J.K. Taussig won an Honorable Mention award for his article in naval magazine *Proceedings* about the supremacy of large fighting ships, namely the battleship.

The United States and Japan were permitted to convert two battle cruisers' hulls to aircraft carriers by the fine print in the Washington Naval Treaty of 1921. The treaty had granted the United States a total tonnage of 135,000 for its aircraft carriers (33,000 tons each). During the London Naval Treaty discussions in 1930—an extension of the Washington Naval Treaty—the United States, Britain, France, Germany, and Italy agreed that there be no further conversions of existing hulls into aircraft carriers and that no new capital ships be built until 1937.[24]

On December 9, 1935, the Second London Naval Conference took place because the terms of the Washington Naval Treaty of 1921 would expire at the end of 1936. One month later, Japan withdrew from the conference and its treaty restrictions. Italy then followed by refusing to sign the new treaty—Second London Naval Treaty—which was signed on March 25, 1936, by the United States, Great Britain, and France. Part of the refusal to be a signatory to the treaty was the public hostility to Italy's invasion of Abyssinia (Ethiopia). In the absence of Japan, a limitation on the number of warships constructed was now counterproductive, so the limitations agreed to involved the size of ships and guns. A departure from the agreements of the treaty was permitted if any signatory's national security was at risk. This treaty's terms were to be in force until 1942. Thus, the 1930s came to a close with the "Sun" (Japan) rising in the east, as the Japanese Navy was fast becoming the premier Navy in the world, and with the "Eagle" (United States) in the west slowly rebuilding its Navy under the Roosevelt Administration.

Looking back, one can appreciate that the visit to Japan by Commodore Perry in July 1853 that opened Japan to international trade—when coupled with the socio-political events of East Asia during the early 1900s—resulted in the unintended consequence of laying the groundwork for eventual conflict between the United States and Japan that was to become a reality 88 years later—on December 7, 1941.

Chapter 4

All Roads Lead to Pearl Harbor

As the 1930s came to a close, Japan's military turned southward. On February 10, 1939, it seized Hainan Island off the southern coast of China. When Germany invaded Poland in September 1939, it was now poised to strike the western nations of Europe. Japan, discerning the world's military and political indifference to Germany's aggression, seized the opportunity to demand that the Dutch government in the East Indies give Japan increased access to oil. The Dutch government refused, fearful that Japan's aggressive moves in China would lead to further aggression in the south.

On May 10, 1940, Germany invaded France; within six weeks, the occupation was complete. Next, Germany set its sights on Britain, and so the Battle of Britain unfolded, from July 10 to October 31, 1940. The drama for air superiority played out in the skies over England. In the end, Britain prevailed, and the victory was best summed up by Winston Churchill's famous quote: "Never in the field of human conflict was so much owed by so many to so few." The British victory caused Adolf Hitler to postpone his invasion of England and finally to cancel it in May 1941, deciding instead to move his bomber groups from the western front to the eastern front in preparation for the invasion of Russia.

On September 29, 1940, Japan, Italy, and Germany signed the Tripartite Pact which formalized the Axis powers' relationship. The pact was seen as a warning to the United States to remain neutral or risk a two-ocean war. Later, Hungary, Romania, Slovakia, Bulgaria, Yugoslavia, and Croatia also signed the Pact. This alliance paid dividends to Japan when Germany aided Japan in coming to an agreement with the German-controlled French Vichy government that permitted Japanese occupation of certain areas of northern Indochina. This political move by Japan closed a major supply route to China from Hanoi, thereby cutting off assistance to the Chinese Nationalistic and communist forces.[1]

In 1940, Roosevelt's intentions to have the United States get involved in the European war with England were almost exposed. A U.S. code clerk in the U.S. Embassy in London named Tyler Kent found secret communications between Churchill and Roosevelt that revealed that the president was determined to get America engaged in the war despite his campaign promises to the contrary. Kent smuggled some of the documents out of the embassy. However, he was caught and tried in a secret British court with the U.S. government's approval and confined to a British prison until the end of the war. Although controversy existed as to whether Kent had passed vital information to the Germans or was innocent of that charge, the existence of correspondence between Roosevelt and Churchill is clear.[2]

In January 1940, the United States named a new Commander-in-Chief of the

U.S. fleet, Admiral James O. Richardson. He was ordered to Hawaii with the American fleet in early spring of that year for naval exercises. His ships were anchored in Lahaina Roads off the northwest coast of Maui by April 10. The anchorage provided easy access to the ocean. It was his expectation that the fleet would return to its permanent base in San Pedro, California. Instead, in mid–May, the Navy Department transferred the fleet permanently to Pearl Harbor on Oahu as a deterrent to a possible Japanese invasion of the Dutch East Indies. The transfer of the fleet from Lahaina Roads to Pearl Harbor was dictated by the assumption that Pearl Harbor was a more secure U.S. naval base than the open waters of Lahaina Roads. In July 1940, Richardson met with President Roosevelt, complaining that the fleet should return to the West Coast. He was rebuffed by the president. On October 8, he again visited the president, who said that the presence of the fleet in Hawaiian waters was a deterrent to Japan expanding her territorial gains. Admiral Richardson replied, "Mr. Roosevelt, I still do not believe it, and I know that our fleet is disadvantageously disposed for preparing for or initiating war operations."[3] Richardson went on to say that the senior officers of the Navy did not have the confidence in the civilian leadership of America required for a successful prosecution of war in the Pacific. It can be said that the Pacific fleet's deployment to Pearl Harbor was as much a provocation to Japan as it was a deterrent.

With this political maneuvering going within the Navy, Congress was faced with the reality that the U.S. Selective Service Act (draft) was due to expire in August 1940, leaving the military weakened by a reduced number of men in the armed forces. Congress would vote to extend the term of the Act to 18 months by the slimmest of margins; the Senate passed the measure 45 to 30, but the bill passed the House by only one vote—203 to 202. World events did not seem to be making an impression on Congress.

In October 1940, Admiral Richardson met with Secretary of the Navy Frank Knox, who proposed a patrol of light ships in two lines extending from Hawaii to the Philippines, and from Samoa to the Dutch East Indies. Richardson vehemently objected, stating that the U.S. fleet was not prepared for such action, nor for a war with the loss of many ships that would presumably result from such action. Knox replied, "If you do not like the President's plan then you should draw up one of your own." On January 5, 1941, Admiral Richardson received orders relieving him of duty.[4]

Japan was formulating its ideas regarding Pearl Harbor. The concept of Japan attacking Pearl Harbor dates back to 1933 when Hirata Shinsaku, a popular Japanese naval author, wrote a book entitled *When We Fight*. In it, he describes an American fleet commander who muses that Japan would send a fast striking force of cruisers and aircraft carriers to attack Pearl Harbor. Within three years of the publication of the book, by 1936, an attack on Pearl Harbor was on the drawing board of the Japanese Naval War College.[5]

This concept was about to become a reality when Admiral Yamamoto Isoroku was placed in command of the Combined Fleet on October 30, 1940, and was charged with developing a strategy of defeating the United States in the event war broke out. Yamamoto, having spent a considerable amount of time in the United States, concluded that Japan's best chance to place America on the defensive was an early annihilation of its fleet. With America's fleet now positioned in Pearl Harbor, this afforded the Japanese their best opportunity to achieve this goal. Hirata's 1933 book popularized the idea, but it was the study by the Japanese Naval War College which gave definition to the concept with an impressive showing by Japanese carrier planes during spring maneuvers in 1940.

However, it was a British naval air attack on the Italian fleet in Taranto Harbor on November 12, 1940, that unwittingly proved that it could be done. If 21 British torpedo bombers could incapacitate three Italian battleships, then 200 Japanese aircraft could certainly damage and sink most of the U.S. fleet anchored in Pearl Harbor.[6] Japan had learned well from Britain's torpedo attack at Taranto and realized that the key to Japanese success in destroying America's Navy at Pearl Harbor was secrecy. Those at Pearl Harbor could have no idea that an attack was coming; however, in January 1941, the secret plan was nearly exposed. A rumor of an attack had originated from a Japanese member of the Peruvian embassy's staff in Tokyo, who had apparently learned of the information from her chauffeur boyfriend. The rumor was brought to the attention of Peru's minister in Tokyo, Ricardo Rivera-Schreiber, that Pearl Harbor was going to be attacked by the Japanese Navy. The minister immediately passed the communication on to Edward S. Crocker, first secretary of the U.S. embassy in Tokyo. Crocker then relayed the information to U.S. Ambassador to Japan Joseph Clark Grew. The news reached Admiral Husband E. Kimmel on February 1, 1941, the day he succeeded Admiral Richardson as Commander-in-Chief of the Pacific Fleet. An assessment was made by Commander Arthur H. McCollum, head of the Office of Naval Intelligence's Far East section in Washington. McCollum concluded, "Naval intelligence places no credence in these rumors."[7]

While American naval intelligence was dismissing the rumor, the Office of Naval Communications was following Japanese naval movements by a combination of code-breaking, direction-finding techniques, and traffic analysis until 1940. During the late 1930s, Japan made several changes to her naval codes, straining American intelligence officers' ability to decipher messages. For example, in 1938 Japan changed the eight-year-old *Blue Book*, resulting in over 4,000 keys being altered and resulting in a new transposition form that now had to be solved. Laurence F. Safford, now a commander and head of the cryptologic section of Naval Intelligence in Washington, assigned the task of solving the revised code to now Commander Thomas Dyer of the HYPO Unit (the U.S. Navy's intelligence unit) in Pearl Harbor.

After one year's effort, progress was being made, but then the Japanese made another major change to their code system. This new code, however, was restricted to flag officers and labeled *AD*. During 1940, there were only 200 messages, a number of which did lend to effective analysis in penetrating the cipher system. The HYPO Unit was restricted to working only on the Japanese flag officer code *AD* from November 1940 until the second week of December 1941. The unit could not spend any time decoding the JN-25 (Japanese Operations Navy Code) or the lesser J-19 code (used by the Japanese consul in Honolulu), nor was intelligence at HYPO privy to any of the Purple traffic (Diplomatic Code). All of the latter functions were restricted to Washington intelligence and other locations such as England and Station CAST in Cavite in the Philippines. This situation left naval intelligence in Hawaii devoid of the ability to obtain critical information that would have been extremely valuable in analyzing Japan's intentions toward Pearl Harbor.[8]

Germany continued to assist Japan, this time by providing Japan with critical intelligence about Britain's attitude toward Britain's territories in the Far East. On

November 11, 1940, a German surface raider captured a British steamer in the Indian Ocean. The Germans acquired top-secret British information that Great Britain would not send a fleet to the Far East nor go to war even if the Japanese invaded Thailand or Indochina. Instead, efforts would be made for the British to leave Singapore and make a deal over Malaya. The reasons why these secret papers were placed on a commercial vessel has never been disclosed. Certainly, it would have been safer to send the secret papers by warship or military aircraft. Britain decided on this plan to leave Singapore because Churchill was unable to persuade Roosevelt to issue a declaration that any attack on British or Dutch territory would result in America's entrance into the conflict. Roosevelt rejected the request because he was not in the political or military position to agree to such a proposition. The threat of force may have worked for Theodore Roosevelt at the turn of the century when the U.S. Navy outnumbered Japan's Navy but now Japan's fleet posed a sizeable threat to the U.S. Navy. As an alternative, Roosevelt proposed that U.S. cruisers show the American flag in the waters off Australia as a show of force designed to influence Japan's military intentions.[9]

With knowledge of Britain's strategy toward her colonies in the Far East now in Japanese hands, American cryptologists continued to work toward gaining Japanese intelligence to learn more about Japanese intentions. Although U.S. intelligence in Hawaii was still struggling to decipher the Japanese fleet code due to the low volume of radio traffic using this code, naval intelligence in Washington was working on the new Japanese naval operations code which became effective on June 1, 1939. This new cipher would later be designated JN-25A because it was the 25th Japanese naval code that they had encountered. The code was a five-numeral, two-part code, which consisted of 33,333 groups in the dictionary book, to each of which were added, by false arithmetic, a five-digit number selected according to the start key from a second book of random additives.[10]

Agnes Driscoll began work on the new code, dividing her approach into three areas: (1) the code itself, (2) the current additive book, and (3) the system of encrypting that was indicated at the beginning of the message, which was the starting point in a stream of additives. Finally in September 1940, after the code had been in use for 18 months, JN-25A was solved.[11]

However, on December 1, 1940, Japan changed the code once again to what was now termed JN-25B. Five successive cipher books were used during the life-span of JN-25A; the fifth cipher book, however, was retained in the new code during the first two months of JN-25B. This helped U.S. intelligence recognize and recover over 2,000 values for the new code book. With the new additives in 1941, deciphering progress slowed but picked up once again with the use of IBM tabulating machines which were introduced in the same year.

During the 1930s, the Army's Signal Intelligence Section (SIS), led by William Friedman, worked on Japan's diplomatic code. In 1935, Japan began ciphers generated by an encryption machine. Mrs. Driscoll quickly developed a manual technique for the decryption for *M1*, as the Japanese called it. However, American army cryptologists were desirous of developing their own machine to decrypt Japanese diplomatic-encrypted messages. SIS began work on a deciphering machine in 1936 which could read Tokyo's diplomatic messages on a regular basis. It was known as the *Red* machine, after the first color of the light spectrum.[12]

In 1939, Japan changed its machine-generated diplomatic code in a very different way that proved unbreakable by the methods inherent in the Red machine. The cover name for the new code was Purple after the opposite end of the light spectrum. Using the Red machine as a prototype, on September 25, 1940, SIS invented the infamous Purple machine, which opened a clandestine door to Japan's secret diplomatic traffic. Eight machines were produced by U.S intelligence: two each for U.S. Army and Navy intelligence, two were delivered to England, and one machine was sent to Station CAST in Cavite in the Philippines. Thought was given to sending U.S. Naval Intelligence in Hawaii (HYPO) a Purple machine in January 1941. Instead, Washington intelligence sent the instrument to Britain, resulting in HYPO never having received a Purple machine prior to the attack on Pearl Harbor. This neglect was to have far-reaching consequences as Washington intelligence deprived Hawaii of vital intercepts it had derived from Purple from late July 1941 until after the attack on Pearl Harbor.[13]

Privately, Admiral Kimmel was in agreement with Admiral Richardson's assessment of Pearl Harbor that the U.S. Fleet was very vulnerable to air attacks while anchored in Pearl Harbor. The harbor was in the shape of a shamrock, with East, Middle and West lochs, and its accessibility was formed by a channel so narrow that only one capital ship could pass through at a time.

On February 18, 1941, Kimmel expressed to Admiral Harold R. Stark, Chief of Naval Operations, his concern that *a surprise attack (submarine, air or combined) on Pearl Harbor is a possibility*. As a result, the Pearl Harbor commander-in-chief divided the fleet into three task forces, keeping 40 percent of the fleet at sea and 60 percent of the fleet in port.[14] The U.S. fleet's movements did not go unnoticed by Japanese agents. It was understood in U.S. intelligence circles that the Japanese Consulate in Honolulu was the center for spying in Oahu. Japanese agents had already been active in Hawaii for some time. When the U.S. fleet was first stationed in Hawaii in May 1940, the Japanese Foreign Office requested information on the size and disposition of the American fleet. Okuda Otojiro, acting Japanese Consul General, went to work checking on the fleet's size and movements and sent the information in code to Tokyo via the telegraph. Later in the year, Seki Kohichi, the Consulate treasurer, took over the job of obtaining information on the fleet. He broke no law as he did not step foot on any military grounds. He was able to keep track of the fleet by visiting the tourist grounds adjacent to the naval base and surrounding airfields.[15]

On March 14, 1941, Kita Nagao, the new Japanese consul general, arrived in Honolulu on the commercial liner *Tatsuta Maru*. Almost two weeks later, a young undercover agent, Yoshikawa Takeo (alias Morimura Tadashi), arrived on the passenger liner Nitta Maru. After six weeks of indoctrination by Kita, he had selected a number of espionage sites, including Aiea Heights and Kamehameha Highway, from which to observe the U.S. fleet and the submarine base. Yoshikawa was cautious not to use a camera or infringe on military territory. All of his spying was done at sites where any tourist could observe the fleet, determine when the fleet was in port or at sea, and on what days of the week. His conclusion was that the bulk of the fleet was in port on Saturdays and Sundays and that the northern sector of the island was rarely scouted for incoming planes.

In May 1941, he was asked to travel to Maui to check out Lahaina Heights, overlooking Lahaina Roads, the American fleet's traditional anchorage which was the original site of the U.S. fleet, to see if any American ships were present. The Japanese preferred this site because the waters were not shallow and any ships sunk in an attack would sink so deep into the water they could not be salvaged. On the other hand, the ships would have had easy access to the sea, but Yoshikawa found no ships present.[16]

In the latter part of 1941, Yoshikawa transmitted his reports to Tokyo on the movements of the Pacific Fleet in the J-19 code. Since the Japanese Consul in Hawaii was not equipped with a Purple system, it used the lower grade J-19 code. This occurrence unwittingly concealed the attack on Pearl Harbor since this code had a lower priority of decryption by Washington analysts than the Purple code in the months preceding the Pearl Harbor attack. Therefore, it would seem that U.S. intelligence in Washington had available to it all of the observations regarding the American fleet that were being sent between the Japanese consulate in Honolulu and Tokyo. Commander McCollum in Washington had refused the request of Lieutenant Commander Edwin T. Layton, intelligence officer for Admiral Kimmel, for Purple intelligence from Washington, and he essentially declined to address the issue of supplying Hawaii with information from the Japanese code J-19. At the same time, Admiral Stark gave the authority to decide the intentions of the Japanese military to Rear Admiral Richmond Kelly Turner, Director of War Plans, and his staff. Turner won a political victory by convincing Stark that he should have that power.

Thus, the authority to decide Japanese intentions was given to men who were not as familiar with Japan, its language, or its armed forces as were those men in the Office of Naval Intelligence. Turner insisted that ONI should be relegated to intelligence gathering only, and their opinions on Japanese military intentions were not to be sought. He would be the only one who would decide the intentions of the Japanese military. Here again, Washington intelligence failed to inform HYPO of critical intercepts, this time from the J-19 code which would have supplied Hawaii with crucial information from the office of the Hawaiian Consulate. The lack of intelligence from Magic and the J-19 code in the last four and half months prior to the assault on Pearl Harbor was to severely hinder Pearl Harbor intelligence's ability to make a proper assessment of the impending attack on that naval base.[17]

On March 31, 1941, Major General Fredrick L. Martin, commander of the Hawaiian Air Force, and Rear Admiral Patrick N.L. Bellinger, commander of the Naval Base Defense Air Force, presented the now famous Martin-Bellinger Report. The document speculated that Japan would send one or more submarines and/or a fast-raiding force composed of carriers supported by fast cruisers. The proposed air attack would be launched from one or more carriers which would approach within 300 miles of Oahu. The Martin-Bellinger solution to this hypothesis was a 360-degree patrol of the Hawaiian Islands. At that time, the Army had sole responsibility for the safety of the naval ships and installations in the harbor but subsequently transferred the long-range aerial reconnaissance plan of the base to the Fourteenth Naval District in Hawaii. Although Rear Admiral Claude C. Bloch, commandant of the Fourteenth Naval District, agreed to this arrangement, he had no patrol planes assigned to his command. The only Navy patrol planes in the Hawaiian area were the 69 planes of Patrol Wing Two, but unfortunately these planes lacked relief pilots and crews. Here, in essence, was the dilemma for those defending Pearl Harbor: the need for a 360-degree arc of patrol without the planes to successfully carry out such a mission.

In the spring of 1941, Major Warren J. Clear of U.S. Army Intelligence was sent to the Far East and learned from high-ranking British officers that Japan was planning an attack on a chain of islands that included Guam and Hawaii. Clear claimed that he sent the information to the War Department in Washington. However, no trace of the communication has ever been found in the National Archives, nor is there any other information to collaborate his story. Interestingly, he was ordered not to appear before the Pearl Harbor Investigation Committee. A copy of an unpublished book written by Clear was sought by his conservator George Farrier but never found.[18]

On April 1, 1941, Naval Intelligence in Washington alerted all naval districts in Hawaii that a Japanese attack could come on a Saturday, a Sunday, or a national holiday, and they should take the necessary steps to be prepared.[19] The warning was vague as to when the attack would come. The Navy in Hawaii certainly did not have enough patrol planes to cover a 360-degree search arc nor was the direction of possible incoming planes certain. What were the necessary steps to be taken that would prevent a surprise attack? The answer lies in the fact that the entire U.S. Army inventory had only 109 B-17s, but 250 B-17s were needed to protect Hawaii with the 360-degree arc.[20] Thus, only a few planes were sent to Hawaii and even those planes were later diverted to the Philippines to bolster its defense. In essence, this series of events meant that at the time there was no adequate land-based air patrol to guard against a surprise air attack on Pearl Harbor.

Meanwhile, the Vacant Sea order authored by Rear Admiral Royal Ingersoll, Assistant Chief of Naval Operations, was issued after Admiral Kimmel disputed an earlier Vacant Sea order of November 22, 1941, which interfered with Kimmel's plans to patrol the North Pacific waters starting on November 23, 1941. As promised, on November 23, 1941, and without White House approval, Kimmel ordered the U.S. Pacific Fleet 200 hundred miles north of Oahu to search for a potential Japanese task force. This search was in the exact area of what turned out to be the intended Japanese launch site on December 7, 1941.[21] On November 25, 1941, Kimmel and San Francisco's Twelfth Naval District received a message from Navy headquarters in Washington directing them to route all transpacific traffic through the Torres Strait. The order was sent about an hour after Nagumo's carrier left Hitokappu Bay and sailed into the North Pacific. The reason given by Rear Admiral Turner, Director of War Plans, for the Vacant Sea order was that the Navy wanted to divert sea traffic so that the track of the Japanese task force would be clear of any other vessels.[22] When White House military officials learned that Kimmel had sent the Pacific warships north of Pearl Harbor, they issued directives that caused Kimmel to rescind his order and quickly return the fleet to Pearl Harbor. This episode in the history of investigation of the Pearl Harbor attack has completely been ignored by every Pearl Harbor investigation including the 1995 congressional probe by Senator Strom Thurmond and Congressman Floyd Spence. The foregoing focus on the Vacant Sea order has been highlighted by Robert Stinnett in his book *Day of Deceit*.

In early May 1941, 21 B-17s had been shuttled from the mainland to reinforce the air-power on Oahu. However, Lieutenant General Walter C. Short, USA, Commanding General of the Army in Hawaii, envisioned a Japanese invasion of the islands preceded by widespread sabotage, not an air attack, designed to sink the American fleet in its harbor followed by an immediate withdrawal. However, he accepted these planes since it was his responsibility to protect the American fleet.[23]

During this time period, Japan's naval leaders were beginning to draft their plan for an attack on Pearl Harbor. Surprise continued to be the key element to the success of the operation. In addition, on April 10 the first important tactical decision was made to form the existing task force into a group of carriers and deploy the supporting ships of fast cruisers and destroyers as a defensive shield for the carrier groups. By mid–April, the Japanese *Pearl Harbor* project had moved into command channels, becoming an authorized subject of staff study. Command of the First Air Fleet fell to Vice Admiral Nagumo Chuichi by seniority and protocol. However, his background was in capital ships, and he was devoid of any connection with air power. The Japanese Navy Ministry appointed Rear Admiral Kusaka Ryunosuke as his chief of staff. Kusaka had a background in aviation, having commanded the small carrier *Hosho* and the big carrier *Akagi*. Nagumo's main responsibility was command of the First Fleet but his staff also headed the First Carrier Division, consisting of *Akagi* and *Kaga*. The Second Carrier Division was commanded by Rear Admiral Yamaguchi Tamon. Nagumo's air officer was Commander Genda Minoru, the only one of the group whose background was rooted in naval aviation. The Pearl Harbor project was the alternative plan to peace, assuming diplomatic efforts failed to resolve the political conflict between Japan and the United States.[24]

In an attempt at peaceful diplomatic solutions, the State Department offered two proposals to Japan in April 1941. One, submitted by two Catholic clergymen, Bishop James E. Walsh and Father James Drought, naïve pacifists, essentially required America to acquiesce to Japan's imperialist demands, including maintaining their occupation of China and Manchuria. America would also recognize Japan's aggression into China and Manchuria as legitimate incursions. Upon closer examination, Secretary of State Cordell Hull perceived the clergymen's proposal as an American capitulation to Japanese demands. He subsequently issued a second proposal to Admiral Nomura Kichisaburo, Japanese Ambassador to Washington, and informed him that all negotiations would occur only through him. Known as the *Four Principles of Freedom*, it advocated that Japan give up its policy of forcible conquest and respect the rights of other countries in the Asiatic area.[25]

On May 5, 1941, the United States came close to losing its diplomatic intelligence advantage over the Japanese. The Japanese Foreign Ministry cabled Nomura that German agents had informed Ambassador Oshima Hiroshi in Berlin that American intelligence was reading Japanese diplomatic mail. Ironically, after a brief investigation, the Japanese refused to believe that the United States could have broken their super-encrypted diplomatic code and continued to use the Purple code unchanged.[26]

Unfazed by the German agent's disclosure, Japan continued to contact Nomura using the Purple code. On May 12, the Japanese responded to the Walsh-Drought draft and Hull's *Four Principles* proposals as though they were submitting a counter-proposal to the Walsh-Drought draft and not to Hull's *Four Principles*. The draft by the clergymen was far more generous than the official U.S. policy toward Japan, leading the United States to reject Japan's counter-proposal.[27]

With attempts at diplomacy being carried out between the United States and Japan, the situation in the Atlantic was deteriorating as German submarines were sinking unprotected merchant ships at an alarming rate. Merchant ships lost their destroyer protection in a dangerous area of the Atlantic where Canadian convoy escorts departed and before British escorts resumed that responsibility. On March 11, 1941, Roosevelt signed House Resolution 1776, a lend-lease destroyer policy (bases for destroyers deal) with Great Britain. England's survival was at stake, and her loss would place America in the position of being the only world power standing in Germany's and Japan's way of dominating the world. With a "Europe first" policy in place, on April 20 the aircraft carrier *Yorktown* and five destroyers were detached from the fleet in Pearl Harbor to the Atlantic and, one month later, the Pearl Harbor–based battleships *Mississippi, Idaho* and *New Mexico* followed the carrier into the Atlantic. The U.S. fleet in the Pacific had now been reduced by 25 percent, leaving Hawaii even more vulnerable to attack.[28]

The United States bolstered its intelligence capabilities in Hawaii by the arrival on May 15, 1941, of Lieutenant Commander Joe Rochefort, who came to Hawaii to command the HYPO Unit. He immediately requested that the title of the unit be changed from Communications to Combat Intelligence Unit for security reasons. Admiral Kimmel, who had limited space aboard the battleship *Pennsylvania,* moved his headquarters to the second story of the headquarters building overlooking the submarine base. This change of location facilitated close cooperation between Lieutenant Commander Layton, Fleet Intelligence Officer, and Rochefort due to the close proximity of the two offices. That summer Rochefort's staff was moved from the upper floors of the main headquarters into its basement with a guard placed at its only entrance.[29]

Rochefort's intelligence unit at Pearl Harbor was by-passed when the Royal Navy code breakers in Singapore turned over all of their information regarding the five-numeral system (JN-25B) to Admiral Thomas Hart's Asiatic Fleet. On March 5, Station CAST in the Philippines, which had already received a Purple machine to decipher Japan's diplomatic code, was now being asked to work on the JN-25B operational code. Until British intelligence delivered the keys to unlock JN-25B to Station CAST in March, OP-20-G (Naval intelligence in Washington) was the only arm of intelligence with the right to work exclusively on the JN-25B operational code.[30]

When Station CAST requested that it be allowed to focus all of its attention on JN-25B, OP-20-G responded that it did not have the statistical machinery and, further, that OP-20-G intended to transfer that function to HYPO. Somehow CAST prevailed, and on May 2, HYPO was notified that it would continue to work on the Admiral Code (AD), not the JN-25B code. CINCPAC intelligence continued to work on the Admiral Code for nine months with little results due to the low volume of radio traffic. Nor, as has been stated, was HYPO provided the current keys for the "J" series of the transposition ciphers which were used for the most secret communications of the Japanese consulate in Hawaii. The only Japanese diplomatic systems given to HYPO were the low-grade ciphers used for routine housekeeping traffic. Thus, not only was HYPO not privy to decipher the "J" series of traffic, but Washington intelligence compounded the problem by leaving most of this traffic unread.[31]

We know that the JN-25A naval code became readable at the end of 1940. Station CAST learned of Japan's intention to push south, just before the Japanese Navy changed its important decrypts to form the JN-25B code. HYPO received its last message in the Purple code on July 20, 1941, due to Rear Admiral Turner's interference. Having won a political victory with the exclusive right to interpret the military intentions of Japan, Turner made sure this change of policy was not printed in the Navy manual, so that if needed politically, he could assign the responsibility for misinterpretation of Japanese intelligence to the Office of Naval Intelligence rather than to his own department. This gave him the flexibility to blame ONI for errors of judgment regarding Japanese intentions. This political maneuvering served Admiral Turner very well, particularly during the post–Pearl Harbor congressional hearings. In the meantime, Turner miscalculated Japan's intention that summer by concluding that they were going to attack Siberia and not move to the south.

Another failure of Washington intelligence under Admiral Turner was its neglect to decipher the WE WE code (a simple substitution system used by Japanese intelligence to communicate information). In late 1940, HYPO had deciphered information from the low priority WE WE cipher that indicated that the Japanese had been building up their military installations in their Pacific mandated islands. Later, this same information was deciphered by Station George in Guam.[32]

The Japanese changed the JN-25A naval code to the JN-25B code in December of 1940. JN-25B deciphering was, for the most part, left to OP-20-G intelligence where only a partial readout was available in the year leading up to the attack on Pearl Harbor on December 7, 1941. It is interesting to note that, although the talented Agnes Driscoll and her colleagues in Washington reportedly could not break enough of the JN-25B code to be of value in 1941, less than four months after having been authorized to work on JN-25B on December 17, 1941, Rochefort and his group deciphered enough of the code for the information to be instrumental in the early American strategic victories in the later battles of the Coral Sea and Midway.

In May 1941, the FBI uncovered the fact that Lieutenant Commander Tachibani Itaru was carrying out espionage activities with his contact man in Pearl Harbor. He worked outside the confines of the Japanese consulate and therefore engaged in illegal espionage. A trap was set by the FBI and Naval Intelligence which led to the arrest of Tachibana in Los Angeles. With negotiations going on between the United States and Japan, his only punishment was to be deported to Japan.[33] This action was taken to avoid upsetting the Japanese at a time of delicate diplomatic negotiations. Tachibani was not the only foreign agent arrested. The United States carried out an overdue house-cleaning of all foreign agents in America but decided to keep the Japanese Consulate open in Honolulu to obtain secret information from their offices. This action was taken in spite of the protests of Robert L. Shivers, a nineteen-year veteran of the FBI, to J. Edgar Hoover and to the attorney general of the United States that all 234 Japanese consular agents in Hawaii were engaged in gathering information for the Japanese Consul and were definitely a source of potential danger.[34] Thus, the Honolulu Japanese Consulate continued its operational espionage activities in Hawaii. Since the Honolulu Consulate used the J-19 code messages which were given a low priority in Washington, the ultimate effect of this action permitted Japanese espionage in Hawaii prior to the attack on Pearl Harbor to be carried out uninterrupted, since there was no legal way to stop the spying.

While the FBI permitted questionable activities to continue on the part of Japanese agents living in Hawaii, the Japanese Navy directed its attention to solving the issue of executing a torpedo attack in the waters in Pearl Harbor. The Japanese Navy realized that the depth of the water in Pearl Harbor was too shallow for their torpedoes not to get stuck in the mud before they reached their targets. Therefore, they went to work on changing the physical characteristics of the torpedo, so that it would run true in shallow water. Studies had shown that the average depth of Pearl Harbor was about 40 feet. A torpedo dropped from an aircraft could sink no lower than 12 feet in order to be effective in an attack on ships anchored in Pearl Harbor. In early

June 1941, Commander Genda Minora, in charge of the First Carrier Division's air wing, initiated the first aerial torpedo program aimed at solving this problem.[35]

Kyushu, the southernmost island of the four main islands of Japan, was chosen as a test site because the locale resembled Pearl Harbor. Since 1933, Japan had been a leader in aerial torpedo techniques, launching from about 300 feet at relatively high speed. There were two main factors that determined how deep a torpedo would sink once launched: plane altitude and design of the torpedo itself. It was discovered that reducing plane speed did influence the depth of water that the torpedo reached upon impact. In 1939, a wooden fin attached to the torpedo stabilized the weapon, but the wooden fin broke off as the torpedo hit the water. A wooden plate affixed to the fin at a slight angle, however, produced promising results. Japan continued its development of a torpedo that would work in the shallow waters of Pearl Harbor.[36]

Kimmel, not realizing that the intensity of Japanese desire to attack Pearl Harbor led them to reinvent the torpedo, believed that Pearl Harbor was too shallow for a torpedo attack against his ships, and that torpedo nets were not needed. With the presumption on Kimmel's part that the depth of Pearl Harbor was not an issue, he met with Admiral Stark about other shortcomings of Pearl Harbor in June of 1941. They discussed weaknesses of the harbor, including the congestion of the ships, the location of fuel oil depots and repair facilities and, most importantly, the existence of only a narrow single channel for ships to leave the harbor, requiring hours for them to reach the sea and sortie. He believed the only solution was for the fleet to be moved somewhere other than Pearl Harbor. However, other than returning to the West Coast, which Kimmel did not recommend, there was no other realistic alternative.[37]

While Kimmel was addressing his concerns to Admiral Stark, Japan's military was trying to decide in which direction its next military move should be. The German invasion of Russia in June 1941 created a dilemma for Japan. Should she join the attack on the Soviet Union by turning her troops north, or should she proceed on her planned southerly direction into Indochina? In July, a conference was held in Tokyo where, although war with the Soviet Union was not ruled out, it was decided that Japan would most likely proceed south. She needed the natural resources of Indochina if she were to proceed with war with the United States. U.S. intelligence in Washington concurred with that expectation, but Admiral Turner felt that the Soviet Union was the direction that Japan would take.[38]

On July 2, 1941, Japan finally made the decision to proceed south into Indochina instead of maintaining the military and political status quo in China and Manchuria, necessitated by the fact that Japan was, at that time, dependent on the United States for 80 percent of its oil supply. By Japan occupying Indochina, she was in position to launch northward against Nationalist China, west against Thailand and Burma, and south toward Malaya. This strategy was based on Japan's need for oil, minerals, and rice as well as for the military protection of its right flank.[39]

Washington intelligence during the Indochina crisis did inform Kimmel with an update from Purple that outlined Japan's timetable to invade Indochina. However, it was directly from CAST that HYPO received important decrypts that Japan had definitely decided to invade Indochina.

HYPO was surprised to learn that Washington intelligence (OP-20-G) had learned this information from Station GEORGE in Guam. That omission was a telling sign that the Navy Department in Washington was either overwhelmed by the volume of traffic it was receiving and the burdens of decrypting and translating, or it was a failure of command structure to ensure that vital traffic was handled in an expeditious manner. The failure of OP-20-G in not informing Kimmel of known vital intelligence in the months prior to the attack by Japan on Oahu certainly seems to point to the latter. Washington intelligence had learned of this communication from Station GEORGE in Guam in June 1941 and had not deciphered this information themselves. The question still lingers: was this failure by OP-20-G to pass on intelligence to Hawaii deliberate in order to insure that Japan would strike the United States first? This action prompted a top-secret message from the CNO to fleet headquarters in Pearl Harbor stating that Pacific Fleet intelligence had information it was not sharing with Washington. Lieutenant Commander Layton responded promptly that he had received the WE WE dispatch from Station CAST and that a copy and the original message were addressed to the CNO. When Kimmel went to Washington to discuss the matter, he found that the CNO and the Director of ONI, Captain Alan C. Kirk, were unaware of the information. On further inspection, they found the raw data in the ONI files untouched. This represented another example of the failure of the CNO and ONI to keep Kimmel adequately informed of significant Japanese intelligence.[40]

On July 24, 1941, with the permission of the French Vichy government, Japan now entered south Indochina which included occupation of the strategic air fields and the use of Saigon and Camranh Bay as naval bases. While the occupation was taking place, President Roosevelt offered Nomura one last chance to reconcile the two countries' differences before America reacted to Japan's movement south. He proposed that Japan have access to Indochina's rice and minerals if she would withdraw from the region. When this action did not occur, President Franklin Roosevelt reacted swiftly with an executive order that immediately froze all of Japan's and China's financial assets in the United States. Eight days later, on August 1, 1941, Roosevelt followed up with an embargo of American high-octane gasoline and crude oil against Japan. This action would jeopardize Japan's financial markets and leave her with oil reserves that were capable of operating her military for only 12 months, creating a point of no return for Japan. The Japanese Naval General Staff now took a closer look at the Pearl Harbor project.[41]

With tensions between the United States and Japan mounting because of Japan's entry into Indochina, Stark notified Kimmel in late July that the president requested that he send a carrier full of planes to one of the Asiatic Russian ports. Kimmel, realizing the potential danger that this course of action presented, vehemently objected, arguing, "If the intent is to provoke war with Japan, let us chose a time and a place that is better suited for the United States."[42]

It is important to repeat that in late July 1941, HYPO in Hawaii was to receive its last piece of Purple diplomatic intelligence from Washington—the probable movements of the Japanese military into southeast Asia. The information derived from the Purple intercepts was invaluable to HYPO because their only assignment was to attempt to break the Japanese fleet code, which provided little formation due to the low volume of traffic. However, traffic analysis and radio directional-finding techniques provided HYPO with enough information that it was able to track some of the ships of the Japanese fleet, revealing that Japan had at least one carrier division in the South China Sea at the time of the Indochina occupation.

The Combat Intelligence Unit (HYPO) was able to ascertain that Japan had two unidentified carriers that were standing by as a show of force while diplomatic negotiations for Japan to secure army and naval bases in Indochina were proceeding between Japan and the French Vichy government. After the war it was confirmed that *Soryu* and *Hiryu* were the two carriers that were present off the coast of Indochina that could not be identified. From this point forward until December 8, 1941, CINCPAC intelligence would not receive any Purple intercepts from Washington, drastically impairing its judgment as to the coming attack on Pearl Harbor.[43]

OP-20-G soon discovered, through analysis of radio traffic, that the newly formed Japanese First Air Fleet had authority over all nine carriers and attached units, together with 16 destroyers. The creation of the First Air Fleet signified that Japan had revolutionized its air power, which presented a formidable threat to U.S. forces in the Pacific, which had only three carriers. However, although aircraft carriers were used as an offensive force in naval fleet war games as early as 1929, in the summer of 1941 battleships still ruled the waves, and many officers in the Navy still saw the carrier function only in a supporting role. This belief led many in the Navy to discount a hit and run carrier attack by Japan on Pearl Harbor.

On July 26, a revised war plan was received by Kimmel from Washington in which the Pacific fleet would now be used to check any attempt by Japan to invade Malaysia, Hong Kong, the Philippines, or any of our outer perimeter possessions. Also with this revision, Kimmel instituted long-range reconnaissance flights 500 miles to the west-southwest toward Jaluit to intercept any Japanese forces that might be sneaking in from their secret bases in the Marshall Islands. When there was no evidence of Japanese forces in that area, the air searches were called off. Nevertheless, the commander-in-chief kept Pearl Harbor on alert, as best he could, for an eventual conflict with Japan.[44]

Another bit of intelligence gathered by the Washington group in late July was that Japan was going to use Indochina as a springboard into the south seas. In early August, Tokyo forwarded to Admiral Nomura Kichisaburo, Japanese Ambassador to the United States, a new set of proposals for the United States to accept. The proposals insisted that Japan would stay in China for at least twenty-five years, adhere to the terms of the Tripartite Pact, and continue its expansion policy to the south for economic and strategic purposes. The proposals demanded that America accept the terms or risk war with Japan.[45] The proposals were rejected by the United States.

On July 31, Magic provided a clear warning of the impact of the United States' oil embargo. It stated that in order to "save its very life," Japan must take immediate steps to "break asunder this ever-strengthening chain of encirclement which is being woven under the guidance and with the participation of England and the United States."[46] The message was from Tokyo to Ambassador Oshima Hiroshi, Japan's ambassador in Berlin. It concluded that Japan must break the United States' and Britain's stranglehold on Japan. The danger that the U.S. oil embargo would actually increase rather than decrease the risk of war between Japan and the United States was completely ignored by those higher up in the U.S. naval command structure and especially by Roosevelt, who actually imposed the oil embargo This act placed Japan in the position of either capitulating to America's demands or invading the countries to the south for its oil needs. The failure by FDR and his inner circle to interpret the true meaning of this Japanese message, or deliberately ignore it, is considered one of the major blunders in U.S. history.[47] The oil embargo meant to deter Japanese aggression in the south Pacific instead became a touchstone of Japan's anger toward the U.S. and Britain, pushing Japan immediately into war. Diplomatic policy—the oil embargo—was dictating military strategy toward Japan, and the United States lacked the naval power to deal with the consequence of that diplomatic strategy—specifically, a war.

The United States was now forced into a secret commitment with Britain whereby an attack on any British possession in the Far East would result in America going to war with Britain against Japan. This deterrent strategy was flawed because neither Britain nor the United States had the naval resources to combat Japanese aggression in the Far East. This agreement was destined to fail by its very nature. On August 7, Roosevelt met with Winston Churchill, Prime Minister of England, in Placenta Bay, Newfoundland. The meeting was most important, with far-reaching consequences, but is still one of history's least understood events. Churchill had just crossed the Atlantic aboard Britain's newest battleship, HMS *Prince of Wales*. Roosevelt reached the site first by sailing on the Presidential yacht *Potomac* and later transferred to the U.S. heavy cruiser *Augusta*. The two met for the first time as president and prime minister aboard the *Augusta*. While Britain had received assistance from the United States by its sending warships into the Atlantic to defend British merchant shipping against submarine attack, the Pacific was another matter. The British delegation was delighted that America's military policy had changed toward Japan as they learned that Washington's oil embargo was forcing the U.S. chiefs of staff to establish a strong naval presence in the Far East as a deterrent against Japan. The change in U.S. strategic policy toward Japan occurred by now making the United States' first line of defense the Philippine Islands rather than Hawaii. The plan was to build up the defense of the Philippine Islands with American aircraft, anti-aircraft guns, and a naval presence that would only serve to strengthen the defense of Singapore and the Dutch East Indies. This aspect of the meeting was kept secret so as not to alarm the public, which up to that time would only support a British/American agreement to uphold Roosevelt's *Four Principles of Freedom* that were later to be incorporated into the United Nations Charter.[48]

The far-reaching military arrangement entered into between the U.S. and Britain—that America would fortify the Philippines and that Britain would send naval forces to Singapore—was not recorded but was instead a silent agreement. The B-17 bombers ear-marked for Britain would now be sent to the Philippine Islands. In addition, Churchill pledged to send a squadron of modern battleships and carriers to Singapore. This policy's weakest link lay in the reality that these countries had neither the air power nor the navy to defend adequately the Philippines and Singapore at the time the plan was implemented, let alone to take the military offensive. Instead of providing a strong military presence, it invited a preemptive strike by Japan on the United States and Great Britain and provided neither protection of the Philippines nor a deterrent to Japan's aggression. It is important to point out that, after this meeting of Roosevelt and Churchill, the Joint U.S. Army-Navy Board chaired by Admiral Stark documented in its minutes that the supreme military council of the United States was working on the premise that an attack on British or Dutch territory by Japan would result in America going to war with Japan! This information, inexplicably, was not shared with the commanders at Pearl Harbor.[49] The first Purple intercept was sent three days before the meeting between Roosevelt and Churchill. It revealed that Nomura had warned Tokyo that the U.S. president accompanied by high army and navy officers had met with Churchill. The second Purple message, not decoded until 1943, revealed that there would be an arrangement for a joint Anglo-American participation in the war. None of this intelligence was forwarded to Kimmel. Three days before the Atlantic Charter was agreed to Japan discovered, through their own intelligence sources, that the meeting was not as much about Europe as it was about the military policy in the Far East.[50]

In spite of this lack of information, Kimmel continued to prepare for war, convinced (from his own intelligence) that Japan would soon strike the south Pacific and target the Philippines. He was also aware that there was a remote possibility that Pearl Harbor could be attacked. He instructed fleet operations to keep at least one task force at sea. At no time in 1941 were all of the ships of the Pacific Fleet in Pearl Harbor. In retrospect, it is apparent that during the period between July 20 and December 7, 1941, it was imperative that Hawaii intelligence receive all of the intercepts that Washington had in order to predict Japanese intentions, but this did not happen. The biggest intelligence loss was from the J-19 codes between Tokyo diplomatic officials and Japan's Honolulu consulate. These intercepts would have revealed to HYPO that Japan's intelligence service was paying special attention to the fleet anchorage and shipping movements at Pearl Harbor. Washington intelligence obviously felt this information would not be valuable to Kimmel in Hawaii. Those working in HYPO were not even aware intercepts such as these even existed. Senior officers directly responsible for the intelligence failures that led to the Japanese success at Pearl Harbor were not court-martialed, reprimanded, or in any other way taken to task for their role in the disaster. The brunt of the blame fell on the shoulders of Kimmel and Short; where lack of foresight contributed for the disaster at Pearl Harbor, for example, the lack of anti-torpedo nets and the clustering all of the parked planes on the airfield.[51]

Admiral Turner had taken control of interpreting all communications intercepts from Navy intelligence in Washington, and as such was responsible for that information being forwarded to Hawaiian intelligence. This power was granted to him by Admiral Stark, Chief of Naval Operations. General George Marshall, Chief of Army Staff, had the deciding authority regarding Army intelligence. After December 7, no one in Washington wanted to accept the responsibility for keeping Hawaii out of the intelligence loop. All of the senior staff officers refused to admit setting the policy that denied Kimmel the critical intelligence gleaned from the Purple and J-19 code. Colonel Rufus Bratton, Chief of Far East section of military intelligence for the Army, stated that he received orders from General Marshall that "...prevented me from transmitting any *Magic* intercepts to overseas commanders."[52]

General Marshall denied the episode and issuing such an order. Admiral Stark also proclaimed he gave no such order of that nature. Stark stated that it was his belief, based on information he received from Admiral Turner, Director of War Plans, that Pearl Harbor had the capability to intercept—as well as translate—Japanese diplomatic messages. Admiral Turner placed the blame on Rear Admiral Leigh Noyes, Director of Naval Communications, saying that he was reassured by Noyes that Kimmel was not only "getting as much as we were" but "he was getting it sooner than we were." When Rear Admiral Noyes was questioned in the Pearl Harbor hearings in 1945, he testified that he never intentionally led Turner to believe that Hawaii was getting any of the messages decoded by the Purple machine. Four months later, Turner was forced to admit that he "was entirely in error as regards the diplomatic codes."⁵³ None of his subordinates, however, was willing to take on this four-star admiral who had successfully masterminded the Navy's wartime amphibious operations. He essentially escaped any damage to his career by denying the unwritten policy that all intelligence coming from the ONI would only be analyzed and interpreted by him. Before Turner gained control over the interpretation on deciphered intercepts, this responsibility fell to the Office of Naval Intelligence. As a result, Turner was often sending out intelligence that was erroneous and based on wild conclusions. Turner's statement at the hearings essentially went unchallenged because Stark and Captain Royal Ingersoll, the CNO's deputy, had refused to place the change in policy in the naval operations manual.⁵⁴

August 1941 brought continuing cooperation between the undercover agents of the Axis powers. For example, when Rear Admiral Abe Koki and his aides had visited Taranto, Italy, in May 1941 to learn everything there was to know about the British torpedo plane raid on that Italian naval base in November 1940, they were accompanied by German intelligence. Coincidently, a British double agent, Dusko Popov, was making one of his routine trips to Lisbon. Popov was born in Yugoslavia where later in his life he was arrested by the Gestapo for advocating democracy. The Germans were able to convince him to join the Abwehr, the Wehrmacht's (highly trained officers of the armed forces responsible for the defense of Germany) intelligence arm. Popov accepted the offer from German intelligence, but he was actually working for MI-6, Britain's secret intelligence service, as a British double agent. His code name was Tricycle. While Popov was in Lisbon, he met with Johnny Jebsen, who was also functioning as a British double agent. Jebsen reported that he was with the German delegation that escorted the Japanese to Taranto. The Japanese official delegation was led by Rear Admiral Abe Koki, and his aides wanted to know every detail of the successful carrier British torpedo raid on Italian battleships in the harbor in 1940. The inquiry lasted from May 18 to June 8. The Japanese visit to Taranto, coupled with the information that the Germans wanted Popov to immediately travel to the United States and organize an espionage ring, prompted him to leave for America. His German orders also stated that once the former was accomplished, he was immediately to travel to Hawaii to secure information about ship deployment in Pearl Harbor, pier installations, number of anchorages, and the depth of the water. This order clearly convinced Popov and British intelligence that Japan was going to attack Pearl Harbor by carrier aircraft.⁵⁵

On August, 10, 1941, Tricycle left for New York after first conferring with MI-6 as to whom in the United States he should notify to pass on this critical piece of intelligence. British intelligence chose J. Edgar Hoover, head of the Federal Bureau of Investigation, as the person to whom he should speak. Popov flew from Lisbon to New York on a Pan-Am flying boat and arrived on August 12, 1941. He met with Percy "Sam" Foxworth, FBI agent in charge of the New York FBI office, with two German secrets in hand. One secret was a sample of the microdot system the Germans were using and the other was a questionnaire. Of the hundred or so questions in the questionnaire, one-third pertained to Hawaii. The microdot contained orders from Germany for Popov to recruit a new German spy in the United States and for Popov to travel to Hawaii, as soon as possible, to report on the U.S. defenses and ship deployment in Pearl Harbor. Popov received a cool reception by the FBI. He stated that he received the information from the British, and he would forward the material to Washington. Foxworth's initial reaction was that the information sounded like a trap. Popov replied the material was from very reliable sources. He insisted on seeing Hoover, and two weeks later, Popov met with the director, who was unimpressed by the information regarding Pearl Harbor. Popov walked out of the meeting feeling that at least he had reported it.[56]

Hoover and the FBI have denied that Hoover and Popov ever met. The FBI reported that it had no record of such a meeting. The double agent then sought the help of William Stephenson, Winston Churchill's secret envoy to the United States, code-named Intrepid, and Sir John Masterman, head of the Double-Cross System in Britain. Both failed to persuade Washington to take the intelligence seriously.

Yet, the fact that Popov's questionnaire was passed on to the proper military authorities and even to President Roosevelt was documented by the discovery of a paraphrased one-page version of the questionnaire that was circulated by the FBI. However, a record of Popov's information suggesting a Japanese air attack on Pearl Harbor has never been found. One fact is certain: Popov went to his grave believing that J. Edgar Hoover was the person responsible for the disaster at Pearl Harbor.[57] Popov was a loyal British double agent, and he hated the Nazis. He is a credible witness because the information he provided to Hoover turned out to be true, and he had no axe to grind against Hoover, as it was MI-6 that recommended Hoover to him. Popov's opinion was based on Hoover's indifference to the information he had received, and the failure by the FBI director to follow up and pursue the critical intelligence Popov had passed on to him.

Incidentally, in 1941 author Ian Fleming met Dusko Popov in a casino in Portugal where Popov was at the baccarat table. Fleming was showing off his limited amount of money at the table while working for British intelligence, when Popov promptly placed $50,000 on the table, leading an embarrassed Fleming to leave the casino. Popov is thought to be the real-life agent upon which Fleming's fictional brainchild James Bond was based.[58]

In early August 1941, the Japanese Foreign Ministry suggested to Nomura that there be a meeting between Prime Minister Konoye Fumimaro and President Roosevelt. Nomura, knowing of America's position regarding the talk, reacted by telling Tokyo that the United States was ready to take drastic action if necessary, depending on Japan's military course of action. At this point, Secretary of State Hull, Secretary of War Henry L. Stimson, and Secretary of the Navy Knox all agreed that appeasement toward Japan was over. In response to the diplomatic decision of America's secretaries, Nomura sent Tokyo a long message in mid–August stating, "There is no doubt whatsoever that the United States is prepared to take drastic action depending on what way Japan moves."[59]

Yamamoto felt at this time that the existing operational plan for war against the American, British, Chinese, and Dutch (ABCD) powers was inadequate. In his opinion, the Pearl Harbor operation was imperative to the successful outcome of Japan's southern Pacific strategy. He concluded that holding war games in September would permit the Naval General Staff a chance to reconsider the idea that an attack on Pearl Harbor become part of their overall strategy in initiating war with the United States. The Pearl Harbor exercise would also allow the operational units a chance to play out their mission and to take account of the problems inherent in the attack upon the United States.[60]

Captain Kuroshima Kameto was given the task to change the Navy General Staff's mind. Rear Admiral Tomioka Sadatoshi headed the Operations Section of the First Bureau of Naval General Staff, and he listed certain reasons for not attacking Pearl Harbor. Included were: (1) difficulty in maintaining secrecy; (2) techniques of refueling at sea needed to be improved; (3) the shallow waters of Pearl Harbor were not conducive to a torpedo attack; (4) the inability of an incoming plane to take action in the harbor; (5) probable anti-torpedo nets in the harbor; and (6) the present poor accuracy and thus the ineffectiveness of horizontal and dive-bomber bombing. No final decision was made for the attack on Pearl Harbor, but Kuroshima had one card yet to play: the threat of a resignation by Admiral Yamamoto. However, he decided to withhold this information, as this was not the right time to play this card for there was time left to persuade the Navy General Staff to his way of thinking.[61]

Later in August, Colonel William F. Farthing, commander of the Fifth Bombardment Group at Hickam Field, his supply officer Major Elmer Rose, and operations officer Captain L.C. Coddington sent a report to Major General H.H. "Hap" Arnold, USA, Commander of U.S. Army Air Forces in Washington entitled *Plan for the Employment of Bombardment Aviation in the Defense of Oahu*. Based on an analysis of Japan's naval capabilities, the Farthing report prophetically predicted that Japan would use six carriers that would arrive at Hawaii from 0 degrees counter-clockwise to 180 degrees around Oahu in an early morning attack. The U.S countermove called for a complete search of the Hawaiian area daily, with a 100 percent coverage during daylight hours and a thorough 360-degree search arc. The purpose of the scouting was to detect incoming enemy carriers before they had the opportunity to launch their aircraft for an attack on Pearl Harbor and its neighboring airfields. In order to carry out these searches, they requested 180 B-17Ds. The problem was that the U.S. Army Air Force only had 109 B-17s in its entire inventory, and many of these had been committed to mainland defense, Britain, and the Philippines.[62]

During the same time frame, General Short decided to order a two-month program to train Hawaiian Air Force personnel as infantrymen. The order did not go over well with members of the U.S. Army Air Force, as there was a shortage of trained pilots, resulting in inexperienced pilots for those aircraft that were available. Many of the pilots at Pearl Harbor had logged in 200 to 300 hours of air time compared to thousands of hours for Japanese pilots. Simply put, the Army Air Force pilots needed more flying time and did not feel their time should be spent training as infantry men.[63]

Nomura, Roosevelt, and Hull met on August 17 to discuss a meeting between the president and the prime minister of Japan, giving Roosevelt an opportunity to seek further clarification of Japan's foreign policy intentions. In spite of their countries' differences, the president remained warm to the idea of meeting the prime minister, but he needed time to study the pros and cons of such a conference. He subsequently scheduled a second meeting ten days later for the three men to discuss the issue. The president in the meantime had concluded that a summit with the prime minister would be a lose-lose situation. If he won every point with the prime minister, the result would bring down the Konoye government, or even his assassination by right wing activists in the Japanese political party. On the other hand, if Roosevelt gave in, a charge that this was another Munich (the city where Britain signed an agreement of appeasement with Hitler in 1938 which basically turned over Czechoslovakia over to the Germans) would be made. This led the president to delay giving Nomura a definitive answer about a meeting with the Japanese prime minister.

On August 15, 1941, while the Japanese ambassador was negotiating in Washington, important Army-Navy meetings were taking place in Japan during which the Japanese Navy brought up for the first time the possibility of an attack on Pearl Harbor. The Japanese Navy's position was to prepare for war while maintaining a wait-and-see attitude during negotiations with the United States. The Army wanted an immediate decision up or down regarding war with America; however, Emperor Hirohito insisted on stressing diplomacy first.

By late August 1941, progress was being made regarding the Japanese leadership positions of the Pearl Harbor attack. Lieutenant Commander Fuchida Mitsuo was chosen leader of the first wave of attack aircraft on Pearl Harbor by Commander Genda, Air Officer of the First Air Fleet; Lieutenant Murata Shigeharu was appointed leader of the torpedo bomber group; Lieutenant Commander Egusa Takeshige was designated leader of the dive bomber group; and Lieutenant Commander Itaya Shigeru was delegated to be the flight leader of First and Second Carrier divisions' fighter group in the Pearl Harbor attack. Up to this time, none of the designated leaders had known of the Pearl Harbor plan.[64]

Yamamoto chose Vice Admiral Shimizu Mitsumi, Commander of the Sixth Fleet (submarines), to command the submarine force in his battle plan for Pearl Harbor. This was the first knowledge that Shimizu had of this daring plan. As of July 29, the leadership positions of the Pearl Harbor plan had been established: Yamamoto, Commander-in Chief of the Combined Fleet; Nagumo, carrier task force commander; and Shimizu, submarine fleet commander. With the leadership established, the process of integrating two forms of attack—from the air and from underwater—began. This plan also afforded the opportunity to test a secret weapon still in the developmental stage—the midget submarine, which weighed 46 tons, carried two torpedoes and two men, and had a radius of 100 miles.[65]

While Japan prepared for war, talks continued with the United States with hope of a diplomatic settlement between the two countries. On September 3, Japan offered its minimum requirements for a negotiated agreement between Japan and America: no interference with Japan's settlements of the China Incident (invasion of north China by Japan in 1937), closing the Burma Road, and no further aid by the United States to the Chiang forces. This package was not new to the United States and left no room for negotiations to continue. A Gallup poll taken that month revealed 70 percent of the U.S. public was willing to risk war with Japan in order to keep her from becoming more powerful. Many in America thought Pearl Harbor was impregnable, but Admiral Kimmel knew that the U.S. fleet was no match for the Japanese Navy, either at Pearl Harbor or elsewhere.[66]

With Nomura providing peace overtures in Washington, supposedly carrying out the emperor's wishes, the reality was such that the Japanese government was actually under the control of the Army which could bring down the prime minister and his cabinet at any time. By regulation, the Minister of War had to be a general on active duty and was chosen by the current Minister of War, the Inspector General, and the Chief of the General Staff. By refusing to name a war minister, the trio could prevent the prime minister from forming a cabinet and could bring down an existing government by reassigning the incumbent war minister.[67]

While the United States and Japan were working on their policy differences, it had become obvious by September 1941 that total victory by Germany in Europe was unlikely. This helped explain Japan's decision not to attack the Soviet Union—the Germany army had stalled in its offensive against Russian cities, allowing the Russians, if needed, to transfer troops from Siberia to Moscow in the west. The Japanese armed forces now significantly stepped up their preparations for war with the United States. Rear Admiral Kusaka Ryunosuke met aboard *Akagi* with key staff officers of the First Fleet: Commander Genda, Senior Staff Officer Commander Oishi Tomatsu, Lieutenant Commander Ono Kenjiro, Lieutenant Commander Sasebe Otojiro, and Commander Sakagami Goro. For the first time, the staff was informed of the proposed Pearl Harbor attack. They now began in earnest to solve these problems; the Navy met aboard the *Akagi* with key staff officers of the First Fleet. From this time forward, the plan emerged as a potential war plan. Genda, Air Officer of the First Fleet, was assigned to report on alternative sailing routes to Pearl Harbor.

The southern route had the advantage of refueling at Wotje in the Marshall Islands, eliminating the need for refueling from tankers at sea, as well as calm seas and proximity to Japanese bases in case of an emergency. The disadvantages lay in the lack of cloud cover for the task force, but more importantly Kimmel's fleet utilized this sea area southeast of Hawaii for training. The central route was ruled out because of the high probability of detection by American submarines. The northern route was recommended by Genda because of the low probability of detection due to weather conditions in this area and the decreased likelihood of encountering a foreign merchant ship. The majority of merchant ships sailing from America or Canada to Japan or to the Soviet Union sailed much farther north of this route. Its disadvantage was the necessity of refueling at sea. In addition, Genda knew—thanks to intelligence from Yoshikawa—that air patrols from Hawaii were weakest in this direction. Now Genda had to convince Nagumo to accept this route, as the admiral preferred the southern route because its refueling advantage.[68]

War games for the attack on Pearl Harbor took place on September 12 at the Imperial Naval Staff College in Tokyo. During the exercises, it was determined that that the Eleventh Air Fleet based on Formosa would attack Major General Douglas MacArthur's (Commander of U.S. Armed Forces Far East) air forces at Clark and Nichols fields in surprise bombing raids. In the meantime, Japan's naval forces would orchestrate an attack on the Philippines, Borneo, and Celebes, and the Japanese army would invade the Malaya peninsula in a three-pronged assault by landings at Singora, Pattani, and Kota Bharu. From these three points the Japanese army would drive through the jungle to Singapore—key to Britain's position in the Far East. It was estimated that it would take two months for the capture of Manila, three months for Singapore, and five months for the conquest of Burma. The rich supply of oil in the Dutch East Indies would be in Japanese hands within four months. Simultaneous invasions were also planned for Guam, Wake, and the Gilbert Islands. One can appreciate the magnitude and scope that these military operations would encompass.[69]

Yamamoto, with some 30 handpicked officers, then moved to the Secret Room to carry out table-top exercises for the attack on Pearl Harbor—code named Operation Z. The first war game spelled disaster for the Japanese fleet if the fleet arrived in daylight and within a 200-mile radius of Hawaii, which led to its detection and destruction by U.S. forces. To correct the situation, Yamamoto changed the arrival time to sunset and kept the Fleet out to a radius of 450 miles from Hawaii. Nagumo would then make a high speed run at Hawaii in the early morning hours of the following day, when America's search planes were still on the ground. This modification in the second war game demonstrated that surprise was achievable.[70]

The arbitrators at the games, however, would tilt the outcomes in favor of the Japanese forces. Too much was riding on the success of the plan for bias to play a role in predicting the outcome of the attack on Pearl Harbor. The Japanese carrier fleet would be vulnerable if surprise was not achieved. Independent of the outcome of the war games, the General Naval Staff still persisted in its opposition to the Pearl Harbor plan for fear that the loss of concentration of forces that would occur by Japan attacking the U.S. fleet and southern operations at the same time would tax the capability of the Japanese Navy and jeopardize the success of both operations. They also felt that an attack on Pearl Harbor would outrage the American public, eliminating any chance for a negotiated peace after the war had begun.[71] Yamamoto himself was tired of the resistance toward his plan to attack Pearl Harbor and stated, "As Commander-in Chief of the Combined Fleet, I will take responsibility for my plan."[72]

A number of issues were discussed at the war games, and a resolution was achieved in some of the cases: the question of the invasion of Hawaii was rejected; orders went out to rush the development of the 16-inch shells and bombs needed to penetrate the thick steel of U.S. battleships; wooden boxlike baffles were added to the fins of the Japanese torpedoes for stability and to prevent the torpedoes from diving too deeply in the water; and pilots began to train intensively in improving their dive-bombing and torpedo dropping skills.[73] One issue that was not reconciled was the number of carriers and battleships that would be involved in the attack on Pearl Harbor. The Japanese military was under pressure to resolve tactical problems facing its attack on Pearl Harbor. Japan could not afford to wait past early December, as the winter in the north Pacific would make an ocean voyage to Hawaii prohibitive. In the south, monsoons began in late October, explaining the army's urgency for an early decision on whether Japan went to war with the United States or continued with its diplomacy.

The United States by September 1941 was also debating the issue of war versus peace with Japan. Secretary of War Stimson felt the time had come for the United States to consider war. The realities of the moment had dictated this position, but Roosevelt was sensitive to the pulse of popular opinion and dodged the issue because the American public was generally opposed to war with Japan. The president had been hopeful of a meeting with Konoye in Alaska or Hawaii. However, the State Department objected to any meeting between the president and Konoye until Japan agreed to withdraw its forces from China and abandon the Tripartite Pact.[74]

A meeting between Konoye and the chiefs of the Army (General Sugiyama Hajime) and Navy (Admiral Nagano Osami) General Staffs was held on September 3 in Tokyo, in which the Japanese military refused to negotiate its withdrawal of troops from China or Indochina. They were willing to guarantee the neutrality of the Philippine Islands, abide by Japan's treaty not to attack Russia, and might be willing to interpret her Tripartite Pact obligations independently, but there would be no other concessions.[75] Emperor Hirohito Michinomiya was not pleased that a preference for war was playing such a major part in the discussions while diplomacy was relegated to an afterthought. He made an unexpected pronouncement when he read a poem to his ministers and senior military officials. The poem, which was delivered in a shrill voice, was written by his grandfather, the enlightened Emperor Meiji Mutsuhito, and dedicated to promoting peace in the world.[76] In the end, the prime minister was given until October 16 to achieve a diplomatic victory, or the negotiations with the United States would come to an end.

Secretary of State Hull and other State Department hardliners misconstrued Konoye's willingness to negotiate with the United States as a sign that the oil embargo was working, and it was only a matter of time before Japan capitulated to U.S. demands. They reasoned, wrongly, that in three months Japan's military leaders would withdraw their troops from the China mainland. Washington disarmament talks of 1921, where playing hardball paid huge diplomatic dividends, were not to take place. Intercepts from Purple were already indicating that Japan, having gained military superiority over the United States, was no longer willing to be pushed into a corner.[77]

While negotiations were taking place in Washington regarding a meeting between Roosevelt and Konoye, the U.S. destroyer *Greer* was attacked by a German submarine on September 4. The ship was sailing off the coast of Iceland delivering mail and passengers. Iceland had been fortified by 20,000 British and Canadian troops for defense against a German invasion of that strategically located island. U.S. destroyers had been peacefully assisting Britain in its war against Germany. A British bomber contacted the *Greer* that a German submarine was stalking her, resulting in the destroyer proceeding to shadow the submarine. In the confrontation, the German submarine fired a torpedo at the destroyer, missing her by just 100 yards. The destroyer then proceeded to unsuccessfully drop depth charges on the submarine. Roosevelt responded by proclaiming, in essence, that America had entered the war in the Atlantic. He stated, "From now on, any German or Italian vessel of war that entered international waters, the protection of which is necessary for American defense, would be to do so at their own peril."[78]

This incident made the front pages of U.S. newspapers, along with the fighting in North Africa and the struggle for Stalingrad, but only a few articles were carried in the inner pages about Japan. The U.S. was officially and unofficially playing down the threat from Japan at the very moment that Japan was planning a huge offensive against the ABCD powers.

On August 26, 1941, while U.S. newspapers were indifferent to the Pacific theater of conflict, the United States began its buildup of the Philippine Islands' defense against Japanese aggression. The first nine B-17s destined for the Philippines landed in Hawaii, after which they would fly northwest to Midway, southwest to Wake, southwest to Ocean Island, south to Australia, and north to the Philippines. All nine B-17s arrived without being detected by the Japanese. The hope was to have 128 Flying Fortresses (B-17s) in the Philippine Islands by February 1942. Consideration was also being given to having 204 long-range bombers in Hawaii by 1942; however, by November only 12 long-range bombers were on Hawaiian airfields.

With the advent of the B-17 bombers, the Philippines became defensible, but only if enough time existed for the production and delivery of more of these bombers to the Philippines. However, many in the U.S. government felt that resources sent to the Philippines should have been diverted for the defense of Hawaii. The decision to move 25 percent of the Hawaiian fleet to the Atlantic in April 1941 was predicated on the availability of the B-17 bomber as compensation for the defense of Hawaii. Kimmel felt that the mission in the Pacific was offensive in nature and not merely the defense of the Hawaiian Islands.

Many in the American press felt that the urgency to build up the defense of the Philippines was unwarranted because Adolf Hitler's difficulties in the Soviet Union made war with Japan less likely than in 1940. Hitler's successes had been on the decline since that time. Admiral Kimmel strongly disagreed with this assessment by the press.[79]

In concert with Admiral Kimmel's beliefs, General Frederick L. Martin, commander of the U.S. Army Air Force, prepared U.S. forces for an attack by Japanese aircraft. He announced plans for joint exercises between the Army and Navy for November 17 to 22, 1941, the purpose of which was to determine if his bombers could find the enemy far out at sea and before they could launch their aircraft in an attack on Pearl Harbor and the nearby airfields. To assist the Army in detecting incoming aircraft, Martin proposed the use of a newly designed radar system, which had yet to be tested in battle. In the exercises, the Army was able to detect an enemy fleet 80 miles off the coast of Hawaii.[80]

The FBI was trying to do its part in the defense of Hawaii by attempting to monitor Japanese agents working out of the Japanese Consulate in Honolulu, the home base of more than 200 sub-consular agents. These Japanese agents mingled with more than 160,000 Japanese-Americans in Hawaii and, as such, disguised their subversive activities. The FBI sorted out the spies from the local population and kept a close eye on them with some success. Another potential spy network existed among the sampan fleet, consisting of several 80-foot diesel-engine fishing boats. Based at Kewalo Basin, about 12 miles from the entrance to Honolulu Harbor, these vessels were frequently seen in the waters south and west of Hawaii where the U.S. fleet exercised. However, none of these activities were illegal, and the FBI and Navy could do little other than observe. The presumed espionage was ongoing, but Washington was mainly concerned about the United States' fragile diplomatic relationship with Japan, so nothing was done. Deporting the agents for suspected espionage was not considered to be an option at this point.[81]

While the FBI was investigating potential Japanese spies in Hawaii, the diplomatic situation with Japan was deteriorating. Roosevelt was hoping to prolong negotiations with Japan for another six months, as the United States built up the defense of the Philippines. However, the freezing of Japan's funds and the oil embargo eliminated any chance for the United States to have the time improve these defenses in the Philippines. Japan's oil reserves were limited, necessitating her decision to proceed with war earlier rather than later to secure oil from the Dutch East Indies. To defend its invasion to the south, Japan needed to protect its left flank against an American counter-attack. This demanded that Japan execute a successful attack on Pearl Harbor. To do so its military leaders needed to know when the U.S. fleet would be in the harbor. They knew that some of the fleet usually left Pearl Harbor on either Monday or Tuesday, and returned on Saturday or Sunday. Lieutenant Commander Tachibana Itaru, the spy whom U.S. officials had refused to prosecute for diplomatic reasons, was now back in Tokyo working on the Pearl Harbor project for Japanese naval intelligence. He would play an important role in the plan's success by assembling the detailed intelligence on Pearl Harbor that was to make the attack possible

On September 24, the Japanese Foreign Ministry, on behalf of naval intelligence, forwarded in the Purple code a significant set of instructions to Yoshikawa to create an invisible grid so he could plot the position of each U.S. ship in its anchorage. This message became known as the "bomb plot" message.[82]

The message was deciphered by Army intelligence and forwarded to Colonel Bratton of Army Intelligence where it drew his attention. When Bratton approached his chief, General Sherman Miles, Assistant Chief of Staff for Intelligence (G2), with the message, Miles was unimpressed. Bratton then forwarded the message to Secretary of War Stimson, Army Chief of Staff General Marshall, and Brigadier General Leonard T. Gerow, Chief of the War Plans Division, without stirring any interest on their part. Undeterred, Bratton discussed the issue with naval intelligence, which reassured him that he need not worry about the message because if and when an attack came, the fleet would not be in the harbor. Two factors dissuaded Bratton from forwarding the message further: (1) the procedure required approval of the Operations Division (which had opposed his meddling in the past), and (2) the Navy historically did not trust Army intelligence. However, Lieutenant Commander Alwin Kramer, head of the Translation Department in Naval intelligence, was somewhat concerned over the communication. He relayed the message to the Director of War Plans, Admiral Turner; CNO Admiral Stark, Secretary of the Navy Knox, and the White House. Kramer also sent the decryption to Admiral Hart in the Philippines, Commander-in Chief Asiatic Fleet (CINCAF). Kramer assumed that since the message went to Hart it would also go to Kimmel. However, Kimmel never received the information. Kramer's superiors showed little interest. Captain Theodore Wilkinson, who had just become the Director of ONI, brushed aside the decryption and later at the congressional Pearl Harbor hearings testified that he barely recollected having seen it. Chief of Naval Operations Stark was unimpressed by the message. He felt that the Japanese were just demonstrating their great attention to detail. Stark never went so far as to ask Rear Admiral Leigh Noyes, Director of Naval Communications, his opinion of the information.[83]

By itself, the "bomb plot" did not definitively prove Japan would attack Pearl Harbor. But taken together with other messages from Tokyo to the consulate in Honolulu, it would have provided evidence of a possible attack. Five days after the "bomb plot" message was sent, Kita Nagao, Japanese Consul General in Hawaii, replied to Tokyo with a suggested refinement of its contents. Washington treated this communication with the same indifference that it had treated the initial information. Kimmel and Short never received either one of these dispatches.[84]

In the early fall of 1941, Kilsoo Haan, an agent for the Sino-Korean People's League, came to CBS' Washington, D.C., office of Eric Sevareid, a foreign correspondent for the network, and told him that the Japanese were going to attack Pearl Harbor before Christmas. His friends in the Korean underground cited that they had conclusive proof that this was the case. One piece of evidence, recalled Sevareid, was that a Korean working in the consulate in Honolulu had seen full blueprints of above-water and underwater naval installations on Oahu spread out on the consul's desk.

Haan explained to Sevareid that he had only been able to visit lower level officials in the State Department, who took a dim view of his information. Late in October, Hann was able to convince Senator Guy Gillette of Iowa that he had discovered that Pearl Harbor would be attacked in December or January. Japan's plan was not only to attack Pearl Harbor but, simultaneously, Guam, Midway, the Philippines, and Wake islands. Gillette alerted the State Department, as well as Army and Navy intelligence.[85]

On Friday December 5, 1941, Hann telephoned Maxwell Hamilton, a Far-East State Department advisor, to inform him that he had been warned by the Korean underground that the Japanese were going to attack Pearl Harbor over the coming weekend. Haan also brought to his attention the Japanese book *The Three Power Alliance and the U.S.-Japan War*, written by Kinoaki Matsuo and published in October 1940. A chapter in the book, entitled "The Japanese Surprise Attack Fleet," stated that there was no doubt in his mind that Japan would grasp the best opportunity to strike the enemy in advance. Hann requested that Hamilton convey his apprehension and send this information to the president and to Army and Navy commanders Hawaii,[86] regardless of how the State Department felt about his evidence.

Ensign Yoshikawa began supplying the necessary information that would comply with the "bomb plot" message. He started by taking a tourist flight to better visualize Kaneohe Naval Air Station, Schofield Barracks, Wheeler Field, Ewa Marine Corps Air Station, the area north of Pearl Harbor, Pearl Harbor itself, and Hickam Field. The air trip's greatest value was that it confirmed his observations from the ground: the mooring sites of the U.S. fleet in Pearl Harbor. U.S. intelligence officers were aware that the Japanese were spying but were helpless to stop it; they were not authorized to censor Japanese mail and dispatches, stop them from taking pictures, nor even arrest them as a suspect.

Senator Gillette of Iowa and Congressman Martin Dies of Texas were aware and concerned about this uninterrupted espionage in Hawaii. Dies was preparing for hearings on the subject, but on September 8 the president, secretary of state, and the acting attorney general all felt quite strongly that hearings would be inadvisable. They felt an investigation would upset diplomatic talks with the Japanese. Dies capitulated to the president after conferring with the White House.[87]

On October 2, 1941, Senator Gillette introduced a resolution for an investigation into Japanese activities in Hawaii. However, Secretary of State Hull vehemently opposed it and implored Gillette to desist from further investigation. He also reasoned that an investigation would hinder U.S./Japanese diplomatic relations. Gillette then backed down from his effort to hold an investigation.

With this decision, Roosevelt and Hull were placing diplomatic relations above national security.[88] Had the United States pursued a policy of rounding up Japan's espionage agents including Yoshikawa in Hawaii, the resulting intelligence loss to the Japanese Navy on the disposition and schedule of U.S. naval forces in Pearl Harbor would have left Japan's Combined Fleet with a precarious strategic decision to make on whether or not to attack Pearl Harbor.

CHAPTER 5

The Jewel of the Pacific

In late September 1941, Commander Fuchida was notified for the first time by Commander Genda that Fuchida would be the leader of the Pearl Harbor attack. Once aboard *Akagi*, Fuchida was questioned about specific aspects of the attack. He responded that torpedo modifications were on-going, but they could not yet be dropped in less than 40 feet of water. The bombs of the dive-bombers were too light to penetrate the steel of the battleships, and pilots of the horizontal bombers needed more training to improve their efficiency. In addition, he was concerned that there could be anti-torpedo nets in the harbor (the latest report on their absence was March 1941).[1]

Within the Japanese Navy, opposition to the Pearl Harbor attack still persisted. Rear Admiral Onishi Takijiru, Chief of Staff of the Eleventh Air Fleet, had by now been persuaded by Rear Admiral Kusaka Ryunosuke, Chief of Staff of the Combined Fleet, to oppose the plan. Onishi felt that Japan could not defeat the United States regardless of how they conducted the war. His belief was that if Japan confined its objective to its southern strategy, America would be angry and might even fight but would remain open to negotiations. But if Pearl Harbor were attacked, the United States would be so outraged that any hopes for a compromise would evaporate.[2]

To appease those who opposed the Pearl Harbor attack, it was agreed by Kusaka and Nagumo that the Eleventh Air Fleet would receive carrier support from the First Air Fleet for its southern operations. Kusaka and Onishi made up their minds to confront Yamamoto on his Pearl Harbor scheme. Nagumo supported the opposition to the Pearl Harbor plan and was delighted to set up a meeting between the opposing parties. Yamamoto listened closely to Onishi, who focused on the need for carriers for the southern operations. When he had finished, Yamamoto asked his staff officer for air operations whether the southern operations could successfully be carried out without carrier support. The answer was in the affirmative. As a result, Kusaka accused the commander-in-chief of taking a great risk with his plan. Captain Kuroshima Osama, senior staff officer of the Japanese Navy, was called upon to refute the arguments against the Pearl Harbor attack, which he did with great vigor. Yamamoto finally stated, "Without this operation I cannot carry out the overall plan of the war in the Pacific."[3] Onishi and Kusaka were moved by the sincerity of Yamamoto, as well as his position in the Japanese Navy; they resigned themselves to carrying out his wishes.

In early October the air officers of each Japanese carrier first learned of the Pearl Harbor attack. This knowledge gave them a sense of purpose in their training and impressed upon them that time was short; there was now a sense of urgency to their mission. At this time, Genda and Fuchida agreed on two attack waves on Pearl Harbor, since it was not possible to launch all planes at the same time. Fuchida would lead the first wave, and Lieutenant Commander Shimazaki Shigekazu would lead the second wave.

Fuchida made certain tactical changes regarding the air attack on Pearl Harbor. He solved the problem of the horizontal bombers by improving their accuracy and ability to penetrate the steel decks of the battleships by arming the planes with 16-inch shells and by having planes fly at 9,800 feet. He also changed the conventional nine-plane horizontal arrowhead formation into a five-plane unit, with a lead plane followed by two planes close together and a closing formation of two planes—all equally spaced from each other. The torpedo bombers would attack in a straight line in four-unit groups, which would suit Pearl Harbor's narrow channel. The dive bombers would now release their bombs at 1,476 feet because that altitude greatly improved bombing accuracy. Genda and Fuchida also concluded that none of the Fifth Carrier Division's airmen would take part in the torpedo attack because of their inexperience. Instead, their dive-bombers and high-level bombers would be restricted to attacking the air bases, which offered much larger targets.[4]

On October 3 (Japanese date), Tokyo received a reply from the United States to Japan's proposals of September 6, 23 and 27 requesting a meeting between the two heads of state. The U.S. response said that it would be doubtful that such a meeting could be held. In view of this development, Admiral Nagano felt that the time for discussions was over and that quick action was needed. A deadline for a settlement was set by Japan for October 15. In Washington, Stimson and Hull agreed that unless Japan withdrew from China and made a commitment not to attack Siberia, there would be no meeting between Roosevelt and Konoye. While Japan was pressing for speed, America was deliberately taking its time to resolve the issues that divided the two countries. Japan needed to know whether it would be proceeding with the southern operation, while Washington needed time to build up its Philippine defenses.[5]

Also in October, the State Department unfortunately drew the wrong conclusion from the Purple intercepts it had received from U.S. intelligence regarding Japan's intentions for a peaceful settlement with the United States. Secretary of State Hull was led to believe that Japan was duplicitous in its intentions, that is, offering a peaceful official response while it conducted a war-like course of action in southeast Asia. In actuality, Japan was still willing to make some concessions to secure peace, but time was running out on the negotiating front. However, the U.S. rejection of the meeting between the president and the prime minister resulted in Konoye resigning his post as prime minister on October 16 since his foreign policy toward the United States had failed to produce a settlement. Emperor Hirohito appointed War Minister General Tojo Hideki to be prime minister. The emperor instructed Tojo to make a last effort for a diplomatic agreement with the United States in order to prevent war. Tojo would remain as a general on active duty and as such, the Army would now have to face the political consequences of its actions. Admiral Shimada Shigetaro was appointed the new Navy minister. He was not considered to be a strong leader and was a questionable choice in view of the ongoing political/military crisis that Japan faced.[6]

In mid–October Chief of Naval Operations Admiral Stark sent Admiral Kimmel a letter apprising him that war with Japan might be imminent based on Purple intercept intelligence. This was the first specific communication by Stark regarding Purple intelligence that the Pacific fleet commander had received since mid–July, when Purple code intercepts ceased being sent to Hawaii for unexplained reasons. U.S. intelligence in Hawaii had not yet received a Purple machine, leaving it dependent on the information that Washington intelligence chose to pass on to it. As a result, when Washington also failed to supply Hawaii with the vital intercepts from Purple that the Honolulu Consul (J-19 code) had received from Tokyo (they contained detailed reports about the fleet anchorage in Pearl Harbor), Navy intelligence in Hawaii was in the dark regarding this key information. This intelligence was available one week before Admiral Stark's letter to Kimmel alerting him about the possible attack on Pearl Harbor.[7] Captain Kirk, Captain Howard D. Bode, head of Foreign Intelligence, and Commander Safford wanted to alert Kimmel of the "bomb plot" intercepts but were unable to because they lacked the authority.

Safford reportedly drafted a letter to Rochefort to begin decrypting the traffic from the local Japanese consulate—the J-19 code. However, the letter never went out because Rear Admiral Noyes, Director of Naval Communication, voiced the opinion that he was "not going to tell any district commandant how to run his job!"[8] It remains unknown why the "bomb plot" messages were never reported by Washington to Hawaii.

Rear Admiral Yamaguchi Tamon, Commander of the Second Carrier Division of the First Air Fleet, was outraged when he discovered that two of his carriers would participate in the southern operation instead of the Pearl Harbor attack. He complained to Kusaka and Nagumo that six carriers were necessary for the Pearl Harbor attack. Genda supported him in his protest. Aboard *Nagato*, Yamamoto for the first time decided that an advanced guard of submarines would operate outside a 600-mile radius of Hawaii and act as scouts. Yamamoto also established the departing location of the fleet: Hitokappu Bay on the island of Etorofu, which was large enough to accommodate the entire Japanese fleet. Fog would offer perfect concealment, and the base was a superior place to sortie. It was decided that the southern operation should not begin until after the attack on Pearl Harbor,[9] so as to prevent any detection of the southern operation fleet on its way to its mission by Allied scouts. Yamamoto also promised significant carrier deployment to the southern operation immediately after the Pearl Harbor attack was over.

In addition to the carrier fleet attacking Pearl Harbor, the question arose as to whether the Japanese Task Force fleet should be reinforced with additional battleships in case the fleet ran into Kimmel's fleet. Yamamoto opposed such a move because the battleships were slow and would be needed in the invasion of Malaya and Singapore to oppose the British threat. On October 13, 1941, in the midst of the naval bickering regarding the decision to attack Pearl Harbor, Yamamoto laid down the gauntlet, stating, "As long as I am commander-in-chief of the Combined Fleet, Pearl Harbor will be attacked."[10]

Yamamoto by this time already had in motion his plan to attack Pearl Harbor. However, he now needed to confirm the data Japan had received about Pearl Harbor from its intelligence agents in Honolulu. One way to accomplish this mission was to send intelligence agents on board a commercial ship liner to Honolulu. But first Japan would have to come to an agreement with the United States because Japan's use of commercial vessels was prohibited under the economic boycott imposed by the United States in July 1941. However, Tokyo continued to negotiate with America to permit its commercial ships to enter U.S. ports. In late August, Hull and Nomura came to an agreement that three passenger ships would be permitted to do so, as long as they carried no commercial cargo. The United States entered into this agreement hoping it would help relations.

Thus, on October 15, the passenger ship *Tatsuta Maru* left Yokohama and arrived in Honolulu for a one-day layover on October 23. Before leaving Yokohama, a sealed envelope was given to the captain of the ship which was to be delivered to Kita as soon as the ship docked. It contained instructions to Kita to prepare a detailed map showing the exact size, strength, and location of every military installation on Oahu. After the ship docked, Kita boarded the liner and picked up the envelope. The ship left the next day and headed to San Francisco.[11]

A second passenger ocean liner, *Taiyo Maru*, was scheduled to leave Yokohama on October 22 and arrive in Honolulu on November 1. Japanese naval intelligence used the opportunity to send its own top-secret spy on this ship, Commander Maejima Toshihide. In addition, Japan sent Sub-lieutenant Matsuo Keiu and Lieutenant Commander Suzuki Suguru to assist Maejima in obtaining information regarding the possibility of using midget submarines to enter Pearl Harbor prior to the air attack on American bases on Oahu. These men were to verify the information Kita had been sending Tokyo via telegrams.

The *Taiyo Maru* would navigate the same route that Nagumo would take to attack Pearl Harbor. They would monitor any other ship movements in the northern Pacific sea lanes as well as the area north of Midway to be sure U.S. patrols did not extend out that far. In addition, the ocean north and west of Oahu was observed for any plane or vessel that could possibly report the task force's approach. Conditions of the sea and weather were also to be recorded.

Commander Maejima assumed the role of a doctor after a crash course in medicine so that he would not be exposed on this mission as a spy for the Japanese government. Suzuki faked the occupation of assistant purser for the ship while Matsuo blended in with the passengers. On their voyage from Japan to Honolulu, the ship operated under radio silence as the three men searched the sea and the sky with high-powered binoculars for intruders. As the liner neared Hawaii, it changed course to approach Oahu from the north. When they were 200 miles north of Hawaii, a patrol plane spotted the liner. Sailing further south, the liner encountered a squadron of U.S. planes about 100 miles from Hawaii, which would be the typical U.S. response to a PBY scouting report in war time. The three summarized their findings on the trip. Sea conditions were rough but manageable. They came across no patrol craft north of Midway, and reconnaissance north of Hawaii extended out to about 200 miles. Most importantly, not a single ship was seen throughout the entire trip. The liner finally reached Honolulu at 0800 on November 1, a perfect time to observe conditions as they would be on a weekend when the attack would occur.[12]

Upon arrival in Honolulu, the three agents did not leave the ship. Kita came on board the first day. On the other days, other members of the consulate would also visit the ship. Yoshikawa was kept away from the liner so as not to disclose his cover. Newspapers were delivered to the ship every day by the consulate. Within the folded newspapers were scraps of paper placed there by the Japanese Consul that contained top secret military information acquired by Yoshikawa. The consul courier, upon arriving at the gate entrance to the ocean liner, would then walk by the security guard who, with just a nod of his head, allowed the visitor to pass by without inspection by any other security guard.[13]

Kita was given a 100-item questionnaire which he forwarded to Yoshikawa to fill out. It covered every aspect of the Pearl Harbor plan. Yoshikawa answered all the questions thoroughly, including making a current check on the Pearl Harbor area. He produced an hourly report of patrol planes, how long they stayed out, the type and number of aircraft used, and the general arc of their search. To the south reconnaissance was fairly good; to the north it was poor. When asked whether he thought the Americans could be caught napping, he responded in the affirmative. No one knows for sure how the questionnaire and maps got back on board the *Taiyo Maru*. The FBI, DIO (District Intelligence Office), Army G-2, and Customs all had the *Taiyo Maru* under observation, yet they detected none of the espionage activity that occurred. One possible explanation is that the Americans were focused on returning and outgoing passengers. For example, customs examined all of the baggage of returning travelers and found nothing. Outgoing passengers received an even closer screening without results.[14] Thus, American attempts to identify Japanese espionage activity were thwarted.

Fuchida continued to review the problems associated the Pearl Harbor plan. Progress on the torpedo problem was being made, but the fliers could do no better than having the torpedoes sink to a level of 66 feet (instead of the required 33 feet). Fuchida, however, was heartened by the news Lieutenant Commander Naito Takeshi brought back after having visited Taranto Bay in Italy in late October. Naito had studied diligently all the details of the successful British torpedo attack on Italian warships in that harbor. Fuchida was impressed and encouraged by the report, concluding that Japan could duplicate in Pearl Harbor the successful British torpedo attack. He concluded that the solution to the torpedo problem now lay in the hands of the technicians.

Research on the torpedoes continued at Yokosuka, revealing that the Model II torpedo was successful in making runs in 37 feet of water, and its fin had been modified so that the torpedo could now run true in a narrow space. Genda improved on the technical changes made on the Japanese torpedo when his pilots discovered that by dropping the torpedo from an altitude of 60 feet and an air speed of 100 knots, a 82 per cent success rate could be achieved. These improvements led to a few of the newly modified torpedoes reaching Fuchida, so that his torpedo bombers could test the new torpedoes in the waters off Kagoshima in late October. The planes dropped the torpedoes in 37 feet of water. One torpedo hit bottom but the other two ran straight and true to hit their targets. These results translated into an expectancy of 27 torpedo hits out of 40 launchings.[15]

By the end of October, many but not all of the problems regarding the Pearl Harbor attack had been resolved. The plan was now ready to be presented to the emperor for his approval, which he subsequently gave.[16] All of this was predicated on the fact that the United States did not have torpedo nets in the harbor. If this were to be the case, the Japanese pilots would dive their planes into the nets in a suicide mission to blast open the nets. Initially, it was believed that industrial giant Mitsubishi could not supply the torpedoes until November 30, but with encouragement from the Naval General Staff, they were delivered by November 17. Meanwhile, the accuracy of the horizontal bombers was improved to 70 percent, adding a new dimension to Japan's naval air strength. Since there was not enough time to train the fliers of the Fifth Carrier Division to fly at night, Fuchida suggested to Genda to have the hour of attack moved from 0630 to 0800, so that all the planes would arrive over the target in daylight. This explains why the Japanese did not attack Pearl Harbor at dawn.

The last major problem involved the refueling of the Kido Butai (Japanese task force) on its way to Hawaii. The carriers *Kaga*, *Shokaku*, and *Zuikaku*, the battleships *Hiei* and *Kiroshima*, and the heavy cruisers *Tone* and *Chikuma* would not require refueling on their voyage from Hitokappu Bay to Pearl Harbor. However, not all task force vessels could get to Pearl Harbor without refueling. Rear Admiral Kusaka was assigned the task of solving this problem. The traditional method for ships to refuel at sea was to have a tanker precede the ship requiring the fuel, and then connect the fuel line between the two vessels. This method often created a problem, however, as large ships needed more space to turn than the tanker, resulting in severance of the fuel line. This dilemma was solved by placing the tanker in the rear of the ship to be fueled, whereby the tanker could more easily follow the lead ship without the fuel hose being severed.

On October 16, when Roosevelt learned that Konoye had resigned his post as prime minister, he called a meeting with Hull, Stimson, Knox, Marshall, Stark, and Harry Hopkins, the president's personal advisor. Stimson wrote in his diary that the United States wanted Japan to make the first overt move in the showdown with America. This would bring public opinion around to favoring a war with Japan. Rear Admiral Turner, director of the War Plans Division in the Navy Department, was concerned about Japan going to war with the Soviet Union because the Manchurian border had been a source of conflict for some time between these two countries. At the time, the Soviet Union's Navy was in home waters in the Baltic Sea, and it had transferred a significant number of troops from the Manchurian border to defend itself against Germany's invasion of its western front. This left Russia's eastern front vulnerable to an attack by Japan, which already had troops in Manchuria. The question was whether Japan would take advantage of this opportunity and attack Russia on its eastern front.[17] If Japan committed the bulk of its military forces to southern operations and to Pearl Harbor in the east, it would be unlikely to have enough military resources to attack Manchuria in the north.

On October 17, Stark sent Kimmel a message that all U.S. shipping was to be re-routed to the south and out of the reach of Japan's territories. Stark also ordered him to take all practical means for the safety of the airfields at Midway and Wake islands. Kimmel responded by sending six submarines to navigate the waters off Japan immediately. He also ordered two submarines at Midway to patrol out to a ten mile radius, dispatched a squadron of 12 reconnaissance planes to Midway for daily patrols, sent six patrol planes to Wake Island, and reinforced Johnston and Wake islands with additional marines, ammunition, and stores. These forces were under strict orders not to attack any Japanese ship or aircraft. The commander-in-chief of the Pacific called upon Stark for two more squadrons of destroyers and asked about bringing the battleships *North Carolina* and *Washington* to Pearl Harbor. Japan was about to commission two new battleships, *Yamato* and *Musashi,* each displacing over 60,000 tons and carrying 18.2 inch guns, making them the fastest and most powerful battleships afloat. Had Kimmel known of this, he almost surely would have been much more alarmed over the balance of naval power in the Pacific.[18]

Also on October 17, Kusaka met with the Naval General Staff and found them not only opposed to the Pearl Harbor plan, but unwilling to commit six carriers to the Pearl Harbor operation. Kusaka was willing to resign but decided instead to talk to Admiral Yamamoto about the meeting. Yamamoto listened intently and then instructed Kuroshima to fly to Tokyo the next day to meet with the Naval General Staff to gain their approval for the Pearl Harbor plan and for the use of six aircraft carriers. When Kuroshima met with Tomioka Sadatoshi of the Naval General Staff, he argued strenuously that the U.S. Navy had enough strength to attack Japan's flank and compromise the southern operations. The United States could also seize the Marshall Islands and weaken Japan's defense perimeter. When Tomioka refused to budge, Kuroshima retorted by saying that he was under instructions from Yamamoto that unless his plan was adopted, he and his entire staff would resign. Tomioka now realized the depth of Yamamoto's conviction and agreed to the following: the Naval General Staff would agree to the use of six aircraft carriers, the Combined Fleet would make no further demands on Japan's air power, and the southern operation would begin as soon as possible after the Pearl Harbor attack.[19]

Tomioka then brought Kuroshima to his superior officer, Vice Admiral Fukudome Shigeru, chief of the First Bureau, who called for an immediate meeting with Chief of the Naval General Staff Admiral Nagano Osami to gain his approval for the Pearl Harbor raid. After discussing the matter, Nagano approved the Pearl Harbor operation on October 19, 1941. The date set for war with the United States was December 8, 1941 (Japanese date).

On October 30, after Nagano's approval of the Pearl Harbor plan, the Japanese government informed the United States that Japan would not pull out of the Tripartite Pact nor would Japan withdraw any troops from Indochina or China. This intention was known as Proposal A and was Japan's first option in negotiations with the United States. It concluded in its statement that an agreement to Hull's Four Principles with the conditions attached was impossible.[20]

The Four Principles demanded respect for the territorial integrity of all nations, support for the principle of non-interference in the internal affairs of other countries, equality of commercial opportunity, and the non-disturbance of the *status quo* of the Pacific.

In early November, Foreign Minister Togo Shigenori and his staff devised Proposal B, in the event that Proposal A failed as part of the negotiation with the United States. It stated that both Japan and the United States would pledge not to make an armed advance into southeast Asia and the south Pacific area, that Japan's access to raw materials from Dutch East Indies would be assured, that trade relations between the two countries would be restored, and that the United States would not take any steps that would hinder efforts for peace between China and Japan.

Emperor Hirohito still wanted peace with the United States, but only if the United States would accept Japan's position on Japanese foreign policy. On November 4, Foreign Minister Togo dispatched a message to Nomura that it was putting forth its last possible offer in Proposals A and B. Togo believed there would be no room for error or misunderstanding and directed that his orders be followed to the letter. The foreign minister gave Nomura until November 25 to accomplish a breakthrough in the U.S. negotiations. Togo then requested that Kurusu Saburo, an experienced diplomat, join Nomura in Washington.[21]

Ambassador Kurusu arrived in Washington on November 15 to bolster Nomura's efforts in seeking a peaceful resolution of the conflict between Japan and the United States. Upon Kurusu's arrival, Nomura received a message from the Foreign Ministry insisting that the cutoff date for negotiations with the United States was November 25, 1941. On November 10, Nomura formally presented Proposal A to Secretary of State Hull. Hull countered that he needed Chiang Kai-shek's approval before the matter of China could be discussed. On November 15, Hull offered some prospect of an agreement on trade concessions, but they would be dependent on Japan's recognition of Roosevelt's Four Principles. Two days later, Japan rejected the conditions of the trade offer and instructed Nomura to proceed with Proposal B, but added that there would be no further concessions. Secretary of State Hull and the two Japanese ambassadors met with President Roosevelt on November 17, but little diplomatic progress was made. The next day, Nomura offered Proposal B to Hull, which stated that Japan might withdraw from Indochina in return for the cancellation of America's freeze of Japan's assets as well as the lifting of the oil embargo. Hull accepted the offer on November 20, Thanksgiving Day, knowing full well from Magic that the proposal was, in fact, an ultimatum. The United States would supply Japan with all the oil it required, lift the freeze, and discontinue aid to China; in return Japan would promise to withdraw from Indochina.[22]

The United States for its part was not in a position to take military action against Japan, so there was a sound reason for peaceful negotiations with the Japanese government to avert war. To this point, Stark and Marshall had sent Roosevelt a joint estimate of military honesty in admitting that the U.S. Pacific Fleet was no match for the Japanese Navy, and that war should be avoided unless Japan took the offensive against a territory of the United States, the British Commonwealth, or the Dutch East Indies. The United States also needed three months to build up its defenses on the Philippine Islands, so that the islands could resist a Japanese invasion and gain an opportunity to go on the offensive with its B-17 bombers.

Hull felt that withholding aid to Chiang Kai-shek would be a problem but would still consider the offer. The secretary of state, however, first wanted Japan to break ties with Germany by withdrawing from the Tripartite Pact, and indicated that a firm American proposal for a temporary agreement would be forthcoming.

The issue with China was discussed with Chinese, British, Dutch, and Australian officials in Washington. Only China balked at the agreement, which did not please Hull. In an attempt to rectify this problem, the secretary met with the Chinese ambassador and explained America's rationale for making this decision in the hope that China would understand America's position in the matter. Regardless, Hull was determined to support the *modus vivendi*—a feasible arrangement in spite of China's objections.[23]

The Japanese government agreed to extend the deadline for the talks to November 29 and communicated this decision to Nomura stating, "This time we mean it, that the deadline absolutely cannot be changed, after that things are automatically going to happen."[24] The intercept was picked up by and deciphered by naval intelligence in Washington and once again critical Purple intelligence was not only ignored by OP-20-G in Washington, but they failed to send the information to naval intelligence in Hawaii.

On November 15, the Foreign Ministry in Tokyo sent a message to its Honolulu consulate stating that since relations between the United States and Japan were at a critical point, the consulate should now report on the number of U.S. ships that were in port twice a week. The report was to be sent to Tokyo on an irregular basis each week and special care should be taken to ensure utmost secrecy. ONI did not translate this message until December 3, but they still had time to alert Hawaiian intelligence. For the first and only time, Tokyo tied the secret Honolulu consular order to failing negotiations between the United States and Japan. The increased interest by Japan in the movements of the U.S. fleet should have alerted Navy intelligence that Pearl Harbor might be a target of the Japanese Navy. Yet despite all these clues, the communication failed to stimulate any interest in Washington about the message, let alone inspire someone in Washington to alert Kimmel or Short.[25]

Yoshikawa, however, did not miss the meaning of the November 15 communication between the Foreign Ministry in Tokyo and the consular office in Hawaii, resulting in his checking on the U.S. fleet's location and schedule on a daily basis. The Japanese agent believed that the Pacific Fleet was still operating on its peacetime schedule. The ships sailed out to sea during the week and routinely returned on weekends. Shore leave was granted to many officers and men. The spy was puzzled by the U.S. fleet adhering to such a fixed schedule with the political situation so tense.[26]

The FBI was not unaware of the espionage engaged in by the Japanese Consul in Honolulu but diplomatic immunity impaired a realistic investigation of their activities. In addition, overt operations against the consul could precipitate a diplomatic crisis with Japan. Yet at this time Captain Irving Mayfield, head of District Intelligence Office (DIO), almost exposed the cover and mission of Yoshikawa. Mayfield was able to persuade David Sarnoff, president of Radio Corporation of America (RCA), to obtain illegal copies of the Japanese consulate's messages in mid–November. These communications were available in the RCA Honolulu office because the nature of the J-19 code required that they be sent via radio waves. The fact that these Japanese transmissions were private in nature and protected by law from being read by other nations did not influence Sarnoff's decision to assist the United States in obtaining this vital intelligence. However, Japan remained lucky, as the Japanese alternated their monthly transmissions among the various radio networks operating in Hawaii; in November they used MacKay Radio, not RCA, for their radio traffic.[27]

On November 16, the first phase of the Japanese Pearl Harbor plan was implemented when the Second Submarine Squadron departed from Yokosuka toward Hawaii. Its seven submarines would cover the areas between Oahu and Kauai and between Oahu and Molokai. Also on November 16, submarine I-10 left Yokosuka and sailed to an area 900 nautical miles southwest of San Francisco. Its mission was to destroy any U.S. ships that might try to get back to San Diego after the attack on Pearl Harbor. The next day, November 17, *Soryu* and *Hiryu* left Saeki Bay on the Kyushu coast and later *Akagi* and *Kaga*, all heading toward Hitokappu Bay in the Kurile Islands. *Zuikaku* and *Shokaku* left Beppu Bay on the island of Kyushu and headed in a northerly direction to the Kurile Islands. *Kaga* was the last ship to leave because it was waiting for the delivery of its modified torpedoes. When they finally arrived on November 18, the carrier proceeded out of Sasebo Bay and on the next day headed toward the rendezvous point located in the islands to the north.[28]

When the Japanese fleet departed from Japan, Rochefort's Combat Intelligence

Unit in Hawaii had lost track of the Japanese carriers. As a result, Rochefort made the assumption that the carriers were possibly in port because, under those circumstances, the fleet would use low-frequency, low-power circuits that could not be heard and where directional-finder bearings couldn't be taken. However, the Kido Butai was now on its way to begin its voyage to Pearl Harbor, and U.S. intelligence had no idea where the Japanese fleet was.

With the Japanese fleet departing for the Kurile Islands, on November 16 the *Taiyo Maru* was returning from Honolulu to Tokyo Bay. The three spies on the ship, Commander Maejima, Lieutenant Commander Suzuki, and Sub-lieutenant Matsuo, immediately reported to the Naval General Staff. All three made their presentations, and in spite of the formidable intelligence they provided, it was felt that the Pearl Harbor plan was still a gamble at best. One question raised during the interview by Captain Tomioka, head of Japan's Operations Section of the First Bureau of the Naval General Staff, was whether the U.S. carriers would be in the harbor on December 8 (Japanese date) or would they have left to carry out a special mission. Suzuki, a representative of the Japanese Submarine Division, had no answer. He did state that on Sundays, the Navy sailors in Pearl Harbor were slow to rise and get into their defensive positions on the ships and in the harbor and that this had been true for the past several months. When Suzuki finished his report, he left Tokyo on the battleship *Hiei* to report to Nagumo in the Kuriles.[29]

On November 18, Japan's Naval Ministry dispatched a message to Consul General Kita in Honolulu to report on the vessels anchored in Pearl Harbor and to do so with great secrecy. The message was in the J-19 code which Washington intelligence had the capability to decipher. Due to the delay in the process of mailing the information, U.S. Army intelligence did not decipher the dispatch until December 5. This communication confirmed that Japan was interested in the location of Kimmel's ships in Pearl Harbor.[30] While the Japanese Navy undertook the most painstaking precautions for communications security, the Foreign Ministry was not as cautious in its conversations. Had Rochefort gained access to the information derived from the J-19 code,—the bomb plot message along with the communications from the other J-19 deciphers—he might have very well have learned that Pearl Harbor was to be attacked.

On the evening of November 20, Japan's main naval radio station transmitted a preliminary war alert message to all fleets: "Carry out second phase of preparations for opening hostilities."[31] This message was intercepted by U.S. Navy's radio intelligence, as evidenced by its decryption in the 250,000 declassified JN-25B codes released by the U.S. government in the 1980s. This decryption was translated by intelligence after the war had ended in 1945. To date, none of the JN-25B code that had been translated by Navy intelligence prior to December 7, 1941, has been declassified. As we know, Safford testified that about ten per cent of JN-25B could be read throughout that year (1941).[32] It is curious that it is this exact percentage that was available to U.S. naval intelligence only months later when they were able to predict the timing and locations of the battles of Coral Sea and Midway. This fact questions whether U.S. intelligence in Washington was truly unable to decipher any significant part of the Japanese naval messages sent in the JN-25B code prior to the attack on Pearl Harbor in 1941.

Even though U.S. intelligence had supposedly done little with the JN-25B code,

British and Dutch intelligence had penetrated it extensively. Britain's efforts took place in their Far East Combined Bureau (FECB) in Singapore, with an outpost on Stonecutter's Island off Hong Kong. However, to date Britain has refused to release or admit they decoded any of the Japanese JN-25B code before or during the war, despite the United States having sent them three Purple decoding machines.

The Dutch had a smaller code-breaking operation stationed at their military headquarters in Bandung on Java. The town of Kamer was the location and designation of the Dutch crypto-analytical unit in the Far East and was under the leadership of Colonel J.A. Verkuyl and his deputy, Captain J.W. Henning. The intelligence section was reading the Soviet diplomatic machine code and the J-19 consular cipher. The Dutch worked in close cooperation with the British. General Hein ter Poorten, the Dutch Commander in Chief in the Far East, is on record asserting that his code breakers gave him reports that revealed Japanese naval concentrations near the Kurile Islands. Unfortunately, all of the files were burned when the Dutch retreated from Bandung. One of the civilian operatives of his intelligence staff reported that this information was derived from a sailing order to the Kido Butai, which was destroyed at the end of the war. However, a recounting of the series of events by Japanese Pearl Harbor survivors confirmed that such an order was indeed transmitted on November 25. It stated, "The task force will move out of Hitokappu Bay on November 26 and proceed without being detected to the evening rendezvous point set for December 3 where refueling and resupply will be carried out as quickly as possible."[33]

An important Japanese message intercepted on November 18, 1941, at 1932 by an unidentified operator with the initials SN at Station H in Hawaii has recently been declassified. This communication is of critical importance as it specifically states that the Japanese carriers were not in the home waters of Japan but in the Kurile Islands—a perfect location for departure for an attack on Pearl Harbor. The decipher clearly spelled out in the communication the words *Hitokappu Bay*, because the Japanese Navy did not have time to develop a code word for that geographic location. The radio message was reportedly translated on May 6, 1946, but it is unknown when the message was actually decrypted. After translation, one learns that Hitokappu Bay is the location of the Japanese First Air Fleet. The communication came in loud and clear and was not affected by atmospheric conditions. It is important to note that the original of this dispatch has not been released by the U.S. government.[34]

However, the existence of a copy of this document clearly substantiates that the message was sent and received by American intelligence and most likely by Dutch and British intelligence as well. The question arises that even if the U.S. communication did not reach Roosevelt's hands, was a copy of the translated intercept brought to his attention by the British or Dutch authorities or actually Churchill himself on the morning of November 26, 1941, at 0300? (details to follow). The seven-day delay in Churchill reporting this information to Roosevelt could be accounted for by the time needed to decipher the message by code breakers. The final answer may not come until Churchill's confidential files are declassified.

In late November, the State Department was working on a compromise proposal. It proposed that Japan would, in return for the United States resuming oil sales for civilian use and other commercial trade, withdraw its troops from southern Indochina, and cease any further armed advancement in that area for three months while negotiations took place between the two countries. This proposal was known as the *modus vivendi*. A copy of the unofficial memorandum was made by Virginia Collins of the State Department which revealed that Hull viewed the *modus vivendi*, a key factor in the negotiations and absolutely necessary in preventing an end to the talks. Secretary Hull felt that the American proposal would give our military the time it urgently needed to get ready to defend a two-ocean war.[35]

On November 22, 1941, while the Japanese fleet had anchored in Hitokappu Bay, Japanese intelligence had overestimated American forces on Hawaii by 50 per cent. In actuality, the U.S. Army aircraft on Oahu consisted of 152 fighters (99 P-40s, 39 P-36s, and 14 P-26s), and all but the 99 P-40s were serviceable due to a lack of spare parts and partially trained crews. Half of the serviceable planes were initially scheduled to be transferred to Wake and Midway islands by the Navy and War departments on November 26, 1941. The directive to send the Army fighters to those islands was subsequently rescinded mainly because of the limited range of the P-40 aircraft.

On November 23, a special conference was held aboard *Akagi*, where the directive for the air attack was issued. They would launch the first wave of aircraft 230 miles north of Oahu, in time to reach Pearl Harbor at 0800. The second wave would be launched 200 miles from Oahu and after the first wave had completed their mission. After the attack, all aircraft would gather twenty miles northwest of Oahu's western tip and fly back to the carriers. Nagumo and Kusaka felt that 350 planes would be enough to effectively destroy U.S. Navy targets and could not conceive of the necessity of a second major strike. They had reached this decision before sailing for the Kurile Islands.[36]

At the same meeting, it was decided to send two seaplanes from the heavy cruisers *Tone* and *Chikuma* to scout Pearl Harbor and Lahaina Roads one-half hour prior to launching the first wave of Japanese aircraft. The first wave would consist of 189 planes: 50 horizontal bombers under Commander Fuchida's charge which would provide the signal *Tora! Tora! Tora!* (Tiger! Tiger! Tiger!) if surprise were achieved; 40 torpedo bombers under Lieutenant Murata Shigeharu; 54 dive bombers under Lieutenant Commander Takahashi Kakuichi; and 45 Zero fighters under Lieutenant Itaya Shigeru. The fighters would first clear the air space over Oahu of any enemy aircraft, following which the torpedo bombers would make their run at U.S. capital ships as the horizontal bombers made its attack from above. The dive bombers would center their attention on Hickam, Wheeler, and Ford Island airfields.

The second wave would follow directly after the first wave with 54 horizontal bombers under the leadership of Lieutenant Commander Shimazaki Shigekazu, 81 dive bombers under Lieutenant Commander Egusa Takashige, and 36 Zero fighters under Lieutenant Shindo Saburo. The torpedo planes would not be involved in the second wave because the loss of surprise would risk too many torpedo bombers being lost. The horizontal bombers would concentrate on Hickam, Kaneohe and Ford Island, while the fighters strafed the same targets as well as Wheeler Field.[37]

November 25, President Roosevelt met with his secretaries of War, State, and Navy along with his service chiefs, Admiral Stark, chief of Naval Operations, and General Marshall, chief of staff of the Army, both of whom had already approved the *modus vivendi*. There is no record that the proposal was rejected that day. To the contrary, American officials had concerns that the Japanese would reject it, and if Japan did not, there was a question of how to deal with the Chinese government protests over the U.S. agreement to withdraw its aid to China for the following three months.

On Wednesday, November 26, war in the Pacific was virtually ordained as the United States abruptly and emphatically turned down any notion of the *modus vivendi*. Instead, it presented an uncompromising ten-point declaration of absolute conditions that bore little resemblance to the original agreement between Japan and the United States. The Japanese negotiators were confounded and angry at America's sudden rejection of the agreement. The ambassadors were unaware of Japan's military decision to go to war if an agreement was not reached between the two countries by November 29. With their expectations destroyed, they interpreted the response as an ultimatum to Tokyo. During congressional investigations in 1945, Hull testified that a tentative agreement by the United States for the *modus vivendi* would have caused a collapse of Chinese resolve to oppose the Japanese militarily in China. Later, in his memoirs, he wrote that his decision to advise the president against a temporary accommodation with Japan was based on Britain's tepid reaction to the agreement, expressed in an overnight cable from Prime Minister Winston Churchill to Roosevelt on November 26.[38]

Notably, later-declassified British cabinet papers indicate that Churchill was apparently satisfied to leave negotiations with Japan to the United States, telling his foreign secretary that he wanted no further expansion of territory by Japan and certainly wanted no war with that country. Confidential British office assessments revealed "...the President and Mr. Hull were ... fully conscious of what they were doing."[39] Churchill tried to suppress a 1943 report by Britain's last ambassador to Japan, which stated, "...had it been possible to reach a compromise with Japan in December 1941 involving the withdrawal of Japanese troops from Indochina, war with Japan would not have been inevitable."[40]

More important than whether war with Japan could have been averted was the question of why Hull deserted the *modus vivendi* so abruptly. The sudden reversal was so dramatic in its political implications regarding the outbreak of war in the Pacific that only the president could have made the decision to order Secretary Hull to abandon the *modus vivendi*. This conclusion is based on the fact that Washington intelligence knew through Purple that this was Japan's last attempt at peaceful negotiations when they set a deadline of November 29 for its Washington ambassadors to complete the deal with the United States. In the absence of an agreement with the United States by November 29, Japan would terminate the meetings. All of this intelligence was known to the United States, as well as the fact that Japan in its communication to its Washington ambassadors stated that after the deadline expired, "things would automatically happen," signifying that war in the Pacific would break out. Churchill tried to distance himself from the decision to abandon the compromise with Japan when he wrote in his memoirs in 1950, "I therefore placed the issue where it belonged, namely, in the U.S. President's hands."[41]

Evidence has come to light that cast doubts about whether Secretary of State Hull was in favor of the reversal of the *modus vivendi*. Landreth Harrison, an aide to Hull, reported that far from initiating the reversal of the policy with Japan, Hull was resistant to implementing the president's order. The secretary came from the White House stating, "Those men over there do not believe me when I tell them that the Japanese will attack us. You cannot give an ultimatum to a powerful and proud people and not expect them to react violently."[42] On November 27, Hull received a letter from Dr. Stanley Hornbeck, head of the Far East Desk, which offered reassurance to the secretary that the action he took the day before would be looked upon by him in years to come with great satisfaction. The letter (which was later removed from the files of the State Department) suggested that the decision was made for the secretary by the president. Hull responded by writing a memorandum to Hornbeck:

> It is no answer to the question of whether this proposal [*the modus vivendi*] is sound and desirable at this most critical period to say that it probably would not have been accepted by Japan in any event; nor to say I would have been widely criticized in the astounding theory of selling China down the river of appeasement. If that sort of demagoguery stuff would be rung into this sort of undertaking, then there could never be a settlement between countries except at the point of a sword.[43]

The evidence appears to confirm that Hull was in favor of the *modus vivendi* until the afternoon of November 26, 1941. Why the policy was changed becomes of greater historical significance than whether its acceptance would have averted war.

According to the Secretary of War's diary, Stimson called Hull on the morning of November 26 to inform him of the protest he had received from Chiang Kai-shek regarding the proposed policy. Hull responding by saying he "had just about made up his mind to give up the whole thing in respect to a truce and simply tell the Japanese [he] had no further action to propose."[44]

Stimson then called the White House to see if the president had received the communication that Japan had started a new expedition from Shanghai toward Indochina consisting of a convoy of 30–50 ships, filled with troops, sighted south of Formosa. The president had not seen the report and was shocked. The secretary of war immediately sent a copy to the White House.[45]

Stimson's chronology of events depends on Roosevelt not having received the Shanghai intercept on the afternoon of November 25. Yet, it is curious that a top-secret decipher containing Magic information was not delivered to Roosevelt upon its receipt. Even more astounding is why the normally volatile Hull did not react to the same communication that afternoon, when the secretary of war called him to tell Hull about the report and that he had sent copies of the G-2 message to Hull and to the president.[46]

What is more unlikely is that this one-day-old intelligence was itself a reason for Roosevelt to reverse the course of United States diplomacy. This conclusion is based on the recovery of the original message that was sent to the White House from G-2. Dated November 25, it cites not 30 to 50 ships but 10 to 30 troop ships leaving Shanghai in the Yangtze River and still located on the river, not in the open sea south of Formosa as had been previously reported. Furthermore, Stimson's diary states this information was available a month before in a prior Magic message, and intelligence estimates did not find this information alarming.[47] The reason for Stimson's exaggeration of the number of Japanese ships involved and their location in the open sea represented his opposition to the *modus vivendi*.

There is now evidence that this Shanghai intercept did reach the White House. The intercept copy, dated November 27, was found in the "Safe File" of the former secretary of war and had attached to it a cryptic note, written by Major General Edwin Watson. He facetiously stated that he had found it "in the inside pocket of a *very distinguished gentleman.*"[48] Although the general did not mention the president by name, the deliberate omission of the person he was talking about suggests that the "very distinguished gentleman" was indeed Roosevelt. It seems very unlikely that

Roosevelt did not have this intelligence prior to November 26, and the finding of the message in the "Safe File" of the Secretary of War casts doubt on Stimson's official account of the circumstances. What is even more revealing in his diary is that the Japanese convoy movement had been known and expected by Washington naval intelligence for over one month and was not considered to be alarming.

Stimson's failure to record in his diary the accurate description of the November 25 Shanghai intercept appears to be a cover story for some more secret information. This line of reasoning arises from the fact that Stimson recorded in his diary that the hand-delivered duplicate of the message contained an additional line: "Later reports indicate that this movement is already under way and ships have been seen south of Formosa."[49] Yet, the G-2 mentions only that the ships were in the Yangtze River and not near Formosa. In addition, there is no evidence that any updated reports followed. Therefore, it is unlikely that this communication caused Roosevelt to alter the course of American policy so abruptly. So the question then is, what new piece of information of significant proportions must have reached the White House between the evening of November 25 and 0900 the next morning to change Roosevelt's opinion regarding the *modus vivendi*.

The first clue is that in 1944, an Army Board of Inquiry received specific evidence dated November 26, 1941, of Japan's intention to initiate offensive action against the United States and Great Britain. However, the Army investigators were not able to link it to Stimson's Shanghai convoy, which was identified in the G-2 report as a "concentration of units of the Japanese fleet in an unknown port ready for offensive action."[50] Thus, the report by Stimson that 30–50 Japanese ships sighted south of Formosa could not be verified by the G-2 and therefore cannot used as a reason for FDR's withdrawal of the *modus vivendi*.

In the Navy Board of inquiry which was being held in tandem with the Army investigation, Admiral Kimmel, in cross-examining Admiral Stark, asked him whether he had received naval intelligence in this regard. Stark replied that for him to answer would disclose information that was detrimental to the public interest, even though the inquiry was held in secret. The court then over-ruled Kimmel and did not allow Stark to answer the question on the basis that the CNO did not have to reveal any state secrets. His refusal to answer indicated that the information Stark received did not come from Army or naval sources. Knowledge of the information must have been restricted to the inner circle of presidential advisors. If Marshall and Stark knew, they were not admitting it, as they avoided answering questions about their knowledge of the reason why the president abruptly abandoned the *modus vivendi*. They both claimed memory loss of the events of that morning.[51]

Although no one knows for certain where the missing intelligence may have come from, there is a clue that Roosevelt may have received the information through the secret conduit of the British security organization, headed by Sir William "Intrepid" Stephenson of the British Security Coordination Office in the United States, which was located in New York City. Colonel James Roosevelt, the president's son, was sent to Stephenson's headquarters in New York City that afternoon with a message that resulted in a telegram to Churchill in London on November 26: "Negotiations off. Services expect action within two weeks." This may have been a reply to some vital intelligence that was received by Roosevelt from Churchill via Stephenson's office in Rockefeller Center. There is another indication that Churchill may have

5. The Jewel of the Pacific

informed the president directly about an impending offensive by Japanese forces. A cover note which was supposedly included with Churchill's telegram to Roosevelt was sent to the American Embassy in London on November 26, and was marked "Most Secret." An apology was offered by the messenger to the Embassy for the late hour of its delivery—at about 0300. Yet, nothing it contained would have warranted waking up the American Embassy at that hour.[52] The question is raised is whether the telegram may had have contained information that the Japanese task force had just left northern Japan for Hawaii.

The question now arises is whether the telegram sent by Churchill to Roosevelt on November 26, 1941, was the only one Churchill sent. At the onset, Roosevelt reportedly sent a telegram to Churchill on the morning of November 25. On the same day, a copy of the FDR's Churchill cable was also delivered to the British Embassy at 1300 in Washington, D.C. The content of these two telegrams, as reported by Layton, included details about the final *modus vivendi* proposal. If this is true, it would be extremely unlikely that Churchill would sent a telegram at 0300 marked "Most Secret" in response to a telegram about the final *modus vivendi* proposal. Yet, if Churchill did send a second cable, it is not found in the files.

Attempts over the years by Layton, the author of a book he wrote after retiring from the Navy, *And I Was There,* to gain access to the classified files were repeatedly rejected by the British cabinet on the claim that it would not be in the national interest. Until they are opened, the question will remain as to whether or not the closed files in London contain information regarding the Japanese attack on Pearl Harbor. [The author researched the release of some of Churchill's confidential files kept classified by the British government for 79 years in 2019. The author found no evidence of a second telegram dated November 26, 1941, in the released declassified files.]

The question is raised as to whether a possible exchange of cables between Churchill and Roosevelt in the early morning hours of November 26 resulted from intelligence that Churchill may have received from a specific, credible, and undisputed source—such as detailed plans of either Japanese Army or Navy war plans. It must be remembered that the 700 copies of Yamamoto's Pearl Harbor initial operational order were in circulation by mid–November, and an even greater number of the Japanese Army's plan were also sent out—including copies to the Japanese embassy in Bangkok. It is possible that British or Dutch agents may have secured a copy of the plans.

Also, Soviet spies had infiltrated the highest level of the Japanese government and their embassies. Master spy Richard Sorge had been arrested a month earlier, but many of the Soviet agents were as yet undetected, including a spy who was a member of the imperial family. In addition, the Russians had also infiltrated the Japanese embassies in Moscow and Bangkok. However, it was not in the Soviet Union's interest to pass on secret Japanese information to the United States as the Soviet Union had withdrawn seven Red Army divisions from Manchuria to defend Moscow against the German juggernaut invading Russia. This transfer of army resources resulted in Manchuria becoming vulnerable to Japanese attack in the east. Subsequently, it would serve the Russian cause best if Japan went to war with the United States in the Pacific, which would deflect Japanese military sources away from its northern border and toward the Pacific and Indian Oceans.

A Japanese transmission that was intercepted by U.S. naval intelligence received a great deal of attention in the congressional hearings held in January 1946. This was the "East Wind Rain" message supposedly broadcast by the Japanese weather service on December 4, 1941. Its relationship to this discussion is not that the message specifically mentions that Pearl Harbor was the target of the Japanese Navy, but rather that the files that are pertinent to the case were missing and that conflicting testimony was given by the witnesses testifying at the hearings. On November 29, 1941, the Foreign Ministry sent a communication to Nomura that in the event that diplomatic relations were severed with the United States, the words "East Wind Rain" would be transmitted daily on the Japanese short wave weather broadcast station. The code message "North Wind Cloudy" would be sent if Japanese-Russian diplomatic relations had been broken, and the cryptic communication "West Wind Clear" would be dispatched if Japanese-British relations had been ruptured.[53]

Although this message did not specify where Japan would open its offensive against the Allies, its reception by Washington intelligence, or lack thereof, received a great deal of attention in the aftermath of Pearl Harbor. The bomb plot dispatch, which was far more significant, documenting that Japanese intelligence in Hawaii was paying serious attention to the anchorage and schedule of the U.S. fleet, received minimal consideration by the same investigators. The question arises as to whether or not the "East Wind Rain" message was ever broadcast by Japan prior to the attack on Pearl Harbor. The dispatch was supposedly not picked up by HYPO, but this assertion is also subject to question. Rear Admiral Layton reported that on November 28, 1941, Washington intelligence sent the "East Wind Rain" intercept to HYPO. This was the first intelligence from Magic sent by Washington in four months. Layton contends that the short wave Tokyo radio message was not a war warning per se, but that U.S./Japanese relations were in danger of collapsing. Washington intelligence placed as little value on this message as it did on a second message, which was sent by Tokyo at the same time as the first message, ordering the embassy to destroy all codes and papers when diplomatic relations with the U.S. were close to collapsing. The one inconsistency in Layton's report is the date of transmission of the second message, November 28, which conflicts with the reported date of its transmission by Safford of December 4.[54]

However, the existence of "East Wind Rain" intercept message—according to Layton—is not subject to doubt. The testimony by Layton is at variance with the official report by Congress's investigation and by sources quoted in Prange's *At Dawn We Slept*, doubting that the "East Wind Rain" message was ever broadcast and received by Washington intelligence.[55] The story of this communication is interwoven with intrigue. Ralph Briggs, a Navy communication officer, was on duty in Cheltenham, Canada, and claims that the "East Wind Rain" message was received by him during the first five days of December 1941. He immediately transmitted the intercept to OP-20G in Washington. The message was received by Safford at Navy intelligence, who then delivered it to his commanding officer, Rear Admiral Noyes. A few days later, Briggs received a bouquet of red roses from Captain Safford as a reward for his good work with a note saying, "Well done."[56]

At the January 1946 Joint congressional hearings on Pearl Harbor, Safford was under pressure regarding his reception of the "East Wind Rain" dispatch. Captain Alwin D. Kramer, head of the translation section of Navy intelligence, testified that he had definitely seen the transmission on December 4. However, when Safford and Kramer tried to find the teletype copy, the station backup copy, and the log sheets, all were missing. Under further questioning, and without proof of his testimony, Kramer later recanted his testimony, emotionally broke down, and was subsequently admitted to the Psychiatric Ward of Bethesda Naval Hospital. Meanwhile, Safford located the operators at Cheltenham and discovered that Briggs had received the communication, which subsequently resulted in a meeting between Briggs and Safford. Briggs had agreed to testify but later received a phone call ordering him to report to Captain John S. Harper, commanding officer of the Naval Security Station. Harper wanted to know why he was not notified that Briggs was meeting with Safford. Harper then ordered Briggs not to meet with Safford, adding that he was not to testify as a witness in the hearing on behalf of Safford. Harper then said, "Perhaps someday you'll understand the reason for this. You understand what I've told you? That is all."[57]

Safford never told anyone of his meeting with Briggs to preserve his communications officer career in the Navy. In 1960, Briggs looked for some proof of the intercept at the depository for all World War II Communications Intelligence. Eventually, he found the log sheet, dated December 2, 1941, which specifically indicated that *RT* (Briggs' operator sign) came on duty at 0500 and tuned his radio to copy the Japanese weather broadcast. The log was dated December 2, but Safford insisted it was December 4, which remains a mystery to this day. The only other person to confirm that Briggs was telling the truth was his chief, with the operator sign of *DW.* However, he declined to do so in the hearings, stating that the intercept was never received. Until the day he died, Safford persisted in his belief that he had received the "East Wind Rain" message.[58]

The "East Wind Rain" message that was sent out did not identify that Pearl Harbor was the target of the attack but signaled that an attack in the Pacific was imminent. However, this message, coupled with the bomb plot decipher, should have alerted the Americans that Pearl Harbor would soon be attacked by Japan. Confirmatory evidence for the existence of the message comes from Captain J.W. Henning, chief cryptanalyst at the *Kamer14* station at Bandoeng, Java. He acknowledged the existence of a "East Wind Rain" message by his intelligence headquarters which was intercepted and interpreted by his group to signify that a Japanese attack in the Pacific was imminent.

Another piece of evidence comes from Lieutenant Commander Cedric Brown, a British Naval Officer, who while interned in a Japanese war camp, met a New Zealand naval officer, Lieutenant H.C. Dixon. Dixon had worked at the Stonecutters Island signal intelligence intercept unit in Hong Kong. Dixon told Brown that he was surprised that the United States was unprepared for the Japanese attack on Pearl Harbor because his intelligence unit had also picked up the "East Wind Rain" message a few days before the attack on Pearl Harbor. This information adds to the evidence that an "East Wind Rain" message was actually sent by the Japanese days before the attack. Since intelligence was shared by the British, Dutch, and with the United States, it is safe to conclude that Safford did receive the "East Wind Rain" message from OP-20-G.[59] On November 25, at 0600 (Japanese date and time), 31 ships (including three submarines) of the First Air Fleet lifted anchor and headed out to the open sea toward Hawaii. The carrier force consisted of *Akagi, Kaga, Soryu, Hiryu, Shokaku,* and *Zuikaku.* These were accompanied by the battleships *Hiei* and *Kirishima,* heavy cruisers *Tone* and *Chikuma,* cruiser *Abukuma,* nine of Japan's newest and best destroyers, a scouting group of three large submarines (I-19, I-21 and I-23), and seven oil refueling tankers. They left from Hitokappu Bay in secrecy with their radio transmission keys reportedly sealed and, in some cases, the radio fuses removed. The ships could receive messages but Genda instructed the Task Force to send no dispatches. However, recently released U.S. declassified documents reveal that radio silence was indeed broken by the Kido Butai. It is interesting that it was on this day that U.S. Navy officials issued the Vacant Sea directive (discussed on page 31). The question arises as to how the three Japanese submarines scouting ahead of the Kido Butai would communicate with the Striking Force if there were complete radio silence. The submarines could communicate directly with Tokyo, which in turn could relay the message to the First Fleet. Or the submarines, using low-powered radio, could send the information directly to Nagumo. In either case, radio silence would be broken. Prange claims that the submarines were brought to within one kilometer of *Akagi*, and communicated with it or the other ships in the First Fleet by signal lamp. However, this explanation seems implausible since Kido Butai was hampered throughout the voyage with low visibility and storms. It is also doubtful that the submarines maintained that position when the fog lifted because the main purpose of their mission was to scout ahead of the fleet and report back the information to Admiral Nagumo.[60]

On the way to Hawaii, Genda tried his best to persuade Admiral Nagumo that multiple air strikes on Pearl Harbor would be the most effective way to neutralize U.S. naval power in the Pacific. He argued that the fuel depots would be destroyed, forcing the U.S. Navy to vacate Pearl Harbor and return to the West Coast. However, Nagumo was rigid in his stance that there would be only one air strike on naval installations on Oahu.[61]

On November 29, Japanese naval intelligence radioed the Kido Butai that the Soviet commercial ship, *Uritsky*, carrying vital lend-lease supplies, had left San Francisco and was heading directly toward the Nagumo force. Following this message, Japan's naval intelligence then sent a dispatch to the Japanese consulate in San Francisco to keep track of any other ships leaving the West Coast and heading into the North Pacific.

What follows has been neglected by every historian except for Rear Admiral Elmer T. Layton. In his book *And I Was There*, Layton points out that in the official Japanese war history entitled *Hawaii Sakusen Senshi Sosho*, Volume 10, there is a first-hand wartime account of the Kido Butai encountering *Uritsky* on its way to Hawaii. In this record, as well as in a Japanese Navy enlisted man's wartime account, *Southern Cross*, it is recorded that the Kido Butai was aware of a Russian freighter which was sailing to the Far East from San Francisco. However, the enlisted man's report made no mention of any actual sighting. It took until 1970 for the government of Japan to publicly admit to the interception of the Soviet freighter. Nine years later, Japanese author Agawa Hiroyuki, in his book *The Reluctant Admiral*, confirmed that a third-world ship was sighted by the task force on its way to Hawaii. It is clear from this text that no action was taken by the Japanese against the freighter.[62] The Russian ship did not radio its sighting of the Kido Butai to anyone on its voyage to Vladivostok, even when it was out of range of the carrier force. One possible explanation is that the Soviet Union had warned Tokyo that the *Uritsky* would be crossing paths with Japan's fleet heading toward Hawaii. But for the Soviet Union to notify Japan of this happening, it had to know that the Japanese task force was in the north Pacific.

The Soviets certainly had spies at the highest levels of the Japanese government, where it would have had ample opportunity to obtain information of the assault on Pearl Harbor. In addition, it was not in the Soviet Union's best interest to prevent Japan from attacking America. The Soviets were fighting Germany on its western front, which resulted in its eastern front being vulnerable to Japanese attack. This was so because many of the Russian Army's divisions in Manchuria were moved west to resist the German threat in that sector. An attack on the United States by Japan would focus Japan's military power to the south and away from the Manchurian border. However, in 2002, Stinnett stated in his book *Day of Deceit* that *Uritsky* was not in the area. After leaving San Francisco, the ship had anchored in Astoria, Oregon.[63]

On November 28, the American carrier *Enterprise* steamed out of Pearl Harbor and headed for Wake Island accompanied by three heavy cruisers and nine destroyers. Its mission was to deliver 12 Grumman F4F-3 "Wildcat" fighters to Wake.[64] One week later on December 5, *Lexington* sailed from Pearl Harbor to ferry 18 Vought SB2U-3 *Vindicator* dive bombers to Midway. However, as *Lexington* approached Midway on December 7, it was learned that Pearl Harbor had been attacked, and the order to deliver the planes to Midway was rescinded.

During the 1945–1946 congressional hearings of the investigation of the Pearl Harbor attack, Chairman (Senator) Alben Barkley, in an effort to determine whether the U.S. government had foreknowledge of the Pearl Harbor attack, questioned whether these carrier deployments were real efforts to reinforce Wake and Midway, or an attempt to move all of the Navy's modern ships out of harm's way. In response to Senator Barkley, Admiral Stark testified that Kimmel had set the dates when the carrier fleets were sent to their respective destinations. The truth is that Stark set the date on November 26, 1941, after having received a direct appeal from General George Marshall to ferry the planes to Wake and Midway.[65] In retrospect, it seems inappropriate that an Army general would give such a directive to the Navy, which had jurisdiction over Wake and Midway, lending doubt as to why the naval forces were removed from Pearl Harbor. With the modern forces at sea, what was left in Pearl Harbor were mostly outdated 27-year-old ships of World War I which ultimately would prove to be expendable.

Kimmel's intelligence had recommended that if there were to be a Japanese attack on Pearl Harbor, it would come out of the west/southwest direction. Therefore, his naval intelligence assumed that the approach would originate from Jaluit in the Marshall Islands, which had a deep water harbor for the Kido Butai. As a result, Kimmel ordered his limited scouting patrol planes to cover the west/southwest area of Hawaii. The Navy had 81 long-range reconnaissance aircraft, which was only one-third of the number of planes needed to cover the arc of 360 degrees. Due to crew and plane maintenance, the number of planes available for daily searches was further reduced to only 30 planes. With each plane covering eight degrees of the arc, this left 120 degrees of the search arc uncovered, particularly in the north and northwest areas.[66]

However, it has been revealed that HYPO unit had intelligence that should have led to a different conclusion as to the direction of the Japanese would attack, namely, a north by northwest bearing. In addition to the Hitokappu message received by Rochefort at HYPO on November 18, which placed the Kido Butai in the Kurile Islands, the leader of the code breakers at HYPO reported that on November 30,

1941, a radio operator picked up a low-powered radio message between *Akagi* and several of its merchant ships at sea. However, Rochefort erroneously concluded that the Japanese carriers were not at sea but in home waters because the low-powered frequencies were unreliable indicators of accurate direction finder assessments by HYPO's fragile system.[67]

Some critics, such as Gordon Prange in his book, have stated that Rochefort could not have picked up the Kido Butai's radio transmissions because complete radio silence was adhered to by Kido Butai. Prange cites the words of Genda, who reported that the transmitter switches were sealed off to prevent the sending of high frequency radio messages and to ensure strict radio silence. However, this admission did not preclude the ships communicating through low-frequency inter-fleet radio. This method of communication was entirely possible in view of the limits that dense fog and bad weather placed on signal lamps and signal flag-waving as means of communication. This was particularly true during the time that the Kido Butai had to refuel in the undesirable weather.

Evidence that supports this point of view is presented by Fuchida in his book *The Battle That Doomed Japan*. He reported that when the Japanese fleet encountered bad weather on its way to Midway, Admiral Nagumo decided to use a medium-wave transmission using a low-powered frequency to communicate between ships. In his book, Fuchida says, "This method is not entirely safe, but it had worked in the past, thanks to enemy carelessness."[68] There is no other historical documentation that the Kido Butai experienced severe weather at sea except when it was on its way to Pearl Harbor, where dense fog and high seas necessitated the use of low-powered radio for inter-fleet communications.

John Toland's book *Infamy: Pearl Harbor and Its Aftermath*, published in 1982, reported that San Francisco's Twelfth Naval District received radio direction finder coordinates that placed the Kido Butai in the Pacific, north of Hawaii, from November 30 to December 4, 1941. The author's source for this information, Robert Ogg, was a special investigator for the Naval District Intelligence Office (DIO). His superior was Lieutenant Ellsworth Hosmer, who obtained radio direction finder bearings during this time and recorded the coordinates on a great-circle map of the north Pacific.

These findings originated from RCA Radio and Globe Wireless and from the Navy's radio direction finder station in Dutch Harbor, Alaska, which picked up the low-powered communications from the Kido Butai in the north Pacific. The radio frequencies used by the Japanese war vessels were low-frequency in the range of 4,000 kilocycles, consistent with the use of low-powered inter-fleet radio. The data revealed that warships were traveling east until December 3, when the ships changed course to a southeast direction toward Hawaii. Hosmer had identified the radio broadcasts as Japanese, as the transmissions were in the unique *kana* telegraphic code of the Japanese Navy. This information was forwarded by Captain Richard McCullough, the District's chief of intelligence, to Washington intelligence by a secure radio circuit, and from there to the White House.[69]

Ogg never was called upon to testify in any of the Pearl Harbor hearings. When his testimony was published in Toland's book *Infamy*, many prominent historians questioned Toland's historical record by citing that the Kido Butai was on strict radio silence during its voyage. Ogg admitted that he had no definite proof of his assertions,

5. The Jewel of the Pacific

as naval intelligence policy prohibited the retention of any classified documents. However, he asserted that records of what he said could be found in the Navy's intercept station at Dutch Harbor. No one ever tried to validate his statements until Robert Stinnett sought copies of these records. When Stinnett's request was denied by the Navy, he sought the records of Station KING, a unit of Rochefort's mid–Pacific direction finder network which was also at Dutch Harbor. When permission was granted, he discovered the following information that completely substantiated Ogg's testimony.

On November 26, 1941, radioman Robert Fox, the traffic chief for KING, picked up a message from *Akagi* to its merchant marine using the low-powered inter-fleet 4963 frequency. The radio direction findings (RDF) clearly document that Japanese radio silence was not maintained and that the location of *Akagi* was in the north Pacific. It was the same frequency message that was intercepted by Station H in Hawaii on the same date, November 26, which also placed *Akagi* and its merchant ships in the northern Pacific.[70]

By December 3, 1941, the Tokyo-based naval transmissions to the Kido Butai had grown in number and were detected by the commercial ocean liner SS *Lurline*, sailing from San Francisco to Hawaii. Normally, low-powered inter-fleet transmissions can travel only about one hundred miles, but a solar storm at that time created an atmospheric medium whereby radio waves could travel thousands of miles due to the effect of these storms on electronic transmissions. This phenomenon led the SS *Lurline* to hear multiple radio transmissions emanating from shore stations in Japan that were directed to the Kido Butai in the northwest Pacific. These communications were then forwarded to the other ships in the fleet by low-powered radio.[71]

Leslie Grogan, the *Lurline's* first assistant radio operator, observed that the Kido Butai's larger ships were repeating messages from Tokyo for copying to the smaller vessels in the fleet. A transcript of the account and the RDF bearings were turned over to Lieutenant George Pease of naval intelligence when the ship docked in Honolulu. However, Pease died in a plane crash in 1945, and the record of how he dealt with the matter disappeared. When the SS *Lurline* returned to San Francisco from Hawaii, the ship's logs were confiscated by Lieutenant Commander Preston Allen from the Twelfth Naval District intelligence unit. The log has never been seen since that time.[72]

Inquiry into the log was made by John Toland, but he was told the log did not exist. However, Lieutenant Commander Allen had filed the log with the port director of the Twelfth Naval District, and in 1958 the port director turned over the files to the National Archives in San Bruno, California. They remained there until the 1970s, when someone, most likely a Navy official (implicated because the files were legally under the Navy's jurisdiction), removed the files without authorization and left a blank withdrawal slip in the files' place.[73]

Station SAIL's records in Seattle confirmed the reports of Hosmer/Ogg and the *Lurline* on December 3, documenting that its radio operators heard strong radio signals emanating from the north Pacific. The next day, three other Navy intercept stations recorded the same findings. Included in the records from Station SAIL are messages from the *Akagi, Kirishima, Tone*, and one dispatch from Admiral Nagumo. Evidence for this accounting was found by Stinnett in the National Archives.[74]

Although the above Japanese naval transmissions were intercepted by U.S.

intelligence between November 28 and December 6, 1941, Stinnett reported that none of these communications were forwarded to Admiral Kimmel, thereby depriving him of vital information that the Japanese Navy was in the north Pacific and heading east toward Pearl Harbor.

Heretofore, the strongest argument that no communications were made by Kido Butai prior to its attack on Pearl Harbor was that the Japanese Navy ordered strict radio silence. This supposition was made by Lieutenant Commander Thomas Dyer, second in command to Rochefort and chief cryptographer at HYPO. Robert Stinnett, however, found evidence to the contrary in the records of Station H, which he included in his book *Day of Deceit*.[75]

The first communication Stinnett found in the records of Station H came from the Tokyo Naval Radio, which warned the Kido Butai of an impending typhoon. On November 30, when the storm subsided, Admiral Nagumo found his fleet dispersed all over the north Pacific.

Signal blinker lamps and flag signals were not an option as the fleet was scattered over the horizon more than 15 miles from the flagship. Due to the previously mentioned solar storms, *Akagi*'s broadcasts to the fleet were detected by U.S. radio interceptors all the way across the Pacific, reaching Oahu, Alaska, the U.S. West Coast, and the SS *Lurline*.[76] Further proof of the effect that the solar storms had on radio transmissions is provided on December 7, 1941, when Fuchida's message, "Tora! Tora! Tora!," transmitted from his plane, was heard in Tokyo over 5,000 miles away.

Layton, in his December 1 report to Kimmel, denied having any knowledge of Japanese carriers transmitting messages. Rochefort confirmed Layton's statement by stating that HYPO intelligence had lost the whereabouts of the Japanese carriers because they had gone on radio silence. However, in the February 15, 1946, hearings, Rochefort modified his statement by saying that he had located them "in a negative sense."[77]

Until October 31, 1941, RDF reports from Washington intelligence were included with the information given to Kimmel and the White House. But beginning on November 1, this data was deleted from the communications sent to Kimmel for unexplained reasons. In fact, Rochefort's original Communication Summaries were found by Stinnett in the National Archives, and each one of Kimmel's copies had the RDF report crudely cut from the bottom page of the record. When Richard A. Von Doenhoff, a specialist in the Pearl Harbor section of the National Archives, was questioned in 1993 by Stinnett, he stated that the deletions occurred prior to the start of the 1945 and 1946 congressional hearings. It now appears that the records presented in the congressional hearings were in this mutilated form.[78]

Evidence has emerged which further challenges the assertion by Rochefort and Layton that the HYPO unit's inability to find the Kido Butai was due to radio silence. There were 129 Japanese naval intercepts detected by Station CAST and H between November 15 and December 6. In contrast to Layton's statement, when Stinnett secured records of these stations, he found that they revealed all categories of carrier messages received by the Kido Butai or transmitted by them during this three-week period. In addition, Captain Duane Whitlock of Station CAST and Homer Kisner of Station H confirmed reception of these transmission messages and their implications. Kisner's reports and intercepts during this time still exist, while Whitlock's records were deliberately burned so that they did not fall into enemy hands when Corregidor fell. However, CAST's records of its RDF reports were sent to Hawaii before Corregidor was taken by the Japanese. Both radio experts, in different interviews with Stinnett, confirmed the validity of the 129 intercepts and their meaning.[79]

Radio silence was further broken when Admiral Nagano Osami, chief of the Imperial Naval Headquarters, broadcast from Tokyo a message to the Eleventh Air Fleet, based in Formosa, that Hawaii was the object of Japan's carrier striking force and that every effort should be taken in Formosa to guard against the United States learning of Japan's military movements before the attack took place.[80] This information was first publicly documented in a postwar article by Commander Shimada Keiichi, an air officer of the Eleventh Air Fleet. Confirmation of receipt of this communication was found by Stinnett in Station H logs and witnessed to by operator *CU*. The intercept was identified by the call letters SI HA 149 and has never been claimed to have been seen by anyone other than Commander Shimada and operator *CU*. Not one of the SI HA 149 intercepts has been declassified.[81]

It is important to remember that Kisner claimed these intercepts were partially readable, which allowed him to decipher enough of the message to understand its content. Kisner then documented his conclusions that Japan intended to attack Pearl Harbor. On the morning of December 6, he delivered the information to HYPO, placing it on Dyer's desk. This critical intelligence package never reached Admiral Kimmel before the attack, and its whereabouts after it reached Dyer's desk remain unknown.[82]

On December 1, the Kido Butai passed the International Date Line and was now 1,700 miles from Hawaii. The seas had calmed down enough from the typhoon for refueling to begin. Radio Tokyo informed the task force that the United States had given Japan an ultimatum regarding the issues that existed between America and the Japan, leading to the conclusion by both military and political figures in Japan that diplomatic relations between the two countries would soon end abruptly.[83]

At that time, Captain McCollum, head of the Far East section of naval intelligence, specifically asked Admirals Stark and Turner if they notified the Pacific Fleet about this Purple intelligence. Both admirals gave him categorical assurance that they had informed the Pacific Fleet to go on a war time footing. This answer gave McCollum pause as he had not heard of any such messages. He advised Stark to send a memorandum to Turner stating it was about time that war warnings be sent to the Pacific Fleet commanders. Yet, in spite of McCollum's request, neither of the two decrypted communications was sent to Admiral Kimmel.[84]

On December 1, 1941, U.S. intelligence learned from a Purple decrypt that the Japanese ambassador to Germany had told the German government, "The time of war may come sooner that anyone expects." This announcement to the Germans was sent to Nomura and Kurusu, the Japanese diplomats stationed in Washington, using the diplomatic code and was deciphered by the U.S. Navy within hours.

In addition to receiving the German announcement, the Japanese diplomats were instructed to keep the information secret. A second cable was sent to the two negotiators in Washington informing them that officials in London, Hong Kong, Singapore, and Manila had been ordered to destroy their code machines. The code machines in Washington, however, were to remain functional until Japan ordered them otherwise.[85]

The Japanese consular officials in the Philippines and in Dutch and British territories were ordered to evacuate their offices and return home. Japanese citizens and diplomats in Canada and the United States were told leave these countries and book passage on steamers that Japan was sending to the West Coast.

During this time, Lord Edward F. Halifax was requested by the Prime Minister of England to visit President Roosevelt to ascertain what the United States would do if Japan occupied Thailand and invaded Malaya. When questioned by Halifax, Roosevelt replied that he wanted a response first from Japan regarding its troop movements heading south out of Shanghai. He was not ready at this time to commit to a joint resolution with Britain against Japan if British colonies in the Far East were invaded by Japanese troops. Roosevelt wanted to make sure Japan took the first major step toward war before making his case to the American people for the United States enter into the conflict. As he went to sleep that night, his difficult political and military decisions were soon to be resolved, not by him but by Tokyo.[86]

On December 2, the emperor of Japan gave his formal approval for Japan to attack the United States. That afternoon, powerful radio transmitters broadcast on four different wavelengths the cryptic JN-25B code message Niitaka Yama Nobore 1208. When the communication was deciphered, it read, "Climb Mount Niitaka," which symbolized that Japan was to climb the highest mountain in its empire, Mount Niitaka Yama. This broadcast signified that the emperor had given his approval for Japan's military to go to war on December 8, 1941 (Japanese date).[87]

The Japanese communication was picked up by the U.S. Navy's communication center on Bainbridge Island in Puget Sound. It was also detected by Station H in Hawaii. According to Layton, intelligence officials in Hawaii never received the communication. However, Layton went on to develop four different stories about the reception of the transmission, implying in each one of them that the message was not received, but in the process raising doubts as to the validity of his assertions. The fact is Joseph C. Howard did intercept the communication on that date. Howard was never asked to testify before any of the Pearl Harbor hearings, but, in 1999, after Layton's death, Howard came forward and publically acknowledged that he had intercepted the message, which subsequently resulted in the Navy censoring Howard and his original records.[88]

In Washington, Lord Halifax was again instructed by Churchill to press President Roosevelt on his commitment to support Britain and Holland in the defense of their colonies in the Far East even if the American territories were not attacked by Japan. Halifax further stated that, until this reassurance was given by the United States, Britain would not take any advance military action against Japan in these areas even if they were attacked by Japan.[89]

On December 3, Togo's cabinet decided that the Japanese government's final response to the United States would be delivered just prior to the attack on Pearl Harbor, since Japan was a signatory of the Hague Convention. However, the 14-page message sent by the Japanese ministry to its emissaries in Washington made no reference to the attack on Pearl Harbor; at best it declared that diplomatic relations with the United States were over.

On December 2, 1941, Captain Johan E.M. Ranneft, the Dutch naval attaché in Washington, visited ONI. He asked Admiral Theodore Wilkinson and other intelligence officers about the deteriorating situation in the Pacific. Since Ranneft was friendly with the agency, they responded in a frank manner when one of the American officers pointed to the map on the wall and bluntly stated, "This is the Japanese task Force proceeding east." The position was halfway between Japan and Hawaii. Astonished, Ranneft wondered how the Americans had managed to track the missing carriers. He immediately cabled Dutch naval headquarters in London and reported the information in person to the Minister of the Netherlands in Washington, Alexander Loudon. He then wrote in his official diary, "Conference at Navy Department, ONI. They show me on the map the position of two Japanese carriers. They left Japan on an easterly course."[90]

On December 3, 1941, while on Bandoeng, Java, Dutch Army intelligence intercepted a Japanese message from Tokyo to their ambassador in Bangkok. The message was encrypted in the consular code, which had been broken by Dutch Colonel J.A. Verkuyl with the help of his wife and a group of students. The message told of the upcoming attacks on Hawaii, the Philippines, Malaya, and Thailand. The signal to begin all operations simultaneously would come from Tokyo in the form of a weather broadcast over Radio Tokyo. General Hein ter Poorten, the commander of the Netherlands East Indian Army, hand-carried the long message to the adjacent building where Brigadier General Elliot Thorpe had his office. Poorten remarked that he had information which was vital to the U.S. government. General Thorpe agreed and stated that he would travel to Batavia to inform the senior State Department officer of the information and make sure that it was sent directly to Washington that night.

Finding the American Consulate closed, Thorpe proceeded to the Hotel des Indies where Dr. Walter Foote, the consul general, and the senior naval attaché, Commander Paul Sidney Slawson, lived. Inexplicably, Foote told Thorpe to forget the information. However, Commander Slawson was impressed and suggested the message be sent immediately in naval code to Washington. When the encoded communication was ready, the two went to the main post office and sent the communication. Since it was in naval code, it had to first go to the War Department through the Navy Communications Center. After the message was acknowledged by the War Department, Thorpe assumed both the Army and Navy had read the message and its warning of an attack on Hawaii.

It is unlikely a coincidence that numerous vital messages and documents concerning Pearl Harbor have disappeared. These include the material confiscated by the U.S. Navy in San Francisco from the *Lurline* on December 10; the General Thorpe and General Ter Poorten message; the questionnaire and other papers Dusko Popov delivered to the FBI; records of the tracking of the Kido Butai by the Twelfth Naval District; and records of Leslie Grogan's original report to the Fourteenth Naval District on December 3, 1941. If one rules out the probable, the improbable becomes strongly suspect as to the alternative explanations as of the course of events. The Kido Butai, now 1,500 miles northwest of Hawaii, ran into a typhoon, curtailing any hope of refueling the ships. There was a significant scattering of the fleet, which required low-powered inter-fleet transmissions to bring the ships together and back on course. Even though Layton, in his book *And I Was There*, took the position that absolute radio silence was maintained by the Kido Butai on its voyage to Oahu, he did report that the radio messages sent by the Japanese Navy's ministry in Tokyo to its fleet during the storm diminished during the day, thereby reducing their chances of detection by U.S. radio intelligence. It can be said that, as a rule, when radio silence is imposed, it applies to the fleet and its units at sea, not to the headquarters in Tokyo which can broadcast without revealing the location of the fleet. Certainly, it has been documented that U.S. radio intelligence detected a signal from the Japanese Navy ministry on December 1 that informed U.S. naval intelligence that a new additive code would be added to the JN-25B fleet code on December 4, 1941 (U.S. date).[91]

On December 3, Kimmel learned for the first time what Purple was. Unaware of the existence of the machine, Lieutenant Commander Herbert Coleman, fleet security officer, explained to Kimmel that Purple was a Japanese electrical coding instrument that permitted the United States to decipher Japanese coded diplomatic messages. The subject of Purple arose because Kimmel learned for the first time that Japanese offices in London, Hong Kong, Singapore, and Manila were ordered to destroy their Purple machines, codes, and ciphers.[92] Kimmel and Hawaiian naval intelligence did not know that Japan's consulate in Honolulu had a Purple machine. However, thanks to the FBI tapping the phone lines in the Japanese consulate's kitchen, it learned that the consulate had been ordered to burn its codes and destroy the Purple machine. This information did not reach Kimmel until the next day.

Admiral Turner in Washington was later to testify in the hearings that he considered the intelligence about the embassies destroying their codes to clearly mean that war was going to break out between the United States and Japan within a few days. However, on December 3 he did not react with that kind of attitude. Turner wanted the original worded dispatch to Kimmel to be cautious and vague in content. It was not until Captain Safford, disregarding all the rules of security, insisted on drafting a message to the Pacific Fleet which, though written in highly technical language, revealed the true nature of the Purple communication ordering the destruction of the Purple machines and the burning of the Japanese codes. Unfortunately, this information came to Hawaii intelligence in a vacuum, without explanation of the context in which it was sent. By itself, its significance was lost on Hawaiian naval intelligence and Admiral Kimmel.[93]

With the preceding intelligence in hand, Roosevelt now felt reassured to give to Lord Halifax the commitment he was looking for, that is, that the United States would provide armed support to Britain and Holland if Japan attacked their territories in the Far East. However, this was a verbal commitment to Lord Halifax and not the public declaration to the American people desired by Lord Halifax.[94]

On December 4 (U.S. date), the Kido Butai again ran into a night of turbulent weather with stormy seas and heavy rain. The ships could not see each other and refueling was impossible. The task force did receive some comforting news in that the ships in Pearl Harbor were the same as they had been described previously in the bomb plot messages sent from the Honolulu consulate to Tokyo. The Japanese task force, having run a course due east since leaving the Kurile Islands, was 1,000 miles north-northwest of Hawaii and now turned southeast toward Oahu.

It is interesting to note that on this date, December 4 (U.S. date), Admiral Nagumo sent a message from *Akagi* to other ships in the fleet that specifically mentions December 8 (Japanese date) as the target date for the attack on Pearl Harbor. The dispatch was reportedly sent by blinker lamp. However, the use of low powered, inter-fleet radio cannot be ruled out in view of the huge storm which would have prohibited ships from seeing the blinker lamp. Robert Stinnett has revealed that Admiral Nagumo sent 60 radio messages from November 15 to December 6 (U.S. date).[95] Was this communication sent by Nagumo on December 4 (U.S. date) one of the 60 dispatches sent by him during this time and picked up by Station H in Hawaii? Since none of these intercepts to date has been released or declassified by the U.S. government, it is impossible to tell.

Chapter 6

Radio Silence Is Broken

On December 5 (U.S. date), Tokyo sent a message to its Washington Embassy to delay Japan's response to the U.S. State Department until 1300 (Washington time) on Sunday, December 7. The Japanese foreign ministry would provide to Japan's emissaries a 14-part communication for the diplomats in Washington to deliver to Hull at that time.

Poll numbers in favor of military action by the United States against Japan were not forthcoming for President Roosevelt. Although 69 per cent of the American public favored stopping Japanese aggression in the Far East, only 51 per cent believed that this would involve military action.[1] Roosevelt needed a direct Japanese attack on American territory to arouse the U.S. public and gain overwhelming support of a war with Japan, and to obtain the full support of Congress for such a war.

At this time, British Admiral Sir Tom Phillips, General MacArthur, and Admiral Hart met in Manila to discuss a joint war plan to deal with the upcoming Japanese threat.[2] MacArthur confidently stated that he had a 125,000-man Filipino army, 112 tanks, and a significant B-17 bomber force to oppose Japan. Phillips agreed to move Britain's Far East naval force to Manila. The meeting was suddenly adjourned when Phillips received an RAF reconnaissance patrol report that a Japanese convoy was sailing around the tip of Indochina.[3] Phillips quickly returned to Singapore and with him went his decision to send the British Far East fleet to the Philippines. Four days later, Phillips lost his life when his battleship *Prince of Wales* and the battle cruiser *Repulse* were sunk by Japanese aircraft in the Gulf of Siam.

Britain appeared to preempt the anticipated public announcement by Roosevelt that the United States would provide armed support to Britain and Holland, even if American territories were not attacked, when Navy Captain John Creighton cabled Admiral Hart that this was the case. With this news in hand, Hart withdrew his Asiatic Fleet from Manila Bay, and sailed it south, out of harm's way. Again, Kimmel was not privy to decisions that affected the strategic policy of the United States in the Pacific.

British intelligence also sent a similar message to its Middle East headquarters in Egypt. When U.S. Army Colonel Bonner Fellers arrived in Cairo, Egypt, he was warmly greeted by Air Marshall Arthur Longmore who told Fellers that he had received a secret message that the United States would be attacked in 24 hours.[4]

It was on this day, December 5 (U.S. date), that the Russian freighter *Uritsky* supposedly intersected the sea lane in which the Kido Butai was sailing and was spotted by the Japanese task force. Since the Soviet Union has never addressed the question of whether the *Uritsky* saw the Kido Butai, it can only be assumed that someone on the Soviet freighter saw the massive Japanese fleet sailing east toward Pearl Harbor. It was customary for ships at sea to report the sighting of each other while en route to their destination. In this circumstance, however, the Russian ship did not report making contact with the Japanese task force sailing toward Pearl Harbor, even when it had sailed out of visual range of the Kido Butai.

The *Uritsky* could have also transmitted the sighting in Russian code, outside the standard frequencies, but supposedly decided to remain silent in its reporting. At the very least, this story tells us that the Soviets had the opportunity—and may have taken it—to inform the Japanese government that the Japanese force heading toward Pearl Harbor was going to run into the *Uritsky*. The fact that Tokyo had alerted the Kido Butai that it would intersect the freighter on its voyage to Hawaii raises the question of who passed the information on to Tokyo. It would certainly appear that the Soviets had alerted the Japanese of *Uritsky*'s path across the northern Pacific because the freighter was loaded with arms and supplies for the Soviet war effort. The Soviets wanted to prevent any encounter where the *Uritsky* would be sunk. What Russia did with its information of the encounter between the Kido Butai and the Russian freighter at sea remains a mystery to this day.[5]

However, Stinnett in his book *Day of Deceit*, published in 2000, discovered that the foregoing tale about *Uritsky* is not true. He discovered that on November 28, 1941, *Uritsky* left San Francisco headed for Petropavlovsk on the Kamchatka Peninsula. Instead, the ship was diverted to Astoria, Oregon, because of the Vacant Sea directive. *Uritsky* left for Astoria and anchored there on December 1 at the mouth of the Columbia River until December 5. The ship then resumed her journey to Petropavlovsk, and by that time the Kido Butai was no longer in the north Pacific. It is interesting that *Uritsky* remained in Astoria until the Japanese task force had completed its part of their journey where they could be spotted.[6]

On December 5 (U.S. date), the aircraft carrier *Lexington*, escorted by heavy cruisers, pulled out of Pearl Harbor and began its voyage to deliver the SB2U dive bombers to Midway. Because the Task Force 12 was concerned about Japanese submarines being positioned along its route to Midway, it sailed for Midway leaving the slow, antiquated battleships, light cruisers, and destroyers behind in Pearl Harbor. On December 6 (U.S. date), *Lexington* was about 400 miles northwest of Pearl Harbor. The lookout on the carrier spotted an unidentified aircraft on the horizon which was confirmed by a second lookout and reported to commanding officer Captain F.C. Sherman on the bridge. After further observation, the plane was determined to be a single engine aircraft. The AA Defense Officer, Lieutenant Jerry O'Donnell, recommended that an aircraft be launched to investigate the contact. Radar detected an intermittent target in the neighborhood of the unidentified aircraft for about ten minutes. The visual sighting and radar detections were passed on to Task Force Commander Rear Admiral John Newton, who was also asked for permission to launch aircraft. No reply was initially given. Finally, an hour later, the task force commander responded, stating that the unidentified aircraft was a twin engine U.S. patrol plane and that no action need be taken. Lieutenant O'Donnell and his AA crew completely rejected that conclusion. Their protests, however, went unheeded. After the Pearl Harbor attack the following day, a request was again made to the task force commander to review the sighting from the day before. His response was negative, as it had erroneously been believed at that time that the Japanese attack came from the southwest. Thus, an opportunity to warn Pearl Harbor a day before it was attacked was lost.[7]

Also on December 5 (U.S. date), U.S. destroyers reported two unidentified underwater contacts just five miles south of Diamond Head. This information came in after an unidentified submarine was reported off the coast of Oahu the night before. One of the destroyers, *Selfridge*, actually made sonar contact with an unidentified submarine, but the commanding officer refused to release any depth charges because the United States was at peace with Japan.[8]

On that Friday, December 5 (U.S. date), the infamous Winds code message was sent by Japan. Although the communication offered no specific mention that Pearl Harbor was the target of the Kido Butai, it received the most attention at the Pearl Harbor hearings. The significance of this message lies in the fact that it demonstrated the length to which the U.S. government would go to cover up any information that might suggest that America would soon be at war and that Japan would strike somewhere in the Pacific. Case in point: in 1945 information surfaced that Captain Kramer, then in the Bethesda Naval Hospital, was persuaded to change his testimony about the existence of the Winds message in favor of the Navy's position under threat of permanent confinement in a psychiatric ward.[9] (The Navy denied that such a message was ever sent.)

On the afternoon of December 6 (U.S. date), the Kido Butai was just 700 miles from Hawaii and within the radius of U.S. patrol planes. However, that weekend no PBYs were scheduled to cover the northern sector of Hawaii. The Japanese task force now turned due south at a high speed toward its launching point, about two hundred and thirty miles north of Oahu. During this part of the voyage, the Japanese submarine I-72 reported that the alternate anchorage site at Lahaina Bay was devoid of U.S. vessels.

The actual *Z* flag, used by Admiral Togo in the Battle of Tsushima in 1905, was flown on the *Akagi* masthead. This was done to signify that the same message that Admiral Togo sent in the great victory in the Tsushima Straits would be applicable in the attack on Pearl Harbor: "The fate of nation depends on this battle—all hands will exert themselves to their utmost." That evening the Japanese task force learned from a Tokyo naval radio message that there were no unusual American movements nor any change in the air patrol surveillance over Pearl Harbor.[10]

While the Kido Butai was steaming toward Pearl Harbor, hostilities in the Pacific actually began to break out near Kota Bharu, Malaya, where an Australian twin engine bomber, having taken off from a neighboring air field, spotted a large Japanese convoy rounding Cambodia and heading southwest toward Malaya. The pilot radioed the sighting just before his plane was shot down and crashed into the Gulf of Siam.[11] This event on December 6, 1941, actually marked the beginning of the war in the Pacific.

In the late afternoon of December 6, while in Pearl Harbor, Layton learned that the Japanese consulate in Honolulu was in the process of burning their codes and official papers, according to information obtained by the FBI tap of the phone in the Japanese consul's kitchen. Layton was also informed by Captain Mayfield of the Fourteenth Naval District Communications Office that he wanted to see Layton the next morning regarding some intelligence Mayfield was to receive later that day. Unknown to Layton, this intelligence centered on a telephone call made from Tokyo to a Mrs. Mori, a Honolulu resident and the wife of a Japanese dentist practicing in the area.

The phone call revealed that she provided information to a supposed Tokyo newsman about dispositions of the U.S. fleet and other military dispositions. However, this disclosure was apparently not seen by Layton until one year later, and as such was not helpful in forecasting an attack on Pearl Harbor.[12]

Prior to December 7, (U.S. date) U.S. naval intelligence in Hawaii came close to deciphering Japanese diplomatic intelligence that would clearly point to an air attack by Japan on Pearl Harbor. By late December 1941, Rochefort's team still was not authorized by Washington intelligence to intercept and decipher any diplomatic messages. OP-20-G had not provided HYPO with a Purple machine.

In 1941, eight Purple machines were in existence. Four machines (two each for Army and Navy intelligence) were in Washington, two were sent to Great Britain, and one was sent to Station CAST in the Philippines. OP-20-G gave some consideration to sending the remaining Purple machine to HYPO in Hawaii, but that option never materialized as Washington intelligence decided that sending a third machine to Great Britain was more important. The explanation for this reasoning is not known.[13]

In addition, Washington naval intelligence did not provide HYPO with any of the latest key recoveries necessary for rapid decryption of a coded diplomatic message. The apparent justification behind this decision was that since HYPO was not authorized to decipher either the J-19 nor the PA-K2 codes, the keys were not given to them.

However, Warrant Officer Farnsley C. Woodward, a cryptologist in Hawaii, did have experience with other diplomatic Japanese cipher systems, so he began to work on the low-grade LA cipher—a code used for routine housekeeping traffic. He worked on this cipher without authorization from Washington but found this effort unrewarding, so on December 2 (U.S. date), he moved on to the J-19 code. But Woodward decided to cease his efforts to decipher the J-19 code because he lacked the current decipher key, which would have shortened the process of decryption of that code.

On December 5 (U.S. date), after they burned their J-19 codes, the Japanese consulate changed to the PA-K2 code for their confidential messages.[14] This act prompted Woodward to shift his emphasis to decoding the easier PA-K2 code. However, this was a significant error in judgment on Woodward's part. Had he continued—even though he did not have the decipher key—and if his efforts were successful in deciphering the J-19 code, he would have learned from the December 2 (U.S. date) communication that Japanese naval intelligence was asking its spies in Oahu to determine the presence of U.S. warships in the harbor, whether or not they were protected by anti-torpedo nets, and whether any observation balloons were in place over the harbor. In turning to the simpler PA-K2 code, he also failed to decipher vital information in time to learn of Fritz Kuehn's (Yoshikawa's agent) method of sending intelligence to the Japanese Army; that is, signaling by lamp from a house on the coast to an off-shore Japanese submarine. Woodward made an egregious error in setting up the message for decryption of the PA-K2 code. He reversed the order of the message text by placing the last part of the message first and the first part of the communication last. This mishandling of the data led to loss of precious time and resulted in his not translating the message until December 10 (U.S. date). The PA-K2 message would have revealed the pronounced attention Tokyo was paying to the disposition of the U.S. Pacific fleet.

On December 3 (U.S. date), the Japanese consul in Honolulu relayed to Tokyo, this time in the PA-K2 code, the elaborate methods by which Yoshikawa's German agent Kuehn was sending his reports to Army intelligence in Japan. In its response to that communication, Tokyo revealed that December 6 (U.S. date) would be the last date that its naval intelligence wanted to know which ships were in or out of Pearl Harbor. In failing to decipher the J-19 code, Woodward missed the vital information from Kita Nagao, Japanese Consul General in Honolulu, that was contained in the two messages he had sent on December 2 (U.S. date): one stated that there were no signs, barrage balloons, or anti-torpedo nets in the harbor; the other dispatch revealed that there was no air reconnaissance being conducted by the fleet arm.[15]

It is important to point out that Washington intelligence had the ability to read the J-19 and PA-K2 codes, and indeed it did. One of the Japanese transmissions dated November 18, which was intercepted by OP-20-G, listed every U.S. warship in the harbor and also detailed the speed, procedures, and time it took for the destroyers to enter in the harbor and settle at their moorings. On December 5 (U.S. date), another message revealed that the consul was requested by Tokyo intelligence to report on the schedules of the ships twice a week and to do so in utmost secrecy. Whether Washington intelligence knew about the exchange of messages between Kita and Tokyo on December 3 is unknown, but certainly if it did obtain this information, the date and location of the Kido Butai's mission would have been known.[16]

On December 5 (U.S. date), U.S. Army intelligence in Washington learned that Kita was to investigate the fleet air bases in Hawaii. On the next day, intelligence derived from Magic revealed that great secrecy was to be used while Kita was carrying out his investigations of the local air bases. In a later translation, another error occurred when Mamala Bay was misinterpreted as Manila Bay by the translator, but clearly Kita was in Hawaii and not in the Philippines. On that same day, OP-20-G learned that Tokyo had instructed Kita to report, for the first time, when there was no movement of ships in the harbor. Washington intelligence completely ignored the fact that the majority of shipping reports intercepted from Purple from August to December involved the naval base of Pearl Harbor. None of the foregoing important decrypts were relayed to Hawaii intelligence for their consideration, leaving those officials once again completely in the dark regarding vital information.[17]

On December 6 (U.S. date), Mrs. Dorothy Edgers, a new recruit working in OP-20-GZ, found a three-week old Honolulu consulate message on her desk waiting to be translated. She received permission to translate the message from her brother Fred Woodrough, who was the leading civilian Japanese linguist in the department. Mrs. Edgers had spent more than 30 years living in Japan and was more fluent in the language than her brother. She pursued her conviction to translate the message with a sense of urgency. When she found some distortions in the dispatch, Mrs. Edgers turned the communication over to the cryptologists to unravel them. The corrected transmission was not delivered back to her until December 6 (U.S. date) at 1230 (Washington EST). She could have left for the weekend but was determined to work on the translation because of its perceived importance.

When the translation was partially completed, she decided to show it to her superior, Lieutenant Commander Kramer, who was unimpressed and felt that the information containing statements about U.S. Pacific Fleet movements did not warrant her staying to complete the translation. Undaunted, she proceeded to bring the interpretation to the attention of her brother, who felt that the partially translated information definitely justified her remaining in the office to finish the job.[18]

She stayed until 1400 to complete the first translation, which revealed that Japanese espionage agents were trying to figure out how to communicate information about U.S. fleet movements to Tokyo intelligence. This was the infamous "light message," in which it was discovered that Japanese spies would transmit U.S. fleet dispositions to a submarine off the Hawaiian coast by the use of light signal from a house near the water. Kramer was not in his office, so she left the translation with Chief Clerk Harold L. Bryant, whose job it was to edit the messages. On Monday morning of December 8, the unread translation was still on Kramer's desk.[19]

In the 1945 congressional hearings, Kramer denied any knowledge of the incident and went on to describe Mrs. Edgers as inexperienced and timid. No attempt was made at the hearings to discover the truth about the incidents as Mrs. Edgers was not asked to testify. Her original worksheet had conveniently disappeared by 1945. The only remaining documentary evidence is Kramer's translation of the message which he completed on December 11 and stamped "Top Secret Ultra." Interestingly enough, even this message was not sent to Hawaiian intelligence even though it was four days after the Pearl Harbor attack, and its translation was approved by Kramer.[20] This evidence demonstrates that even after the Pearl Harbor attack, and although inconsequential, OP-20-G continued to withhold information from Hawaiian intelligence.

On Friday December 6 (U.S. date), the Navy intercepted two Purple messages at Bainbridge Island on Puget Sound. The communication was sent to the Army's Signal Corps Special Intelligence since it was an even-numbered day and therefore their day to cover any Purple transmissions for translation. Colonel Rufus Bratton, head of Army Intelligence, requested help with the translations from the Navy. It was learned from the first dispatch that Nomura was instructed that he would receive a communication in 14 parts and that he should keep this information secret. The second transmission directed him to use an inside typist to do the typing and that extreme caution in maintaining secrecy should be exercised. By 1500 on December 6 (Washington EST), 13 of the 14 parts of the message sent by Tokyo had been translated by the Navy code breakers.

On Friday December 5 (U.S. date), an inventory done by the Registered Publications Section of the Navy Department confirmed that Wake Island held copies of almost every secret code and cipher system in the Navy's playbook. This information was passed on to Captain Safford in Washington, who had the responsibility to maintain the security of naval communications. After reviewing the codes in Wake's possession, Safford worked into the early hours of the morning of December 6 to draft an urgent message to Pacific Fleet command for Wake to destroy all of their code systems "in view of the imminence of war."[21]

On Saturday, December 6 (U.S. date), Safford took the drafted communication to Wake directly to Captain Joseph J. Redman, assistant director of Naval Communications, for permission to immediately release the message to Pacific Fleet headquarters so that they would be aware of the warning to Wake Island headquarters. Initially, permission for the release was refused by the director of Naval Communications, Admiral Leigh Noyes. Learning of this decision, Safford stormed into Noyes' office and wanted to know why the warning was not sent. Noyes responded that he had declined to send the message on the grounds that the Japanese were bluffing. Safford argued, "If the Wake codes are captured by Japan we will never be able to explain it."[22] Noyes finally capitulated to Stafford but the communication was sent only to the Pacific and Asiatic Fleet headquarters and not to Wake Island. In addition, it failed to mention the 13-part message to Nomura that intelligence had intercepted. The final dispatch as written revealed no urgency and was more like a routine administrative message.

Also on December 6, President Roosevelt learned that Japan had two convoys heading toward the Isthmus of Kra, located on the Malaya peninsula. He called for a meeting with Admiral Stark but was unable to reach him. (The admiral was attending a performance of *The Student Prince* at the National Theater, and the President did not want to page him as he felt this would unduly alarm the public.) Roosevelt then sent a telegram to the Japanese emperor describing the Far East situation as a "keg of dynamite" waiting to go off and requesting that the "emperor find a way to dispel the dark clouds hovering over the situation."[23] Since the president was not concerned about security, he sent the cable in the gray code, which although not as secure as the other diplomatic codes, saved time.[24]

Lieutenant Commander Kramer had finally completed translating the 13-part message at 1930 that night. He also was unable to reach Stark, and Admiral Turner was not available either as he was out walking his dogs. Kramer crossed them both off the distribution list, then called his wife to pick him up at the Navy Department and headed directly to the White House. He turned over the locked pouch which contained the 13-part communication to Lieutenant Lester Schultz. The lieutenant then brought the pouch to Roosevelt, who was in his study examining his stamp collection. Roosevelt's response to the content of the pouch was, "This means war." However, the president was determined that Japan must still make the first move in initiating war with the United States.[25]

At 2000 Kramer and his wife reached the Wardman Park Hotel where Secretary of the Navy Knox lived. After studying the 13-part communication, Knox contacted Hull, and they decided to meet the next morning with Secretary of War Stimson in the State Department, as little could be discussed on the phone that night because of security reasons. In addition, Kramer was ordered to be present at the morning meeting to assist in dealing with this crisis.

Kramer then drove to Director of Naval Intelligence Admiral Wilkinson's house in Arlington, Virginia. He was hosting a party, and General Miles, the Army's chief of military intelligence, and Captain John R. Beardall, Roosevelt's presidential naval aide, were present. The group retired to Wilkinson's study to unlock the pouch and to discuss its contents. Surprisingly, only Kramer thought the pouch's contents merited any immediate action. Wilkinson placed a call to Admiral Stark, who by this time had returned from the theater. Stark insisted that the matter did not require any immediate action. When Kramer returned to the Navy Department at 0030, he was told by the watch officer that the fourteenth part of the message had not yet been intercepted. With that information in hand, an exhausted Kramer returned home to get some sleep at about 0100.[26]

Admiral Ingersoll, assistant chief of Naval Operations, and Admiral Turner, head of the War Plans Division, testified in the 1944 hearings that they recalled reading the communication and had also concurred that no action was necessary. This is interesting, as Kramer claimed that he never delivered the pouch to them because they failed to answer his phone call before he set out to hand deliver the pouch.[27]

Colonel Rufus Bratton, head of the Far Eastern Section of Army Intelligence, was executing his responsibility on behalf of the Army by delivering the same Japanese communication to those who were recipients of Magic. Each copy of the message was securely locked up in a pouch. Having delivered the message earlier in the day to the secretaries of State and War and to Army Chief of Staff General Marshall, he returned to his office to await the decrypting and typing up of the fourteenth part of the communication from Tokyo to Nomura. Then about 2200 on December 6 (U.S. date), he delivered the decrypted transmission to Generals Marshall and Miles and Brigadier General Gerow before heading to the State Department. Bratton testified in the Army court of inquiry in 1944 "without equivocation and without qualification, he delivered the intelligence to those generals that evening." Bratton had left the locked pouch with Colonel Bedell Smith, aide to General Marshall, and then went to the State Department where he left the pouch with the watch officer at 2230. As a result of his testimony, General Marshall was issued an indictment for failing to notify Pacific Command of this intelligence.[28]

One year later, Bratton was being pursued by Army personnel to persuade him to sign a sworn affidavit signed by Colonel Smith, General Gerow and other War Department officials that stated that the pouch was never delivered to General Marshall that evening. Confronted by the circumstance and feeling a loyalty to the Army, Bratton reversed his previous testimony and signed the affidavit. It was difficult for him to do so as witnessed by his testimony that he gave to the minority counsel in the 1945 congressional hearings: "I know all of these officers; they are men of honor and integrity, and if they say that they didn't receive the pouches from me—then my recollection must have been at fault and I so admit."[29] Yet, a few months later while in Japan, Bratton stated to Colonel Raymond Orr, a fellow officer on General MacArthur's staff, that Marshall did receive the pouch that night. In addition, he mentioned that earlier in the day he tried unsuccessfully to convince General Marshall to issue another alert to Pacific Command. Marshall refused and retired to his office at Fort Myer telling Bratton that he wished not to be disturbed.

Marshall knew that two large Japanese convoys were approaching the Malayan peninsula and was very cognizant of Roosevelt's commitment to England if British or Dutch territories were attacked. Yet, in his testimony at the congressional hearings in 1945, he had difficulty in recalling the events that occurred on the night of December 6. He evaded admitting whether or not he had received a telephone call or any message by courier that night, and although he could not recall where he was that night, he remained certain that Colonel Bratton had not made a Magic delivery to Fort Myer. In fact, he testified that he went to bed that night without any foreknowledge of the Japanese reply to Washington's demand. Yet, a headline in the *Washington Times Herald* placed him at a reunion dinner for World War I vets that night. The event was held only a few blocks from the White House.

It is improbable that Roosevelt, who spoke to Stark, Chief of Naval Operations, did not try to reach Marshall that evening. James G. Stahlman, a reserve naval officer and a friend of Secretary of the Navy Frank Knox, released a statement that, after returning from Pearl Harbor on a fact finding mission, he returned to the White House on the night of December 6 (U.S. date) to report to the president. According to his statement, Marshall, Harry Hopkins (an advisor to the president), Stimson, Knox, John McCrea (Stark's aide), and Frank Beatty (Knox's aide) were all present.

There is no evidence in the White House official record that the meeting occurred, but that does not mean it did not take place, since given the existing circumstances, a meeting with the president and his military and civilian advisors would be a reasonable course of action for Roosevelt to take. Whether Marshall went to the White House or received a phone call from the president is subject to controversy, but it is doubtful that he went to sleep that night oblivious to the events unfolding around him.[30]

The inappropriate behavior of General Marshall continued into the next morning, when he took an usually long time going horseback riding in the park, which resulted in his arriving at the War Department late Sunday morning. His tardiness played a major role in the failure of the War Department to get a warning to Pearl Harbor in time to notify them that war was imminent. His actions were grounds for dereliction of duty. Indeed, the Army and Navy court of inquiries in 1944 censored both Stark and Marshall for their failure to pass this vital intelligence to Pacific command.[31]

Saturday night, December 6 (U.S. date) in Honolulu, found the U.S. military on low alert. Enlisted men were heading toward the bars and dance halls. At 1630, Lieutenant General Walter Short, Commander of Army Hawaiian Command, was attending a charity dinner-dance at Schofield Barracks, and Admiral Husband Kimmel, Commander-in-Chief of the Pacific Fleet (who had refused an invitation to a cocktail party at the Japanese Honolulu consul), was at the Halekulani Hotel for a small dinner party hosted by his successor to cruiser command, Rear Admiral Herbert F. Leary. Fighter aircraft were lined up wing-tip to wing-tip on the air fields, and station KGMB was ordered to remain on the air to guide the first flight of the 12 B-17s arriving from the West Coast to Hickam AFB. There was only one officer and one switchboard operator on duty at Naval Control Center on Ford Island, and only seven PBYs were scheduled to search the southern sector off Pearl Harbor the next morning.[32]

There was only one new area of enhanced security: the installation of a radar site on the northern coast of Oahu. The unit was ordered to begin operation two hours before dawn the next morning. Even if the radar had been turned on at 1800 that night, the instrument would not have detected the Japanese task force which was then hundreds of miles away because the radar's ground-to-air range was limited to 132 miles. In the midst of this complacency, the Kido Butai was bearing down on Hawaii at a speed of 24 knots.[33]

On December 6 (U.S. date) in Washington, Kramer arrived at OP-20-GZ to find the fourteenth part of the message on his desk. He promptly picked up the communication and delivered it to Commander Arthur McCollum, head of Far Eastern Intelligence Section, who agreed they should take it to Admiral Stark. Even with this intelligence, Stark was unwilling to send it to Pearl Harbor with a warning for them to be on alert for war. Kramer then went to the White House and the State Department to hand-deliver the critical last communication. When Roosevelt received the communication, he remarked, "It looks like the Japanese are going to sever negotiations."[34]

On December 6 (U.S. date) at 0342, an observer on the minesweeper *Condor* in Pearl Harbor sighted a midget submarine about one and three quarter miles from the Pearl Harbor entrance. It was one of the five midget Japanese submarines released two hours earlier from their mother submarine. The minesweeper signaled the destroyer *Ward* to its sighting. Captain William W. Outerbridge, commander of the destroyer, swung his ship around, called on general quarters, and began a sonar sweep. When no contact was made with the submarine, the destroyer returned to Pearl Harbor. The net booms at the harbor entrance were opened and the destroyer entered the harbor, followed by two unseen Japanese midget submarines. The sighting of the midget submarine outside Pearl Harbor by *Condor* was reported to the duty officer at Bishop's Point naval radio station, but assuming it was a false alarm, he decided not to notify anyone in the Naval Control Center.[35]

At 0430 (Hawaii time), the Kido Butai was reassured that the secrecy of their attack was preserved when they learned that station KGMB, which had stayed on the air all night, failed to report any sign that the task force had been sighted. The task force was now 230 miles north of Oahu, and the pilots assembled in the overcrowded briefing rooms. On the blackboard was written the positions of the ships in Pearl Harbor that morning.

Colonel Bratton was reading the fourteenthth part of the Tokyo message in the Munitions Building at 0930 (Washington EST). Moments later, Bratton received a much shorter communication that just had been decrypted, which read: *Will the ambassador please submit to the United States Government (if possible the Secretary of State) our reply to the United States at 1300 on the seventh, your time.*[36]

The dispatch immediately alarmed Bratton because he recognized and was convinced that the time specified in the decipher corresponded to a Japanese surprise dawn attack on an American installation somewhere in the Pacific. It is interesting that Pearl Harbor was not given serious consideration as a target for the Japanese task force, as it was exactly at dawn (0600) that Japan's carriers launched their aircraft for their attack, and the planes would reach their target (Pearl Harbor) at about 1300 (Washington EST). More to the point, when it was 1300 in Washington, it was 0230 in Malaya, 0230 in Manila and 0800 in Honolulu. Pearl Harbor's time zone was clearly the only location that fit into a dawn launching of Japanese aircraft, which is exactly what occurred.

Why this fact did not draw the attention of U.S. Army and Navy intelligence in Washington is a mystery, as U.S. intelligence placed the surprise attack in Malaya or the Philippine Islands. Bratton was determined to send another war warning to Pacific command, so he brought the issue to General Miles. Miles agreed with him, but he still needed the permission of his superior, General Marshall. Bratton placed a phone call to Army headquarters at Fort Myer in an attempt to reach Marshall. However, the general was horseback riding along the Potomac River, and all Bratton could do was to leave an urgent message requesting that the general call him back right away.

Finally, at 1030 (Washington EST), Marshall called the War Department. Bratton offered to take the important communication to Marshall at Fort Myer, but the general refused, preferring to travel to the War Department instead. The latter conversation was not recalled by Marshall in the congressional hearings that followed.[37]

Kramer, who also received the short but critical message about a Japanese deadline to deliver their response to the State Department, also thought that the timing possibly coincided with an attack by Japan on Malaya. Kramer immediately set out to deliver the message to Captain McCollum in Washington. Both men then proceeded to Stark's office. McCollum pointed out to Admiral Stark that the timing of the delivery of the communication to the State Department could represent a surprise attack by Japan somewhere in the Far East or even Hawaii. He suggested that Stark call Kimmel. The Chief of Naval Operations decided instead to first call the president to discuss the situation. When Stark called the president, he was told by the switchboard operator that the president was already engaged. Stark then determined that he would not call Pearl Harbor fleet headquarters.

Rear Admiral Turner had been invited to the meeting with Secretary of the Navy Knox, Secretary of War Stimson, and Secretary of State Hull at the State Department to discuss the implications of the fourteenth part of the Japanese message. He arrived after the meeting had ended, but he later testified in the congressional hearings that he knew nothing of the urgent communication and that all Stark spoke to him about was what the Asiatic Fleet would do if war broke out in the Pacific.[38]

In Tokyo, at 2330 (Japan time) on December 6 (U.S. date), Ambassador Grew requested an immediate audience with Japan's foreign minister, Tojo Hedeki. One hour later, Grew was imploring the foreign minister to arrange for Grew to meet with the emperor. If this demand were granted, then he would have had the reassurance that the president's gray code message (reminding the emperor that diplomatic relations between the U.S. and Japan were deteriorating) would have at least reached the emperor that night.

Exactly at dawn (0600, Hawaii time) on December 7, 1941 (U.S. date), the Kido Butai turned north into the wind to launch its aircraft. Forty-nine high-level bombers, 51 dive bombers, 40 torpedo planes, and 43 Zero fighters took off and moved into formation before they headed on their way to attack Pearl Harbor. Returning to its southerly course, the carrier force then continued to sail toward Oahu. Forty-five minutes later, the carriers again turned into the wind to launch its second wave of planes consisting of 54 high-level bombers, 78 dive bombers, and 35 Zero fighters. This impressive force of 350 planes was now bearing down on Oahu to set into motion the singular event that would ignite World War II in the Pacific.[39]

In Washington, from the time Bratton told General Marshall that he had an urgent message, it took over two hours for the general to arrive at his office. Once there, Marshall insisted on reading the entire 14-part message before looking at the short critical communication that Bratton was anxiously waiting to bring to his attention. Marshall focused on the Philippines as the likely target of Japanese aggression, even though 1300 (Washington, EST) corresponded to 0200 (Philippine time). This conclusion is puzzling since at that time no convoys had been seen leaving Formosa, which would most likely have been the staging area for an attack on the Philippines. In addition, it was an open question whether Japan's bombers had the range to reach Manila from Formosa. An attack on Pearl Harbor was not considered seriously even though the times matched perfectly.[40]

At 1125 (Washington, EST), General Miles, who was also in General Marshall's office, strongly suggested that all commands in the far Pacific (as well as commands in Hawaii, Panama, and the West Coast) be immediately notified to be on alert for aggressive action by Japan at 1300 (Washington, EST). Marshall initially hesitated but eventually agreed to the request, however, the delay caused precious time to be lost in notifying Pearl Harbor. Marshall took more time to write the communication to all commands in the Pacific in long hand rather than have the message typed up. The general then continued to delay sending the message by calling Admiral Stark to discuss what course of action they should take. Stark initially felt that enough war warning had already been sent to these commands. But a few minutes later, Stark reconsidered and recommended a joint dispatch be sent out. Marshall agreed but further delayed notifying Pacific Command by refusing to use the scrambler phone on the basis that it was not totally secure; instead, he decided to send the message by telegram. He later testified that if he had used the scrambler phone, it would have been the Philippines first, Panama second, and Pearl Harbor would have been the last one he would have called.[41] He reasoned that Pearl Harbor was the least likely target of the Japanese task force, since the Philippines were closer to Japan and militarily more vulnerable.

Bratton left the meeting and went directly to the Army Signal Center to send Marshall's warning. When he arrived, Colonel Edward French, who was in charge, notified him that the general's message had to be encrypted before it could be sent. French then told Bratton that the dispatch would take 30 to 40 minutes to be transmitted, meaning that the communication would not reach the Pacific Command by the 1300 (Washington, EST) deadline. When Colonel French learned that heavy static was blocking the Army transmission to Honolulu, he decided to instead send the message through San Francisco via the RCA radio station, using his teleprinter link to the Western Union Office in Washington. French knew that method had four times the power of the Army's link to Honolulu and would transfer faster. However, his belief was based on the fact that RCA had built a direct line to Fort Shafter, but this turned out not to be true, as the telegraph link between San Francisco and Honolulu was still not operational. As a result, the communication reached the Honolulu office three minutes after the deadline 0800 (Hawaii time) expired and had yet to be routed to Fort Shafter.[42]

Even if the warning were received on time, it turned out that Marshall's message was cryptic in nature, considering the circumstances. Although it stated that Japan was going to provide what amounted to an ultimatum to the United States and that the Japanese Washington Embassy was now under orders to destroy their code machines, it misled HYPO by stating that Washington intelligence had no idea of what the 1300 deadline meant. The message concluded that Pacific Command should be on alert accordingly. The statement that Washington intelligence had no idea what the deadline meant and that Pacific Command should be on alert accordingly was misleading at best and totally ignored the real reason for sending the message, which was that war was going to break out in the Pacific at 1300 (Washington time) on December 7, 1941.

At 0600 (Hawaii time), the *Enterprise* was returning to Pearl Harbor after having delivered the *Wildcat* fighters to Wake Island. The carrier was now 200 miles due west of Hawaii.

At 0630 (Hawaii time), Commander Lawrence Grannis of the *Antares*, a supply ship which was pulling a flat bottomed barge, and the helmsman of the destroyer *Ward*, Lieutenant O.W. Goepner, spotted a submerged midget submarine near the entrance channel to Pearl Harbor. Lieutenant Outerbridge of the *Ward* called the ship to general quarters and ordered the destroyer to attain top speed in an attempt to ram the submarine. When the *Ward* neared the submerged vessel, it released its depth charges. He then radioed the commandant of the Fourteenth Naval District of the attack but failed to give details of the incident, namely that a midget submarine was seen, and following the *Ward's* depth charge attack, oil was observed on the surface of the water from the submerged vessel.

The naval radio operator acknowledged the report, but since no details were given, assumed that it was another false alarm. Another episode was reported at 0730 from the pilot of a PBY patrol plane, who stated that he had seen and sunk a submerged submarine one mile from the entrance of Pearl Harbor. Both of these communications did not impress the officer in charge of Bishop's Point of the Fourteenth Naval District, who just logged the reports into the book at 0653 (Hawaii time).[43] The preceding submarine contacts were not even reported to the duty officer at Army headquarters. However, Army headquarters was to receive a critical message from the Opana Mobile Radar Unit stationed at Kahuku Point on the northern tip of Oahu Island. Privates Joseph L. Lockard and George F. Elliott were due to close down the unit at 0700, but the breakfast truck was late, so they kept the radar unit in operation. Elliott detected a large green blip on the radar screen and after ruling out false echoes to explain the observation, concluded it must represent incoming planes. Further calculations revealed that there were over 50 planes, and that they were about 120 miles due north of the island. When Lockard reported the finding to the Information Center, he neglected to mention the number of planes that were represented on the oscilloscope. The duty officer, aware that 12 B-17s were due to arrive from the West Coast, concluded that those planes were the explanation for the findings. The irony was that both the incoming B-17s and the flight of Japanese planes bearing down on Pearl Harbor were using the radio station KGMB music broadcast as a beam to guide them on their approach to the island.[44] Admiral Kimmel was shaving when he received notice of the submarine reports. He felt that the sightings were most likely false alarms, but his instincts sent him hurrying to his submarine base headquarters, skipping breakfast in the process.

In Tokyo at this hour (0300 Japan time), the foreign minister of Japan had obtained permission to travel to the imperial palace to deliver the U.S. president's message to Emperor Hirohito. Despite the late hour, Lord Privy Seal Marquis Kido Koichi awakened the emperor and handed the communication to him. What transpired is unknown, but what is certain is that at this time Japanese forces, having arrived early at Kota Bharu in Malaya, began shelling pill boxes manned by the Ninth Division of the Indian Army at the mouth of the Kelantan River on the north coast of Malaya. This was 23 hours before the attack on Pearl Harbor.[45]

At 1100 (EST) in Washington, Ambassador Nomura utilized Okumura Katsuzo, Secretary of the Japanese Embassy, as his typist. But Okumura was not experienced and thus was slow in typing the last part of the 14th part message. As a result, the ambassador requested an hour delay for his meeting with Secretary Hull in the State Department. This delay caused Nomura to deliver Japan's foreign policy reply regarding Asia to Secretary Hull at 1420 (EST), 87 minutes after the first bombs had fallen on Pearl Harbor.

Controversy exists about whether the U.S. government had foreknowledge of the Japanese attack on Pearl Harbor on December 7, 1941. In order to answer this question, one needs to critically review the evidence that has come to light since that fateful day.

The following body of evidence supports the assertion that members at the highest level of the U.S. government did have advance knowledge of the attack on Pearl Harbor. The evidence can be broken down into three categories:

(1) The warnings

The warnings represent that either unsound judgments were made by U.S. officials or raise questions that the U.S. government was deliberately trying to ignore or cover up the possibility that Pearl Harbor was going to be attacked by the Japanese. The U.S. response to the warnings opens the door for further questions about the possibility of U.S. foreknowledge of the Pearl Harbor attack.

The first potential warning came near the end of January 1941, when a rumor that Japan was going to attack Pearl Harbor was passed on to Ricardo Rivera-Schreiber, Peru's ambassador to Japan. With both persons residing in Tokyo, Rivera-Schreiber informed Grew, U.S. Ambassador to Japan, about the rumor. Grew sent the information first to the State Department and then to the Navy Department, where it ultimately reached the office of Commander McCollum. His official estimation and that of Division of Naval Intelligence was that the rumor was just that, and as such was not credible. What is more significant is that an investigation into the report came to an abrupt halt when it was discovered that Rivera-Schreiber's cook was the source of the information; such a source was not considered credible to U.S. intelligence.[46] Thus, an opportunity to discover the plan that was to unfold on December 7, 1941, was lost. To add to the validity of the rumor is that in Agawa Hiroyuki's *The Reluctant Admiral* published in 1979, Agawa states, "In early 1941 Japan had thought 'that word of the Hawaiian operation had leaked to the Americans.'" Was this failure by Navy intelligence to follow up on the rumor a miscalculation, or a deliberate attempt not to pursue the rumor because President Roosevelt wanted Japan to strike the first blow?

In May 1941, Japanese Admiral Abe Kobe visited Taranto, Italy, to meet with Italian officials and learn everything he could about the British torpedo raid against the Italian Navy in 1940. While in Lisbon, Dusko Popov, the British double agent, learned about the Taranto meeting from Johnny Jebsen, a British double agent (code name "Artist") who was working for the Germans. Popov was then ordered by the Germans to travel to Hawaii on a spy mission for Japan. By combining the information gained about Admiral Kobe's interest in the Taranto raid with his directive to travel to Hawaii to gain information for the Japanese military, the double agent concluded that Pearl Harbor was going to be attacked by Japan. Popov reported this information to British intelligence, which felt this knowledge would be of vital interest to the United States. British intelligence decided that J. Edgar Hoover, director of the FBI, would be the best person for Popov to alert about this intelligence. Stewart Menzies, head of British Intelligence, called Hoover to introduce Popov before they were to meet in New York in mid–August 1941. The double agent initially met with the FBI's agent in charge, Percy "Sam" Foxworth, and disclosed the Pearl Harbor intelligence to him.[47] In addition, Popov revealed to Foxworth German intelligence secrets and an espionage questionnaire given to him by the Nazis, which included questions for Popov to answer while he was in the United States and in Hawaii. Hoover was not available to meet with Popov for two weeks for reasons that are not clear. When the FBI director finally did meet with Popov, he made it clear that he was unhappy with the spy's known wanton way of life. The meeting ended testily, and Hoover apparently dismissed the intelligence because of the way Popov lived his life, which to Hoover precluded the intelligence from being reliable.[48] Thus, no attempt was made by Hoover to follow up on the Pearl Harbor intelligence. Apologists for Hoover and the FBI refuse to acknowledge that Hoover ever met with Popov and claim that whatever was of value in the questionnaire was passed on to responsible military authorities and even to President Roosevelt.

In the book *Codebreakers' Victory* by Hervie Haufler, it is reported that subsequent research found a paraphrased one-page version of the questionnaire in a stack of FBI reports. However, the paraphrased version of the original questionnaire contained only the questions for Popov to answer while he was in the United States, leaving out the questions for the double agent to answer while he was in Hawaii. The only way the FBI could have produced a version of the questionnaire would have been if Popov had met with either Hoover or Foxworth and passed the information on to them.[49]

What is factual is that the intelligence turned out to be true. Hoover was a shrewd and clever person as witnessed by the fact that he remained in office as director of the FBI for 48 years. It seems inconceivable that the explanation given for Hoover for dismissing the Pearl Harbor information is a legitimate one. While it appears to be true that Hoover during the meeting with Popov professed his displeasure with the double agent's way of life, there is no conclusive evidence that Hoover rejected the information on these grounds. The explanation as to why he dismissed Popov's intelligence on Pearl Harbor, if he did, remains unclear. British intelligence officers believed Popov's information on Pearl Harbor and also that his directive from the Germans to travel to Hawaii as a spy for the Japanese was accurate. Apparently, Hoover was unimpressed by the British's faith in Popov. When British intelligence learned of Hoover's dismissal of the Pearl Harbor information, they declined to intervene on the basis that it was up to the Americans to draw their own conclusions from the intelligence given to them by Popov.[50] However, after the war the British government granted Popov citizenship and bestowed upon him the Distinguished Service Medal and the prestigious Order of the British Empire.

The question remains as to whether one should believe the supposed explanation given by Hoover for his dismissal of the Pearl Harbor intelligence, or whether it is possible that he secretly passed on the Pearl Harbor intelligence to the president as the FBI claimed to have done with the questionnaire.[51] The answer to this question will follow in Chapter 11.

(2) American allies had foreknowledge of the attack on Pearl Harbor

SOVIET UNION: On December 5, 1941, the Soviets knew that the Japanese Task Force was heading to Pearl Harbor, a fact publically acknowledged by the Japanese government 25 years after the war.

Could an incident that occurred on December 6, 1941, shed light on how the Soviets had this intelligence? An encounter by the Kido Butai of a ship from a third world nation while on route to Pearl Harbor is described in Agawa's biography of Admiral Yamamoto, *The Reluctant Admiral*. The identity of the ship remains a mystery today other than it was from a third world nation. It is unknown why the Japanese Navy took no military action against the ship, allowing the vessel to leave the area unharmed. The U.S. government never has investigated this important issue, even after Japan's government publically disclosed the intelligence a quarter of a century later.[52]

It is also known that at that time, the Soviet Union had agents in the highest level of the Japanese government, and that the Soviets had also infiltrated the Japanese embassies in Moscow and Bangkok. It has been disclosed that over 700 copies of the Japanese plan to attack Pearl Harbor had been circulated in Japan prior to the attack and that an even greater number of copies of the plan was sent out by the Army to its embassies, including the embassy in Bangkok. Thus, the secrecy of the plan was not what had been previously reported: that it was a closely guarded secret and known to only a few high-ranking Japanese Army and Navy officials.[53]

BRITAIN: Information regarding the role that Britain played in the Pearl Harbor controversy is enlightening. It has already been revealed from Hervie Haufler's *Codebreakers' Victory* that British intelligence recommended to Popov that he disclose his information about Pearl Harbor to FBI director J. Edgar Hoover. This disclosure reveals that British intelligence was aware of Japanese Admiral Kobe's trip to Taranto and found its implications and the intelligence to be credible. So, it appears that Britain was more alert to the possibility that Pearl Harbor was going to be attacked than the United States apparently was.

It is also known that Britain had successfully penetrated the JN-25B Japanese naval code, particularly at their Far East Combined Bureau (FECB) based in Singapore. It was revealed in the three-volume official history *British Intelligence in the Second World War*, published in 1993, that Britain was able to keep track of Japan's naval movements as far back as 1939.[54]

In a 2006 book by Ian Pfennigwerth entitled *A Man of Intelligence: The Life of Captain Theodore Eric Nave*, he reveals information pertinent to the intelligence gained from FECB. Eric Nave was a code-breaker at FECB and later was in command of the Special Intelligence Bureau in Australia. In 1989, Nave stated in an interview that Churchill had sufficient evidence to have concluded that Pearl Harbor was the target of the Japanese on December 7, 1941.[55]

Additional evidence that the British had prior knowledge of the attack on Pearl Harbor is provided by Colonel Bonner Fellers, a military observer for the United States, who testified at the Pearl Harbor hearings. He stated that when he arrived in Cairo, Egypt, on December 5, 1941, he was greeted by Air Marshall Sir Arthur Longmore, who stated, "We have a secret signal Japan will strike the United States in 24 hours."[56] Colonel Fellers considered notifying Washington headquarters but concluded that if the British knew, the United States must also know.

If it is true that Churchill had enough intelligence to conclude that Japan was going to attack Pearl Harbor, would Churchill not have alerted Roosevelt? The British have refused to release any of their records in this regard, nor have they set a date for the release of either the Japanese "Ultra" reports or Churchill's records regarding the Far East intelligence, even though 78 years have elapsed since their interception.

To the previous point, there is a document of a transatlantic phone call between Churchill and FDR that occurred on November 26, 1941, where the prime minister warns FDR that a Japanese task force is heading east to attack Pearl Harbor. The phone conversation was picked up by a German intelligence monitoring station located in Holland. Since the authenticity of the document has been questioned, details of the controversy will be discussed in a later chapter.

Holland: The Dutch had a smaller code operation than FECB on Java. Colonel Verkuyl was in command of this crypto-analytic unit which was reading Soviet Union diplomatic communications, the Japanese J-19 consular code, and its five-digit Japanese fleet system. They worked in close cooperation with the British and, although they could not read Japan's Purple messages, which they passed on to the British intelligence headquarters in Singapore, they did pass on the decipher that Japan had concentrated naval forces near the Kurile Islands. General Hein ter Poorten, Dutch Commander-in-Chief of the Far East, is on record as saying that his crypto-analytic unit on Java provided him with intelligence that revealed "Japanese naval concentrations near the Kurile Islands" in late November 1941.[57]

Unfortunately, all Dutch records of the report were burned in order to prevent them from falling into Japanese hands when the Dutch retreated from Bandung. In addition, all the Japanese naval orders to the Kido Butai while they were anchored in the Kurile Islands were also destroyed after the war, so these communications are not available. However, Captain Fuchida revealed that on November 25–26, 1941, communications were sent to Kido Butai by Tokyo naval headquarters, ordering the task force out of the Kurile Islands and to a secret rendezvous point for refueling.[58]

There is proof that another Kurile Islands message was sent by Japan to the Kido Butai on November 18, 1941, and it exists in the declassified files of the U.S. National Archives. This evidence proves that Japan was sending messages to the Kido Butai in the Kurile Islands. It is therefore reasonable to assume that Japan had also sent an order to the Kido Butai to leave the Kurile Islands on November 26, 1941 (U.S. date). Dutch intelligence had the capability to decipher 30 percent of the JN-25B code, so we can take General Poorten's word that he had passed the information (that the Kido Butai was in the Kurile Islands) on to British intelligence, which most certainly would have passed this crucial knowledge on to the United States.[59]

(3) Foreknowledge

The question arises as to whether or not the United States government had sufficient intelligence to deduce that Pearl Harbor was the intended target of the Kido Butai. This discussion can be divided into five areas:

(A) What was General George Marshall's role?

Was General George Marshall derelict of duty as charged or did he have foreknowledge of the attack on Pearl Harbor? Emphasis is placed on the whereabouts of General Marshall on the night and morning of December 6–7, 1941, and is related to the fact that the U.S. Army—and not the Navy—had sole responsibility for the protection of the U.S. Pacific Fleet and air bases in Hawaii. Was General Marshall the only person with the authority to alert Hawaii? The answer is supplied by examining the chain of command of the War Department as of December 7, 1941. President Roosevelt, as commander-in-chief, had ultimate authority over military forces

6. Radio Silence Is Broken

in Hawaii, followed by Secretary of War Stimson and then Chief of Staff, General Marshall.

On the afternoon of December 6, Marshall received the pilot (initial) message decoded from Purple that a 14-part message to the Japanese emissaries in Washington would follow, giving them instructions on how to deal with the present negotiations with the United States. Marshall then disappeared and was not seen until the next morning.[60]

To this day the mystery persists of where Marshall was during this time. In testimony he gave to the congressional committee investigating the Pearl Harbor attack in 1945, Marshall, whose living quarters were at Fort Myer, stated that he could not recall where he was on the evening of December 6. Testimony given by his wife shed little light as to General Marshall's whereabouts. Forest Pogue, Marshall's official biographer, in his book *Ordeal and Hope*, stated that Marshall was at home all evening, but offers no evidence to substantiate that assertion. The author claims in his book that an orderly—who may have corroborated this claim—was on duty at Marshall's quarters but the orderly was not asked to testify at the congressional hearings. To date, Pogue still has not offered any definite proof of where Marshall was either in the evening of December 6 or the morning of December 7.[61]

Marshall's denial of Bratton's assertion that he received the 13-part message on the evening of December 6 was cover for the account he went horseback-riding the next morning: that if he had no knowledge of the communication, there would be no reason for him not to do so. It also freed him of responsibility for his lack action of that night.

There are two accounts of where General Marshall was on the morning of December 7, 1941. One is that he was horseback riding in Rock Creek Park in Washington, a very open area where he might have been easily observed. A second account placed Marshall on a more secluded horseback riding path on the Virginia side of the Potomac River. Regardless of where he was riding when he finished his outing, he returned to his quarters in Fort Myer, changed his clothes, and then went to his Munitions Building office in Washington. There were three different accounts given by three people testifying before the congressional committee in 1945. One account had him arriving at 0900, the second at 1000 and the third at 1120—the earlier times implied that Marshall had up to three hours to alert Hawaii. As it was, the telegram did not reach the Honolulu cable office until 0803 (Hawaii time), ten minutes after the Pearl Harbor attack had begun. When Marshall arrived at his office, he insisted on reading the long 14-part message sent to Nomura. Bratton had to wait for Marshall to finish reading the entire message before explaining to the general that he had just received an additional urgent transmission sent to Nomura from the Navy ministry in Tokyo. It stated that the ambassador had a 1300 EST deadline to deliver Japan's response to America's rejection of the *modus vivendi*.[62]

Marshall seemed to use faulty reasoning in his interpretation of the 1300 deadline. In spite of the fact that 1300 Washington time corresponded to 0800 Hawaii time, Marshall persisted in his opinion that the attack would occur in the Philippines, Malaya, or at the Panama Canal. This deduction appears to defy logic as Washington 1300 EST corresponded to 0200 in the Philippines and Malaya where it would have been dark, and 1300 EST in the Panama Canal, where both time and the logistics of reaching Central America were improbable. These locations would have been inconsistent with an air attack from Japanese aircraft carriers.

When he finished reading all of the communication, he decided to forward the message by telegraph, instead of calling General Short directly. Marshall decided not use the scrambler phone, which would have saved a great deal of time. There was no evidence that Japan had broken the U.S. code and certainly the telegraph offered no more guarantee of confidentiality than the scrambler telephone. This action taken by Marshall is another example of his apparent efforts to delay notifying Hawaii, and also explains his belief that Japan might become aware that the U.S. had learned about Japan's intentions. Foreknowledge of this intelligence by Japan would most likely have led the Japanese to cancel their attack on Pearl Harbor.

A cancellation of the attack on Pearl Harbor by Japan was not well-suited to America's foreign policy, which was to give military support to British and Dutch colonies in the Far East, but the main objective was to unite with Britain in its war against Germany. In 1941, there was little political support in the United States for an offensive war against either Axis power, Germany or Japan. Thus, the United States needed Japan to strike the first blow against it. Even with that occurrence, the United States did not simultaneously declare war on Germany but waited for Germany to declare war on America, which it did four days after the Pearl Harbor attack, on December 11, 1941. It is not inconceivable that Marshall took every possible action to delay his communication to Hawaii so that Japan would strike the first blow in the Pacific, which would result in full political support of the American people for the war in the Pacific and provide a vehicle for the United States to enter the war against Germany.

The telegram was sent by Marshall to Hawaii close to 1230 EST and was not marked "Urgent." The telegram was also cryptic in nature, indicating that Marshall did not know what the 1300 time specification might signify, but only that Pearl Harbor should be on alert accordingly. In addition, Marshall relegated the priority of the alert to Pearl Harbor to fourth place in the notification order in which the alert order was sent out. The Philippines were first, the Panama Canal was second, the third location is not cited, and Pearl Harbor was the fourth.

This subjugation of the Pearl Harbor alert to fourth place further delayed the time in which the information would be received by Pearl Harbor, and ensured that the intelligence would not reach Admiral Kimmel before the attack occurred. The information on the pecking order of the alert messages was derived from a photostatic copy of the times and places of the transmission by Captain Safford in Washington. In 1963, Safford circulated this intelligence to those who, at that time, were questioning the official government version of the events surrounding the Pearl Harbor attack.[63] By examining Marshall's actions on these days, it is difficult to conclude that this high-ranking officer would behave in such an inappropriate way to the circumstances at hand, if not on the night of December 6, certainly on the morning of December 7. Marshall was aware that Japanese convoys had been spotted in the South China Sea. To remain unavailable that morning by taking a horseback ride, or otherwise, defies explanation unless he was trying to delay getting out an alert message to Pearl Harbor. The question also arises as to why Army intelligence officer Colonel Bratton would claim—and later retract—that he contacted General Marshall on the night of December 6.

Although Marshall testified at the hearings that he did not recall where he was on that night, he definitely ruled out any contact with Bratton. On Sunday morning, he was supposedly taking a longer-than-usual horseback ride, which left him unreachable even though he knew that two Japanese convoys were closing in on the Malayan Peninsula. It took Marshall two hours to reach his office, in spite of the fact that Bratton told him he had an urgent message to reveal to him.

When the general arrived, he did not want to hear about the urgent message until he had read the entire 14-part communication.[64] The fact that the 1300 Japanese deadline coincided only with a dawn attack on Pearl Harbor apparently did not occur to him, or he purposely ignored the obvious true meaning of the time.

One would question whether this behavior was consistent of a man with the title of Army Chief of Staff, or if Marshall actually knew of the impending attack on Pearl Harbor which he was trying to conceal. Evidence to support the latter is provided by Robert Sherrod, a well-respected war correspondent for *Time* and *Life* magazines covering the war in the Pacific. His credentials were on a par with famed war correspondents Clark Lee and Ernie Pyle. Sherrod was recognized many times for his accuracy in reporting events of the war in the Pacific. In his book *I Can Tell It Now*, published in New York in 1964, he revealed that on the morning of Saturday, November 15, 1941, the War Department called a secret meeting for seven of the most trusted war correspondents, including Sherrod, in Washington. There General Marshall disclosed that Japan would attack the United States in the first ten days of December 1941.[65] The general was not specific about the source of this intelligence but did reveal that it came about by the ability of U.S. intelligence to intercept and decode Japanese messages. This information could only have evolved from decryption of the JN-25B code, as there is no evidence that an attack on Pearl Harbor came from diplomatic transmissions. After the war, according to Hanson Baldwin of the *New York Times*, Marshall told him that Sherrod's account "is apparently accurate." (Although Marshall died in 1959, it is highly likely he was interviewed by Sherrod long before Sherrod's book was published.)

In 2001, Robert Stinnett said in his book *Day of Deceit* that he discovered, within the Navy records of HYPO, information revealing that radio messages from Admiral Nagano were intercepted in Hawaii on November 5 and 13, 1941. The communication records disclosed that Rochefort documented these intercepts in his Communications Summary, and that his intercept radio-operators decoded three radio dispatches from Admiral Nagano to three of his naval commands: (1) Admiral Yamamoto, (2) Commander in Chief of Japan's China Area Fleet and (3) Chief of Staff of Japan's carrier divisions. This intelligence summary was passed on to Station U.S. in Washington. Two of the coded messages intercepted by HYPO were in the Japanese "kana" code (modified International Morse code adopted to Japan's unique syllabary known as katakana) and indicated war with the United States would begin in the first part of December 1941. These messages apparently were the source of Marshall's assertion at the press briefing that Japan would attack the United States in the first ten days of December 1941.[66] Only one of these secret communications by Admiral Nagano—to Yamamoto on November 1, 1941—has been released to the National Archives. Eight hundred and forty-two messages from Admiral Nagano are missing from Station H files.[67]

It is noteworthy to point out that the other Japanese messages were most likely in the JN-25B code and although HYPO was directed by OP-20-G *not* to work on JN-25B code prior to the Pearl Harbor attack, it did not mean Rochefort's unit was not independently working on the JN-25B code. Evidence for this is to be found in the fact that after the Pearl Harbor attack, HYPO was given clearance to work on the JN-25B code on December 10, 1941. In just nine days after that on December 19, 1941, Rochefort's unit intercepted, decoded, and translated Admiral Nagumo's report in the JN-25B code on his devastating attack on the Pacific fleet.[68] This revelation supports the conclusion that the JN-25B code was readable prior to the Pearl Harbor attack, at least by Rochefort's team. It would be unlikely that a highly regarded war correspondent like Sherrod would provide false testimony in his book. Also, documentation of British, Dutch, and U.S. intelligence regarding the location of the Kido Butai in the Kurile Islands provide evidence that the Kido Butai was breaking radio silence on its way to Pearl Harbor. In addition, the discovery of the bomb plot message and Popov's warning, both of which were available to Marshall, points to the fact that Marshall knew that the Pearl Harbor attack was coming sometime in the first week of December 1941.

In January 1942, the Roberts Commission was convened by presidential executive order and decided to exonerate General Marshall of any wrongdoing. However, in October 1944, an Army Court of Inquiry heard testimony from 151 witnesses from Hawaii, San Francisco, and Washington that led the court to censure Marshall for (1) failing to keep General Short advised of the worsening situation; (2) failing to reply to Short's "sabotage alert"; (3) not forwarding to Short on the evening of December 6 and on the morning of December 7 critical information Marshall had in hand; and (4) not determining the state of readiness of the Hawaiian command. One month later, the politically motivated Clausen Investigation sought to overturn the Army Court of Inquiry's decision. It was a secret investigation that relied on affidavits rather than direct testimony. The investigation yielded no public report. Since that time, an alternative point of view has come forth, that Marshall knew of the attack on Pearl Harbor and was using delaying tactics so as not to prevent the attack by alerting U.S. forces to intercept the Japanese task force. This explanation more rationally explains Marshall's behavior on the night of December 6 and the morning of December 7, 1941.[69]

It is curious that President Roosevelt, after receiving the 13-part Purple message, made every attempt to contact Admiral Stark, who had no authority to send war warnings to Pearl Harbor, rather than attempting to reach General Marshall. The military had already stipulated that war warnings to Hawaii would emanate from the office of the Army Chief of Staff. If President Roosevelt tried and could not reach Marshall, why did he not reach Stimson, who was Marshall's superior? If, on the other hand, Stimson was reached, why did he not send war warnings to Hawaii? Stimson suffered a heart attack during the congressional hearings; his written testimony answered only some of the questions asked of him. The substance of his responses is not available.

In the absence of Marshall, Roosevelt could have ordered Stimson to send the critical intelligence to Pearl Harbor, or if Stimson were unavailable, the president could have sent the warning himself. What is a fact is that neither Roosevelt, Stimson, nor Marshall ever sent a warning to Hawaii that night, and Marshall did not send the information to Hawaii until about 1230 on Sunday morning (December 7, 1941). As I stated earlier, he placed it fourth in the notification order of telegraphic transmissions to the bases in the Pacific.

On November 25, 1941, Secretary of War Stimson wrote in his diary information which further implicates Roosevelt in wanting Japan to take the first step in the war in the Pacific. The diary reveals that the White House held a strategy meeting on the threat of war in the Pacific on that date. In that meeting, Stimson cites Roosevelt as saying that the question arises is how we should maneuver them (the Japanese) into the position of firing the first shot without allowing too much danger to ourselves.[70] This statement clearly indicates that Roosevelt did not want to take the first action against Japan for political reasons (in view of its isolationistic tendencies, America would not support a war where the U.S. took offensive action) and that he was willing to sustain the first blow against our country for that same reason. If Hawaii had been alerted earlier, the results would likely have been in either Japan calling off the attack or the United States striking the first blow in the war in the Pacific.

(B) Was Washington intelligence deliberately withholding critical information from HYPO?

To initiate this discussion, one must first state that there is no denial that U.S. intelligence in Washington withheld critical Purple information from Navy intelligence in Hawaii. A perfect example of this neglect is the *bomb plot* message that would have alerted Hawaii to a possible attack on Pearl Harbor.

On September 24, 1941, Japan's naval intelligence requested that Yoshikawa, their spy in the Hawaiian Japanese Consulate, create an invisible grid over Pearl Harbor, so that placements of the ships in the harbor could be defined.[71] Five days later, Yoshikawa cabled back to naval intelligence a more effective modification of the initial bomb grid. Using Purple, both branches of the military intelligence services intercepted and decoded the communications. The Army broke the first bomb plot signal on October 9, 1941, and the Navy decoded the second signal on October 10. Clearly, these communications raised the possibility that the information was needed by Japan for a planned bombing attack on Pearl Harbor. Common sense dictates that this intelligence should have been passed on to naval intelligence in Hawaii. This neglect is inexplicable, as is the failure of multiple congressional and military hearings following the attack to fully address the bomb plot issue at the hearings.

It is important to understand that OP-20-G not only failed to send the bomb plot communication to the HYPO unit, but also deprived Hawaiian intelligence of a Purple machine (Britain was given three) to decipher the Japanese diplomatic code. In addition, the Hawaiian intelligence unit was ordered not to decipher the JN-25B (naval code) and the J-19 and PA-K2 (low grade Japanese consular diplomatic codes). It is also revealing that HYPO was only permitted to work on deciphering the Admiralty Code (AD), a minor code used for personal matters by flag officers. This process was unproductive and never produced significant intelligence, yet no attempt was made by OP-G-20 to change that directive. The foregoing information, taken together, provides further evidence that Washington intelligence was either grossly incompetent or that it deliberately withheld pertinent intelligence to Hawaii.

(C) Did Japan break radio silence on the way to Pearl Harbor?

To answer the question of whether Japan broke radio silence in the Kurile Islands or on its way to Hawaii, one must refer to the evidence presented by Stinnett in *Day of Deceit*, where he utilized the Freedom of Information Act of 1979 (FIOA). He discovered that in mid–November 1941, Japan had arranged a special communication zone known only to senior commanders assigned to the First Air Fleet in Hitokappu Bay in the Kurile Islands.[72] Usually, a five-numbered code was used to send secret messages, but that code was periodically changed. When Japanese intelligence discovered that there was no cipher for the words Hitokappu Bay, they decided to transmit those words in the clear, not encrypted.[73]

On November 18, 1941, U.S. intelligence intercepted a communication sent by the Japanese Navy in the operational code JN-25B. In the message, the word Hitokappu Bay was blatantly spelled out in the clear.[74] The message included the following statement: "Please arrange to have Suzuki, who was sent to the 1st Air Fleet on business, picked up on about 23 or 24 November at Hitokappu Bay by the ship of your secondary naval station." This communication is not to be confused with the message intercepted by the Dutch on November 25 on Java that ordered the Kido Butai to depart from the Kurile Islands the next day and head out to sea. In his book Stinnett presents factual data that Japan's naval command had sent a communication to the Kido Butai in the Kurile Islands. He was able to obtain a copy of this message under FOIA. This communication was received at Station H in Hawaii by an unidentified operator with the initials SN at 1932 hours on November 18, 1941. A date in the right hand corner reveals that the transmission was translated or transcribed on April 4, 1946, but it is the decryption of the message that is at issue here, not the translation. Some critics have claimed that the original of this communication was not received until after December 7, 1941, but the date on the copy is clear that it was received on November 18. To date the original of this communication has not been released by the U.S. government.[75]

Certainly, intelligence at Station H in Hawaii could read Hitokappu Bay which was spelled out in katakana, a code with which they were familiar. The location of Hitokappu Bay, if not already known, could have easily been determined. Thus, there is now definitive evidence that Japan's naval command in Tokyo did not observe complete radio silence and that U.S. intelligence in Hawaii had the transmission that would have enabled them to locate the Kido Butai in the Kurile Islands.

As to the question of whether or not the Kido Butai actually maintained complete radio silence on its voyage to Hawaii, recent evidence from declassified documents shows that this was not the case.

The foregoing data clearly refutes the long-held view that Japan's naval command in Tokyo maintained radio silence while the task force was in the Kurile Islands, but there is also evidence that the Kido Butai broke radio silence on the way to Hawaii. There are two ways in which the Kido Butai could have broken radio silence. One way was for them to have radioed naval command in Tokyo; the other was for the task force to use inter-fleet radio communication. Radio silence appears not to have been broken by the former method, but there is definite evidence that radio silence was broken by the latter.

Although most of the ships in the First Fleet were well-equipped with radio receivers to receive messages from Tokyo, the height of the radio antennae on the ship played a significant role in its ability to receive radio communications. Thus, it was necessary for the task force flagship to go on the airwaves to communicate the information sent from Tokyo to other ships in the Kido Butai. These transmissions from late November to December 5, 1941, were picked up by British and Dutch naval radio stations in Singapore and in Java as well as by Station CAST in the Philippines. Captain Duane Whitlock, radio traffic analyst at CAST, confirmed the transmission of these broadcasts in an interview with Stinnett in 1993. His information is consistent with the testimony given by the British and Dutch Navy radio stations. Since the American, Dutch, and British records were destroyed as Japanese forces advanced on Corregidor, Java, and Singapore, the truth was subject to question.

Despite Stark's testimony during the joint congressional investigation in 1945–1946 that he knew of the intelligence regarding Hitokappu Bay prior to the attack on Pearl Harbor, questions remained.[76]

Stinnett has clarified the issue of whether or not the Kido Butai broke radio silence during its voyage to Hawaii. He has provided the following documentation from declassified information in *Day of Deceit*. From November 30 to December 4, 1941, San Francisco's Twelfth Naval District secured information from the Navy's directional finder station at Dutch Harbor, Alaska, that placed the Kido Butai in the North Pacific. Robert Ogg, who was on the staff of the naval District Intelligence Office (DIO) as a special investigator, was requested by his boss Lieutenant Hosmer to plot the radio direction finder bearings on a great circle chart of the North Pacific. This plot placed the Kido Butai in the North Pacific heading east. Certain that these findings represented Japanese warships, Hosmer reported these findings to the DIO in San Francisco. According to San Francisco's District Intelligence Chief, Captain Richard McCullough, the DIO then passed on the intelligence to the OP-20-G in Washington and from there to the White House. Documentation for this account is provided by that the U.S. Navy's direction finder station at Dutch Harbor, where Stinnett discovered them in declassified material released by the U.S. government.

The Japanese communications by the Kido Butai in the North Pacific were also detected by the SS *Lurline*, a U.S. commercial ship, and has been discussed earlier. It is mentioned here because it lends support to the fact that the First Fleet did not maintain radio silence. The fact that the Japanese task force broke radio silence on its way to Hawaii is further confirmed by information supplied by Stinnett from other declassified documents. He found that between November 15 and December 6, 1941, 129 radio messages were intercepted by U.S. naval monitoring stations. This information was found in the records of Stations H and CAST. The evidence provided that among the 129 messages, Admiral Nagumo had sent 60 transmissions, his carriers 20 messages, and Tokyo radio naval command 24 messages to the Kido Butai on its way to Hawaii.[77]

It is of interest that Fuchida, in his book *Midway*, acknowledged that Admiral Nagumo broke radio silence again when the First Air Fleet ran into foul weather during its voyage to Midway. He stated, "This occurrence was not the first time, and that Nagumo had successfully broken radio silence before, due to enemy carelessness."[78] The only other opportunity prior to the June 1942 Battle of Midway that the First Fleet had to break radio silence due to weather conditions was when the Kido Butai was headed to Pearl Harbor. Fuchida's statement has been overlooked as possible corroborating evidence that radio silence was broken by the Kido Butai on its way to Hawaii.

(D) How much of the JN-25B code was U.S. intelligence able to decipher prior to the attack on Pearl Harbor?

Was U.S. intelligence in 1941 Washington able to decipher enough of the JN-25B to learn that Pearl Harbor was the intended target of the Japanese Navy and, if not, how was U.S. intelligence in Washington and Hawaii able to predict the Japanese air attack on Rabaul a month later and the Battle of the Coral Sea five months later?

Captain Safford subsequently testified that throughout 1941, his section could decipher about ten percent of JN-25B code.[79] Although this is not a large amount of Japanese naval code deciphered, it could provide enough information for naval intelligence to determine that Pearl Harbor was the objective of the Kido Butai. Certainly, it was exactly this percentage, ten percent, that allowed Navy intelligence to predict the dates and locations of the Japanese air attack on Rabaul in January 1942 and the battles of the Coral Sea and Midway in May and June of the same year respectively. The HYPO Unit had been ordered by Washington naval intelligence not to engage in deciphering JN-25B code prior to December 7, 1941, but on December 10, 1941, Rochefort's group was finally given permission by OP-20-G to work on the JN-25B code.[80]

Less than one month later, in January 1942, Rochefort, in spite of limited decryption of the Japanese code, was able to accurately predict the Japanese strike against Rabaul several days in advance. On March 25, 1942, he and his group concluded from an intercept that Port Moresby would be attacked by Japanese forces. Thus, in only about four weeks working on the JN-25B code, Rochefort was able to predict the Japanese invasion on Rabaul. And in March 1942, he accurately predicted the attempted Japanese invasion of Port Moresby. By contrast—if we are to believe the testimony of OP-20-G officials—U.S. naval intelligence in Washington was able to decipher only 10 percent of JN-25B over a one year period, which effectively produced no results in predicting a Japanese attack on the Pearl Harbor. In addition, by June 4, 1942, Rochefort and his group accurately predicted that Midway was the target of the Japanese Navy. Not only that, with the ability to decipher only ten percent of JN-25B, Rochefort predicted the location and date of the attack on Midway.

It has also been documented that in early 1942, Britain was capable of passing on to the United States vital intelligence regarding Japanese carrier dispositions in the Indian Ocean and, more importantly, that Japan's Carrier Division Five was on its way to Truk to support the invasion of Port Moresby.[81] Although most of British intelligence's role in breaking JN-25B before December 7, 1941, is still classified, the subsequent ability of both U.S. and British intelligence, in just four months after December 7, 1941, suggests that their intelligence units prior to Pearl Harbor actually had the ability to extract information from the JN-25B code. This capability had heretofore been denied by some intelligence officers in Washington.

Is one to conclude that U.S. Navy intelligence—having the capability to decode only ten percent of JN-25B before the attack on Pearl Harbor—were able to predict accurately the location and date of the Japanese air attack on Rabaul and the battles of Coral Sea and Midway but not the attack on Pearl Harbor?

The foregoing also provides a new perspective has to how HYPO was able to determine that Midway was the target of the Kido Butai on June 4, 1942. Namely, that a strong foundation had been formed based on the prior experiences HYPO had gained in detecting the date and locations of Japan's air attack on Rabaul and the battle of the Coral Sea.

(E) What was the real reason for the Vacant Sea directive?

The fact that this directive came out on the exact day that the Kido Butai was leaving the Kurile Islands, November 25, 1941, has to be more than a coincidence. The order cleared the northern Pacific of any U.S. or allied ships that might discover the Japanese Task Force.

The reason given for the order by Rear Admiral Turner stated it was in order to track the Japanese Task Force if it took the northern route. This explanation is curious since the official position of the U.S. government and the Navy was that if a Japanese attack on Pearl Harbor would occur, it would come from the southwest. Turner's directive implies that the United States was already aware that a northerly route was being taken by the Japanese Navy and that Pearl Harbor was its target. This conclusion is supported by the fact that Admiral Kimmel, while on fleet maneuvers north of Oahu, was ordered by his superiors in Washington out of the exact area where the Japanese would launch its air attack on Pearl Harbor and directed Kimmel to return to Pearl Harbor.[82]

As the foregoing events were unfolding, Japan's first wave of 183 aircraft were within 25 miles of its targets in Pearl Harbor and the military airfields on Oahu. The sequence of events that were to follow would set into motion the beginning of World War II in the Pacific.

Chapter 7

The Die Is Cast

Japan's tactical design for the Pearl Harbor attack was to launch its carrier planes in first and second waves. The two waves of aircraft would take off one hour apart, and together would comprise the first strike offensive against the U.S. fleet in Pearl Harbor and the nearby U.S. airfields. Consideration would then be given to a second strike offensive against U.S. oil depots, repair facilities, and the submarine base on Oahu.

The first wave of 183 planes, having been launched from all six Japanese carriers north of Oahu, was flying due south. These aircraft were under the overall command of Commander Fuchida. With his mission of surveying Pearl Harbor accomplished, a pilot from a *Chikuma* (cruiser) float plane radioed back to the Kido Butai that there were nine battleships and six light cruisers anchored in Pearl Harbor. Shortly thereafter, a scout plane from *Tone* (cruiser) reported that there were no U.S. warships in the Lahaina anchorage on the west coast of Maui. There was no evidence of any U.S. aircraft carriers in either location.[1]

The time was 0739, and the first wave of Japanese planes was now only 20 miles from Pearl Harbor. Fuchida's radioman gave him a message transmitted from the Kido Butai that informed Fuchida of the reports from the two scout planes' reconnaissance missions. When the planes arrived at the northern tip of Oahu (Kahuku Point), they turned southwest as Fuchida gave the order for the planes to deploy in their attack positions.

It was at this point that the plan devised by Fuchida would be implemented. He would release one flare from his rocket pistol to signify that surprise had been achieved. If he released two flares at two to three second intervals, that would signal that the Kido Butai had been detected.

The single flare would direct the torpedo bombers to begin their descent toward Pearl Harbor, as the fighters gained control of the air. The accompanying dive and high level bombers would then immediately proceed to their targets. On the other hand, if the enemy were on alert, the torpedo bombers would wait until the dive and high level bombers gained the attention of Pearl Harbor anti-aircraft fire, following which the torpedo bombers accompanied by fighters would begin their attack.[2]

With the knowledge that surprise had been achieved, Fuchida fired off one flare. When Lieutenant Suganami, one of the fighter group leaders, failed to move into proper attack formation, Fuchida concluded that the fighter pilot had failed to see the first flare, so the flight leader shot off a second flare. Lieutenant Takahasi, leader of the dive bomber group, misread the second flare to signify that surprise was not obtained. He immediately broke formation and headed toward the airfields at Ford

Island and Hickam Army Air Force Base. The remainder of the first wave of Japanese aircraft continued to fly southwest toward Barbers Point, on the western side of the Oahu. Still feeling comfortable about the tactical situation, Fuchida ordered his radioman to send the following message over the airwaves to naval headquarters in Tokyo: *Tora! Tora! Tora!*—the code words that the Japanese had caught the U.S. Pacific Fleet unaware.[3]

As the remaining part of the first wave flew southwest to Kaena Point, the other group of *Val* dive bombers and Zero fighters, which had not misread the second flare, veered off toward the southeast to attack Wheeler Army Air Force Base. Several of the Japanese fighters went on to assault Kaneohe Naval Air Station located on the southeastern corner of the island.

When the torpedo and the level bombers reached Kaena Point, they split into two groups. The "Kate" torpedo bombers hugged the coast on their way around to Barbers Point, and the *Kate* level bombers, though following a similar route, flew further west and south of Barbers Point as they also continued toward Pearl Harbor. As these planes now turned east toward Pearl Harbor, six Japanese Zero fighters, which had been providing cover for the torpedo bombers, peeled off to strafe Ewa Marine Corps Air Station in the southwest corner of Oahu. This was the first action taken by the Japanese in the Pearl Harbor attack.[4]

All of the 40 torpedo planes in the attack, which had been launched from four of the six Japanese carriers, gathered northwest of the Ewa Air Station. After Fuchida gave the general order for all planes to attack, the torpedo planes divided into two formations. One was a squadron of 16 torpedo bombers that split into two groups of eight planes each as they increased their speed to approach the west side of Pearl Harbor. These planes, launched from *Hiryu* and *Soryu*, were led by Lieutenants Nagi Tsuyoshi and Matsumura Heita. The time was 0752. As one group of torpedo planes neared *Utah*, a battleship commissioned in 1911, the aircraft unwittingly launched two torpedoes against the old ship. Shortly thereafter, *Utah* began to capsize. The cruiser *Raleigh* was the next to be severely damaged by torpedoes. One *Kate* bomber flew across Ford Island and unleashed its torpedo at the *Oglala*, flagship of the Pacific Fleet Mine Force. The torpedo went under the *Oglala* and struck the *Helena*, a light cruiser, damaging both ships.[5]

The second formation of torpedo bombers, which were northwest of Ewa, divided into two groups of 12 planes each. These planes were launched from *Akagi* and *Kaga* and were under the leadership of Lieutenants Murata Shigeharu and Kitajima Ichiro. The aircraft flew initially southeastward, then turned north and northwest over Hickam Field to come into a direct line with Battleship Row. Lieutenant Matsumura, having attacked the ships on the west side of Ford Island, now began his second run against Battleship Row on the east side of Ford Island. This time his torpedo struck *West Virginia* and inflicted significant damage. The attack was immediately followed by Lieutenant Murata releasing and striking *West Virginia* with a second torpedo.[6]

At 0805, *California*—the most southward ship in Battleship Row—received two torpedo hits, leaving the battleship listing in the water. The inboard battleships now became the objective of Japan's horizontal bombers. After Fuchida gave the signal for his horizontal bombers to attack the battleships, he fell back to an observation position where he could witness the attack directed toward *Oklahoma*, which was

Aerial view of Naval Operating Base, Pearl Harbor. Looking southwest on October 30, 1941, Ford Island is in the center, with Pearl Harbor Navy Yard just beyond it across the channel. The airfield in the upper left center is the Army's Hickam Field (Naval History and Heritage Command).

outboard of *Maryland* and in an exposed position. Lieutenant Goto Jinichi from the second squadron spotted the vulnerable battleship and steered his torpedo bomber from *Akagi* toward *Oklahoma*. He inflicted a direct hit on the battleship. Shortly thereafter, there were two additional hits on *Oklahoma*, followed by one which struck the battleship in its middle causing her to take a large list. At this time, a torpedo sped under the repair ship *Vestal* which was outboard of *Arizona* and inflicted a direct hit on *Arizona*.

The battleship then sustained a direct bomb hit close to the Number Four turret on the starboard side of the quarterdeck (usually located on the main deck and reserved for official functions).[7] At 0805, *California* received two torpedo hits, leaving the battleship listing in the water.

Fuchida observed the inboard battleships, which were now the objective of Japan's horizontal bombers. On the first pass of the formation, air turbulence prohibited their proper sighting of the battleships. However, the third plane in the formation actually had its bomb shaken loose by enemy fire, which then fell harmlessly into the water. Just then, the fuselage of Fuchida's plane sustained a number of direct hits, causing his plane to shudder but still able to function normally.[8]

When a fourth torpedo struck *Oklahoma*, the ship shook, then capsized. Father

7. The Die Is Cast 107

Tugs and other ships trying to keep the *California* afloat, soon after Japanese torpedoed and bombed the battleship at Pearl Harbor (Naval History and Heritage Command).

Aloysius Schmitt, a Catholic priest who directed *Oklahoma* sailors to squeeze through an available porthole to safety, was himself unable to fit through the porthole. The priest quietly returned to the bowels of the ship. His body was never found. He was one of the first American chaplains killed in the Pacific war.[9]

During this time, *Arizona* received a direct bomb hit on its forward magazine near the Number Two turret, resulting in such a massive explosion that 1,000 men were killed in an instant. The bridge was on fire as the ship began to descend to the bottom of the harbor. The order was given to abandon the ship. *Vestal*, being on fire from two direct bomb hits from *Kate* bombers, was saved by the huge concussion sustained from *Arizona* which surprisingly put out the fires of *Vestal*. A total of eight bomb hits and multiple torpedo attacks made the *Arizona* untenable at 1032. Of the 1,400 men on board, less than 200 survived.[10]

West Virginia, still afloat, sustained two direct bomb and six torpedo hits by *Kate* bombers. Smoke and flames abruptly encompassed the battleship. *Tennessee*, in spite of receiving two direct bombs hits, sustained more damage from the debris flying over from *Arizona*.

Enterprise, having left Wake Island on December 5, was now 300 miles from Oahu and ran into an unexpected gale which slowed the speed of the fleet in half. In the absence of the storm, *Enterprise* would have arrived in Pearl Harbor on Saturday night and would have been vulnerable to attack by Japanese planes. *Lexington*, which

The *Arizona* ablaze, immediately following the explosion of its forward magazine (Everett Collection/Shutterstock).

was returning from Midway, was southeast of Midway, about 500 miles away from Pearl Harbor, and thus was spared as well.

Nevada, which had thus far escaped the attention of the Japanese attackers, was anchored in a northeast mooring in Battleship Row but was in an exposed position with no ship outboard of it. At 0802, a Japanese torpedo struck the port bow of the ship and flooded a number of its compartments. With counter-flooding measures taking place, the ship moved out into the narrow channel. At this point, Lieutenant Murata's torpedo bombers, having released all of their torpedoes, headed north back to the carrier *Kaga*.[11]

At the same time (0752) that *Utah* was being assaulted by torpedo bombers, Kaneohe Naval Air Station, in northeastern Oahu, was being attacked by 11 Zero fighters. The Air Station housed Naval Patrol Wing One, which consisted of three squadrons of 12 PBY *Catalina* flying boats. Three PBYs were on patrol west of the island, four flying boats were anchored in the bay at their moorings, and four PBYs were in their hangars. The remaining 25 planes were lined up on the ramp. When the Zeros finished firing their guns and 20 mm cannons, they had destroyed 27 PBYs and damaged six.[12]

On December 7 at 0740, *Enterprise,* which was now 215 miles west of Oahu, launched 18 SBD (VB-6 and VS-6) dive bomber aircraft to scout ahead of the task force. Earlier the carrier had launched two SBD dive bombers, one of which was the

The light cruiser *Phoenix* is steaming down the channel off Ford Islands' Battleship Row, past the sunken and burning *West Virginia* on the left and *Arizona* on the right (Naval History and Heritage Command).

The *West Virginia* afire forward, immediately after the Japanese air attack (Naval History and Heritage Command).

Nevada **seen aground and burning off Waiipo Point, at the end of the Japanese air raid (Naval History and Heritage Command).**

leader of the 18 plane group and the other was his wing-man. The two pilots flew directly to Ford Island Air Field. At 0820, the two aircraft arrived over Pearl Harbor as the first wave of the Japanese attack was raging and ran into a hail of U.S. antiaircraft fire. Both planes, however, were successfully able to land on the Ford Island airstrip. Shortly thereafter, the remaining 18 SBD planes arrived. One was shot down by U.S. antiaircraft fire and landed in the sea; however, the pilot and gunner were rescued unharmed. Four SBD aircraft were downed by Japanese Zeros, one SBD pilot parachuted to safety west of Ewa Air Field, and another crash-landed at Burns Field in Kauai. The remainder of the planes landed safely at either NAS Ewa or NAS Ford Island.

At about the same time, 12 B-17 bombers arrived over Hickam Army Air Force Base from Hamilton Field in California. The final destination of these planes was to be the Philippine Islands. Suddenly, the group was attacked by Zero aircraft, and the B-17s scattered in every direction in an attempt to land safely, which they did. As the B-17s scrambled to land, 17 *Val* dive bombers launched from *Shokaku*, accompanied by 18 Zero fighters, arrived on the scene. The B-17s, flying without ammunition, were unable to defend themselves.

The dive bombers had flown east of Haleiwa in northwestern Oahu and then turned south in a mostly eastern direction toward Hickam Field. When they reached Hickam, the planes turned southwest toward the airfield and destroyed over half of the numerous parked aircraft on the field, as well as inflicting heavy damage to the

A U.S. Army B-17E at Hickam Air Field has landed safely at the time of the Japanese raid. Smoke can be seen rising from burning ships at Pearl Harbor in the distance (Naval History and Heritage Command).

facilities on Hickam and on Ford Island. Although the attack only lasted ten minutes, over 182 men were killed or missing.[13]

Twenty-five dive bombers, which had been launched from Zuikaku, had flown to Oahu with 26 dive bombers from their sister carrier Shokaku. As the combined dive bomber group neared Kahuku Point, they veered southwest to a point just east of Haleiwa. As the dive bombers from Shokaku headed southeast to Hickam Field, the 25 dive bombers from Zuikaku attacked Wheeler Army Air Force Base, setting the hangars on fire. The accompanying eight Zero fighters then destroyed at least half of the 153 Wheeler Field aircraft, which were lined up in front of the hangars and under armed guard to prevent sabotage.[14] An ill-advised order from General Short to arrange the aircraft close together, rather than scattering the planes, made the aircraft easy targets for destruction by Japanese Zeros. Wheeler Field, which was once the main army fighter base on the island, sustained a lethal blow.

At 0815, the Japanese fighters and dive bombers, having completed their attack on Wheeler and Hickam Army air fields, now turned their attention to Ewa Marine Corp Air Station. The base had already been attacked by six Zeros at 0753, which destroyed over half of Ewa's aircraft on the ground. At 0820, the Zeros and Vals dove down to strike the remaining aircraft on Ewa's airfield. Among the 48 aircraft on the ground at Ewa were the newest Dauntless SBD-3 dive bombers and Wildcat F4F-3 fighters. In the end 33 of the existing 48 planes were either destroyed or damaged by Japanese aircraft.[15]

The only effective initial U.S. air power response lay in the hands of Lieutenants George S. Welch and Kenneth Taylor, Army pilots who had spent the night at Wheeler Field attending a dance and playing poker until 0800 December 7. When they realized that the Japanese were attacking Wheeler Field, they immediately called Haleiwa Air Field where their P-40 fighters were parked and ordered them to be ready for take-off.[16] Having reached Haleiwa Field, they flew their P-40s to Barbers Point where they did not find any Japanese aircraft in the skies. The pilots then decided to head to Wheeler Field to rearm their aircraft. As the planes were being armed, Japanese aircraft arrived on the scene, and the maintenance crew ran for cover. Taylor and Welch climbed into their planes and took off. The pilots headed directly for the incoming Japanese planes, and the two U.S. pilots shot down six to eight Japanese aircraft. The Zeros had planned to strafe Haleiwa Air Field, but because of Taylor and Welch's ability to intercept numerous Japanese fighters, Sub Lieutenant Fujita Iyozo turned their attention away from the airfield to the two U.S. planes. Thus, Haleiwa Air Field was the only U.S. airbase not attacked during the Japanese Pearl Harbor raid.[17] Welch suffered no injuries but Taylor was superficially wounded in the left arm and leg by Japanese bullets. Both pilots landed their planes safely after engaging the Japanese aircraft and subsequently received multiple military awards for their heroic efforts.

As the attack raged at Pearl Harbor, it was 1300 in Washington. Secretary of the Navy Knox had just returned to his office from a meeting with Secretary of State Hull and Secretary of War Stimson. Knox was subsequently joined by Chief of Naval Operations Stark and Director of War Plans Turner for an hour-long conference. When the meeting was over, the three men then entered the office of Knox's confidential assistant John H. Dillon, when a naval commander brought them a message from Pearl Harbor that read, "We are being attacked. This is no drill."[18]

Ninety minutes after the first wave of Japanese planes took off, the second wave of aircraft was launched. When Fuchida cried out "Tora! Tora! Tora!" at 0740, the second wave was about 110 miles from Oahu. The flight of aircraft now heading toward Pearl Harbor consisted of 36 fighters, 54 high-level horizontal bombers, and 78 dive bombers for a total of 168 planes. The missions of the aircraft were as follows: the fighters were to strafe Ford and Kaneohe airfields, the horizontal high level bombers (all from *Zuikaku* and *Shokaku*) were to attack Hickam and Ford fields, and the dive bombers which were launched from *Akagi*, *Kaga*, *Soryu* and *Hiryu* were to destroy the remaining battleships.[19]

The second wave of Japanese aircraft reached Oahu about one hour after the first wave had arrived and about 30 minutes after it had departed. At 0850, the second wave, under the overall command of Lieutenant Commander Shimazaki Shigekazu, having reached Kahuka Point, turned southeast for ten miles. Some of the high level bombers and fighters attacked Kaneohe Naval Air Station while the other high level bombers and fighters looped around the southeast corner of Oahu as they headed for Hickam Field and Ford Island. The dive bombers veered southwest just north of Kaneohe Naval Air Station and flew toward Pearl Harbor.

By this time, anti-aircraft firing on the island had substantially improved and created a problem for the attacking planes. Eighteen Zeros split into two groups of nine planes each near Kaneohe. Nine fighters dove down to strafe the floatplane

A Japanese Navy Type 97 carrier attack plane (*Kate*) flies high over Hickam Army Air Field during the attack. Pearl Harbor is in the background with smoke rising from burning ships off Ford Island and at the Navy Yard (Naval History and Heritage Command).

installation on Kaneohe, then turned west to attack Wheeler Field. The other nine aircraft flew south past Kaneohe toward Bellows.

The Zeros reached Bellows Field at 0900. The planes set fire to a gasoline tank truck, destroyed one plane as it was trying to take off, and later shot down the only two planes that had been successful in getting airborne. One of the 12 incoming B-17s, having earlier turned away from Hickam Field, attempted to land at Bellows and was severely damaged in the process. Then, the aircraft was repeatedly strafed by all nine Zeros even though it had been totally disabled by its crash landing.[20] The Zeros then returned to Kaneohe where the high level bombers had already destroyed the hangars and the aircraft they housed. The fighters strafed everything in sight including homes, cars, and pedestrians.

The pilots of the high-level bombers, all on their maiden combat mission, headed toward Hickam Field. They were escorted by 16 Zero fighters. Upon arrival, the bombers inflicted heavy damage on two hangars. Meanwhile, the dive bombers directed their attention to the remaining U.S. battleships. Each plane held one 250-kilogram bomb, so each plane had one chance to be successful in scoring a direct hit. However, once the dive bombers reached Pearl Harbor, they found the targets obscured by heavy black smoke and an intense amount of anti-aircraft fire which now filled the air. The dive bombers could only attack the ships that might be visible and accessible in

A view looking down Pier 1010 toward Pearl Harbor Navy Yard's Dry-dock Number One. In the center, one can see battleship *Pennsylvania* (BB-38) and burning destroyers *Cassin* (DD-372) and *Downes* (DD-375) (Naval History and Heritage Command).

view of the heavy flack from U.S. guns. *Nevada*, the only battleship able to get underway, had just moved past *Arizona* and *Oklahoma*. Sinking the *Nevada* in the channel would have blocked any escape route out of Pearl Harbor. *Nevada* received five direct hits on the forepart of the ship, the superstructure (the part of a ship above the main deck), and the forecastle (part of the upper deck forward of the mast nearest the bow). At 0910, the battleship grounded its hull in the mud at Hospital Point. By 1045, tugs had moved the ship to the western part of the Pearl Harbor entrance.[21]

At 0902, Lieutenant Commander Egusa Takashige's dive bombers made a direct hit on *Pennsylvania* and five minutes later a second bomb landed on the starboard side of the main deck. In spite of the fact that the battleship was in an exposed position in the dry dock of Pearl Harbor, the battleship sustained little serious damage. However, the nearby destroyer *Shaw* had its whole bow blown off, and destroyers *Cassin* and *Downes* were so badly hit that their magazine and torpedo compartments blew the ships apart, the two destroyers being in the same dry dock as *Pennsylvania*. *California* was sinking, but *Maryland*, being inboard of *Oklahoma*, was protected from torpedoes, and thus had the least amount of damage of all the battleships.[22]

At 0908, *Raleigh*, still reeling from the first wave of torpedo attacks, received a direct hit by a dive bomber near its aviation gasoline storage tanks. A second dive

The repair ship *Vestal* (AR-4) was beached in Pearl Harbor after having been struck by a Japanese bomb during the raid (Naval History and Heritage Command).

bomber missed the ship, 100 feet to port. The direct bomb hit caused enough damage that the cruiser had to remove 60 tons of topside weight to keep from capsizing.

At 1000, *Oglala*, which was severely damaged, finally rolled over and sank. The repair ship *Vestal* was moved away from the burning *Arizona* by a tug. When *Vestal* began to take on water, it was decided to beach the ship on a coral reef.[23]

St. Louis, a light cruiser, shuddered as a bomb landed near light cruiser *Honolulu*, which was moored alongside. *St. Louis* immediately made preparations to get under way and head out of the harbor. At 1004, the cruiser was doing 22 knots in an eight-knot zone as it cleared the channel. At that moment, two torpedoes were sighted heading straight for the cruiser. The ship took immediate evasive action, and both torpedoes missed. Suddenly, a midget submarine was seen and fired upon by *St. Louis*, apparently hitting its conning tower. The escape of St. *Louis*, and its encounter with a Japanese midget submarine, was the last major ship action in the attack on Pearl Harbor.[24]

The U.S. Navy suffered severe damage or the destruction of eight battleships, three light cruisers, three destroyers, and four auxiliary craft as well as 13 fighters, 21 scout bombers, and 46 patrol planes. The Army's losses were even greater with the loss of four B-17s, 12 B-18s, two A-20s, 32 P-40s, 20 P-36s, four B-26s, two OA-9s, and one O-49. An additional 86 pursuit planes, six reconnaissance aircraft, and 34 bombers were damaged, but 80 percent of these planes were salvaged. Of the 12 B-17s

A chart of Pearl Harbor which identifies U.S. ships' moorings, recovered from a downed Japanese Navy Aircraft (Naval History and Heritage Command).

arriving from California at the time of the attack, one was destroyed and three were damaged.[25]

Two thousand and eight sailors died in the attack on Pearl Harbor. The Marines lost 109 men and the Army 208. In addition, 68 civilians were killed during the attack. A total of 2,400 people died in the assault on Pearl Harbor, and 1,178 people were wounded. The total cost to the Japanese was the loss of 29 planes, a large submarine, five midgets submarines, and 64 men.

At 1000 in Washington, Captain John Beardall, the president's naval aide, presented to Roosevelt the 14th part of Japan's message which stated that diplomatic relations between the United States and Japan had come to an end. About three and half hours later, Secretary of the Navy Knox informed the president that Pearl Harbor had just been attacked by Japan. At 1405, Roosevelt called Secretary of State Hull to inform him of the attack and instructed that he should receive Ambassadors Nomura and Kurusu but not mention anything about Pearl Harbor. Then, Hull could indifferently escort them out the door.

At 1420, Kurusu and Nomura were received by Hull. They informed him that their reply to the present state of U.S. negotiations with Japan should have been delivered by 1300. The Secretary of State then responded to the ambassadors that their diplomatic reply was full of more untruths and distortions that he had ever seen in his 50 years of service. The envoys left his office with their heads down. Nomura was to learn shortly thereafter that Pearl Harbor had been attacked by Japan, and he was stunned.[26]

At 1600 a press report came in that Japan had declared war on the United States, just as President Roosevelt was working on his famous "Day of Infamy" speech in the White House. Secretary of War Stimson wanted Roosevelt to also declare war on Germany, but the president declined because he knew Germany would soon declare war on the United States. The day ended with Roosevelt working on the speech that he would give at 1230 the next day in Congress. In that speech, the president would offer a concurrent resolution requesting that the U.S. declare war on the empire of Japan.[27]

In Hawaii, Commander Charles Coe, Operations and War Plans officer for the Navy, was trying to contact Army Air to discuss from what direction the Japanese carriers had attacked Pearl Harbor. Communication was impossible as lines were down, and confusion was widespread. Even if the direction could be discovered, Army Air was not in position to retaliate. The Opana Station had plotted a clear northbound direction of the Japanese aircraft returning to their carriers at 1027 and 1029. However, this information was overlooked until the Japanese fleet was well out of range of U.S. air power. Thus, Admiral Kimmel, who believed the Kido Butai originated from the Marshall Islands, sent his surface ships in a westerly direction to find the Japanese task force. A single B-17 took off from Hickam and flew south to look for the Kido Butai, but instead of finding the Japanese task force, the plane discovered *Enterprise* in the area. When a map was discovered in a downed Japanese aircraft, it documented a northwesterly direction for the Japanese task force. The planes that were finally sent in that direction found nothing but empty ocean.[28]

Slowed down by road blocks and traffic, the Radio Corporation of America (RCA) telegraph messenger Tadeo Fuchimaki could not deliver to the Army Signal Center until 1145 (Hawaii time) General Marshall's cryptic message warning U.S. forces in Hawaii to be on alert. After the communication was decoded, it finally reached General Short's office at 1458 (Hawaii time). When the message was delivered to General Short, he was furious that he had not been notified sooner. When Admiral Kimmel received the dispatch from General Marshall, he threw the message in the trash can in disgust. As these events were taking place, rescue operations in the harbor were under way, and the military was on high alert for another Japanese attack.[29]

At 1010 (Hawaii time), the first wave of Japanese planes was returning to their carriers. The weather had deteriorated, and high seas made it difficult to recover the returning aircraft. As Commander Fuchida was homing in on *Akagi*, thoughts of an additional strike on Pearl Harbor entered his mind. The fuel farms, the vast repair and maintenance facilities, and the submarine base had not been targeted during the first strike but remained targets for a possible subsequent strike which would complete the mission. Commander Genda, planner of the Pearl Harbor attack, had been waiting for him to return and report on the results of the first wave strike. Genda was then summoned to meet with Admiral Nagumo and shortly thereafter, when Fuchida landed, he was requested to report on the results of the attack. Gathered in the room, in addition to Genda, were Rear Admiral Kusaka Ryunosuke, Chief of Staff of the First Fleet; Captain Hasegawa Kiichi, Commander of the *Akagi;* Commander Oishi Tomatsu, First Fleet Staff member; and Admiral Nagumo.[30]

Divers in front of a decompression chamber while working on salvaging ships (Naval History and Heritage Command).

Fuchida reported that four battleships were sunk and that the U.S. Pacific Fleet would not be able to leave Pearl Harbor for six months. Kusaka wanted to know what the next targets should be, to which Fuchida replied that the fuel tanks and dockyards would be appropriate targets but not the battleships, which were already incapacitated. Fuchida then reassured Kusaka that Japan had control of the sea and skies over Oahu but added that the U.S. carriers by this time would be looking for the Japanese carriers. Genda added that if the American carriers were in the area, "Let the enemy come! If he does, we will shoot his planes down."[31]

With this information in hand, the discussion turned to whether there would be a second strike on Pearl Harbor. The Japanese task force had achieved only 20 per cent of its tactical mission, since the fuel depots, repair facilities, and submarine base were left untouched. Fuchida, Genda, and the pilots favored a second strike to complete the mission but Nagumo and Kusaka, who had opposed the idea of a Pearl Harbor attack in the first place, were reluctant to grant permission for a second assault. They felt that since the American carriers *Enterprise* and *Lexington*'s locations were unknown and thus a counterattack could be expected, to pursue a second strike would risk the loss of a now-intact Kido Butai. In addition, the weather was poor for launching and recovering aircraft. Another significant factor entered into the decision not to proceed with a second strike. In preparing for a second assault, the carriers would be required to change the planes' armament—which was now ready for an attack on ships at sea—to land-based ordnance. This is the same scenario that Japan would later face at Midway. However, there is a significant tactical difference between the two conflicts, namely, that the Japanese carrier force at Pearl Harbor outnumbered the U.S. carrier force by at least 6:1 (at that time, only *Enterprise* was in the area, *Lexington* was almost 400 miles away) as opposed to Midway, where the ratio of Japanese to U.S. carriers was only 4:3 in favor of Japan. The odds for success by Japan to destroy the one or two U.S. carriers in the area (*Enterprise* and *Lexington*) and then complete their mission against the U.S. fuel tanks, repair shops, and submarine base would never be better in the entire war. This plan was exactly what Genda proposed. He had recommended that the Japanese task force refuel, launch reconnaissance aircraft to locate the missing U.S. carriers, and then, after the American carriers were eliminated, the Kido Butai could complete their mission at Pearl Harbor.[32]

After listening to the discussion, Admiral Nagumo, who had already made up his mind that there would not be a second strike when the Kido Butai was still in the Kurile Islands, declared that there would not be a second Japanese attack on Pearl Harbor. Admiral Yamamoto, who was stationed in Japan, had a policy of leaving those decisions to the commander in the field. However, Admiral Yamamoto was to lament in late 1942 that, had Japan launched a second strike on Pearl Harbor, the early course of the war in Pacific would have been dramatically changed.[33]

Commander Genda was still hoping that Admiral Nagumo would change his mind and order a second strike on Pearl Harbor. At 1300, the Kido Butai had turned due north to escape detection by U.S. aircraft. Nagumo ordered a full 360-degree search the next day, covering a radius of 300 miles, to search for the American carriers. His main purpose, however, was to protect the escape route of the Japanese task force, as they were still vulnerable to a U.S. counterattack. At 1530, the air patrol search revealed no trace of an American task force out to a radius of 300 miles. In fact, the only U.S. carrier in the area was *Enterprise*, which was searching an area southwest of Oahu. *Lexington* was still 300 miles from Pearl Harbor. Without confirming the location of the U.S. carriers, Genda concluded that another attack on Pearl Harbor would be improbable. This conclusion was in stark contrast to a decision that would be made at Midway, where the Kido Butai proceeded with an air attack on the atoll without first confirming that there were no U.S. carriers in the area.[34]

There certainly were risks involved in a second assault on naval installations in Oahu, but the rewards would have far outweighed any loss to the Japanese carriers. Had the fuel depots been destroyed (they were all above-ground) by Japanese aircraft, the U.S. fleet would have been forced to retreat to the West Coast. With U.S. naval forces concentrated in San Diego, and given the great distance from that naval base to Midway (3,490 miles) and to the Coral Sea (7,640 miles), U.S. engagement in the battles of the Coral Sea and Midway would have been, at the very least, logistically difficult.

Also, with the U.S. submarine base in Hawaii left intact, severe damage was subsequently inflicted on the Japanese merchant marine fleet. Otherwise, Japan would have had complete naval superiority in the Pacific and Indian oceans, and Australia would have been cut off from its allies. The opportunity for a second strike on Pearl Harbor was a once-in-a-lifetime opportunity which would have had profound effects on the war for months to come. That opportunity was missed.

The question arises as to whether the Japanese attack on Pearl Harbor was really a tactical success. The failure to damage or destroy any of the U.S. carriers was clearly a tactical failure. True enough, nine U.S. battleships were either sunk or damaged. However, the battleships were old and slow and could not keep up with the speed of the U.S. carriers. Thus, those ships would have played no role in the carrier warfare that was to come. *Arizona, Oklahoma,* and *Utah* were sunk or damaged beyond repair. *West Virginia, California, Tennessee, Pennsylvania,* and *Maryland* were relegated to playing significant but supportive roles in the war in the Pacific. *Nevada*, which initially played a supportive role in the Pacific, was transferred to the Atlantic in 1943, where the battleship escorted U.S. convoys; in 1944, *Nevada* bombarded the German batteries at Normandy on D-Day. Admiral Nimitz later observed that the destruction of the U.S. battleships at Pearl Harbor turned out to be an advantage for the United States.

The next question is whether the attack on Pearl Harbor was a strategic success. As cited above, the loss of the U.S. battleships played no role in America's defensive posture in the early days of the war. It was the lack of U.S. carriers in the Pacific that was responsible for creating the tactical situation existing at the time. There were only seven carriers in the entire U.S. Navy at the time of the Pearl Harbor attack. and four of those were stationed in the Atlantic. The United States had only the *Enterprise* and *Lexington* stationed at Pearl Harbor. *Saratoga*, which had just left Bremerton, Washington, after repairs, was entering San Diego Navy Yard on the West Coast to prepare for deployment. One of the reasons the attack was a strategic failure, simply put, is the fact that the fuel depots were not destroyed, which would have forced the U.S. Pacific Fleet back to San Diego.

As stated above, the loss of the old U.S. battleships at Pearl Harbor played no role in the conduct of the early days of the war in the Pacific because they were slow and could not keep up with the carriers. Remaining unscathed, the U.S. carriers were free to roam around the Pacific at will. Another reason why the attack on Pearl Harbor was a strategic failure is that the assault on Pearl Harbor unified America in its determination to defeat Japanese aggression in the Pacific and led to the U.S. demand for an unconditional surrender from Japan as a prerequisite to end the conflict.

As the Japanese carrier force headed west to Japan, the U.S. threat to the Japanese task force diminished exponentially. By December 9, the Kido Butai finally felt free of retaliation by U.S. carriers. At 2100 on that date, Nagumo received orders to consider an attack by the Task Force on Midway Atoll on his way home. After deliberation with Genda, Maeda Minora, and Captain Yamaguchi Bunjiro, Nagumo decided not to attack Midway due to the perceived risks to the fleet and the future strategy of Japan in fighting the war. This directive is not to be confused with the fact that on its way to Pearl Harbor, the Kido Butai had detached two destroyers *Sazanami* and *Ushio* to bombard Midway. On December 7, at 1828, Midway's radar detected ships approaching Midway from a distance of three miles. Three hours later at 2130, the destroyers opened fire on Midway's Sand Island. Two hundred and ten shells were unleashed on the atoll. As the destroyers closed in on the islands, a large Japanese flag became visible, and moments later Midway's gun batteries opened fire, hitting both destroyers a total of five times. The damage on Midway included an airplane hangar, a PBY aircraft, the laundry building, and, most importantly, the Marine Command Post on Sand Island. It was at the Marine Command Post that First Lieutenant George

Cannon, USMC, died from wounds sustained during the attack. Cannon was the first Marine awarded the Congressional Medal of Honor in World War II.[35]

Since the attack on Midway was virtually ineffective, the atoll needed to be attacked again, raising the question of whether the two destroyers should return to Midway alone, or should the entire Japanese task force be used to attack Midway. Genda recommended that Nagumo bypass Midway on the way back to Japan and instead head for Truk Lagoon in the Caroline Islands. There the task force would replenish supplies, overhaul the fleet, and pick up Navy and Army troops from the Caroline and Marshall Islands. They would then head east to take Wake Island, then Midway and the Johnston Islands. Seizure of these islands would form a bridge across the Pacific for the Japanese to seize the Hawaiian Islands. This plan would surely bring out the U.S. carrier fleet to challenge the Kido Butai and, with the U.S. forces outnumbered, would result in destruction of the U.S. Pacific Fleet. Genda felt that this would be the perfect opportunity to destroy U.S. forces as the United States would still reeling from the assault on Pearl Harbor.[36]

On December 16, the decision of whether to attack Midway either in force or by two of its destroyers became irrelevant. On that date, the First Air Fleet received orders to immediately dispatch the Second Carrier Division (*Hiryu* and *Soryu*) to Wake Island. U.S. forces on Wake were thus far successfully resisting Japanese advances to occupy the island. The cruisers *Chikuma* and *Tone* and destroyers *Tanikaze* and *Urakaze* were sent to accompany the carriers. The carriers' planes had the ability to make only one bombing and strafing pass on Wake Island's installations. Japan desired to occupy the island before returning to Japan. During the encounter, Japanese horizontal bombardier Kanai Noboru, who was credited with releasing the bomb that exploded *Arizona*, was shot down and killed over Wake.[37]

On December 17, Nagumo dispatched the damage report of the attack on Pearl Harbor to the Combined Fleet headquarters in Tokyo. The initial reaction was one of elation, but upon further introspection it became obvious that the attack did not succeed in locating and destroying the U.S. carriers. This was a huge disappointment to the staff. However, they felt that Southern Operations could still be carried out as the United States repaired Pearl Harbor.

On December 23 at 1830, the First Air Fleet dropped anchor in Hiroshima Bay. There Admiral Yamamoto congratulated the pilots but warned them that Pearl Harbor was one of many battles that would be fought in the war, and that they should be wary of over-confidence as a result of their victory.[38]

On December 24, Genda visited Admiral Yamamoto aboard *Nagato* in Hiroshima Bay. He learned that on December 9, Captain Yamaguchi and Rear Admiral Maeda had presented his plan to expeditiously attack the Midway Islands and Hawaii to Vice Admiral Fukudome Shigeru, Chief of the First Bureau, and Rear Admiral Tomioka Sadatoshi, Chief of the Operations Section of the Naval General Staff. However, both admirals emphatically rejected the plan on the basis that Japan's first priority should be a commitment to conquer the fertile resources of Southeast Asia for its own needs. Plus, Hawaii would be very difficult to support logistically, even if Japan were able to successfully invade those islands.[39]

What Fukudome and Tomioka did not take into account is that with a subsequent attack on Pearl Harbor, the destruction of the oil tanks by Japanese aircraft would have forced the U.S. fleet to retreat back to San Diego for lack of fuel and that

Japanese occupation was not strategically necessary. Thus, at a time when the United States had just three carriers (*Enterprise, Lexington,* and *Saratoga*) in the Pacific (*Yorktown* had just passed through the Panama Canal toward the Pacific on December 16) and the Japanese had at least eight carriers to commit to the battle, Japan lost a strategic opportunity to attack Midway and destroy the three or four U.S. carriers in the Pacific that would eventually come to Midway's defense.

Only four days after Japan's attack on Pearl Harbor, Rear Admiral Noyes, the Navy's director of communications, instituted a 54 year censorship policy that confined all pre–Pearl Harbor Japanese military and diplomatic intercepts to Navy vaults where they would be free from public scrutiny. In addition, he ordered the following: "Destroy all notes or anything in writing." His actions allowed for the exclusion of pre–Pearl Harbor Japanese military intercepts from the upcoming presidential-appointed Roberts Commission and subsequent investigations. Later, Noyes denied giving the order to his subordinates. He said, "I may have instructed my subordinates to destroy personal memoranda. Nothing was said to destroy official records." However, personal memoranda written by Navy officials in the offices of the Navy belong to the people of the United States if the files concern naval matters. They cannot be destroyed except by the authority of Congress.

During December 1941, there was a movement in Congress to have a congressional investigation to determine who was at fault in the failure of the United States to be prepared for the Japanese surprise attack on Pearl Harbor. President Roosevelt feared that the code-breaking ability might be compromised and that the revelation of Lieutenant Commander memorandum would be made public. McCollum's report had been sent in October 1940 to two of Roosevelt's trusted advisors, Captains Walter S. Anderson and Dudley W. Knox. Anderson was director of the Office of Naval Records and Library and had direct access to the White House, and Knox was a naval strategist and chief of the ONI library. The paper trail ended with endorsement of McCollum's eight-action plan. The very next day, McCollum's proposals were put into effect by Roosevelt.

To circumvent the exposure of the two preceding issues, FDR called upon Associate Justice Owen J. Roberts of the U.S. Supreme Court to create a five-man board to investigate the matter. None of the U.S. Navy's intercept operators testified or produced radio logs and documents. Roosevelt approved the Roberts Commission report of January 24, 1942, which concluded that all the blame fell on Admiral Kimmel and General Short. General Marshall and Admiral Stark were cleared of any wrongdoing.

From July 24 to September 27, 1944, a Navy Court of Inquiry headed by Admiral Murfin G. Orin was held. The Court concluded that Admiral Stark had failed to provide Admiral Kimmel with all the information he had in Washington on Japanese intentions, preventing Kimmel from having a complete picture of the situation. Therefore, it was decided that Kimmel acted appropriately given the restricted information he received from Stark.

At the same time from July 20 to October 20, 1944, the Army Pearl Harbor Board convened. While the board was critical of General Short, General Marshall and the War Department were censured for the first time for the following: failing to keep General Short up to date on the gradual breakdown of relations between Japan and the United States, failing to make the November 29 warning clear and concise, and failing to see that the joint Army-Navy plans were properly implemented.[40]

Secretary Stimson and Secretary of the Navy James Forrestal were displeased that the shift of blame had now been placed from the local commanders to their superiors in Washington. Thus, on May 14, 1945, Forrestal requested that a Navy inquiry convene with a one-man investigation, headed by Admiral W. Kent Hewitt, USN. However, no report from the inquiry was ever published. Instead, on August 29, 1945, Forrestal issued an announcement: "Kimmel and Short failed to exercise the superior judgment necessary to exercising command commensurate with their rank and duties."[41]

In September 1944, author and journalist John T. Flynn published a 46-page booklet entitled *The Truth About Pearl Harbor*, which launched the Pearl Harbor revisionist movement. In September 1945, he wrote a 15-page report entitled "The Final Secret of Pearl Harbor" where he charges that Roosevelt was to blame for diplomatic mismanagement, for keeping the Pacific Fleet stationed at the insecure Pearl Harbor base (over the objections of Admiral James O. Richardson, Commander-in-Chief, Pacific Fleet), and for stripping Pearl Harbor of needed defensive equipment.

On November 15, 1945, through May 31, 1946, a concurrent resolution of Congress established a Joint Congressional Committee of the Pearl Harbor attack, which seated a majority of Democrats (six Democrats and four Republicans), without which much of Pearl Harbor's narrative would not have been made public. Flynn provided private funds for staffing the minority, who were not provided with their own staff. Evidence was extracted from the witnesses that contradicted the Roberts report. The majority report concluded that Japan had brilliantly planned and executed the attack and that there was no evidence that Roosevelt's cabinet had engineered the Japanese into launching a first strike, so that Congress would declare war on Japan and Germany. Secretary of State Hull and Secretary of War Stimson had done everything possible to avert war with Japan.

Sole blame was placed on the shoulders of the local commanders in Hawaii. The report did suggest that the War Department should have notified General Short that his sabotage alert measures were not enough and that Army and Navy intelligence should have realized the significance of Japanese efforts to ascertain the location of U.S. warships in Pearl Harbor (the bomb plot messages that had actually been decoded). Finally, the War and Navy departments should have been on a higher state of alert in the 48 hours prior to the attack and alerted Pearl Harbor about the impending diplomatic break scheduled to take effect at 1300 (Washington time) on December 7 between Japan and the United States.

In 1947, George Morgenstern, a Phi Beta Kappa graduate of the University of Chicago and a captain in the Marine Corps, wrote *Pearl Harbor: The Story of the Secret War*, which was published by Devin-Adair Company. He noted that the 1932 Navy exercise revealed that Pearl Harbor was open to air attack by carrier-based aircraft, which led him to explore in detail how the fleet was moved to Pearl Harbor in the first place in May 1940. Opposition to Roosevelt's order, which moved the U.S. fleet from the west coast of Maui to Pearl Harbor, came from Admiral Richardson, who was relieved of his command by Roosevelt four months later. He was replaced by Admiral Kimmel.

In 1995, a Senate hearing encouraged by the Kimmel family was held to consider restoration of Admiral Kimmel's rank from a two-star admiral to a four-star admiral.

He had been demoted after the Pearl Harbor attack. The resolution passed the Senate, but the House was not in session to take a vote. In May 26, 1999, the Senate voted to clear the names of the two officers, Short and Kimmel, who were accused of dereliction of duty. The vote was 52 to 47. The Senate requested that the president restore his rank to four stars. Neither President Bill Clinton nor any subsequent president has honored this request.

CHAPTER 8

Wake Island's Heroic Defense

Wake Island is a coral atoll located about 2000 miles directly west of Hawaii. The atoll is made up of three islands surrounding a central lagoon. Shaped like the letter V, it is situated in a northwest by southeast direction with twelve miles of coastline. The largest of the islands is Wake, with Peale and Wilkes Islands being smaller and together make up only about twenty percent of the size of Wake.

In 1568, the Spanish discovered Wake Island but found it worthless and did not actually claim the atoll for Spain. In 1796, the British also found the atoll and came to the same conclusion. In 1898, however, the United States gained control of the atoll presumably as a result of the Treaty of Paris Agreement which ended the Spanish-American War. Wake was acquired by the United States as a way-station for the Trans-Pacific Cable Company to establish telegraph communications between San Francisco and the Philippines.

In the mid–1930s, Pan American Airlines (Pan Am) decided to establish an air route across the Pacific Ocean. Boeing Aircraft Company had introduced the *China Clipper*, a flying boat which would facilitate this ambition. The obstacle confronting the airline was the huge distance between Midway and Guam (2,800 miles). The airline's research discovered a small uninhabited island named Wake, halfway between Guam and Midway. The island was a U.S. territory but was felt to have no value. Wake was about 1,200 miles from Midway and a perfect refueling and resting place for the *China Clipper* and its passengers. The air journey across the Pacific was now established as follows: San Francisco to Honolulu—2,300 miles; Honolulu to Midway—1,140 miles; Midway to Wake Island—1,260 miles; Wake Island to Guam—1,560 miles; and Guam to Manila—1,610 miles. The total distance was 7,870 miles from San Francisco.

In 1935, Pan Am began the process of developing air bases and housing facilities on Midway, Wake, and Guam. One year later, Pan Am was ready to transport passengers from San Francisco to Manila. The airbases that Pan Am built on Midway, Wake, and Guam would prove to be of enormous strategic value not only for the airlines but for the United States military as well. These bases permitted refueling of commercial and military planes in their flights across the Pacific, without which these flights would not be possible.[1] The airbases at Midway, Wake, and Guam allowed the U.S. to reinforce the Philippine Islands with B-17s prior to the outbreak of war with Japan on December 7, 1941.

In early 1941, as the winds of war with Japan began to blow across the Pacific, a Marine garrison was sent to Wake Island. Wake had strategic value because it represented an advance base where military planes headed to Guam and the Philippines

Approaching Wake Island from the northeast on May 25, 1941 (Naval History and Heritage Command).

could rest their crews. In addition, U.S. patrol planes could scout the western Pacific for Japanese naval ships, which would prove to be vital at the outbreak of war in the Pacific. Thus, large quantities of fuel needed to be stored on Wake, adding to the necessity of maintaining an airbase on the island.

On October 12, 1941, (Wake date) Major James Devereux, USMC, was assigned to command all the personnel on Wake including the senior naval officer. On November 19, however, Commander Winfield Scott Cunningham arrived on Wake to take over as commander of the 449 Marines from the First Defense Battalion on the island. On December 4, *Enterprise* delivered 12 F4F-3s to improve the air defense on Wake.

Four days later (December 8), the Marines on Wake Island learned that the Japanese had just attacked Pearl Harbor. The defenses of the atoll were immediately placed on full alert. At noon, 34 Japanese Mitsubishi G3M2 Type 96 land-attack planes attacked Wake from their air base in Roi on the Kwajalein Atoll in the Marshall Islands, 700 miles south of Wake. The atoll had no radar, so the local defenses were totally dependent on sight of incoming aircraft. Four F4Fs had taken off that morning to patrol the skies over Wake Island for incoming Japanese planes. The remaining eight F4Fs were grounded on the airfield when the Japanese bombers arrived over Wake.[2] All eight planes were either destroyed or damaged by attack planes' bombs. These air raids would continue almost on a daily basis until December 23.

8. Wake Island's Heroic Defense

[On December 10, news of Guam's surrender reached Washington. Guam was an American possession ceded to the United States by Spain at the end of the Spanish-American War in 1898. It is situated at the southern tip of the Mariana Islands, about 3,700 miles west-southwest of Honolulu. Its size is 212 square miles. On December 8, 1941 (Guam date), over 5,000 Japanese troops overwhelmed the 540 U.S. Marines on Guam. Two days later, at 0600 on December 10, Guam surrendered to the Japanese invasion force.]

In the evening hours of December 10, Rear Admiral Kajioka Sadamichi, commander of the Wake Island invasion convoy which had sailed from Kwajalein two days earlier, was nearing Wake Island. When the Japanese striking forced approached Wake on December 11, 1941, the Marines' artillery shells hit the Japanese light cruiser *Yubari* 11 times. The artillery guns also found their marks on the Japanese destroyer *Hayate*, which sunk after receiving several direct hits. In addition, U.S. F4F fighters inflicted a direct hit on destroyer *Kisaragi*'s storage site of depth charges, which led to its sinking. However, two of U.S. fighters were lost by sustaining hits from the destroyer's anti-aircraft fire. In view of bad weather and the casualties sustained by the Japanese invasion force, Admiral Kajioka ordered the force to retreat back to the Marshall Islands. News of the Japanese retreat from Wake provided a ray of light in an otherwise dark period for the United States.[3]

On December 14, Admiral Nagumo, while returning from Pearl Harbor, cancelled his attack on Midway when he received word that he was to detach carriers *Hiryu* and *Soryu* to Wake. On December 20, *Hiryu* and *Soryu* were ordered to attack Wake with their remaining operational aircraft from the Pearl Harbor attack as a preliminary step to an invasion by Japan on Wake between December 20 and December 23. (The two carriers lost 3 Zeros and 4 dive bombers over Pearl Harbor, while 20 Zeros, 23 dive bombers, and 3 torpedo bombers were damaged.)[4]

In Pearl Harbor, Admiral Kimmel was considering reinforcing Wake and evacuating non-essential civilians on the atoll. For this mission, the seaplane tender *Tangier* was available because it sustained only minimal damage in the attack at Pearl Harbor. The seaplane tender would be escorted by the carrier *Saratoga* which, having left San Diego on December 8 (California date), was delayed by bad weather in reaching Pearl Harbor. The carrier and its accompanying cruisers and destroyers did not reach Pearl Harbor until the morning of December 15 (Hawaii date).

Williams Ward Burroughs (a transport), which had departed from Pearl Harbor on November 29, 1941, was bringing to Wake, along with munitions and supplies, critically needed SCR-270 air search radar. On December 7, the ship, which was now only 425 miles east of Wake, was ordered by Rear Admiral Claude Bloch, Fourteenth Naval District commandant, to abort its mission to the atoll because the transport had no escort. By December 13, *Williams Ward Burroughs* then received orders to return not to Pearl Harbor but to Johnston Island, as the ship was no longer in the plans for the relief of Wake.[5]

At 1001 on December 14 (Hawaii date), Task Force 11 (which included the carrier *Lexington*, flagship *Indianapolis*, heavy cruisers *Chicago* and *Portland*, destroyers *Phelps, Aylwin, Dewey, Dale, MacDonald, Farragut, Worden, Monaghan, Hull* and the oiler *Neosho*), was placed under the command of Vice Admiral Wilson Brown. The task force sortied from Pearl Harbor and headed southwest for a raid on the Marshall Islands. Once at sea, 21 Brewster F2As, 32 Douglas SBDs, and 15 Douglas TBDs

Wrecked F4F-3 Wildcat fighters on Wake Island airstrip, sometime after its capture by the Japanese on December 23, 1941. There appear to be at least seven aircraft (Naval History and Heritage Command).

landed on *Lexington's* carrier deck, having taken off from Ford Island. The fleet's mission was to raid Jaluit, the center of Japanese naval activity in the Marshall Islands, to create a diversion to Task Force's relief effort of Wake. These orders, however, were subject to change as circumstances dictated, meaning that Admiral Brown could change the target of the mission to other installations and forces in the Marshall Islands or withdraw without any attack at all.[6]

Rear Admiral Frank Jack Fletcher, a non-aviator, was assigned by Admiral Kimmel to command Task Force 14 on board his flagship cruiser *Astoria*. Task Force 14 also included cruisers *San Francisco* and *Minneapolis* and destroyers *Mugford, Selfridge, Patterson*, and *Ralph Talbot*, seaplane tender *Tangie,r* and oiler, *Neches*.

On board *Saratoga* were 13 Grumman F4F fighters, 43 Douglas SBDs, and 11 Douglas TBDs. The carrier was assigned to deliver 14 Brewster F2A-3 fighters to Wake and to escort *Tangier* on its way to Wake. Fletcher's prime mission was to ensure that *Tangier* would safely transport 207 Marines of the Fourth Defense Battalion, three- and five-inch antiaircraft guns, ammunition, one M-4 director (mechanical computer to calculate firing solutions for and transmitting pointing data to an antiaircraft gun), one range finder (to calculate range for an antiaircraft gun), 200 tons of dry goods, and two SCR-268 radar units to Wake. The ship would then transport 650 civilians and wounded from Wake to Pearl Harbor.[7]

As stated above, on December 8 (U.S. date), *Saratoga* left San Diego and docked in Pearl Harbor seven days later on December 15 (Hawaii date) to refuel, needing 24 hours to complete the process. In the late afternoon on that day, *Tangier*, oiler *Neches*, and destroyers *Porter, Mahan, Lamson,* and *Flusser* sortied out of Pearl Harbor just as Vice Admiral William F. Halsey's Task Force 8 was entering the harbor.[8]

On December 16 (U.S. date), Admiral Kimmel received notice that he was being relieved of command by Vice Admiral William Pye, his former military advisor and commander of the battleship *California.* The decision had come from the CNO Admiral Stark. On that same day, Task Force 14, now fully refueled, left Pearl Harbor and headed west to catch up with the reinforcement fleet that had sailed the day before.

During that time, Admiral Nagumo had placed the Japanese Wake Reinforcement Force under the command of Rear Admiral Abe Hiroaki, Commander of the Eighth Cruiser Division, and its air command under Rear Admiral Yamaguchi. Admiral Nagumo continued west toward Japan, as Rear Admiral Abe's fleet sailed southwest toward Wake.

On December 17 (U.S. date) Fletcher's fleet caught up to *Tangier* and *Neches,* uniting Task Force 14 for the first time. Fletcher then had to slow the speed of the fleet to about 13 knots to accommodate the oiler's best speed as the task force steamed southwest toward Wake.[9]

On that day, U.S. radio intelligence was able to decipher the naval code and learned that the Cruiser Division 8 (*Tone* and *Chikuma*) and Carrier Division 2 (*Hiryu* and *Soryu*) were connected to the 24th Flotilla of Japan's Fourth Fleet. This was further evidence that U.S. naval intelligence was able to decipher enough of Japan's naval code to gain critical intelligence in December 1941.[10]

In Pearl Harbor on December 19 (Wake date), Vice Admiral Pye had learned from naval intelligence that Japanese Carrier Division 2 and Cruiser Division 8 were linked to the Japanese Fourth Fleet, which had been assigned to capture Wake. The addition of the carriers *Hiryu* and *Soryu* to the Japanese Wake Invasion Force significantly raised the risks to the United States attempting to reinforce Wake Island. Admiral Pye felt he could not afford to lose a carrier at this time. The foregoing knowledge, in addition to decoded Japanese radio communications (revealing that Japan was establishing an air base in the Gilbert Islands and already possessed a submarine force on Jaluit in the Marshall Islands), led Pye to question his decision to reinforce Wake. Admiral Pye did not know that *Hiryu* and *Soryu* had lost three Zero fighters and four Type 99 carrier bombers at Pearl Harbor. In addition, 20 Zero fighters, 23 Type 99 carrier bombers, and 3 Type 97 carrier attack planes sustained varying degrees of damage at Pearl. The losses and assorted damage to the Japanese planes on *Soryu* and *Hiryu* left both carriers with 51 undamaged aircraft.[11]

Vice Admiral Brown of Task Force 11 was now faced with the fact that Japan had air bases in the Gilbert and Marshall islands that could threaten his force. Therefore, he decided to refuel and take the time to reconsider his objective to attack the Marshall Islands. Meanwhile, Fletcher's Task Force 14, which was moving steadily toward Wake, was now 1,020 miles away from the atoll.

On December 19 (U.S. date), Halsey's Task Force 8 left Pearl Harbor toward a position south of Midway and west of Johnston Island. Their mission was to remain in that location and reinforce Task Force 11 and Task Force 14 if an engagement between U.S. and Japanese carriers in the Wake area ensued. On board *Enterprise* were 14 Wildcat fighters and one F2A Buffalo fighter. (The exact number of SBDs and TBDs aboard the carrier is not certain but was close to 37 SBDs and 18 TBDs.)[12] The United

States now had three carriers, *Enterprise, Lexington,* and *Saratoga,* scattered in the Pacific, east of Wake and southeast to southwest of Midway.

On the morning of December 21 (Wake date), Rear Admiral Kajioka's Sadamichi fleet left the Marshall Islands. On the same day, the *Hiryu* and *Soryu* turned into the wind to launch their aircraft. Dive bombers and fighters took off from *Soryu* and *Hiryu's* flight decks and headed toward Wake. At 0900, the planes arrived over Wake and focused on the shore installations. The carrier attack caught the Americans by surprise. The only Marine aircraft available (VMF-211) were on the ground but escaped damage from the incoming carrier planes.[13]

On December 21, Vice Admiral Brown's Task Force 11 (*Lexington*) was continuing toward the Marshall Islands. The voyage was interrupted when Admiral Pye, who had now become concerned that carriers *Hiryu* and *Soryu* were in the Wake area and who also had intelligence that there was increased Japanese air patrols over Jaluit, decided to cancel Task Force 11's mission against the Marshall Islands. Admiral Pye then ordered Vice Admiral Brown to divert his fleet toward Wake to support Task Force 14 in the event that the Japanese would carry out a carrier attack against *Saratoga*. At that time the three U.S. carrier fleets were operating independently of each other, so Pye ordered the task forces to close the distance between themselves and thus concentrate his carrier forces heading for Wake.

On the same day at 0700, *Soryu* launched 9 fighters and 14 Type 99 carrier bombers, and *Hiryu* launched 9 fighters and 15 Type 97 carrier bombers (a total of 47 planes). Their mission was to attack the military installations on Wake. Leading the Type 97 attack planes was Lieutenant Kusumi Tadashi, who was credited for dropping the bomb that ignited the *Arizona* at Pearl Harbor. The defenders of Wake sent the two operational Marine fighters on the atoll to intercept the incoming Japanese planes. Both pilots faced overwhelming odds while engaging the 39 Japanese planes in the skies over the atoll. In the engagement, both U.S. fighters were lost in combat with Japanese Zeros. Commander Cunningham informed CINCPAC that Wake Island was now without any air protection.[14]

Rear Admiral Fletcher's Task Force 14 had slowed to 13 knots as a result of heavy seas and the slow movement of oiler *Neches*. On December 22 and 23 (Wake dates), Fletcher further delayed the fleet's progress toward Wake by refueling the destroyers. On the evening of December 22, Admiral Fletcher received a message from Admiral Pye that he was not to approach any closer than 200 miles off Wake. From there, Fletcher could fly off the carrier the 14 Marine F2A-3s to the atoll.[15]

A controversy has existed since Rear Admiral Samuel Eliot Morison, author of *The U.S. History of Naval Operations in World War II* published in 1949, criticized Rear Admiral Fletcher's decision to refuel his destroyers on December 22 and his decision to disregard the operational plan when he first found out that Wake had been attacked by Japanese carrier planes on December 21. Morison felt that Fletcher should have left the U.S. destroyers, seaplane tender *Tangier,* and oiler *Neches* behind even if they ran out of fuel and proceeded at high speed (20 knots) with *Saratoga* and heavy cruisers *Astoria, San Francisco,* and *Minneapolis* as escorts, to intercept the Japanese invasion forces on the morning of December 23. Morison's judgment has been questioned recently by historian John Lundstrom in his books *The First Team* and *Black Shoe Carrier Admiral* published in 1984 and 2006, respectively.[16]

The first issue in the controversy is whether Morison's recommendation that

Saratoga and the three heavy cruisers attack the Japanese invasion force would have been a sound tactical decision. The Japanese invasion force did include the two carriers, *Hiryu* and *Soryu*, to one carrier for the United States. However, the United States had the element of surprise, as they later did at Midway. In addition, the Japanese carriers' aircraft had sustained some losses and damage in the attack on Oahu, and some of the Japanese pilots on board were inexperienced. Although Lundstrom does attempt to refute the advice given by Morison on its own merits, his main compelling rebuttal is on the refueling issue and that Fletcher was ordered by Admiral Pye not to approach Wake any closer than 200 miles. Morison's tactical advice is debatable, but it did offer the United States the one chance it had to improve the military conditions on Wake.

This brings us to the refueling issue, that is, that Fletcher needed to refuel the destroyers in order to operate at high speed during combat conditions. Morison argued that the destroyers should have been left behind if they ran out of fuel and that *Saratoga* with heavy cruisers *Astoria*, *San Francisco*, and *Minneapolis* should have continued to attack the Japanese carrier force. On December 21, Task Force 14 was sailing northeast of Wake in order to be positioned outside the 700-mile perimeter of the Japanese scout planes located in the Marshall Islands and was not sailing directly west, closing in on Wake. At dawn on December 22, Fletcher was still 515 miles northeast of the atoll. At midnight on December 23—the day of the Japanese invasion force attack—he was still refueling at sea, 440 miles from Wake. His task force would not be 180 miles away from Wake until December 24, one day after the attack. Morison's point is that the delay in refueling the destroyers and in heading northeast of the atoll prevented Fletcher from being in position to attack the Japanese invasion force on the morning of December 23. In Morison's view, the best possible plan for the United States to retain control of Wake would have been for *Saratoga's* planes to arrive before the Japanese invasion forces assaulted the island.

Lundstrom points out that even the cruisers needed refueling, citing Rear Admiral Fletcher's own words as his source. The fact is that neither the heavy cruisers nor *Saratoga* were ever refueled, and Fletcher is cited by Lundstrom and John L. Cressman as saying that he was ready for action when the mission for Wake's relief was cancelled on the morning of December 23.[17] (It is true that in high speed combat conditions the fuel consumption is greatly increased, and that naval standard operating procedure "expected" the fleet to be refueled before engaging in such combat. However, the key word in the directive is "expected" and not "required.")

More to the point is the analysis of the cruising range of *Saratoga* and the heavy cruisers after their fuel tanks were topped in Pearl Harbor. The distance from Pearl Harbor to Wake Island is approximately 2,000 nautical miles. *Saratoga* could sail for 10,000 nautical miles at 10 miles. (No mention is made by historians of fueling *Saratoga*.)[18] Heavy cruisers *Astoria*, *San Francisco*, and *Minneapolis* had a greater cruising range than *Saratoga*: 14,000 nautical miles at 10 miles/hour and a range of 5,280 nautical miles at 20 miles/hour[19] Assuming the heavy cruisers ran at high speed (20 miles/hour in catching up to *Neches* and *Tangier* after leaving Pearl Harbor, a distance of 240 nautical miles), the heavy cruisers' fuel reserve would still be 12,240 nautical miles at 10 miles/hour by the time the ships reached Wake. This reserve would still allow for 4,388 nautical miles for high speed (20 miles/hour) combat conditions, clearly much better than the ability of the fully refueled destroyer (3,000 nautical miles at 20 knots) and enough to engage the Japanese task force. However, a case can be made that the destroyers needed to be refueled, so the question arises whether one would risk the U.S. carrier force approaching the atoll without its destroyers for the sake of saving Wake. That question is yet to be resolved.

It is true that Admiral Pye ordered Task Force 14—which was then 635 miles northeast of Wake—to remain clear of the 700-mile radius that included Japan's air bases at Rongelap in the Marshall Islands. However, Fletcher was authorized to approach Wake from the northeast on December 21, which was beyond the 700-mile radius range. There was also was an opportunity for Fletcher to sail directly west, if he had decided it was a reasonable, to approach Wake at high speed and intercept the Japanese invasion forces on December 23, notwithstanding Admiral Pye's order for *Saratoga* not to get any closer to Wake than 200 miles on the night of December 22. Had *Saratoga* and its heavy cruisers moved at high speed toward Wake on December 21, the task force would have been within a 100-mile range (traveling at 20 knots]) of the atoll at midnight December 22, and not the 440 miles it actually was.

The key to a successful mission by U.S. naval forces in reinforcing Wake Island was that Task Force 14 arrived before Japan invaded the atoll on the morning of December 23. As shown above, only if Fletcher had disregarded Admiral Pye's order not to come within 200 miles of Wake on the night of December 22, and only if he had not decided to refuel his destroyers, would he have been able to intercept the Japanese invasion force the morning of December 23. As events turned out, Fletcher's decisions to refuel the destroyers and not to approach nearer than 200 miles of Wake resulted in Task Force 14 arriving on December 24. It was one day too late to prevent the Japanese invasion of Wake, one day too late to deliver the 14 Brewster *Buffalo* F2A-3 fighters to the Marines on the atoll. In addition, it seems clear—as Morison argues—that certainly the *Saratoga* and the three heavy cruisers had enough fuel to engage in high speed combat conditions. The destroyers, which had a range of 6,500 nautical miles when fully fueled, had a reserve of 4,500 nautical miles after reaching Wake. Leaving 2,000 miles for their return trip back to Pearl Harbor, that would have left 1,111 nautical miles for high speed combat conditions. Thus, it is reasonable to assume that even if the destroyers had run low on fuel, they could have been refueled by *Neches* on their return to Pearl Harbor.

On December 22, Admiral Pye, learning about the difficult circumstances that Commander Cunningham was facing on the atoll, ordered *Tangier* to detach from Task Force 14 and depart for Wake to evacuate the civilian contractors and reinforce the Marines. Task Force 11 (Vice Admiral Brown) and Task Force 8 (Vice Admiral William Halsey) were also ordered to move in closer and support Task Force 14.[20] On this date, *Saratoga* was 515 miles from Wake, with *Lexington* being 750 miles southeast, and *Enterprise*, 1,100 miles east of Wake. However, this decision by Admiral Pye was to be short-lived. At 0245, on December 23, Japan landed its troops on the southwestern part of Wake Island, just west of Peacock Point. Japanese forces also went ashore on Wilkes Island at the western end of Wake to establish a beachhead. As the Japanese moved inland, communication wires to the command posts where Major Devereux and Commander Cunningham were stationed were cut, severing communications with Camp One (located where Wake borders Wilkes Island), with Major Paul Putnam, commanding officer of VMF-211, near the airstrip, with Second Lieutenant Robert Hanna at his command post on south beach on the southwest tip of

Wake, and with Battery A, located at Peacock Point. The last words from these sectors described a hopeless situation in trying to defend their areas.[21]

At 1100 on the morning of the invasion, *Soryu* lifted off 9 fighters and 17 Type 99 carrier bombers, and *Hiryu* launched 9 fighters and 16 Type 99 carrier bombers (a total of 51 aircraft) to assist the Japanese forces invading Wake Island. When news of the arrival of Japanese forces on Wake reached Admiral Pye in Pearl Harbor, he directed that the relief ship *Tangier* be sent back east, thus suspending the relief effort on Wake Island.[22]

Pye was faced with a dilemma. Should he risk a major engagement between the Japanese invasion forces and Task Force 14 (*Saratoga*) with the inherent risk of losing the carrier, or should he withdraw this carrier force? Pye considered that if Task Force 14 could surprise the Japanese force, heavy losses could be inflicted on the enemy. On the other hand, he could have Task Force 11 (*Lexington*) join up with Task Force 14 by the next day and use Task Force 8 (*Enterprise*) as a cover for the two carriers' (*Saratoga* and *Lexington*) retirement. Another alternative option would be to have Task Force 8 join the two carrier groups to form a powerful three-carrier force and come to the aid of Wake the next day. Even if the Japanese carrier force was gone on December 24, U.S. ground forces with air support could contain and capture Japanese forces on Wake. This action would have—at least temporarily—kept Wake in American hands. In addition, under these conditions *Tangier* could deliver its reinforcements to the atoll. On the other side of the coin, U.S. pilots on *Saratoga* lacked combat experience, which would make questionable a decision to confront the Japanese carrier force at Wake. Admiral Pye was unaware that some pilots, observers, and radio-gunners on *Soryu* and *Hiryu* had no combat experience, as they were to be used as backups in anticipation of heavy aircraft losses that would have been sustained in the Japanese attack on Oahu.

Before Admiral Pye had come to a decision, he received an order from CNO Admiral Stark that Wake Island was expendable. Pye was not to proceed with the attack on the Japanese fleet because the loss of even one American carrier would leave Hawaii more vulnerable to another attack by Japan's carrier fleet. Thus Fletcher, less than 440 miles from Wake, turned around and headed back to Pearl Harbor. The Japanese had won Wake Island precisely because it was considered expendable by the U.S. naval top command.

The White House was not pleased with Admiral Pye's decision to cancel the relief effort for Wake. There was anger and displeasure with Pye's vacillation and final decision to abort the relief effort. President Roosevelt had been following the events surrounding the relief effort closely. Secretary of the Navy Knox acknowledged that the president took the news of not fighting for Wake worse than the Pearl Harbor attack. Presumably, the president felt that, while the Japanese had overwhelming air superiority and the element of surprise in its attack on Pearl Harbor, the United States had a reasonable chance to defend and hold on to Wake had they taken the initiative to the Japanese. As a result, the president maintained a lifelong wrath toward Pye over his decision not to relieve Wake.[23]

On December 23, Japanese forces were encroaching on the south side of the U.S. airstrip on Wake, but U.S. forces near the runway at Camp One repelled them. Elsewhere on the island, Japanese forces were able to move freely in the areas they had captured. The situation on Wilkes Island had also improved, as U.S. forces vigorously fought back. Unfortunately, neither the information from Wilkes Island nor Camp One on Wake could be delivered to Devereux and Cunningham, as communication lines to them had been severed.[24]

On the same day, *Soryu* and *Hiryu* launched five waves of attacks on Wake. The results of the air attacks were indecisive. Devereux and Cunningham, with communication lines cut, believed that the island had fallen. Unaware of the favorable tactical situation both on Wilkes Island and at Camp One, Cunningham ordered Devereux—who did not resist the order—to surrender Wake Island to the Japanese forces. It took some time to inform the Japanese command of the surrender, but at the end of the day, Wake was in Japanese hands.[25] A total of 449 Marines, 68 Navy and 5 Army personnel, and 1,146 civilians were captured.

On January 12, 1942 (Wake date), U.S. prisoners of war from Wake Island were transferred by ship to concentration camps in Japan and China until the end of the war. Most of the prisoners of war survived, but some Marines, sailors, soldiers, and civilians died in the concentration camps as a result of brutal treatment they received at the hands of Japanese guards. In September 1942 the last of the Americans were taken off Wake by the Japanese and placed in concentration camps in Japan. Civilian construction workers that remained on the island were all executed by the Japanese on October 3, 1943, out of fear that one of them would escape and reveal to the United States that Wake Island under Japanese control had weak defenses.[26]

Wake's main value, like Midway, was its naval air station and the Marines assigned there to defend it. Therefore, a Navy commander had been placed in charge of both Midway and Wake. Commander Cunningham never received recognition for being in overall command of Wake. Instead, Cunningham's command was ignored by the U.S. press for unknown reasons and the U.S. Navy's Public Relations Office added to the misconception that Devereux was in charge of Wake by failing to acknowledge that Cunningham was in command. These actions resulted in Major Devereux receiving all the credit for the valiant defense of Wake. In addition, Devereux never made any verbal or written statements to dispel this falsehood. Documentary film of the surrender of Wake left no doubt that the commander of Wake Island was Commander Cunningham.[27] In the aftermath of the Wake surrender, the Japanese press got it right, but to this day the U.S. Navy has been slow to acknowledge who was in command of Wake Island.

During the remainder of the war, Wake was attacked by U.S. air power and Navy ships, but it was not retaken by the United States until the after war had ended. After the war, Captain Sakaibara Shigemitsu, who gave the order to execute the remaining U.S. civilians on Wake, was placed on trial and executed on June 18, 1947. The bravery and heroism exhibited by U.S. Navy and Marine forces at Wake Island in December 1941 were an inspiration to the nation at the time, and its story remains a legacy in the annuals of U.S. naval and American history.

Chapter 9

Southern and Central Pacific Operations

At about the same time that Japan attacked Pearl Harbor on December 7, 1941, the Japanese army invaded the Malaysian Peninsula, Thailand, Borneo, and the Philippine Islands. On December 10, Japanese aircraft sank the British battleships *HMS Prince of Wales* and *HMS Repulse* in the waters east of Malaya.

The Philippines were the strongest U.S. military position in the Far East. They consist of 7,107 islands that were created by earthquakes and underwater volcanic eruptions over the millennia since the formation of the earth. They are generally divided into three major geographic areas, running from north to south: the Luzon, Visayas, and Mindanao groups of islands. Geographically, Taiwan is located just north of the Philippines; Vietnam, west of the Philippines, is separated from the archipelago by the South China Sea; Borneo and Indonesia are located south and southwest of the islands and are separated from the Philippines by the Celebes Sea; and the Philippine Sea borders the islands' east coast. In 1521, Ferdinand Magellan discovered the Philippine Islands and claimed them for Spain. In 1898 when Spain lost the Spanish-American War, the Philippines were ceded to the United States.

By July 1941, with the threat of the United States going to war with Japan, these islands were considered prime targets of the Japanese military. To defend the Philippines, the United States assigned Lieutenant General Douglas MacArthur to the task. He had one U.S. Army division (about 7,000 men) and 10 Philippine army divisions. The U.S. Army Forces Far East (USAFFE) was commanded by Major General Lewis Brereton. It had 107 modern P-40s and 35 long range B-17s, which were expected to play a major role in the defense of the islands. Admiral Thomas Hart was placed in command of the small Asiatic Fleet, consisting of his flagship heavy cruiser *Houston*, light cruiser *Marblehead*, 23 destroyers, 1 destroyer tender, 1 yacht, and a formidable force of 29 submarines. If war were to come to the Philippines, a major threat to the islands was a pre-emptive strike by Japanese aircraft. An operational radar intercept center at Nielson Field in Manila was established to warn U.S. forces against that possibility.[1]

Major General Jonathan Wainwright headed the North Luzon Force, defended the northern beaches, and protected the airfields in his sector. Major General George Parker commanded the South Luzon sector; Brigadier General William Sharp was assigned to defend the airfields in the Visayas and the B-17 bases at Del Monte, Mindanao; and Major General George Moore were charged with protecting Manila Bay in southeastern Luzon. As stated above, Major General Brereton was placed in overall command of the USAFFE.

Japan's strategy was to capture Luzon and then capture the remaining islands at a leisurely pace. Japan's military leaders accurately evaluated that the U.S. forces were the ones to be feared in the Philippines and not the Filipino army, which was ill-trained and ill-equipped to fight the Japanese. In view of this perceived weakness in the Filipino army, which made up 90 percent of the troops in the Philippines, Japan decided to relegate the less-experienced 16th Division in China and the 48th Division (which had never seen action) to the Philippine Campaign. At the same time, Japan decided to gain air superiority over the Philippines and then use the airfields to extend the radius of action of their aircraft. The Japanese Navy's land-based Zero fighters were assigned targets farther south from the Lingayen Gulf because of their greater range. The Army would support the initial landings in northern Luzon. No Japanese aircraft carriers were to be used in the Philippine operation. The initial air attacks would originate from Formosa and concentrate on Clark and Iba airfields on Luzon. The invasion was set for December 8, 1941 (Philippine date).[2]

At 0220 on December 8 (Philippine time and date), Admiral Hart and General MacArthur learned independently that Pearl Harbor had been attacked by Japanese aircraft. At 0300 at his Manila headquarters, Admiral Hart was notified that Pearl Harbor had been attacked, but he apparently did not pass the information on to General MacArthur. (There is some controversy over whether or not Admiral Hart notified MacArthur.) Brigadier General Richard Sutherland, General MacArthur's chief of staff, having learned about the attack on Pearl Harbor from reports on commercial radio, notified MacArthur in his Manila Hotel at 0340. At 0530, General Marshall sent a radiogram to MacArthur that war had broken out between Japan and the United States. In addition, Marshall instructed MacArthur to execute war plan *Rainbow Five*, which specifically stated that MacArthur should carry out air raids against Japanese bases. MacArthur also received a phone call from Major General Henry "Hap" Arnold, chief of the Army Air Force in Washington. He warned MacArthur not to have his aircraft caught on the ground as the planes were in Hawaii when the Japanese attacked.[3]

Japan's attack of the Philippine airfields from Formosa the morning of December 8 was delayed because of fog over the airfields, which prevented the pilots from taking off. As a result, the Japanese pilots feared that the element of surprise was lost. They also became concerned that U.S. aircraft would attack the airfields in Formosa while their planes were still on the ground. However, an American attack on Formosa never happened, and at 0845, when the fog lifted, the Japanese planes took off and headed south toward the Philippines.[4]

At 0500, General Brereton arrived at MacArthur's headquarters to request permission to attack Formosa. He was told by Sutherland that MacArthur was in conference and could not be disturbed; however, Southerland said he would try to obtain permission for the attack from MacArthur. At 0715, with time being of the essence, Bremerton returned to Sutherland's office to obtain an answer. Once again, he was rebuffed by Sutherland, who stated that as of yet there was no answer to his request for an attack. It was apparently MacArthur's belief that the war warning given on November 27, that the United States desired Japan to initiate the first overt act, was still in effect and that was the reason why MacArthur did not authorize Brereton to attack Formosa. The attack on Pearl Harbor, the bombing of Davao, a port in the Philippine Island of Mindanao, and the order to execute *Rainbow Five* apparently did not influence MacArthur's decision to withhold permission for the air raid. Had Brereton been allowed to attack Formosa at that time, U.S. aircraft would have caught Japan's planes on the ground due to the fog. MacArthur's failure to take the initiative against the Japanese resulted in the loss of his air force seven hours after the Pearl Harbor attack.[5]

At 0800, (Philippine time) Brigadier General Gerow in Marshall's office confirmed with MacArthur that he had received news of the Pearl Harbor attack. Fifteen minutes later, the radar control center at Nielson Airport in Manila, which was headquarters of USAFFE command, detected about 30 Japanese aircraft heading toward Clark Field. In Manila. U.S. fighters at Clark were immediately given orders to take off and fly north to intercept the incoming planes. Fighters at Nichols Field, also in Manila, were sent to cover Clark Field. B-17s were ordered to take off to avoid being caught on the ground. By 1130, not having encountered any Japanese aircraft, all the planes returned to their respective air bases to refuel and get ready for the next mission.[6]

At around 1100, for reasons that are still not clear, MacArthur finally gave Brereton the authority to bomb Formosa later that day. While the B-17s were being serviced and the fighters refueled, radar detected another large formation of Japanese planes over northern Luzon. Telephone and telegraph reports by Filipino observers confirmed the sighting. Warnings were sent to the fighter command at Clark Field, but for unknown reasons none were sent to the bomber command at Clark. Thus, no action whatsoever was taken regarding the 18 B-17s sitting on the ground at Clark. At 1230 (Philippine time) as U.S. fighters reached their takeoff positions, Japanese bombs began to fall on Clark. None of the incoming Japanese aircraft were intercepted by any U.S. plane. The airfields at Nichols, Iba, and Del Carmen were also targets of the Japanese bombers and fighters. On this day, December 8, the United States lost 53 P-40s, 18 B-17s (all on the ground), and 35 other aircraft in the Japanese air attacks. On December10, the Japanese aircraft returned and destroyed half of the remaining P-40s. The surviving 15 B-17s in the Philippines were transferred to Australia on December 17.

Thus, by December 17 all U.S. air power in the Philippine Islands ceased to exist. There was never any military or congressional investigation into why so many U.S. aircraft were lost on the ground ten hours after the Pearl Harbor attack, in spite of repeated warnings from Washington for MacArthur to make sure that no U.S. aircraft were caught on the ground. Why MacArthur escaped scrutiny, while the actions of General Short and Admiral Kimmel at Pearl Harbor were censored by Congress, has never been adequately explained.[7]

On December 10, the Japanese landed troops on the northern, northeastern and northwestern sector of the Luzon peninsula. Finding no significant resistance, the invasion forces then moved southwest toward Lingayen Gulf. MacArthur had only one division consisting of the North Luzon Force to oppose the Japanese invasion. On December 22, weather limited the number of Japanese troops that could land on the east coast of Lingayen Gulf. However, all the troops were able to land close enough to their initial objective. The Japanese Lingayen troops united with Japanese forces moving south from northern Luzon and drove U.S./Filipino forces to a position ten miles south of the Lingayen Gulf.[8]

On December 24, Japanese forces landed at Lamon Bay, a body of water on the east coast of the Luzon peninsula that connects with the Pacific Ocean. This pincher movement forced the United States to withdraw to the Bataan Peninsula to defend the Philippines. On Christmas day, Admiral Hart turned over the small Asiatic Fleet to Rear Admiral Francis Rockwell, commander of the Sixteenth Naval District in the Philippines, and left by submarine for Java to establish a new headquarters. MacArthur had hoped for U.S. reinforcements to assist in defense of the Philippines. Even though he had the support of General Marshall, the U.S. Navy was not supportive of his plan to reinforce the Philippines. However, it is more likely that senior civilian and military leaders in Washington did not send reinforcements because America was committed to a Europe-first policy and the Philippines, like Wake Island, were expendable.[9]

The retreat to Bataan was not easy, with the U.S./Filipino armies using delaying tactics as they moved their troops backward toward the Bataan Peninsula in Manila Bay. The withdrawal was completed by January 6, 1942.

Bataan was perfect for a defensive position with its three major mountain ranges, rudimentary in-roads, the lack of landing beaches, and the jungle which covered the entire peninsula. At this point, there were 80,000 U.S. and Filipino soldiers on Bataan and 26,000 civilians. The main defensive position stretched from Bagac on the west coast to Orion on the east coast. In January, repeated efforts by Lieutenant General Homma Masaharu, commander of Japanese forces in Luzon, were unsuccessful in dislodging the Americans from their defensive perimeter. Finally, on February 8, Homma withdrew his forces to the north where they would remain until April 3, 1942.[10]

During the lull in the fighting, many U.S. and Filipino soldiers were lost though disease and malnutrition. Reinforcements of food or military hardware were wanting, and morale faded as it became evident that the United States was not going to reinforce the Philippines. This became more evident when President Roosevelt on February 23 ordered MacArthur to move his headquarters to Australia.[11] On March 11, MacArthur, his wife, and son were taken from Corregidor to Mindanao by PT boat. There, B-17s met him and flew his family to Australia. Upon landing, MacArthur uttered the words, "I shall return."[12]

MacArthur left Major General Jonathan Wainwright in command of the troops on Bataan, who, by this time, were decimated by malnutrition and disease. On April 3, General Homma's refreshed troops attacked the left flank of U.S. defense perimeter, which resulted in the collapse of the U.S. position. The situation for U.S. and Filipino forces rapidly deteriorated. On April 9, Major General Edward King, commander of U.S. forces on Luzon, against the orders of Generals MacArthur and Wainwright, surrendered 75,000 starving troops—65,000 Filipino and 10,000 American—to the Japanese. Two days later, close to 400 officers were executed either by the samurai sword or by bayonet thrusts. The remaining prisoners were then marched 61 miles to a railway that took them to Camp O'Donnell in the Philippines. This was the infamous "Bataan Death March." Along the way, prisoners were beheaded, stabbed to death by bayonets, raped, or beaten by gun butts for minor infractions, such as not being able to keep up with the march or for possession of a Japanese yen. Five to ten thousand Filipinos and about 650 Americans died during the march. After arriving in Camp O'Donnell, over 1,600 U.S. prisoners and 16,000 Filipinos died as a result of disease, malnutrition, and cruel treatment.[13]

The remaining U.S. troops had withdrawn to Corregidor, an island off the southeast corner of Bataan. As the days wore on, Japan's artillery shells compelled U.S. forces to move into the Malinta Tunnel, an underground bomb-proof bunker built by the Army Corps of Engineers which also served as a hospital. After holding out for a month against Japanese bombardment and with a severe shortage of food, U.S. forces in the Philippines surrendered to the Japanese on May 9, 1942. Thus, the Philippines, another U.S. territory considered expendable by U.S. high command, fell into Japanese hands.

Simultaneously with the attacks on Pearl Harbor, Wake, and the Philippines, the Japanese Army was moved down the Malaya Peninsula toward Singapore. Two days after the attack on Pearl Harbor, Japanese shore-based naval aircraft sank *HMS Prince of Wales* and *HMS Repulse*, mainstays of the British Far Eastern Fleet, in the waters east of Malaya. Thailand's occupation followed, and the Borneo oil fields were on their way to being captured by the Japanese occupation of Miri on December 16, 1941. Makin and Tarawa in the Gilbert Islands were seized on December 23, 1941, the same day that the Japanese Pearl Harbor attack force, minus aircraft carriers *Hiryu* and *Soryu*, were arriving at Hashirajima Bay, the initial staging location.

With the first phase of operations successfully underway, Japanese eyes turned toward the invasion of Rabaul and Kavieng in the Bismarck Archipelago, located just northeast of New Guinea. On January 5, 1942, carriers *Akagi, Kaga, Shokaku,* and *Zuikaku* moved out from the Inland Sea with their accompanying escorts and sailed toward the Bismarck Archipelago. The task force reached its destination on January 20, where aircraft from all four carriers attacked Rabaul. The next day, Kavieng was the target of planes from *Akagi* and *Kaga* while aircraft from *Zuikaku* and *Shokaku* attacked airfields on Lae and Salamaua on the east coast of New Guinea. The number of Japanese carrier aircraft involved in the assault on Rabaul was superfluous, as targets on the Archipelago and the neighboring seas were few. On January 21, Rabaul and Kavieng surrendered to the Japanese without any resistance.[14]

After the Bismarck Archipelago was conquered, Nagumo's carrier task force retired to Truk in the Carolina Islands, northeast of New Guinea. On February 1, the four-carrier task force was scheduled to attack the Celebes Islands, located southwest of the Philippine Islands in the Celebes Sea. The mission was aborted when the Nagumo force received word that the Marshall Islands were being attacked by U.S. naval aircraft. The carriers were immediately ordered to travel at high speed toward the Marshall Islands, even though the islands were over 1,200 miles away from Truk. On February 2, while en route, the Japanese task force picked up U.S. radio broadcasts that the Marshall and Gilbert islands had indeed been successfully attacked by U.S. carrier aircraft. With that information, Nagumo turned the task force around and headed back toward Truk.[15]

The Japanese reacted to the U.S. attack of the Gilbert and Marshall Islands by ordering the *Shokaku* and *Zuikaku* to detach from the four-carrier task force and patrol the waters east of Japan for possible U.S. carrier raids. This measure unwittingly but seriously weakened the integrity of the six-carrier unit, the most powerful task force in the Pacific Ocean. It had the ability to engage and destroy any enemy naval force in the Pacific, including the undamaged U.S. carrier force.

Japanese Combined Naval Headquarters now turned its attention to northern Australia, which posed a threat to Japan's invasion and occupation of the Dutch East

Indies. A plan for an amphibious landing at Port Darwin in northern Australia was rejected by Japan's Naval General Staff. The only option open to the Combined Fleet was air strikes on installations in the Port Darwin area. The mission was to be carried out by *Akagi* and *Kaga* (Carrier Division I) and *Hiryu* and *Soryu* (Carrier Division 2). The latter carriers were ordered by Admiral Nagumo to join *Akagi* and *Kaga* in the Palau Islands east of the Philippine Islands as *Shokaku* and *Zuikaku* (Carrier Division 5) broke away from Carrier Division 1 and headed for home.[16]

Soryu and *Hiryu* had returned home from Wake Island where they received orders to support amphibious operations in the Banda Sea area north of Timor, an island located between the Indian Ocean and the South China Sea. On January 24–25, Carrier Division 2 carried out pre-invasion strikes on the Ambon Islands northeast of Timor. *Hiryu* and *Soryu* then departed for a key Japanese naval base at Kendari, a small town in the southeast Celebes. On February 4, the American-British-Dutch-Australia (ABDA) fleet commanded by Dutch Rear Admiral Karel Doorman was proceeding to intercept the Japanese invasion convoy headed for Surabaya on the northern coast of Java. This city was the main naval base for the Dutch in the Far East. Planes from *Soryu* and *Hiryu* joined land-based medium bombers from Kendari in an attack on the ABDA fleet (four cruisers and seven destroyers) in the Java Sea, just south of Kangean Island. The ABDA fleet was forced to retreat after a Japanese air attack severely damaged two U.S. cruisers, *Houston* and *Marblehead*.[17]

On February 15—the day on which Singapore fell into Japanese hands—battleships *Hiei* and *Kirishima*, heavy cruisers *Tone* and *Chikuma*, light cruiser *Abukuma*, and nine destroyers left from Palau and headed for Port Darwin. This formidable force met little resistance and found only 20 planes grounded on the airfield. A strike force of 188 aircraft attacked the airfield, a few waterfront buildings, and the only existing pier with relative ease. In the end, 11 Australian ships were sunk in the harbor, all 20 planes on the ground were destroyed, and all base installations were effectively disabled[18] After the attack on Port Darwin, Nagumo's task force retired to the Staring Bay on the southeast coast of the Celebes, but their stay was short-lived as the Japanese army's invasion of Java was to begin on March 1. Nagumo's task force, strengthened by Admiral Kondo Nobutake's Southern Force, which included four battleships, was to sortie to the south of Java to cut off any allied ships that tried to escape or reinforce Java. Kondo was commander of Japan's Second Fleet in Southeast Asia.

The carrier task force left Staring Bay on February 25 and moved through the Ombai Strait to the Indian Ocean. On March 3, 180 planes were launched from all four carriers in an attack against the south Javanese port of Tjilatjap, where about 20 allied ships were sunk. On March 5, Japanese aircraft sank three allied destroyers and 14 transports. The raid was successful and on March 9 Java surrendered. The invasion of Java ended the southern operations mission for Japan, and the Nagumo task force was subsequently ordered back to Staring Bay to await further orders.[19]

The Japanese army had been successful in taking the island of Sumatra, located in western Indonesia just north of Java. In the latter part of March, the Andaman Islands in the Bay of Bengal also fell into Japanese hands. In addition, Japan had succeeded in taking Rangoon in Burma. In view of these successes, Japan needed to protect its newly won acquisitions from the British navy. The British naval force in the Far East was formidable and included two carriers, two battleships, three heavy cruisers, and four to seven light cruisers. In addition, Britain possessed about 300 shore-based planes.

Admiral Kondo assigned this mission to Admiral Nagumo's task force including Carrier Division 5 (*Zuikaku* and *Shokaku*), which had previously been ordered to patrol the waters east of Japan, and Admiral Kondo's battleships. Sailing from Staring Bay on March 26, the ships (minus *Kaga*, which had been sent home for repairs) sailed into the Indian Ocean and assaulted Colombo, Ceylon, with a surprise air attack on April 5.

The first wave of planes took off 30 minutes before dawn, about 200 miles south of Ceylon. This force consisted of 36 fighters, 54 dive bombers, and 90 level bombers for a total of 180 aircraft. A British flying boat spotted the task force the day before and most likely radioed the information back to its base before it was sent crashing into the sea by Japanese aircraft.

As the Japanese planes neared their target, 12 British torpedo bombers were spotted. The British Swordfish torpedo bombers, flying at a lower altitude, did not see the vast armada of aircraft flying above them. The British aircraft were unaccompanied by any fighter escort. The Japanese fighters dove down and attacked the unsuspecting torpedo bombers from above, destroying every one of them. Since it was now obvious that forces on Colombo had spotted the Japanese task force, it was decided that the first wave would fly north of Colombo and then south to attack the city. The Japanese found the city devoid of any fighters in the air or on the big airfield southeast of Colombo. It appeared that available planes had flown south to engage the oncoming Japanese task force.[20]

There were not any British warships in the harbor, but there were many cargo ships which were subsequently attacked by Japanese dive bombers, resulting in great damage to the cargo vessels. The fighters then moved on to strafe the airfield. With their mission accomplished, a radio message was about to be sent back to Nagumo that a second wave would not be necessary. Just then, a radio message from a Japanese float plane reported that two enemy cruisers were heading south toward Nagumo's force. With this information, the carrier aircraft accelerated their return to protect the fleet from the oncoming cruisers. Twenty British Hurricane fighters then appeared, approaching the returning first wave of Japanese aircraft from the south. The Japanese fighters separated from the first wave of planes to intercept the Hurricanes, as the remainder of the aircraft headed back to the carriers.

When the planes returned, it was discovered that the British cruisers were actually trying to flee the Japanese task force. The second wave of 80 Japanese aircraft, already on its way, caught up to the cruisers. *Dorsetshire* and *Cornwall* were overmatched in a very short time, and both cruisers were sent to the bottom of the ocean. After recovering the second wave, Nagumo's force retired south beyond the range of Ceylon-based air patrols.[21]

On April 9, the Japanese task force headed north to assault the important British naval base at Trincomalee, on the east coast of Ceylon. As in the raid against Colombo, the first wave consisting of 180 planes was launched in the pre-dawn darkness. However, before the Japanese planes reached their target, they were intercepted by British Hurricane fighters, apparently as a result of detection by British radar. Japanese Zeros quickly removed the British fighters from the sky as the remainder of the first wave headed toward its target. In spite of heavy antiaircraft fire over the target, the mission was highly successful. The Japanese planes destroyed a number of carrier-type aircraft on the ground, as well as damaging airfield installations and naval base facilities. Upon completion of their mission, the first wave of planes headed back to their carriers.[22]

On their way back to the carriers, there was a replay of what occurred on their Colombo strike. That is, a Japanese patrol plane had discovered two enemy ships heading south. This time one of the ships was an aircraft carrier and the other a destroyer. Upon hearing this news, the first wave of aircraft increased their speed as they headed back to its carriers. Fortunately, the second wave had not yet taken off for Trincomalee and thus was given orders to take off and attack the two British ships heading their way.

Upon landing on the carriers, the first wave of planes was refueled and rearmed, with the level bombers rearmed with torpedoes. The combat air patrol continued to fly over the carriers to protect them against any enemy planes that might appear. Just as the *Akagi* ordered its men to take anti-aircraft action, six bomb explosions occurred off the ship's bow, four explosions to starboard and two to port. Six British Wellington bombers had caught the combat air patrol by surprise. After the British planes made their run on the *Akagi*, they were all shot down by Japanese Zeros.[23]

By this time, Japanese dive bombers from the second wave reached the British carrier *Hermes*. In 15 minutes, both the carrier and the lone destroyer were sent to the bottom of the sea by Japanese dive bombers. No planes were seen on the carrier, and it became apparent that those aircraft had been sent to the airfield on Trincomalee, where they had been destroyed by Japanese planes earlier. This action closed the Indian Ocean chapter and the first phase of Japan's southern operations. Nagumo now headed eastward toward the Strait of Malacca and onward to Japan. On their way home, *Zuikaku* and *Shokaku* were detached and ordered to Truk Atoll, located northwest of the Marshall Islands, to participate in the battle of the Coral Sea which would take place in early May.[24]

The Nagumo force had covered almost 50,000 miles of ocean, ranging from Hawaii to the shores of India from December 7 to mid–April 1942. During this time, Japan had multiple victories extending east to Hawaii, west to Burma, north to Manchuria, and south to New Guinea. In reviewing the southern operations, it is apparent that the Nagumo's full naval forces were not necessary for the success of these operations. The assigned naval forces without the carriers would have been more than adequate to provide the necessary naval power to ensure the operation's success. What is more important is that Japan lost sight of the fact that the remaining U.S. carrier force, with its accompanying heavy cruisers, was the main threat to Japan's naval success in the Pacific. Japan's Naval General Staff and the Combined Fleet should have ordered all six carriers of the Nagumo force, accompanied by seven battleships and numerous heavy cruisers, to seek out and destroy the remaining U.S. naval carrier fleet in the Pacific. Instead, the battleships were moored in Hashirajima Bay, and the Nagumo force turned its attention unnecessarily to the success of the southern operations. It was the inability of Japan's Naval High Command to recognize that, in spite of its success at Pearl Harbor and its accomplishments against allied warships in the southern operations, the carrier was now the new potent weapon of success at sea, and the battleship was now obsolete. The United States was quick to learn the new role of the carrier in naval warfare because all its battleships were destroyed

9. Southern and Central Pacific Operations 143

or damaged at Pearl Harbor. Even if the Pearl Harbor attack had not been successful, the battleships were too old to keep up with the speed of the carrier and heavy cruisers. Thus, Japan failed to seize the moment to exploit the opportunity to destroy the remaining U.S. forces in the Pacific. The outcome in a confrontation with the U.S. carrier fleet would have favored Japan, with Nagumo's forces having six carriers with a protective cover of seven battleships and heavy cruisers, and the United States having three carriers accompanied by heavy cruisers but without a protective battleship antiaircraft shield. In addition, Nagumo would not have been confronted with having two objectives at the same time—assaulting Midway and the destruction of the remaining U.S. carrier force. The end result would most likely have been the loss of all three U.S. carriers in the conflict. That outcome would have seriously altered the outcome of the war in the Pacific.

After Japan attacked Pearl Harbor, the Kido Butai was able to successfully avoid detection by U.S. naval forces by retiring to the northwest. The American task forces were looking in the wrong direction for the Japanese fleet. On the evening of December 7, Admiral Halsey's Task Force 8 (*Enterprise*, CV-6) was searching for the Japanese carriers southwest of Oahu. Rear Admiral John Newton's Task Force 12 (*Lexington*) was returning from Midway and was alerted to look for the retiring Nagumo force. *Saratoga* was searching the sectors southwest of Oahu. This area should have been on the route that a Japanese task force would have taken after departing from Pearl Harbor and heading to the Marshall Islands. In reality, Admiral Nagumo's force was northwest of Hawaii, taking the northern route home.

Enterprise task force returned to Pearl Harbor to refuel on December 8 after finding no evidence of the Japanese fleet. The carrier then departed at 0420 on December 9 for waters north of Oahu. The *Enterprise* task force ran into Japanese submarines aiming torpedoes at the U.S. vessels, and destroyers dropping depth charges. The results were insignificant, as no ship or submarine was hit.[25]

On December 8, Vice Admiral Brown replaced Rear Admiral Newton as commander of Task Force 12. The fleet now raced toward Johnston Island in anticipation of encountering the enemy. Instead, the chase turned out to be a false alarm. From December 8 to December 13, Task Force 12 operated south and west of Oahu. The oiler *Neosho* was sent to fuel Brown's ships in order to maintain the fleet at sea. But rough waves prevented the refueling, necessitating the task force's return to Pearl Harbor for refueling.[26]

Saratoga (CV-3) had just finished a routine refit at the Puget Sound Navy Yard and had departed for San Diego. When the carrier arrived on the morning of December 7, news was received that Pearl Harbor had just been attacked. *Saratoga* immediately prepared for wartime operations and the next morning got under way for Pearl Harbor. Rear Admiral Aubrey Wray Fitch was assigned as commander of the newly formed task force (Task Group 16.2) and used *Saratoga* as his flagship. He learned from Admiral Kimmel that his carrier would be joined by Task Group 16.1, an escort group consisting of heavy cruiser *Minneapolis* and four destroyers, which had left Pearl Harbor on December 10. Together, the ships would meet up at Pearl Harbor on December 14.[27]

The mission of the three U.S. carriers in the relief of Wake Island from December 14 to December 23 has been discussed in Chapter 8. As December 1941 came to a close, all three carrier task forces, which included *Enterprise, Lexington,* and

Saratoga, operated west of the Hawaiian Islands. *Enterprise* (Task Force 8) was assigned to cover Midway until the seaplane tender *Wright* arrived. *Lexington* (Task Force 11) and *Saratoga* (Task Force 16.2) were delayed by rough seas in returning from their positions in relief of Wake Island. On December 30, Admiral Chester W. Nimitz took command as Commander-in-Chief Pacific Fleet (CINCPAC). On December 29, *Saratoga* (Task Force 16.2) docked in Pearl Harbor, with *Enterprise* returning to Oahu on December 31, and *Lexington* returning three days later.[28]

Saratoga departed from Pearl Harbor on January 2 to safeguard the Midway area. The policy implemented by Admiral Pye of having only one U.S. carrier in port at one time in Pearl Harbor was continued by Admiral Nimitz with *Enterprise* arriving after *Saratoga* had left.

On January 3, *Enterprise* sailed out of Pearl Harbor to cover an important convoy coming in from the West Coast of the United States, as well as carrying out gunnery exercises along the way. On January 7, *Lexington* departed Pearl Harbor and sailed southwest toward Johnston Island to carry out surveillance operations against Japanese submarines. A number of visual contacts were made between U.S. aircraft and enemy submarines, but no confirmed damage was reported.[29]

On January 11 *Saratoga* was heading southeast 270 miles from Johnston Island toward a rendezvous with *Enterprise*. At 1915, a Japanese torpedo from submarine I-6 slammed into the carrier. A list to port was quickly corrected by damage control. Although severely damaged, *Saratoga* was able make 16 knots as it headed back to Pearl Harbor. The carrier was without power for a short time due to water contamination in the oil tanks. On January 13, *Saratoga* limped into port. The question now was whether the ship could be repaired in Pearl Harbor. On January 17, the decision was made to send the carrier back to the West Coast for repairs. *Saratoga's* fighter squadron, which flew off the carrier prior to its entry into Pearl Harbor, landed at Ewa Marine Corps Air Station, where it remained.[30]

On January 16, *Lexington* returned to Pearl Harbor to prepare for raids on the Marshall Islands and offer naval support for reinforcement of Samoa. Admiral Nimitz's first priority was to honor the prior commitment made in January 1942 by CINCPAC to reinforce the U.S. garrison in Samoa, in the central South Pacific half-way between Hawaii and New Zealand. CNO Admiral Stark had directed the Second Marine Brigade to depart from San Diego in January. *Yorktown* (CV-5), stationed in Norfolk, Virginia, would escort the convoy carrying the Marines to Samoa.[31]

Yorktown was commissioned in 1937 as the Navy's first modern U.S. carrier. The carrier had been on loan to Admiral Earnest J. King's Atlantic Fleet. The flat-top had previously served in the Pacific as Admiral Halsey's flagship. In April 1941, *Yorktown* was transferred to the Atlantic to assist Britain in its battle against the German navy in the North Atlantic. When *Yorktown* arrived in Norfolk, it prepared for extended operations in the Atlantic. The fighter squadron (VF-5) aboard *Yorktown* still had bi-winged aircraft; these planes were scheduled to be replaced by the single-wing F4F-3. When the air group commander left for what was to be temporary shore duty, the fighter squadron (VF-42) from USS *Ranger* was called upon to temporarily replace the aircraft on *Yorktown*. These aircraft were composed of the new F4F-3 just released by the Grumman factory on Long Island. Fighting Group Five never returned, and VF-42 accompanied *Yorktown* on all its subsequent missions in the Atlantic and the Pacific until June 7, 1942, when the carrier was sunk northeast of Midway.[32]

On June 28, 1941, *Yorktown* left Norfolk for the first of its four scheduled Neutrality Patrols in the North Atlantic. The first two Neutrality Patrols were without incident, but on the third cruise in September, the carrier ran into heavy fog and rain off the coast of Newfoundland, and the mission proved to be unproductive. In its fourth and final cruise, the flattop escorted convoys within 700 miles of Brest, France. On December 2, *Yorktown* pulled back into port in Norfolk for vital maintenance.

On December 7, 1941, the carrier was in port in Norfolk while its aircraft were parked at NAS Norfolk's East Field. Upon hearing of the bombing of Pearl Harbor, the men assigned to the aircraft scrambled to return to the carrier. When the planes arrived at the airfield near the carrier, they were moved to the ship's dock and hoisted aboard the ship. *Yorktown*, however, was not ready to leave, as the repairs to the underwater portion of her hull were still not complete. Cooler heads prevailed as the high command rescinded the order for the carrier to immediately get underway. The planes returned to East Field to make final preparations to become combat ready. Self-sealing gas tanks and fitted pilot seat armor were placed in each fighter.[33]

On December 16, *Yorktown* and her escorts departed Norfolk and sailed for the Panama Canal. On December 22, the carrier passed through the canal with VF-42 providing combat air control and headed northwest into the Pacific Ocean. Eight days later, as *Yorktown* neared the California coast, the air group took off and landed at NAS San Diego. Hours later, *Yorktown* arrived secure in San Diego harbor. The Samoa convoy ships were also in the harbor: three ocean liners acting as transport ships and a fleet oiler. On January 1, 1942, Rear Admiral Fletcher and his staff boarded *Yorktown*. They had flown in from Pearl Harbor to form the new Task Force 17 with *Yorktown* as its flagship. The carrier would carry 101 aircraft for the upcoming Samoan operation.[34]

On January 6, *Yorktown*, heavy cruiser *Louisville*, light cruiser *Saint Louis*, four destroyers, a fleet oiler, and the convoy's four ships departed from San Diego and headed for the South Pacific. On January 11, Halsey's Task Force 8 with three heavy cruisers and seven destroyers set sail from Pearl Harbor to join Fletcher in escorting the convoy to Samoa. Task Force 8 then would unite with Task Force 17 and take offensive action against Japanese bases in the Marshall and Gilbert islands in the first week in February. The convoy's voyage to Samoa was completed without incident. Now the carriers counted time to prepare for their offensive missions in February.[35]

On January 19, Brown's Task Force 11, made up of *Lexington* with three heavy cruisers and nine destroyers, sailed from Pearl Harbor to patrol the seas northeast of Christmas Island in the central Pacific Ocean. The next day, Brown was ordered by Nimitz to prepare for an air strike on Wake Island. The oiler *Neches* was assigned to Task Force 11 for the mission. Brown was to refuel on January 27 from the oiler and then raid Wake Island. He sent the destroyer *Jarvis* to escort the oiler. On January 23, however, before *Jarvis* could reach the oiler, Japanese submarine I-72 torpedoed and sank *Neches*. Nimitz therefore recalled Task Force 11 to Pearl Harbor, and an opportunity was lost to exact revenge against the Japanese for their capture of Wake Island.[36]

Nimitz wanted Task Force 11 to join Task Forces 8 and 17 in the United States' first offensive counterstrikes on Japanese island bases. He made this decision after learning from U.S. naval intelligence in Washington that the Japanese carrier striking force was located deep in the southwest Pacific.[37] The ability for U.S. intelligence to decipher the Japanese naval code just six weeks after the attack on Pearl Harbor is another example that U.S. intelligence had the ability to read the Japanese naval code prior to the attack.

On February 1, *Enterprise* and *Yorktown* were closing in on the Gilbert and Marshall islands, which Japan had received as a bonus for siding with the allies in World War I. Nimitz felt that Japan had weakened its military position in the Marshall Islands to support its operations in the southwest Pacific. He felt this would be the ideal time to deliver the mandated islands a crushing blow which would divert Japan's attention from Australia. Halsey would make his run from an easterly direction against Kwajalein in the northern Marshalls and attack Wotje and Maloelap in the northern Gilberts. Fletcher was assigned Jaluit in the central Marshalls and Mili and Makin in the Gilberts. *Yorktown* would approach Jaluit also from the east but south of Halsey.[38]

The air defense of the Marshall and Gilbert islands was provided by Rear Admiral Goto Fiji's 24th Air Flotilla, which consisted of 33 carrier fighters, 9 land-attack planes, and 9 flying boats. The mainstay fighter protection was located on Roi in the Kwajalein Atoll, where there were 18 carrier fighters available, and on Taroa in the Maloelap Atoll, where 15 carrier fighters were stationed.[39]

U.S. intelligence had identified the most potent Japanese air base on the Kwajalein Atoll. As a result, *Enterprise's* dive bombers were assigned to attack the Kwajalein air base, while 9 torpedo planes armed with bombs sought out any ships in the atoll's lagoon. The important bases at Wotje and Taroa in the Gilberts were left to the carrier's fighters since no other aircraft were available to do the mission. The cruisers and destroyers in Task Force 8 (*Enterprise*) would then bombard the two atolls' air bases. Six fighters under Lieutenant Commander Wade McClusky took off from *Enterprise* and headed for Wotje, only 36 miles away. Six additional fighters under Lieutenant Jim Gray were assigned to attack the air base on Taroa on the Maloelap Atoll. This base was considered to have few, if any aircraft, although definitive intelligence was lacking. The heavy cruiser *Chester* and two destroyers would follow up the air strikes by also bombarding the base. At 0445 on February 1, 12 Combat Air Patrol (CAP) fighters, followed by 37 dive-bombers and the 9 bomb-armed torpedo planes, lifted off *Enterprise* and headed out on their mission. One hour later, 12 fighters assigned to Wotje and Taroa lifted off *Enterprise*, so that by 0620 the first wave of 58 aircraft were on their way to achieve the United States' first counter-offensive action in the war in the Pacific.[40]

At 0700, McClusky and his five accompanying fighters bombed and strafed Wotje's airfield and buildings. No planes, however, were seen in the air or on the ground. Soon the heavy cruisers and two destroyers arrived on the scene to bombard the air base. With one of his fighters lost to an accident, Gray's remaining five fighters came upon Taroa. To Gray's surprise it was not a small sleepy seaplane base but a complex, well-equipped airfield resembling Ford Island. In actuality, Taroa was one of the main enemy bases in the Mandates. Gray found numerous aircraft including twin-engine bombers parked on the runway. He dropped his bomb on the runway and continued to strafe the island.[41]

The Japanese had already sent up its CAP to cover the atoll. Two Japanese fighters spotted a heavy cruiser heading their way, but their attack on *Chester* was ineffective. Lieutenant Wilmer Rawie, following Gray's lead, attacked the airstrip but then ran into the two fighters that had attacked *Chester*. The first Japanese plane, flown by Lieutenant Kurakane Yoshio, was promptly shot down by Rawie. Rawie's plane then dove on Atake Tomita, Kurakane's wing-man. In a head-on run, the result was a mid-air collision. Atake's plane was forced to land, but Rawie's aircraft, though damaged, was still flyable. When Rawie discovered that all four guns on his plane were inoperable, he headed back to *Enterprise*.

Gray, having completed his mission, left the area at 0720, just as *Chester* began to pound the atoll. The bombardment was ineffective, as Japanese planes were seen taking off from the Taroa airfield. This observation caused *Chester* to vacate the area. In the process, the cruiser was superficially hit by a bomb from a Japanese fighter.[42]

At 0705, *Enterprise*'s dive bombers reached the twin island of Roi-Namur, just north of Kwajalein Island. The anti-aircraft guns on Roi were prepared to open fire as Japanese fighters readied to take off from the airfield. Two SBDs were lost in a melee with airborne Japanese fighters. The dive bombers caused some damage to the airfield and nearby buildings.

VT-6, the *Enterprise* torpedo bomber squadron, arrived over the lagoon armed with torpedoes because Japanese carriers were erroneously reported in the area. The unopposed torpedo bombers damaged one light cruiser, one submarine, and seven other ships.[43]

At 0905, the aircraft from the Kwajalein strike returned. Halsey was determined to make two more strikes against the Taroa air base stronghold. Lieutenant Richard Best, *Enterprise*'s dive bomber squadron (CV-6) executive officer, led nine SBDs on the third mission. The SBD pilots destroyed two Japanese fighters in the process of attacking the Taroa atoll. After the melee, the U.S. planes returned to *Enterprise*.

The island of Wotje was next in line for attack from *Enterprise* aircraft. This target was easier because it lacked enemy fighter support. Eight SBDs and nine torpedo planes armed with bombs severely damaged the island's installations and ships in the harbor. No U.S. aircraft was lost on the mission.[44]

The 24th Air Flotilla was slow to respond but at 1330, five land attack bombers spotted *Enterprise* northeast of Wotje. The Japanese bombers made a glide-bombing run on *Enterprise*, releasing all their bombs. However, *Enterprise* eluded all the bombs dropped including a near miss. Lieutenant Nakai Kazuo, who led the Japanese twin engine bombers in the attack on *Enterprise*, suddenly discovered that both engines on his plane were on fire, so he headed straight for the carrier. His right wing tip scratched the port edge of the flight deck, tumbling the aircraft into the sea. Other attempts by Japanese aircraft to damage *Enterprise* were unsuccessful. At 2000, Halsey turned Task Force 8 away from the Gilbert and Marshall islands and back toward Pearl Harbor.[45]

To the south, *Yorktown*, along with heavy cruiser *Louisville* and light cruiser *Saint Louis*, forged ahead toward Jaluit, Mili, and Makin. Turbulent weather prohibited any aircraft from attacking Jaluit. Mili was empty of any military targets. On Makin, two Japanese flying boats and an auxiliary vessel were discovered and destroyed. Fletcher had hoped to launch another attempt at Jaluit in the afternoon, but the weather worsened considerably, preventing the mission. That evening, Halsey ordered Fletcher to withdraw from the area and return to Pearl Harbor.[46]

On January 22, *Lexington* returned from its attempted relief of Wake Island to Pearl Harbor, with Fighting Three (recently replenished with the new F4F-3s) replacing Fighting Two on the carrier. U.S. naval policy permitted squadrons from one U.S. carrier to be transferred to another carrier. Japanese carrier policy did not allow for this flexibility.

On January 31, Brown's Task Force 11, which consisted of *Lexington,* heavy cruisers *Minneapolis* and *Indianapolis,* seven destroyers, and *Neosho,* was assigned to meet and assist Halsey's Task Force 8, thought to be low on fuel after its raid on the Marshall Islands. This assumption turned out to be incorrect (this fact is supported by the data on fuel consumption by carriers and cruisers cited in the previous chapter), and thus Brown's task force was ordered to escort a convoy on its way toward Canton Island, halfway between Hawaii and the Fiji Islands.[47]

On February 6, Task Force 11 was ordered into the South Pacific to cooperate with the recently created ANZAC (America, New Zealand, and Australia Command) naval forces command under the U.S. Navy's Vice Admiral Herbert Leary in order to thwart Japanese plans to disrupt the line of communication between Pearl Harbor and Australia. Brown's plan was to attack Rabaul, Japan's naval stronghold on New Britain.[48]

On February 9, *Saratoga* departed from Pearl Harbor and headed toward Bremerton naval base in Washington state for repairs. The carrier would remain there to repair damage inflicted on her by a Japanese torpedo on January 11, 1942. The Saratoga would remain under repair for about five months and miss both the battles of Coral Sea and Midway.

On February 14, Brown and task force 11 had to leave the ANZAC Squadron commanded by the Royal Navy's Rear Admiral John G. Crace. The squadron consisted of heavy cruiser *Chicago,* two light cruisers, and two destroyers. Brown was not able to spare any Task Force 11 fuel for Crace's ships. U.S. intelligence from CINCPAC advised Brown that the Japanese carriers were operating near the Dutch East Indies. On February 17, Brown's task force was reinforced with heavy cruiser *Pensacola* and two destroyers, *Clark* and *Bagley*.[49]

The Bismarck region was defended by the Japanese South Seas Force, which had attacked and captured Wake Island. The area's air defense was provided by the 24th Air Flotilla, which also operated out of Truk Island, north of New Guinea, and the Marshall Islands.

At 1030 on February 20, as *Lexington* steamed north of the Solomon Islands preparing to turn southwest toward Rabaul, the carrier was detected by a Japanese Kawanishi flying boat. The plane radioed back to Rabaul its discovery of Task Force 11. At 1112, fighters from *Lexington*'s combat air patrol dove down on the flying boat with their guns blazing, sending the plane careening into the sea. A second Japanese flying boat arrived on the scene and also was promptly shot down. Task Force 11 was now 460 miles from Rabaul.[50]

With the Japanese sighting of the American task force, Brown called off the air raid on Rabaul. Instead, he decided to turn the fleet southwest as if he were going to continue his assault on the Japanese naval bastion, in the hope that this maneuver might deter the Japanese from attacking the Dutch East Indies. Brown knew the task force would come within range of Japanese bombers and readied the CAP for their arrival.

9. Southern and Central Pacific Operations 149

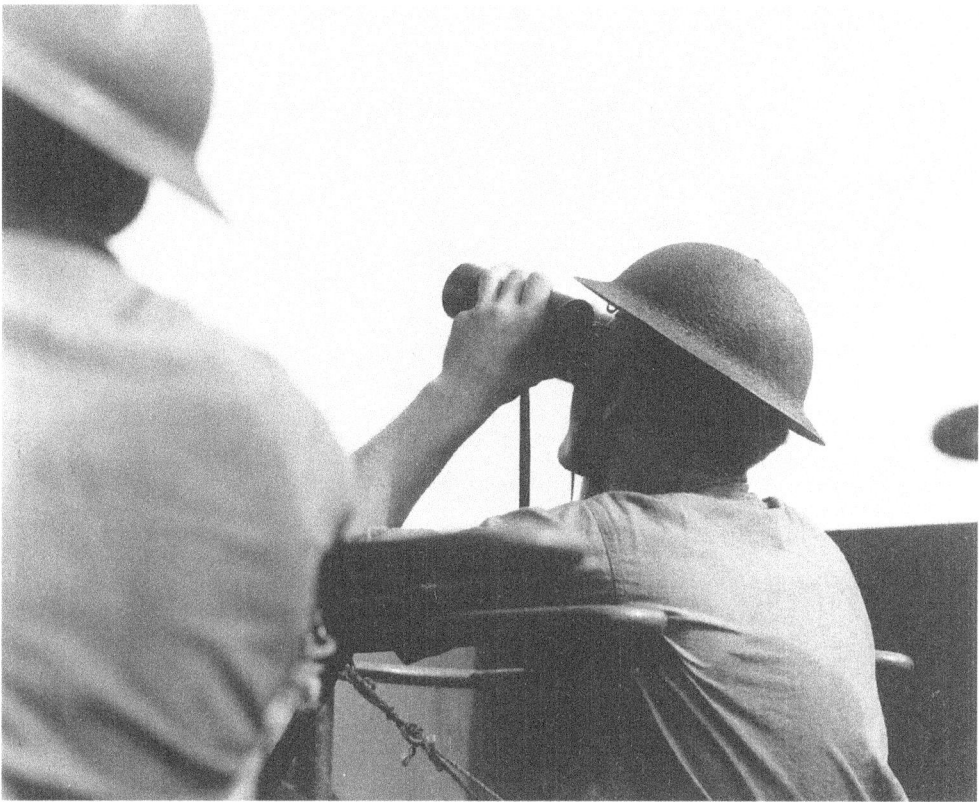

A view taken from the *Enterprise* showing a lookout peering through his binoculars for signs of Japanese air activity during a Wake Island raid on February 24, 1942 (Naval History and Heritage Command).

Nine G4M1 Betty twin engine bombers arrived on the scene at 1635. Five of the bombers were shot down before they reached *Lexington*. The other four bombers reached the carrier and released their bombs, but none came closer than 3,000 yards. The surviving Japanese aircraft then returned to their base on Rabaul.[51]

At 1700, eight more Betty's spotted the U.S. carrier task force. Lieutenant Commander Edward "Butch" O'Hare and his wingman were assigned to intercept the incoming bombers. O'Hare's wingman's guns jammed, leaving O'Hare alone to attack the incoming Japanese bombers. O'Hare dove in on the planes, shooting down three Betty's and damaging two. The surviving two damaged aircraft and three undamaged planes continued toward *Lexington*. As they neared the carrier, Ensign Edward R. Sellstrom from combat air patrol attacked one bomber, causing it to ditch. Another Betty was lost trying to crash dive into *Lexington*. Of the three remaining Japanese bombers, one came close to hitting *Lexington*, dropping its bomb within 100 feet of the carrier. With the release of its bombs, the three Japanese bombers then returned to Rabaul, landing safely at 1950.[52]

On February 5, *Enterprise* returned to Pearl Harbor from its raid on the Marshall Islands. The carrier subsequently underwent maintenance repair in dry dock. On February 14, with its maintenance completed, *Enterprise* and Task Force 16 headed out of Pearl Harbor. Accompanying the carrier were two heavy cruisers including

A Douglas TBD-1 torpedo plane from the *Enterprise* (CV-6) flies over Wake Island during a U.S. raid. The view appears to be from the west-northwest, with Wilkes Island in the center and Peale Island on the right (Naval History and Heritage Command).

Northampton and seven destroyers. The task force's mission was to attack Wake Island in the central Pacific. This would be the first attack on that atoll since it fell into Japanese hands on December 23, 1941.[53]

The weather worsened as Task Force 16 closed in on Wake. On February 23, the heavy cruisers departed from Task Force 16 to head northwest of the atoll. Halsey felt that bombardment by the cruisers would surprise the Japanese garrison on the atoll. At 0647 the next day, 37 bombers, 9 torpedo bombers armed with bomb ordinance, and six fighters were launched from *Enterprise*, 120 miles north of Wake and thirty minutes behind schedule. When the aircraft reached Wake, they found no Japanese planes on the air strip or in the air. Two Japanese Kawanishi Type 97 flying boats were spotted in the lagoon and quickly sunk. The harbor was free of any major ships, so the planes attacked buildings and installations. Between 0948 and 1014, the planes returned to the carrier.[54]

When the heavy cruisers and destroyers reached Wake at 0707, they were attacked by three Japanese Type 95 float planes. Air support for the cruisers was nowhere to be found because of the delay in *Enterprise*'s launching its aircraft. At 0742, after the float planes were successfully evaded, the heavy cruisers began to pound Peale Island but were not able to destroy its gun batteries. With its mission unsuccessful, the heavy cruisers and their escorting destroyers headed northeast to

9. Southern and Central Pacific Operations

A Dauntless SBD-3 of VB-6 preparing to take off from the *Enterprise* on a Wake Island raid, February 24, 1942 (Naval History and Heritage Command).

rejoin Task Force 16. The attack on Wake Island was largely ineffective, but it did serve to point out the weaknesses in U.S. planning and coordination.[55]

On February 25, Admiral Nimitz ordered Halsey to attack Marcus Island, which was northwest of Wake and just 1,000 miles from Japan. *Enterprise*, along with two heavy cruisers, made a high-speed run toward Marcus Island to a point 175 miles northeast of the island. Then, on March 4, *Enterprise* closed to 125 miles from Marcus to accommodate the short range of its dive bombers. The carrier launched a predawn air strike at 0446 consisting of 32 SBD dive bombers and six fighters. Disappointingly, no aircraft was found on Marcus Island, so the planes were relegated to strafing the runway. The mission again pointed out lessons to be learned in combat engagement and intelligence but did little damage to the enemy. The planes returned to the carrier, which then returned to Oahu. On its way, *Enterprise* ran into turbulent weather with high seas and winds and arrived in Pearl Harbor on the morning of March 10.[56]

On February 16, after Halsey had left Oahu to attack Wake, *Yorktown* left Pearl Harbor with cruisers *Astoria* and *Louisville*, six destroyers, and oiler *Guadalupe* and sailed to the Canton Island area in the Phoenix Islands, in the central Pacific east of the Gilbert Islands. There, Fletcher would be in position to support either Halsey or Brown in the southwest Pacific.[57]

On February 27, Fletcher was ordered to join Task Force 11, 300 miles north of New Caledonia, to execute a second attack on Rabaul. Since the first attack on Rabaul did not catch the Japanese by surprise, Brown recommended to Admiral King, now Commander-in-Chief, United States Fleet and Admiral Nimitz, Commander-in-Chief, Pacific Fleet, that a second attack should not be considered unless two carriers were involved. *Lexington* was already heading southwest toward the Coral Sea. When the two task forces united on March 6, Brown now had two carriers, eight heavy cruisers, and fourteen destroyers under his command. The plan was to attack Rabaul from the south on March 10.[58]

On the evening of March 7, a sighting from a Royal Australian Air Force patrol plane changed the plans to attack Rabaul. It discovered a large Japanese convoy, including one cruiser, several destroyers, and a numerous transports, off Buna on New Guinea's northeast coast. On March 8, confirmation of Japanese invasions of Lae and Salamaua up the coast from Buna were received by U.S. intelligence. Additional information was received from an Australian patrol plane that there were no ships in the Rabaul harbor. As a result, Brown broke radio silence on March 8—he had every reason to believe the Japanese had been alerted to his location—and broadcast a change in targets from Rabaul to the villages of Lae and Salamaua on New Guinea's coast. He was hoping to find Japanese ships in the adjacent waters unloading supplies and troops.[59]

In attacking the villages from the south, the carrier's aircraft would have to fly over the rugged Owen Stanley Mountains, with some peaks reaching 15,000 feet. The mountainous area was well known for its bad weather and poor visibility. However, reconnaissance aircraft determined that there was a pass in the mountain range at 7,500 feet and that usually the weather cleared in the morning from 0700 to 1100.[60]

The carriers launched their planes at 0800 on March 10, 45 miles offshore in the Gulf of Papua, just north of Port Moresby on the southeastern corner of New Guinea. *Lexington*'s aircraft would strike first, followed 20 minutes later by *Yorktown*'s planes. One hundred and four aircraft were sent, consisting of 18 fighters, 61 dive bombers, and 25 torpedo planes. Although most of *Lexington*'s planes made it easily over the 7,500 foot mountain pass, the carrier's torpedo bombers—laden with heavy torpedoes—barely made it. However, U.S. planes found no Japanese aircraft in the skies or on the runway at Salamaua or Lae. It was later determined that the Japanese did not plan to land fighter aircraft on the airstrip on Lae until a few days later.[61]

There were 16 Japanese vessels in the waters off these coastal villages. The 18 dive bombers from *Lexington* attacked three transports and a light cruiser, *Yubari*. The fighters from *Lexington* strafed the runway on Lae and eliminated the Japanese shore batteries. One float plane that the Japanese were able to get airborne was valiant in its efforts to avoid being shot down by U.S. fighters but eventually met its demise.[62]

Yorktown's planes had no trouble getting over the Owen Stanley Mountains. The 17 dive bombers of Bombing Five singled out *Yubari*, and at 1005 the 13 SBD dive bombers of Scouting Five continued the attacks on the Japanese transports. Contributing to the attack were 8 B-17E Flying Fortress heavy bombers from the 19th Bombardment Group flown up from their base at Townsville, Australia, on the northeastern coast. In the end, U.S. aircraft sank three transports, caused medium damage to the transport *Kokai Maru* and seaplane tender *Kiyokawa*, as well as minor damage to *Yubari*, minelayer *Tsugaru*, and destroyers *Asanagi* and *Yunagi*. One hundred and thirty Japanese were killed and 245 wounded.[63]

9. Southern and Central Pacific Operations

At 1050, *Lexington* and *Yorktown* began recovering their strike forces. At noon, both carriers were withdrawing from the New Guinea area. One of the Japanese flying boats spotted the task forces and radioed the information back to Rabaul. However, bad weather set in, preventing the 24th Air Flotilla from launching a counter-attack on Brown's forces, which was now free to leave the area. On March 11, the carriers headed southeast into the Coral Sea. Brown was instructed by Nimitz to return *Lexington* to Pearl Harbor and leave *Yorktown* in the south Pacific.

After refueling, *Yorktown* headed northwest for the New Hebrides Islands to guard the lines of communication between Australia and the United States. Fletcher had heavy cruisers *Astoria* and *Portland* and five destroyers patrolling the Coral Sea to confront any Japanese forces that might come out of their naval bastion in the Bismarck Islands. *Lexington* arrived in Pearl Harbor on the morning of March 26.[64]

The raid on the villages of Lae and Salamaua on March 10 are little remembered but were to have profound implications on the outcome of the Battle of Midway three months later. The raid inflicted the greatest number of losses on the Imperial Navy in the war thus far. This forced Vice Admiral Inouye Shigeyoshi, commander of Fourth Fleet/South Seas Forces, to postpone the invasions of Port Moresby and Tulagi for over a month. But more importantly, it caused him to request carrier support from the Combined Fleet for the invasion of Port Moresby. This action resulted in placing the assigned carriers, *Zuikaku* and *Shokaku*, in harm's way in the upcoming Battle of the Coral Sea. If these carriers were to lose their ability to participate in the Battle of Midway, the Kido Butai would have just four carriers to confront U.S. carrier forces at Midway.

This is exactly what happened. *Shokaku* was damaged in the Coral Sea battle. *Zuikaku* was left with a depleted complement of aircraft. Thus, the prelude to the Battle of Midway began with the Battle of the Coral Sea because of the profound effects that the latter battle had on the Japanese carrier force at Midway.

Analysis of the root causes of Japan's defeat at Midway and its consequences have been fully described in my book *Victory at Midway: The Battle That Changed the Course of World II* published in 2019.

Chapter 10

The Final Analysis of the Japanese Attack on Pearl Harbor

In the final analysis of the December 7 Japanese attack on Pearl Harbor, a rational case can be made that the U.S. government had foreknowledge of the attack. This deduction is based on the examination of the facts that follow, derived from archival and historical military and intelligence records. In other cases it is eyewitness testimony, with the last piece of potential evidence having been derived from captured German documents (yet to be authenticated).

The Vacant Sea Directive

During the time leading up to November 25, 1941, most ships sailing between Japan and the continental United States generally avoided the northern route in the Pacific because it was colder, foggier, and filled with heavy seas. We now know that the Japanese fleet had chosen the northern route to attack Pearl Harbor because it was the best way to reach Hawaii undetected. With this in mind, it is important to reconsider the Vacant Sea directive.

On November 25, 1941, a directive was issued by Captain Ingersoll, assistant to the Chief of Naval Operations. The directive was sent to Admiral Kimmel in Hawaii and to San Francisco's Twelfth Naval District. Known as the Vacant Sea directive, it directed both commercial and military ships crossing the Pacific to utilize the southern Pacific route through the Torres Strait, located in the South Pacific between Australia and New Guinea. rather than the northern route. Thus, the northern Pacific route would be clear of any sea traffic except Japanese naval vessels. There is evidence that the Vacant Sea directive was the result of information received by the U.S. government that a Japanese carrier force had departed northern Japan for Pearl Harbor on November 25, 1941 (to be discussed below), and the fact that on November 23 Admiral Kimmel had ordered his warships to search the area north of Hawaii. By coincidence, this location was very close to the area where the Japanese task force launched its attack on Pearl Harbor.[1]

Referring to the Vacant Sea directive, Rear Admiral Turner, Navy War Plans Director, admitted in 1941, "We were prepared to divert traffic when we believed that war was imminent. We sent the traffic down via Torres Strait, so that the track of the Japanese task force would be clear of any traffic." Pearl Harbor Part Transcript (PHPT) page 444, 1941.[2]

The Vacant Sea order was never brought up in any of the original Pearl Harbor hearings from 1941 to 1946, nor was it brought up by Kimmel at the 1995 hearing sponsored by Senator Strom Thurman and Congressman Floyd Spence. The reasons for its omission in the hearings remains unknown.[3]

The Bomb Plot Messages

On August 21, 1941, Morimura, the Japanese spy stationed in Oahu, having complete freedom to survey the ships anchored in Pearl Harbor, was able to complete a map showing the location of every ship. Morimura also determined the grid coordinates for the ships to assist the Japanese dive bombers and torpedo bombers in their attack. He sent the intelligence to Ambassador Nomura in Washington. The encrypted bomb plot communication was intercepted that day by a monitoring station set up by the U.S. Army's MS-5 at Fort Shafter. General Short had not been cleared for Magic transmission, nor had he been made aware of MS-5's existence. Since Navy intelligence in Hawaii did not have a Purple machine, this intelligence was to have been flown to Washington on August 21, 1941. However, the planned Pan American flight was cancelled due to bad weather, so the information was sent by ship. It arrived in Washington on October 6 and was decrypted by S.I.S. (Army's Signal Intelligence Service) three days later. On the Japanese side, the bomb plot grid message was encrypted in the J code and sent by the Japanese via RCA radiograms from Honolulu to Japan's embassy in Washington with a request that the intelligence be forwarded to Tokyo.[4] On the same day, the message was transferred to Navy Intelligence. Realizing that the bomb plot could mean that there could be an air attack on Pearl Harbor, Captain Alan Kirk, the new chief of the Office of Naval Intelligence (ONI), urged that the intelligence be sent to Admiral Kimmel. Rear Admiral Richmond Turner, Chief of War Plans, objected. Turner refused to budge on his opinion even after Captain H.D. Bode, Head of Foreign Intelligence, sided with Kirk. Turner turned to Admiral Harold Stark (CNO), who backed Turner's decision. The message was never sent to Kimmel. In addition, Kirk and Bode were "detached" from Naval Intelligence in Washington, D.C. and reassigned elsewhere.[5] The reason for Kirk's and Bode's reassignment and Turner's and Stark's herculean efforts to deprive Hawaii of vital intelligence has never been satisfactorily explained. One fact is certain: in spite of the critical importance of the information in the bomb plot message, Stark and Turner were responsible for the fact that Kimmel never received this vital Washington intelligence.

The Hitokappu Bay Message

On November 18, 1941, (Japanese date), the Japanese unwittingly sent a message which contained the words "Hitokappu Bay" clearly spelled out. As stated earlier, Hitokappu Bay was located in the Kurile Islands and was the place where the Japanese warships would rendezvous and head for Pearl Harbor. On November 18, the ships of the Kido Butai located in various ports in Japan began their departure for the Kurile Islands.[6]

The Hitokappu Bay message was intercepted by Station H. This fact was later confirmed by examination of H's records by Stinnett, though Captain Duane Whitlock, the radio analyst at CAST in the Philippines, denies such an message was sent. Other warships anchored in their Japanese naval bases went on the air to rebroadcast the same message. British naval monitors at Singapore and their Dutch counterparts in Java reported intercepting the same message. General Poorten, Commander of the Netherlands Army forces in the Dutch East Indies, stated his cryptologists at Kamer 14 had evidence that "showed Japanese naval forces concentrated near the Kuriles."[7]

Stinnett reported that on November 19, 1941, Rochefort did not inform Admiral Kimmel of the intercepted Hitokappu message in his Communication Summary—the logical date for his disclosure. Instead, Rochefort wrote that Japanese naval transmission circuits in the far north were intercepted. In the 1945–46 congressional hearings, Rochefort stated he knew of the Hitokappu Bay rendezvous point prior to December 7, 1941. However, the message was never presented at the congressional 1945/46 hearings or made available to the 1995 Senator Strom Thurmond inquiry.[8]

Stinnett presented two versions of the intercepted message in his book *Day of Deceit*: one with and the other without blacked-out code numbers. The one with redactions was released in 1979 under a Presidential Executive Order by President Jimmy Carter. The unredacted message was intercepted at 1932 hours on November 18, 1941, and decrypted, translated, and transcribed in 1946. The message stated, "Suzuki who was sent to the First Air Fleet on business was to be picked up about November 23 or 24 at Hitokappu Bay by an unidentified ship of your secondary Naval Station," a designated sea defense area which is regulated by its commandant. The key to the importance of the message is not when it was translated or its contents except for two words—Hitokappu Bay—which identified the location of a Japanese Fleet in the Kurile Islands. The spelling of Hitokappu Bay in the clear should certainly have warranted the communication being translated on November 18, or at the very least signify that Hitokappu Bay had to mean that Japan had warships in the north Pacific whose probable destination was Pearl Harbor.[9]

The SS Lurline *Incident*

On November 29, 1941, the SS *Lurline*, pride of the Matson Line, left San Francisco after picking up passengers in Los Angles and then sailed toward its destination in Honolulu. The name of the radio operator on the SS *Lurline* was Leslie Grogan. What follows is Grogan's recollection of the events that unfolded on the voyage, as written in his journal. The journal was given to Toland by the Matson Line and described by him in his book *Infamy*, published in 1982.[10]

On December 1, 1941, Grogan, with little to do, decided to move the dial of his radio receiver and surprisingly discovered a faint signal in the northwest Pacific that he could not identify. He wondered what any ships would be doing in those rough waters. He strained to listen more closely and was able to determine that the call sign was "JCS," the shore station in Yokohama in Japanese code. Commercial call signs such as "JCS" were not normally used by Japan to address warships; rather they were used for commercial vessels. When Japan addressed warships, radio station JCS changed procedure and used the call sign HA FU 6 (the same transmitter as JCS) to reach the units of the Hawaiian strike force.[11]

The radio transmissions were determined to be emanating from Japan by RDF. When the SS *Lurline* docked at Aloha Tower in Honolulu on December 3, Grogan and Chief Radio Operator Rudy Asplund rushed down Bishop Street to the downtown office of the Fourteenth Naval District located in the Hotel Alexander Young Building. Introducing themselves to Lieutenant Commander George Pease of Navy Intelligence, they turned over the transcript of the broadcasts and RDF bearings to him. He promised to turn the information over to his superiors in Navy Intelligence, but there is no record that he ever did so. The narrative ends here, as Pease died in a plane crash in 1945 and it is not known whether he ever submitted the report that the *Lurline* had located Japanese ships northwest of Hawaii. What is known is that the Grogan's transcript was never found.[12]

On December 10, the ship returned to San Francisco and was boarded by Lieutenant Commander Preston Allen of the Twelfth District Intelligence unit. Allen entered the radio room and requested the ship's radio log. Asplund insisted that Commodore C.A. Berndtson, the ship's captain, be the one to hand over the radio log to Allen. They went to see Berndtson, where the radio log book was turned over to Allen.[13]

While researching for his book *Day of Deceit*, Robert Stinnett discovered that Allen filed the log in the records of the Port Director of the Twelfth Naval District. Because of this, it remained hidden during the Pearl Harbor investigations. Stinnett learned that in 1958, the Port Director files were transferred to the Federal Records Center (FRC) in San Bruno, California, a division of the National Archives. Stinnett also discovered that in 1970, an unknown person removed the log from the National Archives and left a withdrawal slip in its place. The caption on the slip referred to the *Lurline*'s radio log but the slip was not signed or dated. The aging yellow color of the withdrawal slip indicated that it was probably about 20 years old, which was about the time author Toland made his FOIA request for *Lurline*'s radio log. At the time, the log was under the physical custody of the Federal Records Center but under the legal custody of the Navy. Kathleen O'Connor, an archivist at the San Bruno Center who found the slip in 1991, stated that since only naval personnel had access to the log, only Navy personnel could have been responsible for the removal of the log book from the file and the placement of the withdrawal slip in its place.[14] Thus, a highly significant piece of information relevant to the attack on Pearl Harbor had been removed from the National Archives and away from public awareness.

The veracity of Grogan's journal is documented by the fact that the United States had established five listening posts—Stations ITEM (San Diego), CAST (Philippines), H (Oahu), KING (Dutch Harbor), and SAIL (Bainbridge Island, Washington)—to monitor radio messages in the Pacific. On December 3, 1941, all five listening posts and SS *Lurline* detected radio transmissions coming from the North Pacific. The discovery of radio signals by the five U.S. stations were logged in the official Navy reports and forwarded to Washington. In addition, Robert Orr, who was on the staff of the District Naval Intelligence Office (DIO) as a special investigator, related to Toland and to Navy Historian Commander Irving Newman that the bearing he obtained from November 30 to December 4, when plotted on the chart, disclosed Japanese warships in the North Pacific. Orr also related to Toland that a verification of his account could be found in the Dutch Harbor records. In 2000, Stinnett reported in *Day of Deceit* that he found the records at Dutch Harbor which verified Orr's account of the discovery of Japanese warships in the North Pacific during the dates cited.[15]

Critical intelligence of Japanese ships located in the North Pacific heading east was once again withheld from Admiral Kimmel and his Pacific Fleet in Hawaii. Again, credit goes to Stinnett for discovering the actual records of Station CAST and Station H that document that 129 radio naval intercepts were detected between November 15 and December 3, 1941.[16]

The foregoing is conclusive proof that the Japanese did not maintain radio silence on their way to Hawaii and that the Japanese task force, as a result, was detected by the U.S monitoring stations and the SS *Lurline* before the attack on Pearl Harbor.

The Enterprise *and* Lexington *Leave Pearl Harbor*

It is of interest to know who ordered the only two U.S. operational carriers in the Pacific to leave Pearl Harbor on November 28 and December 5, 1941, respectively. Research traces the origin of the order for the movement of the two carriers out of Pearl Harbor and to Wake and Midway directly to General Marshall. Thus, the directive to move *Enterprise* and *Lexington* oddly originated from an Army source and not a Navy one. Why did the Army wade into the waters of the Navy's responsibility? Could it be that the motive was to move the United States' only two carriers out of harm's way in the impending Pearl Harbor attack?

On November 26, Admiral Kimmel received a directive from Admiral Stark at the Pentagon that they had reached an agreement with the War Department regarding the reinforcement of the Midway and Wake islands. The directive was weakly worded and stated, "It will be necessary to send these aircraft by carriers to their destinations, if you consider this order feasible and desirable." Following the orders, Kimmel ordered *Enterprise* to leave Pearl Harbor on November 28 and sail to Wake Island to reinforce that base with 12 Marine F4F fighters (Fighter Squadron 211). *Lexington* was directed to sail to Midway on December 5 to deliver 18 SB2U-3 Vindicator dive bombers. Since the orders to Admiral Kimmel contained the words "if you consider it feasible and desirable," it was clearly meant to be a suggestion and not a direct order. However, also on November 26, President Roosevelt proclaimed that negotiations with Japan were off and that war was imminent in the Pacific theater. There appears to be an inconsistency in the accepted version of the explanation of why the directive was issued. The stated reason for the movement of *Lexington* and *Enterprise* by Admiral Stark was to reinforce Midway and Wake islands, but the weak wording of the directive was curious for the circumstances. However, there could be another reason for the directive, namely to get the carriers out of Pearl Harbor and out of harm's way. Coincidently or not, it is of interest that on November 26, the Japanese task force left the Kurile Islands for Pearl Harbor. It is noteworthy that General Marshall was censured in the 1944 Army Pearl Harbor Board hearings for failure to keep General Short in Hawaii informed of critical Washington Army intelligence prior to the attack:

Critical Intelligence Omitted

In the bomb plot message on August 21, Tokyo intelligence requested an invisible grid outlining the locations of all the naval ships in Pearl Harbor. The English version of the message is dated September 24, 1941, but it is in error because U.S. censors excised the priority designator contained in the original Japanese text from the congressional printing. The date given of August 21, 1941, for the bomb plot message is based on the 1943 interrogation of Richard Kotoshirodo by Navy intelligence officers in Hawaii. Kotoshirodo was a consulate clerk who drove Morimura around in the consulate's 1937 Ford sedan to the high vantage points overlooking the Pearl Harbor. When confronted in 1943 by Navy intelligence, he admitted to doing so but denied responsibility for his part in the attack because he had no idea that Japan would use the information for an attack on Pearl Harbor.[17] Hawaii intelligence failed to receive a Purple machine, which made it possible to encipher Japanese diplomatic messages, while Britain received three Purple machines.

1. After July 1941, Admiral Kimmel in Hawaii never received any intelligence obtained directly from Magic or from U.S. command officials in the Philippines.
2. Japanese intelligence requesting minute-by-minute berthing of U.S. ships in the harbor from their spy stationed in Hawaii.
3. Washington senior military officials sent warnings to Hawaiian and Philippine commands on November 24, 27, and 29, 1941. The message on November 24 pointed out that war was imminent, with an attack on the Philippines or Guam as a possibility but with no mention of a possible attack on Pearl Harbor. The November 27 warning was cryptic in nature, stating that the U.S. wanted Japan to take the first hostile action and any action taken by Kimmel should not alarm the Hawaiian civil population. Again there was no specific mention of a possible Pearl Harbor attack. The November 29 message to Kimmel stated that the communication was a war warning, as negotiations with Japan had ceased and that war could break out in the Philippines, Thailand, Kra Peninsula, or possibly Borneo. Kimmel was ordered to execute a defensive deployment. Again no mention of Pearl Harbor being a target was ever made.[18]

In Frederick Parker's 2013 monograph for the Center for Cryptologic History, *Pearl Harbor Revisited*, Parker listed the three November dates—November 24, 27, and 29—as "warning messages" from Washington high command. Parker, however, fails to mention that none of those messages ever mentioned a possible attack on Pearl Harbor but rather indicated just the opposite: that the forthcoming attack would be directed at the Philippines, Thailand, or even Borneo. The November 27 dispatch from Admiral Stark read: "This dispatch is to be considered a war warning. Negotiations with Japan looking toward stabilization in the Pacific have ceased and an aggressive move by Japan is expected within the next few days. The number and equipment of Japanese troops and the organization of naval task forces indicate an amphibious expedition against either the Philippines, Thai or Kra peninsula or possibly Borneo. Execute an appropriate defensive deployment preparatory to carrying out tasks assigned in WPL 46. Info District and Army authorities. A similar warning is being sent by War Department. SPENAVO (Special Naval Observer in London) inform British. Continental districts Guam, Samoa directed to take appropriate measures against sabotage."[19]

To emphasize the preceding point, the 1945 Joint Congressional Pearl Harbor hearings charged Marshall, among other individuals, with being culpable for the disaster at Pearl Harbor.[20] The previous statement will have more significance as this narrative unfolds.

Eyewitness Testimony: Joseph Clark Grew

The first person whose testimony bears advance witness to the surprise attack on Pearl Harbor is the American Ambassador to Japan, Joseph Clark Grew. He sent a documented report to Secretary of State Hull in Washington on January 27, 1941. It stated:

> My Peruvian colleague told a member of my staff that he had heard from many sources, including a Japanese source, that the Japanese military forces planned, in the event of trouble with the United States, to attempt a surprise mass attack on Pearl Harbor using all their military facilities. Although the project seemed fantastic, the fact that it was heard from many sources prompted me to pass on the information.[21]

The information was passed on to Admiral Kimmel by the Office of Naval Intelligence on February 1, 1941, the day he assumed command of the Pacific Fleet. With the report came a message from Commander McCollum of the Office of Intelligence Far East section that "naval intelligence places no credence in these rumors."[22] It was a surprising response since the Navy War Plans Division was clearly concerned that "if war eventuates with Japan, it is believed easily possible that hostilities could be preceded by a surprise attack upon the Pacific Fleet in the naval base of Pearl Harbor."[23]

It should be noted that Commander McCollum is the same person who wrote the famous McCollum memorandum which detailed an eight-step plan to provoke Japan into attacking the United States first:

    1. Make an arrangement with Britain for the use of British bases in the Pacific, particularly Singapore.
    2. Make an arrangement with Holland for the use of base facilities and acquisition of supplies in the Dutch East Indies (Indonesia).
    3. Give all possible aid to the Chinese government of Chiang Kai-shek.
    4. Send a division of long-range heavy cruisers to the Orient, Philippines, or Singapore.
    5. Send two divisions of submarines to the Orient.
    6. Keep the main strength of the U.S. Fleet, now in the Pacific, in the vicinity of the Hawaiian Islands.
    7. Insist that the Dutch refuse to grant Japanese demands for undue economic concessions, particularly oil.
    8. Completely embargo all trade with Japan, in collaboration with a similar embargo imposed by the British Empire.[24]

Over the course of 1941, President Roosevelt implemented all eight steps of McCollum's recommendations, including placing an oil embargo on Japan which would leave that country without oil and in the position of either capitulating to U.S. demands or going to war.

On December 7, 1941, the goal of the recommendations was met when Japan attacked the United States. McCollum was one of President Roosevelt's most trusted advisors. The foregoing raises the question of why the Grew report was so easily dismissed when the War Plans Division itself had predicted that Japan could make a surprise attack on Pearl Harbor to initiate the war in the Pacific.

On February 3, 1941, one week after the Grew report, Rear Admiral Turner of the War Plans Division expressed his opinion of the report in a memorandum. Turner was dismissive, stating the report was not credible. Turner was to later claim that he predicted that Japan might attack Oahu with planes launched from "a striking force of carriers."[25]

In spite of the War Plans Division's concern over Japan striking Pearl Harbor to begin the war, throughout 1941 Admiral Stark, General Marshall, and Admiral Turner all gave orders preventing transmission of Magic intercepts to Admiral Kimmel. Later, all three men in testimony denied such orders were ever given. One fact remains certain: intercepts of Magic transmissions were never sent to Kimmel.[26]

According to Kimmel's former intelligence officer Layton, in 1941 Turner was in constant conflict with Captain Kirk, of the Office of Naval Intelligence (ONI), over issues involving intelligence analysis and interpretation. In these disagreements, Turner almost always had the complete backing of Admiral Stark. The main issue beginning in the spring of 1941 and continuing during the year was that, according to the Navy operational manual, ONI had the authority to analyze and interpret coded Japanese interceptions. However, Turner had issued an oral directive that he alone would analyze and interpret the intelligence gathered by ONI. Thus, ONI would be relegated to only collecting Japanese intelligence. In view of the circumstances, Stark and Captain Ingersoll, the CNO's deputy, had refused to change the manual to accommodate Turner's order because the nature of the admiral's directive was questionable at best.[27]

In the 1944 naval court of inquiry, Turner initially denied that he alone would have access to Purple intercepts. When the congressional investigation committee gained access to the secret records of naval court of inquiry on December 21, 1945, Turner was called back to answer questions regarding the obvious conflict in his testimony between Noyes, who testified in the 1944 naval inquiry that Turner unintentionally gave the order, and Turner's own denial in the inquiry that he had issued such an order. At the congressional hearing, Turner was forced to admit he had done so. He escaped punishment by skillfully obfuscating the issue and denying an unwritten policy that all intelligence coming from the ONI would *only* be analyzed and interpreted by him. His statements were left unchallenged because Stark and Ingersoll had refused to incorporate the directive into the Navy manual and members of ONI refused to testify against him. Thus, he escaped punishment for his actions in this matter.[28]

The obvious question is how, in spite of the War Plans Division's position in Washington and the introduction of the Martin-Bellinger Report (which follows), could the United States have been unprepared for a surprise attack on Pearl Harbor?

Martin-Bellinger Joint Estimate

Major General F.L. Martin, head of the Hawaiian Army Air Corps, and Rear Admiral Patrick L.N. Bellinger, head of the Hawaiian Naval Air Patrol, issued a joint report on March 31, 1941, on Pearl Harbor stating in part: "At present an attack would most likely be launched from one or more carriers which would probably approach inside of 300 miles." The attack would occur at sunrise and have a high probability of occurring as a surprise. With this report, the bomb plot message, and Ambassador Joseph Grew's intelligence of Japanese intentions to attack Pearl Harbor as a background, it is difficult to conceive how high-ranking Washington government officials, including the president, were surprised by the Japanese attack on Pearl Harbor.

Further evidence for this conclusion are the statements previously cited, that Kimmel and Short were deprived of vital Japanese intelligence, and the oddity that HYPO did not receive a Purple decoding machine while the British received three (two for Britain and one for Singapore).[29] These reasonable questions have never been satisfactorily answered by supporters of the conventional position that the United States had absolutely no advance knowledge of the Japanese attack on Pearl Harbor.

Dusko Popov

The second eyewitness is Dusko Popov (code name Tricycle), the British double agent from Yugoslavia. As explained earlier, he was first recruited by the Germans but, being a patriot, he offered his services to MI-6 in British intelligence. In May 1941, Japanese Admiral Abe and his aides had visited Taranto, Italy, in search of information regarding the successful 1940 British torpedo raid on the Italian fleet anchored in the Taranto Harbor. In the summer of 1941, while on one of his routine visits to Lisbon, Popov learned the details of Admiral Abe's visit to Taranto from Johnny Jebsen, another double agent working for the British. Popov then met with the German spymaster Ludovico von Karsthoff, who gave Popov a telegram which contained questions about Pearl Harbor in the microdots of the "i's" of its wording. A separate typewritten questionnaire was also given to Popov which duplicated the same questions. The reason for the duplication is uncertain. The Germans wanted Popov to travel to Hawaii to gain information on the deployment of ships in Pearl Harbor, the harbor's pier installations, its number of anchorages, and the depth of its waters. He concluded, along with British intelligence, that Japan was going to attack Pearl Harbor by carrier aircraft.[30] The following is excerpted from John Toland's *Infamy*, published in 1982, page 359.

It is a summary of the complete questionnaire given to Popov, and, as translated from the German by British Secret Service.

The questionnaire included the following questions and statements: The naval ammunition and mine depots at Pearl Harbor, the total Army ammunition reserve.

- The total Army ammunition reserve at Crater Aliamanu.
- A detailed sketch of Aerodrome Lukefield.
- Details about Kaneohe's hangars, depots and seaplane dispositions.
- Details about Army aerodromes Hickam and Wheeler Fields.
- Details about airports Rodgers and Pan American Airways.
- Details about the U.S. submarine base.
- Details about Dry Dock No. 1 and the new one being built.
- What are the number of anchorages in Pearl Harbor?

10. The Final Analysis of the Japanese Attack on Pearl Harbor

- How far has the dredge work progressed in the entrance and in the east and southeast locks?
- How deep is the water in Pearl Harbor?
- How far has torpedo net protection been introduced in the harbor?

The questions regarding the airfields on Oahu, petrol depots, water depth of Pearl Harbor's waters, and torpedo nets make it perfectly clear that Japan was seriously considering an attack on Pearl Harbor and its air bases in the ensuing months.

As previously pointed out, Stewart Menzies of British intelligence decided that Popov should meet with FBI Director Hoover. On August 12, 1941, after landing in New York, he met with Percy "Sam" Foxworth, agent in charge of the FBI's New York Office. There Popov presented the questionnaire and the telegram to him. One third of the questions were related to Pearl Harbor, specifically about the defenses on Oahu, including Hickam, Wheeler, and Kaneohe airfields, the piers and dry docks at Pearl Harbor, and the depth of the water. Popov felt he received a cool reception because Foxworth thought his information was a trap since Popov was a double agent. Initially, Foxworth felt that Popov's intelligence was unreliable. With time, the FBI bureau chief began to appreciate the information Popov was offering and even supported Popov's suggestion that he could assist the U.S. government in its efforts against German espionage.[31]

Two weeks later, on August 26, 1941, Popov presented to Hoover the two pieces of evidence previously cited to Fox: namely, Japan's interest in the British Taranto raid and the German questions about Hawaii, for which he was to obtain answers. Germany and Japan were axis powers, so it was in both of their interests to assist each other. In spite of the evidence, Popov left the meeting feeling that Hoover was unimpressed and with good reason. Popov recalled Hoover's parting words: "Good riddance."[32]

Prior to the attack on Pearl Harbor, Popov sought the aid of William Stephenson, Churchill's secret envoy to the United States, and Sir John Masterman, head of Britain's Double-Cross System. Both failed in their efforts to have the FBI take the intelligence seriously. However, the information was passed on by the FBI to the proper military authorities and to Roosevelt. Eventually, the FBI circulated a paraphrased one-page version of the Popov questionnaire. Nonetheless, the FBI until 1983 vigorously denied that Popov ever met with Hoover or the FBI. Up to that time any definitive evidence to the contrary had not been discovered or was supposedly still classified.[33]

The FBI denial of the Hoover meeting raises questions as to why the FBI would do this. If Popov did meet with Hoover, then the cause for the denial is obvious: the warning was unheeded and the attack did occur. Popov had spoken to MI-6 for assistance, and the British intelligence agency sent Dick Ellis, British intelligence officer, and Stephenson to speak to Hoover about the veracity of Popov's intelligence.

However, since the U.S. government did not act on Popov's intelligence, it has been concluded that either Hoover did not pass the information on to military intelligence and the president, or he did but the intelligence was not acted upon by those who received it. The forthcoming discussion will resolve this issue.

After the war, Hoover and the FBI continued to deny that Hoover ever met with Popov, nor was there any record of such a meeting. In 1974, after Popov released his memoirs, the FBI in turn released 1,400 pages about its relationship with the double agent (but at least several hundred pages were not released). The main purpose of the FBI releasing the information was to document the denial that Hoover ever met with Popov. However, a highly credible source—Sir John Masterson, head of Britain's Double-Cross System (where captured German agents in Britain were induced to become double agents and serve the Allies)—has presented evidence to the contrary.[34] Masterson stated that when he met privately with Popov in 1941, Popov confirmed that he had met with Hoover and discussed the questionnaire in detail. As a result, Stephenson had no doubt that Popov was telling the truth because the questions in the questionnaire were specialized and detailed, indicating that the Japanese plan to attack Pearl Harbor had reached an advanced state.[35]

Popov went to his grave believing Hoover was responsible for the disaster. In 1983, the truth about the meeting was unintentionally released by the FBI. It came too late for Popov—who died on August 18, 1981—to appreciate that his story about the contents and existence of the meeting with Hoover and the FBI had been validated. On April 2, 1983, an article in the *Washington Post* by George Lardner, Jr., reported that newly released declassified documents by the FBI revealed information that was contrary to the standard narrative expressed by the agency about Popov up to that time. Lardner reported that the FBI had just declassified documents relating to the issue of whether Popov met with the FBI regarding Pearl Harbor. The article stated that the FBI obtained a questionnaire from a double agent that revealed that Japan had an intense interest in the defense installations at Pearl Harbor and the Army and Navy airfields on Oahu.

The article added that Assistant FBI Director Roger S. Young released six classified internal FBI memos that would clear Hoover of charges that he had failed to pass on Popov's intelligence to Navy and Army officials intelligence or to Roosevelt. Young was quoted as saying that the agency had indeed informed the offices of Navy and Army Intelligence and President Roosevelt in the months preceding the Pearl Harbor attack and provided the double agent's intelligence in August 1941.[36]

The FBI had released the long-kept secret records in 1983 in response to an article, "Pearl Harbor, Microdots and J. Edgar Hoover," by two Michigan State University historians, John F. Bratzel and Leslie B. Rout, Jr. They reported in the December 1982 issue of *American Historical Review* that Hoover only told the White House about the microdots and the innocuous portion of Popov's questionnaire. It was implied that Hoover took this action only to demonstrate how the FBI was staying on top of German espionage.[37] This statement has not been proven to be true as Hoover's communication to Roosevelt about the microdots has not been found at the Hyde Park Roosevelt Library, FBI files, or the National Archives.

One of the declassified documents was an FBI memo from D.M. Ladd, head of the bureau's Intelligence Division, dated September 30, 1941. It stated, "Information contained in the questionnaire furnished to Popov by the Germans had been paraphrased and given to U.S. Naval and Army intelligence." Another document showed that further details on the enemy inquiries concerning Pearl Harbor were supplied to naval intelligence. The Navy in turn gave false information about the anti-torpedo nets to Popov to affirm that he was loyal to Germany and to pass on disinformation to the Germans and to the Japanese as well.[38]

The release of declassified intelligence by the FBI cleared Hoover of the charges of negligence that had been brought against him. At the same time, it proved that Popov did meet with the FBI and that Popov provided the agency with significant intelligence that Japan was going to attack Pearl Harbor in the coming months.

Kilsoo Haan

The third eyewitness is Kilsoo Haan, an agent for the Sino-Korean People's League. The narrative that follows is derived from Toland's book *Infamy* and is based on his interviews with the participants and their families. Haan came to the Washington office of Eric Sevareid, a CBS foreign correspondent, and made him aware of the information he had that Japan was going to attack Pearl Harbor before Christmas. His colleagues in the Korean underground reported that they had conclusive proof that the intelligence was accurate. Sevareid stated in Toland's book that Haan had told him that the Korean underground discovered that a Korean working in the Japanese consulate in Honolulu had seen full blueprints of U.S. above-water and underwater naval installations at Pearl Harbor spread out on the consul's desk. Also, according to Sevareid, Haan said that he had previously visited low-ranking State Department officials and told them of this report.

Late in October 1941, Haan convinced Senator Guy Gillette, Iowa Democrat, that he had discovered that the Japanese were not only going to attack Pearl Harbor but also simultaneously invade the Philippines, Wake, Guam, and Midway. Gillette immediately alerted the State Department as well as Army and Navy intelligence.[39]

On December 5, 1941, Haan telephoned Maxwell Hamilton, an official at the State Department, to tell him that the Korean underground had informed him that the Japanese were planning to attack Pearl Harbor over "this coming weekend." Haan also brought to Hamilton's attention a Japanese book, *The Three Power Alliance*, written by Matsuo Kinoaki and published in October 1940. In the book the author describes the "Japanese Surprise Attack Fleet," leaving no doubt in Haan's mind that Japan would seize on the opportunity to strike the United States first. However, Matsuo did not specify an attack on Pearl Harbor. Haan recommended to Hamilton that he send the intelligence to the president and to the Army and Navy commanders in Hawaii to help alleviate his apprehension of the implication of this information. According to Haan, he followed up with the report to Hamilton that stressed the following points:

 1. In the November 22, 1941, issue of *Nippu Jiji*, the Japanese daily paper circulated throughout the Hawaiian islands, a U.S. Army air maneuvers time table "was published every day except Sundays and holidays."
 2. The Italian magazine *Oggi* on October 24, 1941, contained an article that predicted war between Japan and America with a Japanese air attack on the Hawaiian Islands. The article stated "that there will be a surprise attack on the fleet in Pearl Harbor in the month of December and perhaps on the first Sunday in December."[40] Haan reiterated his request that the information be sent to the president and military and naval commanders in Hawaii, as he had previously said on the phone.[41]

This narrative is another example of eyewitness accounts by individuals who state that they warned the U.S. government (President Roosevelt, Office of Naval

Intelligence, and the State Department) that Japan was planning on attacking Pearl Harbor in early December—information that was either negligently or willfully ignored or carefully taken into consideration by those who were in high official positions.

Colonel Elliot Thorpe and General Hein Ter Poorten

The fourth and fifth eyewitnesses are Army Colonel Elliot Thorpe, who was serving as a U.S. military attaché in Dutch-controlled Java (Netherland Indies) in early December 1941, and General Poorten, commander of the Dutch East Indies Army. Dutch Army intelligence, through the efforts of Colonel Verkuyl—with the help of his code-breaking wife and a group of students— had broken the Japanese consular code broadcasted on November 19, 1941. According to Toland, they intercepted a Japanese message in consular code which revealed that Japan was planning an attack on Hawaii, the Philippine Islands, and Thailand.[42] The message stated that the signal to begin the attacks would come from Tokyo in the form of a weather broadcast which was to become known as the infamous Winds Code. Poorten hand-carried the intercepted message to Colonel Thorpe. According to Toland, Thorpe's communication had the gravity of a message that should be sent to Washington immediately. Thorpe went at once to the U.S. Consulate in Batavia to have "our senior State Department representative send it directly to Washington tonight." The message was sent but Thorpe didn't receive a response from Washington. He sent a second message and again received no reply. He then sent a third message through Consul General Dr. Walter Foote.

Toland reported in *Infamy* that two of the four messages sent by Thorpe have been found in the War Department files: the censored one signed by Foote and his own final message to Miles. Both arrived in the War Department without the paragraph warning of the Pearl Harbor attack. The reason for the deletions never has been fully explained.[43] The other two messages have never been found. If one believes Thorpe's account of sending the messages, it follows that the two remaining messages were either lost, altered, or destroyed. This issue will be resolved in the next chapter.

The foregoing are examples of U.S. intelligence rejecting outright information containing details that Hawaii was going to be attacked, and the subsequent failure to forward the intelligence to senior officials in Hawaii. Why did senior leaders in Washington decline to consider such information—even as a possibility—and alert the commanders in Hawaii? It is difficult to believe that U.S. intelligence lacked that ability to do so, which leads to the obvious question: did they already know that Pearl Harbor was going to be attacked?

Ensign Yoshikawa Takeo

The sixth eyewitness is the Japanese spy on Oahu, Ensign Yoshikawa Takeo (alias Morimura Tadashi).

According to Layton's book *And I Was There*, Yoshikawa was posing as a consul official but actually was the sole Japanese spy in Hawaii. On August 21, 1941, a Mackay

10. The Final Analysis of the Japanese Attack on Pearl Harbor

```
2 Dec.,      The following Japanese Diplomatic message
1941         of Comcardiv 2 despatch of 4 Nov 1941 regarding preparation
             for torpedo firing against anchored capital ships
"From: Tokyo                              #123   2 Dec, 1941
 To  : Honolulu
       (Secret outside the Department).
 In view of the present situation, the presence in port of
 warships, airplane carriers and cruisers is of utmost importance.
 Hereafter, to the utmost of your ability, let me know day by day.
 Wire me in each case whether or not there are any observation
 balloons above Pearl Harbor or if there are any indications that
 they will be sent up. Also advise me whether or not the warships
 are provided with anti-torpedo nets".
```

Tokyo's diplomatic message to the Japanese Honolulu Consul on December 2, 1941, questioning the presence of balloons and torpedo nets in and over Pearl Harbor (National Archives).

```
6 Dec.,      The following very significant despatch through
1941         diplomatic channels is the reply to Japanese
             diplomatic #123 from Tokyo dated 2 December.

From: Honolulu                         #253   6 December, 1941
 To  : Tokyo
Re the last part of your #123a.
1. On the American Continent in October the Army began
training barrage balloon troops at Camp Davis, North Carolina.
Not only have they ordered four or five hundred balloons, but
it is understood that they are considering the use of these
balloons in the defense of Hawaii and Panama. In so far as
Hawaii is concerned, though investigations have been made in
the neighborhood of Pearl Harbor, they have not set up mooring
equipment, nor have they selected the troops to man them.
Furthermore, there is no indication that any training for the
maintenance of balloons is being undertaken. At the present
time there are no signs of barrage balloon equipment. In
addition, it is difficult to imagine that they have actually
any. However, even though they have actually made prepara-
tions, because they must control the air over the water and
land runways of the airports in the vicinity of Pearl Harbor,
Hickam, Ford and EWAb, there are limits to the balloon defense
of Pearl Harbor. I imagine that in all probability there is
considerable opportunity left to take advantage for a surprise
attack against these places.
2. In my opinion the battleships do not have torpedo nets.
The details are not known. I will report the results of my
investigation.
a - not available.
b - kana spelling.
(ARMY #25877-JD-7178)
```

Japanese diplomatic message answers on December 6, 1941, to Tokyo's questions about the presence of balloons and torpedo nets in Pearl Harbor (National Archives).

cable from Captain Kanji Ogawa (Tokyo Intelligence) was delivered to the Japanese Consulate in Honolulu. Yoshikawa was instructed to create a grid system for Pearl Harbor's military installations, including information on the exact location of U.S. ships in the harbor, for the benefit of Japan's torpedo and dive bombers. Yoshikawa was instructed to carry out this mission for Consul General Kita Nagao. Yoshikawa discovered he had the freedom to observe and later record the military installations, including the ships in Pearl Harbor. By taking tour guides into the Pearl Harbor basin, touring around the island by car and bus, and by flying commercial tour aircraft, he was able to obtain the needed intelligence to develop his grid system.[44] The FBI and military intelligence tracked Yoshikawa's activities but were unable to arrest him because of orders originating in Washington prohibiting them from doing so on the basis that it might upset the loyalty of the island's dual-nationality population. This seems implausible in view of the obvious potentially catastrophic effect that an air attack would have on the U.S. naval fleet at Pearl Harbor.

Arresting him was one issue, but another issue is that the intelligence obtained from the FBI shadowing Yoshikawa's activities was ignored by certain FBI agents who were able to draw the proper conclusions about his obvious actions. We are left with the conclusion that either the FBI lacked the ability to grasp the significance of Yoshikawa's activities or that the FBI's lack of action in arresting Yoshikawa and/or alerting U.S. intelligence was another attempt by the FBI to keep an impending Japanese air attack on Pearl Harbor a secret.

Colonel Rufus S. Bratton, USA

The seventh eyewitness is Colonel Bratton, the Army's Far East Director of Military Intelligence. On Friday, December 6, 1941, the Navy intercepted two Purple messages on Bainbridge Island in the Puget Sound which were being sent by Japan to the Japanese embassy in Washington. That day, it was the Army's turn to decrypt any Purple coded transmissions. However, Colonel Bratton requested assistance from Navy intelligence for translation of the messages. He learned from the initial dispatch that a 14-part transmission was forthcoming and that the Japanese embassy was instructed to keep it secret. The second transmission directed Nomura Kichisaburo, diplomatic envoy representing Japan in Washington, to use an inside typist to perform the typing and that extreme caution in maintaining secrecy should be exercised. By midnight, 13 of the 14 parts of the message sent by Tokyo had been deciphered by the Navy's code-breakers.[45]

At 2200 on December 6, Bratton delivered the decrypted messages from the first 13 parts to Generals Marshall and Miles and Brigadier General Gerow, chief of the Army's War Plans Division. Bratton left the locked pouch with then-Colonel Walter Bedell Smith, aide to General Marshall, before heading to the State Department where he left the locked pouch containing the intelligence with the watch officer at 2230. This testimony was given at the Army Court Inquiry in 1944 and resulted in Marshall being censored for failing to notify Pacific Command of this intelligence.[46]

One year later, Bratton was persuaded by now Major General Smith to sign an affidavit that recanted the testimony he presented in 1944 and stated that Bratton never delivered the intelligence to General Marshall that December evening in 1941.

However, while serving in Japan in 1946, Bratton stated to Colonel Raymond Orr, a fellow officer on General MacArthur's staff, that he did indeed deliver the intelligence to Marshall that night and that earlier in the day he tried unsuccessfully to convince Marshall to alert Pacific Command. Marshall refused and returned to his office at Fort Myer, telling Bratton he wished not to be disturbed.[47]

Although Bratton recanted his initial testimony that he delivered the intelligence to Marshall, the question arises as to why he would give false testimony about Marshall. There is no logical reason for Bratton to lie about such a high-ranking Army officer. The conclusion based on Marshall's behavior on the night of December 6 and the morning of December 7, 1941, is that Bratton told the truth in his initial testimony.

As stated earlier, during the 1945 congressional hearings Marshall could not recall where he was on the night of December 6, but he was adamant that Bratton had not made a Magic delivery to him at Fort Myer. In fact, Marshall testified that he went to bed that night without any knowledge of the Japanese reply to Washington's demand. Yet, on Sunday December 7, 1941, a headline in the *Washington Times Herald* placed him at a reunion dinner for World War I vets that night. The event was held only a few blocks from the White House.[48]

In addition, there is testimony from James G. Stahlman, a Naval Reserve Officer. Stahlman recalled that he, along with Secretary of the Navy Knox who had just returned from a fact-finding mission on Pearl Harbor, Marshall, Stimson, Knox's aide Frank Beatty, and Stark's aide John McCrea, all met at a meeting in the White House on the night of December 6. However, an official record of the meeting is not available. Whether Marshall went to the White House that evening or received a phone call from the president is still subject to controversy, but it is doubtful that Marshall was unaware of the events that were taking place.[49]

The 14th and final part of the diplomatic message was received and deciphered at OP-20-GZ at 0630 on Sunday morning, December 7 (Washington time and date). Bratton arrived in the Munitions Building just before 0900. He had read the 14th part of the Tokyo diplomatic message and tried to reach Marshall but as described earlier, he was out horseback riding. Within moments, Bratton received a shorter decrypted Japanese diplomatic message which read: "Will the ambassador please submit to the United States Government (if possible the Secretary of State) our reply to the United States at 1300 on the seventh, your time." Finally, at 0930 Bratton reached Marshall and offered to take the documents to him at Fort Myer, but Marshall refused. The general instead insisted on traveling to the War Department.[50]

It took Marshall two hours to arrive at the War Department, even though Bratton had told Marshall that he had a urgent Japanese message. When Marshall arrived at 1130, he insisted on reading the entire 14-part message before looking at Bratton's urgent communication. Marshall took more time to write the communication to all commands in the Pacific in longhand rather than have the message typed. He delayed further by placing a phone call to Chief of Naval Operations Stark to see what course of action the CNO would advise. After hesitating, Stark agreed to notify all commands in the Pacific with a joint dispatch signed by both men. Marshall then, strangely, refused to use the scrambler phone on the basis it was not secure system and instead decided to send the message by telegram.[51]

As reported earlier, due to various communications delays, the highly important message did not reach Honolulu until three minutes after 1300, and the message had yet to be transferred to Fort Shafter.

Marshall's message, even if it had been delivered on time, was cryptic in nature, stating, "Japanese are presenting at one p.m. eastern standard time today what amounts to an ultimatum. Also they are under orders to destroy their code machines immediately. Just what significance the hour may have we do not know but be on alert accordingly. Inform naval authorities of this communication. Marshall."[52] The statement that Marshall could not place any significance on the 1300 deadline seems disingenuous at best. Most importantly, the statement also failed to mention that war was expected to break out in the Pacific by 1300 on December 7, 1941 (Washington time and date). [See Appendix A.]

Why Marshall did not act expeditiously at this critical juncture on the morning of December 7 is difficult to explain. His memory loss regarding the night of December 6, requiring two hours to reach the War Department on December 7, his demand that he take the time to read first the 13 parts of the 14-part decrypted diplomatic transmission and, finally, sending the message to Hawaii by the slow process of a telegram—rather than by phone—to notify the Pacific commanders are all factors that delayed the notification to those commanders until after the attack had begun. There was no mention in Marshall's message that Pearl Harbor may have been in danger of a surprise attack by the Japanese. Also, it was misleading for Marshall to state that he didn't know what the 1300 deadline meant, and the telegram made no suggestion whatsoever that Pearl Harbor was going to be attacked by Japan. The cessation of diplomatic ties with the United States at 1300 Washington time corresponded with 0800 Hawaii time, 0230 Malaya time, and 0230 Philippine time. A Japanese attack at 0230 Malaya and Philippine time would not be effective due to darkness, but not so for an 0800 attack on Pearl Harbor. Thus, the content of Marshall's telegram demonstrated gross negligence, if not deceit.

During the congressional hearings in 1944, Marshall was censured for failing to notify Short that U.S./Japanese relations had taken a downward turn. This failure was critical because Marshall had previously warned Short to assume a defensive posture against sabotage. It was the Army's position and that of Secretary of War Stimson, Marshall, and Rear Admiral Turner that sabotage was the main threat to Pearl Harbor. They had all predicted that "with adequate air defenses, enemy carriers and their naval escorts would come under air attack at a distance of 750 miles from Hawaii." Short's response to Marshall's warnings was to position Army aircraft wing-tip to wing-tip, which presented an easy target for Japanese fighters on the day of the attack.[53]

What was not discussed during the 1944 congressional hearings was that Admiral Stark's November 26, 1941, directive to Admiral Kimmel to send *Enterprise* to Wake and *Lexington* to Midway to reinforce those islands required General Marshall's approval. This was so because the War Department was ultimately under the authority of Marshall as Army Chief of Staff.

There is evidence that the idea to move the carriers out of Pearl Harbor originated with Marshall and the Army rather than with Stark and the Navy. This is based on the initial request by Stark to Kimmel that Army fighters be sent to Midway and Wake islands, an unlikely choice originating with the Chief of Naval Operations. Indeed, after Kimmel received the directive, he changed the type of aircraft being sent to the specified islands from Army to Navy aircraft.[54]

It is interesting to note that Stark's directive to Kimmel occurred on the exact date—November 26, 1941 (Hawaii date)—that the Japanese task force left the Kurile Islands for Hawaii. We know this because on the same day as Stark's directive, Station H in Hawaii partially decrypted extensive radio exchanges between Vice Admiral Nagumo and Japan's Central Pacific commander, as well as the Japanese submarine commander in the Pacific, while the task force was en route to Hawaii.[55] Thus, as of November 26, 1941, Hawaiian naval intelligence was generally aware that a Japanese naval force was heading toward Hawaii.

Was this another series of coincidences or a deliberate course of action taken by Marshall? This question can't be answered in a vacuum: one needs to take all the acts surrounding General Marshall's behavior (previously discussed), as well as his decision-making and analyze them together. Marshall was appointed Chief of the Army Staff in 1939 by Roosevelt and subsequently appointed Secretary of State and Secretary of Defense during Harry S. Truman's tenure as president. He served with distinction and intellect throughout his military career. This was not the type of man who couldn't comprehend the meaning of the 1300 diplomatic deadline, and it is unlikely that he neglected the significance of the information he possessed. Thus, it would be unreasonable to conclude he was negligent with regard to the Pearl Harbor warnings. A more rational explanation for his behavior and decision-making is that he had advanced knowledge of the attack on Pearl Harbor on December 7, and in keeping with FDR's policy of going to war only after Japan attacked the United States first, reacted accordingly.

Franklin Delano Roosevelt

The last witness is Franklin Delano Roosevelt, president of the United States at the time of the Pearl Harbor attack. The initial evidence for his knowledge of the attack was considered to be inferential and not worthy of discussion. However, new evidence has come to light that seriously questions that position. Was Roosevelt a man who could be deceitful in order to justify an end?

In May 1942, Roosevelt stated to Secretary of the Treasury Henry Morgenthau, "I may have one policy for Europe and one diametrically opposed for North and South America. I may be entirely inconsistent, and furthermore, I am perfectly willing to mislead and tell untruths if it will help us win the war."[56] FDR was not the first or the last president to fabricate the truth to the American people. To that end, on March 11, 1941, Roosevelt signed the Lend-Lease bill into law, permitting increased military aid to Britain—a policy that violated U.S. neutrality and international law. In April, he authorized U.S. troops be sent to Greenland. On May 27, he violated international law by sending military aid to the Soviet Union. In July 1941, he sent troops to occupy Iceland. Lastly, in September of 1941, he granted permission for U.S. naval ships to attack German and Italian ships on the high seas.[57]

On October 27, 1941, FDR spoke to an audience on Navy Day in Washington. In the initial part of his speech, he declared that German submarines had fired upon destroyer *Greer* on September 4 and upon *Kearny* on October 17. What Roosevelt failed to say was that the German submarines were first attacked by the U.S. destroyers, and the German torpedoes were fired in self-defense. Hitler had no desire to go to war with the United States. At the time, most Americans were significantly opposed to U.S. involvement in the European conflict.[58] FDR stated he had in his possession a secret map made by the German government. He pointed out that the map was of South America and the Panama Canal and was divided into five vassal states under German domination. He declared, "That map, my friends, makes it clear the Nazi design is not only against South America but against the United States." However, the map was a forgery created by British intelligence in Canada. William Donovan, U.S. intelligence chief, had passed it on to President Roosevelt.[59] The previous revelations give testimony to the length to which Roosevelt was willing to go to deceive the American people for political reasons. When Japan invaded Indochina on July 25, 1941, Roosevelt froze all of Japan's assets with a net worth amounting to $53 million. On August 1, Roosevelt placed an oil embargo on Japan which depended on the Unites States for about 80 percent of all its oil imports. When Rear Admiral Turner learned of the oil embargo, he stated:

> "An embargo would probably result in an early attack on Malaya and the Netherlands East Indies, and possibly would involve the United States in an early war in the Pacific." His advice that "trade with Japan not be embargoed at this time" was forwarded by CNO Stark to Roosevelt with a note, "I concur in general."[60] Their advice was ignored by the president. This was not the first time that FDR disregarded military advice. In January 1941, he relieved Admiral Richardson as Commander-in-Chief of the U.S. Fleet because Richardson believed that the Pacific fleet was vulnerable at the Lahaina anchorage at Maui, let alone in the confines of Pearl Harbor, and that the fleet should be relocated to the U.S. West Coast.[61]

Thus, in spite of being forewarned, Roosevelt kept the oil embargo in place, knowing full well that Japan had a stronger military than the United States and that America needed at least a six month delay in any war with Japan if the United States was to be able to compete militarily. Roosevelt told the American people that the oil embargo was necessary because the United States had a shortage of oil. This statement was a half-truth. While it was true that there was a shortage of oil on the East Coast, there was a glut of oil on the West Coast with no easy way to get the oil from the West Coast to East Coast. Thus, the problem persisted in spite of the oil embargo.[62]

FDR must have realized that Japan had only three options in response to his oil embargo:

1. Suffer and endure the consequences.
2. Capitulate to U.S. demands to counter Japan's aggression.
3. Go to war with the United States.

Japan chose the last option.

But the question remains, why would Roosevelt provoke war now? One must keep in mind that Roosevelt must have believed in a "Europe First Policy" before his meeting with Churchill aboard the *Augusta* in Placentia Bay on August 9 and 10, 1941. It was at this meeting that he formally consented to the policy. However, Roosevelt was faced with that Gallop poll in 1941 claiming to show that more Americans had come to favor war with Germany, but that question was never actually asked by the pollster. Rather the question asked if the individual favored helping Britain, invalidating the intended purpose of the poll.

One must also consider another important factor that on June 22, 1941, Germany invaded the Soviet Union and was making great gains in pushing into the interior of that country. Roosevelt was an internationalist who predicated his policy on continued Soviet-American cooperation. The Soviet Union in the summer of 1941 was pleading for Britain and the United States to launch a second front against Germany, even though America was not at war with Germany.

It has been documented that Harry Dexter White, assistant secretary of the Treasury, was, in fact, a Soviet spy. This was confirmed in 1995 when the National Security Agency declassified *Verona*, the U.S. government's program to decode Soviet spy messages before and during World War II. The FBI had been told in 1945 by Elizabeth Berkley and Whitaker Chambers (both Soviet spies) that White was a Soviet spy, but *Verona* confirmed it.[63]

On November 26, 1941, Washington and Tokyo were deeply involved in a diplomatic struggle about the U.S. view toward Japanese aggression. A U.S. diplomatic note was sent to Tokyo making various demands and offering proposals which were described by the Army Pearl Harbor Board (June to September 1944) as, "The document that touched the button that started the war."[64]

This was so because "The Note" demands were considered by the board humiliating and impossible to meet. Of critical importance is the fact that White wrote the first, second, and third parts of "The Note," which would have been approved by Secretary of State Hull and probably FDR before it was sent. This is an indication of the influence that White possessed in the Roosevelt administration. It is now known from FBI records that White was at the center of Moscow's Operation Snow, a 1941 plan to influence America's foreign policy against Japan. One must also keep in mind that Germany had invaded the Soviet Union[65] and as stated earlier, the Soviets were pleading for the United States and Britain to begin a second front. The United States knew from reading Japanese Ambassador to Germany Oshima Hiroshi's reports to Tokyo that Germany would declare war on the United States if the United States declared war on Japan, thus opening the door for America to assist Soviet Union in its fight against the Germans.

Analysis of the foregoing reveals that FDR had a proclivity to use untruths to justify his ends. It also documents that White had clearly influenced FDR's foreign policy toward Japan, even to the point that FDR acted against the military advice of his top commanders and against the best interests of the United States.

On November 25, the FDR administration was seeking a *modus vivendi* to buy three months' time in the Pacific. The reason for this was that the United States was in no position to defend its possessions in the Pacific because America needed more time to build up its depleted military. On November 26 (note date), Roosevelt dispatched his son Colonel James Roosevelt to seek out "Intrepid" Stephenson, the head of the British Security coordination organization in New York. Roosevelt was carrying the president's cable message, which stated, "Negotiations off. Services expect action within two weeks."[66]

On November 26, Churchill sent a cover note to Roosevelt that supposedly enclosed Churchill's "thin diet for Chiang Kai-shek" telegram marked "Most Secret." It arrived at 3:00 a.m. at the American Embassy in London, but Layton in his book *And I Was There* has reported "...yet nothing it contained, at least as we now see it, could have warranted disturbing the American embassy in mid-slumber. It could have waited until London office hours the next morning and still reach Washington at the start of the 26 November business day."[67]

Layton goes on to say that Churchill's cable specifically refers to a message from Roosevelt "received tonight. If—as the official record would have us believe—this was the 'President to Former Naval Person' (as the two familiarly addressed one another) message detailing the initial *modus vivendi* proposals, there is a glaring inconsistency. Roosevelt's message had been delivered to Downing Street by the American embassy messenger that morning and the foreign office copy of the same cable was received directly from the British embassy in Washington at 1300 that afternoon."[68]

Churchill would not likely confuse information from the White House that was nearly 24 hours old with a message that required an immediate response—even to the point of waking up the American embassy at 3:00 o'clock in the morning. Yet, if there was a second cable, as Churchill's response seems to indicate, that cable is not in the files. It is important to mention that on November 26, 1941 (Japanese date), the Japanese fleet sortied from Hitokappu Bay in northern Japan and headed toward Pearl Harbor. Could this intelligence be the source of Churchill's reported 3:00 a.m. cable that the Prime Minister was trying to pass on to FDR?[69]

During an online search for the missing cable, this author was able to obtain from the office of the Historian of the Secretary of State the official record of the telegram sent by Churchill at 0300, which reached Roosevelt at 0900 on November 26. The telegram's content revolves around the danger of China collapsing. It stated: "What about Chiang Kai Shek? Is he not on a very thin diet? Our anxiety is about China...." This phrase appears to mean that China was not being supplied with economic or military aid by the United States or Britain, and its fall would make the situation in the Far East much worse.

This author also made inquiries to the British Archives, but was unable to obtain find any telegrams sent by Churchill on November 26, 1941. To add to the confusion, there is a cable during this time frame to Lord Halifax marked "Secret" and dated November 26, 1941, from the British Under Secretary of State in Washington in which he acknowledges that a secret message was exchanged between Roosevelt and Churchill. Given the historic date in question, it is reasonable to ask what world event could have been so significant that prompted Churchill to immediately send FDR a secret message at 3:00 a.m. Certainly, the Japanese task force leaving northern Japan for Hawaii comes to mind. However, based on the evidence at hand, this conclusion is yet to be proven.

There are those who say Churchill could not have known that the Kido Butai was leaving northern Japan for Hawaii because the Japanese fleet maintained radio silence on its way to Pearl Harbor. As previously stated, on November 26, Station H picked up extensive radio exchanges between Admiral Nagumo and his Central Pacific commander, as well as his submarine forces in the Pacific. Certainly, it was possible that these same Japanese radio messages were detected by Britain's listening station in Singapore. In addition, the British listening station also had the capacity to locate the Japanese task force by virtue of its directional finders. In May 1994, the British government declassified documents that showed that it could freely read the Japanese fleet code (JN-25A) in 1940. Fortunately, when it was changed in October 1940 to the JN-25B, the Japanese retained the reciphering table and indicating systems, allowing for new code groups to be discovered immediately. This error of omission by the Japanese made it easier for the cryptologists to decode JN-25B messages.[70] These facts lay the groundwork for the possibility that Churchill, on November 26, 1941, was aware that a Japanese task force was in the North Pacific heading to Hawaii. With this critical intelligence in hand, it is reasonable to deduce that Churchill would send an urgent message to Roosevelt at 3:00 a.m. on November 26.

The following also gives credence to the foregoing. Robert Ogg, a special investigator for the Twelfth Naval District, disclosed to author Toland his role in locating the Japanese task force northwest of Hawaii between November 30 and December 3, 1941. His superior, Lieutenant Hosmer, obtained radio direction finder bearings on the Japanese warships. He then asked Ogg to plot the findings on the great-circle chart of the North Pacific that was in their office. Once plotted, the bearings revealed that the warships were in the North Pacific. He could not prove his assertions later because Navy intelligence personnel were forbidden to retain classified documents. He assured his detractors that confirmation could be found in the records of the Navy's intercept station at Dutch Harbor, Alaska. But no one looked there until Robert Stinnett (*Day of Deceit*). In 1984, Stinnett requested to see the 4,000 kilo-cycle records of Dutch Harbor for November and December 1941, but he was turned down. Navy historians George W. Henriksen and Commander Irwin Newman reassured him that there were no such records in the National Security Group Command files.[71] Trying a different tack in October 1985, he went to the National Archives and looked for the 4,000 kilo-cycle records from Station KING, which was a unit of Rochefort's Mid–Pacific Direction Finder Network in 1941. There he found 129 transmissions, which presented irrefutable evidence that the Japanese warships transmitted 129 messages on their way to Pearl Harbor. Of note is that Station H in Hawaii intercepted an *Akagi* broadcast on November 26, when the carrier utilized 4,963 kilo-cycles as it began its journey east toward Hawaii. Again, the foregoing date is identical to the date that the mysterious Churchill message was sent at 3:00 in the morning.[72] This evidence does not prove that the early morning urgent message was about the Japanese task force leaving Japan for Pearl Harbor on November 26, but it certainly suggests that it is a possibility.

This author visited the National Archives in College Park, Maryland, in September 2018 and reviewed the 188 Japanese Navy (JN-25B) messages released by the NSA in 1979 that were intercepted between September 1 and December 4, 1941, but were not deciphered until 1946. Although Pearl Harbor is not mentioned by name in these messages, there are a number of clues that a Japanese carrier force would attack battleships in a shallow-water harbor. In addition, the following group of diplomatic messages is also significant. It can be found in National Archives files as follows: Group 457, SRH 406, Pre-Pearl Harbor Japanese Dispatches, declassified October 1991, page 000110.

The following dispatch—part of Group 457—was sent from Honolulu to Tokyo on December 2, 1941, by diplomatic channels in reference to the balloon defense of Hawaii and the torpedo nets in Pearl Harbor. It is further evidence that Japan was obtaining information for the Pearl Harbor attack.

    1. "They have not set up mooring equipment, nor have they selected the troops to man them. Furthermore, there is no indication that any training for the maintenance of balloons is being undertaken…. I imagine that in all probability there is considerable opportunity left for a surprise attack against these places."

    2. "In my opinion, the battleships do not have torpedo nets."[73] Tokyo replied through diplomatic channels as follows:

"In view of the present situation, the presence in port of warships, airplane carriers and cruisers is of utmost importance. Hereafter, to the utmost of your ability, let me know day by day. Wire me in each case whether or not there are any observation balloons above Pearl Harbor or if there are any indications that they will be sent up. Also advise me whether or not the warships are provided with anti-torpedo nets."[74] Diplomatic message intercept, Group 457, SRH 406, p. 000115.

These two messages are very significant because they were sent through diplomatic channels using the J-19 consular code and not the code system employing the Purple machine. U.S. intelligence had given the J-19 code system a lower priority than the Purple system. The latter message was intercepted at 0707 on December 2, 1941, but not mailed to ONI, which had a Purple machine, until December 11. The intelligence did not reach Washington until December 26 and was decrypted on December 30, 1941.

In addition, Captain Safford, father of naval cryptology and head of OP-20-G (NEGAT) section of the Office of Naval Communications responsible for intercepting and breaking radio traffic of foreign navies, has stated from memory (Group 457, SRH 406, Pre-Pearl Harbor Japanese Naval Dispatches) in August 1970, "By December 1, 1941, we had the code solved to a readable extent." On May 17, 1945, Safford discussed OP-20-G's reading ability in a memorandum stating: "Station CAST was considered most reliable ... not only because CAST had better reception but because Com 16 was currently reading messages in the Japanese Fleet Cryptographic System (5-number or JN-25B) and was exchanging technical information and translations with the British Singapore unit (FECB)). As regards the JN-25 system, the current version (JN-25B) had been in effect since December 1, 1940 and remained in effect until May 27–31, 1942, and was partially readable in November 1941."[75]

This quote is certainly a departure from the previous testimony given by a number of witnesses that less than ten percent of the JN-25B code was readable prior to December 7, 1941. In addition, Winston Churchill contradicted a long line of reports that U.S. intelligence could read no more than ten percent of encrypted JN-25B messages in 1941. The Prime Minister states in his book *The Grand Alliance*: "From the end of 1940, the Americans had pierced the vital Japanese ciphers, and were decoding large numbers of their military and diplomatic telegrams."[76]

The question arises as to whether Britain had broken the Japanese Naval Code JN-25B prior to or even after December 7. British intelligence had focused its intelligence unit on JN-25A code at Bletchley Park in England until December 1939 when the task was reassigned to the British naval base in Singapore and designated as the Far East Combined Bureau (FECB). In the first volume of the officially sanctioned history text *British Intelligence in the Second World War* is the following statement, "In September 1939, beginning with the fleet cipher, the new ciphers began to yield." This reference, combined with a footnote in the second volume, states that the FECB was able "to keep track of *her* main naval movements." It is important to note that this ability was related to the JN-25A version of the Japanese naval code. On December 1, 1940, the Japanese introduced the JN-25B version of their naval code. Significantly, is the fact that when the Japanese changed the JN-25A to the JN-25B code, they did not change the additive groups which were added to the main code. For example, if the code for *Kaga* was 01905 and the additive was 00989, the final super-enciphered form was 01894. When adding 01905 and 00989, the Japanese eliminated the first digit in the addition of each column of the 5 digit equation, if there were one. Thus, when one adds 0989 to 905 (the 01 is eliminated), the sum of the two numbers is 01894 instead of the original 02894.

When the Japanese introduced the new code book for the JN-25B in December 1940, they retained the deciphering table and indicating system used in the prior JN-25A code. This oversight led to a much easier process for the allies to decipher the JN-25B code with this information unchanged.[77]

One fact is certain: on December 10, 1941, "'Intelligence reached the FECB that the *Prince of Wales* and the *Repulse* had been spotted and would be attacked from the air, four hours before the attack occurred. However, by the time the Japanese signals were decoded, the air attacks had occurred."[78] This disclosure documents that only three days after December 7, the British had the ability to decipher the JN-25B code (if not prior to that time). To this point, *The Emperor's Codes*, written by *Daily Telegraph's* defense correspondent Michael Smith and published in 2000, claims that Britain broke the JN-25B Japanese Fleet code before the Americans. Britain had been deciphering the Japanese codes as early as 1926.[79]

Credit for cracking the JN-25B code is given to John Tillman, a cryptographer who worked at Bletchley Park. Within weeks of JN-25A inception in June 1939, Tillman had deciphered the code. This was many months before the Americans would crack the code. In May 1941, the policy of complete exchange of radio intelligence between the United States unit at Corregidor and the British unit at Singapore showed that the British were well ahead of the U.S. regarding JN-25B code results. This prompted the Americans to begin a program of expansion. With the expansion of the American intelligence program, the Singapore and Corregidor units began to work in close cooperation with Army intelligence but not with Navy intelligence until both Singapore and Corregidor were overtaken by the Japanese in the first half of 1942.

The issue regarding *when and if* Britain could read the JN-25B code was finally settled in May 1994, when the British government declassified the fact that it freely read the Japanese Fleet Code (JN-25B code) in November 1941.[80] In addition, in Warren F. Kimball's *Churchill and Roosevelt,* he reports that Churchill's draft of a British warning arrived on the same day as the news of the Japanese attack on the American naval base at Pearl Harbor, signifying that British intelligence had knowledge of the attack on that date, and most likely beforehand.[81]

There is another piece of evidence indicating advance knowledge of the Japanese attack on Pearl Harbor. The disclosure was published in Gregory Douglas's book *Gestapo Chief* in 1995 and consists of a transcript of an intercept of a trans–Atlantic scrambler phone conversation between Roosevelt and Churchill on November 26, 1941. In 1996, when the U.S. government declassified all German files, they released evidence that Roosevelt and Churchill discussed the attack on Pearl Harbor in this conversation.

Background

In 1937, the American Telephone & Telegraph Company put into use a telephone scrambling device known as A-3. This device, which permitted telephone conversations to be scrambled at one end and descrambled at the other, effectively prevented interception of the conversations en route. The German *Reichpost* (state postal organization responsible for the telephone and telegraph systems in Germany) had purchased the A-3 system from AT&T before the war for its use on lines in service between Germany and the United States. However, each set of scrambling devices was different so that the possessors of one set of scrambling devices could not intercept the transmission of another. Trans-Atlantic phone calls could be intercepted because they used radiotelephone technology in which the telephone communications were broadcast as radio waves.[82]

The A-3 system in use between Roosevelt and Churchill was located on one end in the United States a secure area of the AT&T offices at 47 Walker Street in New York; the British counterpart was in London. Roosevelt's calls to Churchill were routed through the New York office where the conversations were listened to by technicians to make sure the transmissions were unintelligible after passing through the scrambling devices. Churchill and Roosevelt could not use the secure AT&T trans–Atlantic undersea telephone cable line because it did not exist until 1955.

In September 1939, the A-3 system was in use by the White House. The Germans were well aware that FDR used the scrambling device phone system through an article published in the *New York Times* entitled "Roosevelt Protected in Talks to Envoys by Radio Scrambling to Foil Spies Abroad." German Minister of Post Dr. Wilhelm Ohnesorge appointed Kurt Vetterlein, a specialist in scrambling technology, to unscramble the conversations between FDR and Churchill. By 1940, Vetterlein and his team had effectively broken Roosevelt's and Churchill's secure system.[83] Vetterlein built a device that could unscramble each conversation without the loss of any words. This resulted in Ohnesorge ordering that an intercept station be established in the occupied Dutch coastal town of Noorwijk aan Zee, just north of Haag. The operation was designed to intercept and transcribe all of the trans–Atlantic radio telephone traffic 24 hours a day.[84]

The first intercept occurred at 7:45 a.m. on September 7, 1941. There were between 30 to 60 intercepts a day. Significant intelligence was transcribed in the original English and then sent by courier either to Hitler's military headquarters or to Heinrich Himmler in Berlin. In March 1942, Ohnesorge sent the following letter to Adolf Hitler to which a copy of the intercepted conversation was attached:

> Mein Fuhrer!
>
> The research section (*Forschungsanstalt*) of the German *Reichspost* has, as the latest of its efforts, completed a unit designed to intercept the telephone message traffic between the United States and England, which had been rendered unintelligible by their use of current communications technology. Because of the significant work of the technicians, the *Reichpost* is the sole agency in Germany that is now able to make immediate interception and decoding of these hitherto unintelligible conversations.
>
> I will present these results to the *Reichsführer-SS-Pg* Himmler who will forward them to you on the 22nd of March [1942]. It is my intention, pending your approval, to strictly limit the circulation of these communications in order that no news of our success reaches the English. This might seriously jeopardize future intentions.
>
> Heil mein Führer!

The following is a copy of the conversation between Roosevelt and Churchill that was intercepted by the Germans on November 26, 1941, and reported in Douglas's *Gestapo Chief Secret State Matter.*

10. The Final Analysis of the Japanese Attack on Pearl Harbor

No. 321/41
Time: 26.11.41
Hour: 13.15
Conversation Participants
A Franklin Roosevelt, Washington
B Winston Churchill, London

B I am frightfully sorry to disturb you at this hour, Franklin, but matters of a most vital import have transpired and I felt that I must convey them to you immediately.

A That's perfectly all right, Winston. I'm sure you wouldn't trouble me at this hour for trivial concerns.

B Let me preface my information with an explanation addressing the reason I have not alluded to the facts earlier. In the first place, until today, the information was not firm. On matters of such gravity, I do not like to indulge in idle chatter. Now, I have in my hands, reports from our agents in Japan, as well as the most specific intelligence in the form of the highest level Japanese naval codes [conversation broken] for some time now.

A I felt this is what you were about. How serious is it?

B It could be worse. A powerful Japanese task force comprising [composed of] six carriers, two battleships and a number of other units to include [including] tankers and cruisers, has sailed yesterday from a secret base in the northern Japanese Islands.

A We both knew this was coming. There are also reports in my hands about a force of some size making up in China and obviously intended to go [move] South.

B Yes, we have all of that. [Interruption] … are far more advanced than you in our reading of the Jap naval operations codes. But even without that, their moves are evident. And they will indeed move South but the force I spoke of is not headed South, Franklin, it is headed East.

A Surely you must be … will you repeat that please?

B I said to the East. The force is sailing to the East … towards you.

A Perhaps they set an easterly course to fool any observers and then plan to swing south to support the landings in the southern areas. I have….

B No, at this moment their forces are moving across the northern Pacific and I can assure you that their goal is the [conversation broken] fleet in Hawaii. At Pearl Harbor.

A This is monstrous. Can you tell me … indicate … the nature of your intelligence? [conversation broken] reliable? Without compromising your sources.

B Yes, I will have to be careful. Our agents in Japan have been reporting on the gradual [conversation broken] units. And these have appeared from Japanese home waters. We also have highly reliable sources in the Japanese foreign service and even the military.

A How reliable?

B One of the sources is an individual who supplied us the material on the diplomatic codes that [conversation broken] and a Naval offices [sic] whom our service has compromised. You must trust me, Franklin and I cannot be more specific.

A I accept this.

B We cannot compromise our code breaking. You understand this. Only myself and a few [conversation broken] not even Hopkins. It will go straight to Moscow and I am not sure I want that.

A I am still attempting to … the obvious implication is that the Japs are going to do a Port Arthur on us at Pearl Harbor. Do you concur?

B I do indeed. Unless they add an attack on the Panama Canal to this vile business. I can hardly envision the canal as a primary goal, especially with your fleet lying athwart their lines of communications with Japan. No, if they do strike the canal, they will first have to neutralize [destroy] your fleet [conversation broken].

A The worst form of treachery. We can prepare our defenses on the islands and give them a warm welcome when they come. It certainly would put some iron up Congress' ass [asshole].

B On the other hand, if they did launch a bombing raid, given that the aircraft would only be of the carrier-borne types, how much actual damage could they inflict? And on what targets?

A I think torpedoes would be ruled out at the onset. Pearl is far too shallow to permit a successful torpedo attack. Probably they would drop bombs on the ships and then shoot [conversation broken] damage a number of ships no doubt the Japs would attack our airfields. I could see some damage there but I don't think an airfield or a battleship could sink very far. What do your people give you as the actual date of the attack?

B The actual date given is the eighth of December. That's a Monday.

A The fleet is in the harbor over the weekend. They often sortie during the week.

B The Japs are asking [conversation broken] exact dispositions of your ships on a regular basis.

A But Monday seems odd. Are you certain?

B It is in the calendar. Monday is the eighth. [conversation broken]

A ...then I will have to consider the entire problem. A Japanese attack on us, would result in war between us ... and certainly you as well ... would certainly fulfill two of the most important requirements of our policy. Harry has told me repeatedly ... and I have more faith in him than I do in the Soviet ambassador ... that Stalin is desperate at this point. The Nazis are at the gates of Moscow, his armies are melting away ... the government has evacuated and although Harry and Marshall feel that Stalin can hang on and eventually defeat Hitler, there is no saying what could transpire [happen] if the Japs suddenly fell on Stalin's rear. In spite of all the agreements between them and the Japs dropping Matsuoka [foreign minister], there is still strong anti–Russian sentiment in high Japanese military circles. I think we have to decide what is more important ... keeping Russia in the war to bleed the Nazis dry to their own eventual destruction [conversation broken] supply Stalin with weapons but do not forget, in fact he is your ally, not mine. There are strong isolationist feelings here and there are quite a number of anti-communists.

B Fascists.

A Certainly, but they would do all they could to block any attempt on my part to more than give some monetary assistance to Stalin.

B But we too have our major desperations, Franklin. Our shipping upon which our nation depends, is being sunk by the Huns faster than we could ever replace [conversation broken] the Japs attack both of us in the Pacific? We could lose Malaya which is our primary source of rubber and tin. And if the Japs get Java and the oil, they could press south to Australia and I have told you repeatedly, we cannot hold [conversation broken] them much but in truth I cannot deliver. We need every man and every ship to fight Hitler in Europe ... India too. If the Japs get into Malaya, they can press on virtually unopposed into Burma and India. Need I tell you of the resultant destruction of our Empire? We cannot survive on this small island, Franklin, [conversation broken] allow the nips [nips?] to attack, you can get your war declaration through your Congress after all. [conversation broken]

A ...not as capable as you are at translating their messages and the army and navy are very jealous of each other. There is so much coming in that everyone is confused. We have no agents in place in Japan and every day dozens of messages are [conversation broken] that contradict each other or are not well translated. I have seen three translations of the same message with three entirely different meanings [conversation broken] address your concern about British holdings in the Pacific ... if the Japanese do attack both of us, eventually we will be able to crush them and regain all of the lost territories. As for myself, I will be dammed glad to be rid of the Philippine [sic].

B I see this as a gamble [conversation broken] what would your decision be? We cannot procrastinate over this too long. Eleven or twelve days are all we have. Can we not agree in principle now? I should mention that several advisors have counseled [advised] against informing you of this and allowing it to happen. You see by my notifying you where my loyalty lies. Certainly to one who is heart and soul with us against Hitler.

A I do appreciate your loyalty, Winston. What on the other hand, will happen here if one of our intelligence people is able to intercept, decipher and deliver to me the same information you just gave me? I cannot ignore it ... all of my intelligence people will know about it then. I could not ignore this.

B But if it were just a vague message then?

A No, a specific message. I could not just sweep it under the rug like that [conversation broken].

B Of course not. I think we should let matters develop as they will.

A I think that perhaps I can find a reason to absent [leave] myself from Washington while this crisis develops. What I don't know can't hurt me and I too can misunderstand messages, especially at a distance [conversation broken].

B Completely. My best to you all there.

A Thank you for your call.

Citations: Nr. 321/41 gRs

The key question: *Is this transcript authentic*? The transcript as published in *Gestapo Chief* did not come from an official archive and as such cannot be documented by historians. Therefore, evidence will be presented both for its potential illegitimacy as well as its potential authenticity.

Evidence Against Authenticity

The following are statements for the fraudulent nature of the document:

    1. The fact that Roosevelt and Churchill called each other by their first names. In most conversations, Churchill was referred to as "the former naval person" and FDR as "Mr. President."

    2. The assertion that their conversation would never have been authorized or allowed on the trans–Atlantic radiotelephone link has been made by John Lukacs in his article "The Churchill-Roosevelt Forgeries" for *American Heritage* in November/December 2002.

    3. The Pearl Harbor attack date in the transcript is December 8, 1941.

    4. As far as is known, neither Kurt Vetterlein, the German who ran the intercept program, nor any of his colleagues ever mentioned this particular intercept in post-war interviews.

    5. The following is the most compelling evidence that the transcript is fraudulent: Vetterlein told American author David Kahn in his book *The Code Breakers*, published in 1967, that AT&T changed the bandwidth on its a=3 encryption/decryption device, resulting in a "blackout period" from late fall 1941

to early winter of 1942, during which they were unable to descramble phone calls. If true, the strong implication is that the document is a forgery.

6. The historical record shows that at *Reichpost* did not begin making English language transcripts until 1943; all known 1942 transcripts are in German only.

7. The author of the transcript used American English, not British English, as was common in Europe at that time.

8. The document exhibits no underlining or writings in the text margins, as many *Reichpost* transcripts did.

9. One problem with the transcript is that Churchill does not correct Roosevelt about his assumption that Pearl Harbor's shallow depth of 45 feet would mitigate against any potential Japanese torpedo attack in the harbor. As reported previously, a year earlier Britain successfully attacked Italian battleships anchored in the 40-foot depth of the waters at the Italian naval base in Taranto Bay. The success of the British mission was its ability to modify the British torpedo to handle the shallow depth. Thus, the possibility would exist that Japan could do the same to its torpedoes, which is exactly what happened.

Evidence for Authenticity

1. The fact that Churchill and Roosevelt called themselves by their first name does not by itself prove that the transcription is a forgery. While doing research in the FDR Research Library in Hyde Park, New York, in 2018, this author found a correspondence between Roosevelt and Churchill, written in 1941, in which FDR referred to Churchill as Winston. In another source, *Roosevelt and Churchill*, Loewenheim, et al. (editors), FDR again refers to Churchill as Winston. In addition, Churchill is referred to by FDR as Winston on October 15, 1941, and on March 18, April 3, and April 16 of 1942 in correspondence at the Hyde Park FDR Library.

2. The following testimony appears to refute the premise that the telephone call would never have been authorized by security. "On November 13, 2014, Ruth Ive, assistant to Churchill who was authorized to listen in and transcribe the Churchill/FDR trans–Atlantic conversations, remarked to the BBC that in 1942 that was her task. She stated: 'When possible, they signaled 24 hours beforehand that they wished to speak and they set out on numbered paragraphs the subject that they wished to discuss. Consequently, they never mentioned the actual subject, they just referred to the number of the paragraph and went on from there.'"[85] Therefore, it appears that the topic of discussion was not initially known to the listener. The AT&T link was also used by American and government officials. General Marshall repeatedly warned Roosevelt and Churchill that the trans–Atlantic link was not secure and advised them to be more discreet in their phone conversations. In addition, Churchill had the power to override any objection to any given phone call for national security reasons.

3. The Pearl Harbor attack date of December 8, 1941, is consistent with the fact that the intelligence Churchill received was obviously transcribed from Japanese sources, thereby utilizing Japanese dates. This conclusion is confirmed in

the early part of the transcription where Churchill states that a powerful Japanese task force had sailed from the northern Japanese Islands y*esterday*. The date of the conversation between Churchill and Roosevelt was November 26 (November 27 Japanese date), and yesterday would be November 26, 1941 (Japanese date). This consistency explains the December 8, 1941, date in the transcription. It appears from the transcription that Churchill and Roosevelt were not aware that the sources of intelligence Churchill received were written with Japanese dates in mind—an understandable oversight.

    4. The German *Reichpost* did have a trans–Atlantic telephone call interception and decryption operation and did prepare transcripts of intercepted calls. The fact that he does not recall seeing the document does not in and by itself rule out that the document is not authentic.

    5. "Blackout for Six Months": upon closer scrutiny of David Kahn's book *The Code-Breakers*, published in 1967, he states that the time it took to solve the encrypted phone messages from start to finish was only a few months. By September 1, 1941, the solution was in hand and within a few more months the German deciphering unit established an intercept and voice-cryptanalysis station on the Dutch coast. No mention of a "Black Out" is cited.[86] In Kahn's "*Hitler's Spies*" published in 2000, he states, "All was not entirely cut and dry. Once the AT&T engineers changed the sub-band widths, compelling Vetterlein to repeat some of his analysis." That is the only reference made to the issue that involves decryptions of the trans–Atlantic telephone calls.[87] It is unlikely that Kahn would not have made reference to a delay of almost six months in his books. Thus, one of the strongest cases to be made for the transcription's illegitimacy is now in doubt.

    6. Language, Margin Writing, and Ink and Paper Questions: According to an article written by Thomas Kimmel, Jr., the grandson of Admiral Husband Kimmel, and two coauthors in August 2009 and published in the *Journal of Intelligence and National Security* entitled "A Diplomatics [sic] Analysis of a Document Purported to Prove Prior Knowledge of the Attack on Pearl Harbor", trans–Atlantic phone transcripts were not transcribed into English until 1942.[88] The exception would be if the original 1941 German translated transcript was copied into English after 1941. The paper [A-4] and the pitch of the transcript [2.5 mm European, not Imperial 10–12 characters per inch] are both consistent with those used by the Germans during World War II, as is the classification stamp. The general style and layout of the document is consistent with authentic transcripts of *Reichpost* intercepts of calls. The document is written with a metric pitch, characteristic of a European style typewriter on aged A4–sized paper. Although governmental research and investigative agencies in Germany and the United States have been invited by author Gregory Douglas to study the original 1941 Churchill-Roosevelt transcript with chemical and physical techniques for assessing the date of the ink and paper, to date this analysis has not been performed. In 2009, the original transcript was placed in the hands of Thomas Kimmel, Jr. by Douglas.[89] The document may have been copied after the war (1945), explaining the why it was typed in English, the lack of underlining and marginalia, and the use of American English rather than British English.

    7. Churchill Fails to Correct FDR on Torpedo Bombers Ability to Operate in Pearl Harbor. One plausible explanation as to why Churchill deliberately did not

correct FDR on this point is that the president was already concerned about the potential damage that could be inflicted on the ships in the harbor. The addition of another potent offensive weapon in Japan's arsenal to inflict further destruction on ships in the harbor might be enough to persuade Roosevelt to warn Pearl Harbor and intercept the oncoming Japanese Task Force, and in so doing, cause Japan to abort its attack on the base and return home, thus preventing the United States from entering the war against Germany.

Other Factors

The date and time attributed to the transcript is plausible, which was about 12 hours after the Japanese Task Force sailed from the Kurile Islands to attack Pearl Harbor and corresponded to 0735 time in Washington—about 15 hours after the Japanese fleet sailed.

One should keep in mind that the transcript of the recorded conversation was reportedly taken from the files of Heinrich Muller, head of Hitler's secret police, the *Gestapo*, in 1948 by U.S. Army intelligence and kept classified until 1996. Therefore it is reasonable to assume that any forgery that might have occurred would have been created before 1948, since the document was kept classified and kept in the secret U.S. government files until 1996. However, it is important to note that the details and accuracy of the information in the document were little known by the Germans and the rest of the world until 1955, when Fuchida Matsuo published the intelligence in his book *Midway*.[90]

This former statement speaks against the transcript being a forgery during that time period (1941–1955). The document's critics have acknowledged that a great many details and circumstances of the transcript are accurate. In addition, it appears unlikely that a forgery was created and planted among the documents captured by the allied forces and then kept in secret U.S. intelligence files until 1996.

The following is a list of the documented facts that are discussed between Roosevelt and Churchill on November 26, 1941.

1. A powerful Japanese Task Force did leave the Kurile Islands for Hawaii on November 26, 1941 (U.S. date).[91]
2. The records at Station KING in Dutch Harbor and Station H in Oahu reveal that Akagi's radio broadcast to several merchant ships using 4963 kilocycles were intercepted en route to Pearl Harbor on November 26, 1941.[92]
3. Winston Churchill did send a telegram marked "Most Secret" to FDR at 3:00 a.m. on November 26, 1941.[93]
4. William Casey, in his book *The Secret War Against Hitler*, states, "As the Japanese storm began to gather force in the Pacific, the most private communications between the Japanese government and its ambassadors in Washington, Berlin, Rome and other major capitals were being read in Washington. Army and Navy cryptographers, having broken the Japanese diplomatic cipher, were reading messages that foretold of the attack. The British had sent word that a Japanese fleet was steaming east toward Hawaii."[94]
5. President Roosevelt departed from his more conciliatory *modus vivendi*

policy to a more aggressive attitude toward Japan for otherwise unexplained reasons on November 26, 1941.[95]

6. On November 27, 1941, Admiral Stark (CNO) sent a warning to Pearl Harbor that relations between the United States and Japan were about to be severed.[96]

7. On Friday, November 28, 1941, Roosevelt left Washington for Warm Springs, Georgia, and was there until December 1, when he was urgently recalled by Secretary of War Henry Stimson and Secretary of State Cordell Hull.[97] The reason for FDR's recall to Washington was based on the fact that on November 28, 1941, U.S. Magic diplomatic intelligence revealed that our relations with Japan were teetering on the brink of war.[98]

Academic Support for the Document's Authenticity

The document was believed to be authentic by Anthony D'Amato, Leighton Professor of Law at Northwestern University of Law, and Dr. Frank Thayer, chairman of the Department of Journalism and Mass Communications at New Mexico State University. On June 19, 2003, D'Amato filed a motion in U.S. Federal Claims Court asking not to dismiss his case of *Achenbach v. United States*.[99] The case revolved around the personal injuries suffered by his clients in World War II at the hands of the Japanese on several Pacific islands. His case was based on the fact that the U.S. government in the six months preceding Japan's attack on Pearl Harbor on December 7, 1941, "deliberately left them in harm's way by preventing them from securing passage back to the United States despite overwhelming probability if not the virtual certainty of Japanese attack." In the brief, D'Amato asserted that the defendant (U.S.) had in its possession a "smoking gun" that proved his theory that the U.S. government had foreknowledge of the Japanese attack on Pearl Harbor and therefore was culpable for the injuries suffered by his clients. He stated, "The U.S. government has in its possession transcripts of the trans–Atlantic telephone conversations of June through December 1941. These transcripts have been kept secret despite the inquires and requests for information from many historians." In 2005, Thayer wrote in full support of the authenticity of the FDR/Churchill document as the author of the foreword in Gregory Douglas' *Gestapo Chief*. These endorsements by significant academic professors have lent considerable additional credibility to the validity of the documents.[100]

Another interesting aspect of the transcript's potential authenticity is its historical accuracy, as described by Kimmel and his two coauthors in the article cited above. They reported that government research and investigative agencies in Germany and the United States had been invited by author Gregory Douglas to study the 1941 Churchill/Roosevelt transcript in an attempt to authenticate it. As of 2019, this has yet to be done. Reasons cited by Kimmel in his article for not testing the transcript are that the typewriter is of European origin and that the paper is A-4 in size and appears to be old. He concludes that if the paper were tested, it most likely would be genuine Third Reich stationery. However, Kimmel also points out that it is still possible to obtain genuine Third Reich stationary, typewriters, typewriter ribbons, and even authentic Geheime Reichssache stamps from collectors of Third Reich memorabilia in Germany. Thus, the value of testing the transcript would be to prove the transcript was not written on authentic paper or an European typewriter or that the stamp was not legitimate. This process could definitively prove that the transcript was a forgery. It is interesting that, as of this writing, an analysis of the transcript has not been done by the German or U.S. governments.

In summation, it appears that November 26, 1941, was the real Day of Infamy, when a number of clues indicating foreknowledge of the attack on Pearl Harbor intersect. The examination of these intersected clues can lead one to conclude that the truth about the bombing of Pearl Harbor in December 1941 was that it was not a *surprise* attack, as those the world over have been told for generations.

Chapter 11

Connecting the Dots

In order to support the idea that both the United States and British leaders knew of the Japanese plan to attack on Pearl Harbor, one must first address the critics of this position. The most compelling arguments against prior knowledge of the attack are as follows:

1. The Japanese maintained complete radio silence on their way to Pearl Harbor.
2. Officials at the highest levels in the military and civilian branches of our government could not or would not possibly have been involved in a cover-up.
3. No concrete evidence that there was advance knowledge of an attack on Pearl Harbor exists.
4. Denial of the existence of newly declassified intelligence which indicating that there could have been prior knowledge of the attack.

None of these arguments takes into account recent declassified intelligence that provides objective evidence that the United States unequivocally had knowledge that Japan would attack Pearl Harbor. The real question is why the United States did not act on this intelligence. The answer to this question is one of two possibilities: either U.S. intelligence grossly failed to act through ignorance, or that the U.S. government had a reason for taking no action. Namely, it was a way for America to enter a war that an overwhelming percentage of the U.S. population opposed and did not want to get involved in. This statement is supported by the fact that Congress only renewed the Selective Service Act by one vote in the House of Representatives on August 12, 1941.

The Warnings

There is no controversy that the United States clearly received a number of warnings that Japan was interested in an planned attack on Pearl Harbor. Some of the sources of the warnings are more credible and clearer in defining that Pearl Harbor was the target than others.

Warning Number 1

On January 27, 1941, U.S. Ambassador to Japan Grew provided information to Director of War Plans, Rear Admiral Turner that Japan was planning a major attack with all of its resources against Pearl Harbor. Turner dismissed the information as only "rumors" and no further action was taken.

Warning Number 2

In the fall of 1941, Kilsoo Haan visited Eric Sevareid, CBS foreign correspondent, and provided Korean underground intelligence that Japan was going to attack Pearl Harbor in December 1941 and perhaps even on the first Sunday in that month. Hann was convinced the information was accurate. He also presented evidence to Senator Guy Gillette (D–Iowa) who then submitted the intelligence to the State Department and to Army and Navy intelligence. No preemptive actions were taken based on this information.[1]

Warning Number 3

The most compelling war warning came from double agent Dusko Popov. On August 11, 1941, Popov, while working for the British intelligence agency as a double agent, brought information to MI-6 that the agency concluded warranted a meeting with the FBI. At the behest of MI-6 and with their assistance, Popov set up a meeting with the FBI. This has been detailed earlier in this book (Chapter 10) and elsewhere, but what has not received much attention is this: Popov claimed that he met with the FBI in New York and with J. Edgar Hoover in New York to offer his knowledge about Japanese interest in the British attack on the Italian navy at Taranto. He disclosed to the FBI and Hoover that the intelligence in his possession included a questionnaire and questions in microdot on a telegram which the Germans provided for him to obtain answers. Included in the questionnaire and microdot were inquiries about the depth of the Pearl Harbor waters and whether there were any torpedo nets in place. For over 42 years, the FBI denied that Hoover had ever met with Popov. But in 1983, the FBI declassified documents that proved otherwise. For example, one such document exonerated Hoover from the charge that he had not passed on Popov's information to U.S. intelligence. In so doing, the FBI substantiated that Popov had met with the FBI and revealed that Popov's initial intelligence included questions about the depth of the waters in Pearl Harbor and the presence of torpedo nets.[2]

This author's review of the FBI files in December 2018 discovered a memorandum dated December 11, 1941, from the Assistant Director of the FBI D.M. Ladd to FBI Director Hoover stating that ten days before the attack on Pearl Harbor, Japanese radio intercepts had been obtained by HYPO in Hawaii. Unable to break the consular code, HYPO sent the unencrypted coded message to Washington intelligence, where Army G2 deciphered the message. The decryption revealed, "A message was sent by Army radio to the Hawaiian Islands, *setting forth* this entire plan for the Japanese attack on Pearl Harbor to the authorities in Honolulu."[3] Included in the FBI files was intelligence that Japanese code words would be sent to its fleet, that the date had been established, and that the code words would be used as a signal to attack. This code words would be repeated three times. The code worded message should have alerted U.S. intelligence that the attack would come on Saturday (December 6 U.S date) or Sunday (December 7 U.S. date). This information was also sent by military radio to the Hawaiian Islands. However, an investigation by Supreme Court Justice Owen Roberts, chairman of the 1941 Roberts Commission, questioned Colonel Kendall Fielder and Lieutenant Colonel George Bicknell of Army Intelligence in Hawaii.

December 12, 1941

MEMORANDUM

At about 5:00 P. M., Honolulu Time, on Friday afternoon, December 5, 1941, a Dr. Mori in Hawaii talked by telephone to a relative in Japan. The exact identity of the relative to whom he talked was not known, but it is known that Dr. Mori has a close relative who is an Admiral in the Japanese Navy.

The transcript of this telephone call disclosed that the party in Japan inquired concerning weather conditions in the Hawaiian Islands for the past few days and was advised that the past few days had been very cold, with occasional rainfall, and that the wind was blowing very strongly, which was an unusual climatic phenomenon. The party in Japan inquired about the U. S. Fleet and was told that Dr. Mori did not know much about the fleet but that it was "deemed small." Dr. Mori indicated that some of the fleet had left the Hawaiian Islands. The party in Japan also inquired whether there were many searchlights in the Hawaiian Islands and whether they were used on planes which flew around at night. The answer to these inquiries was negative. Other inquiries of the person in Japan concerned the morale of the Japanese people, a direct inquiry as to whether there were any big factories in the Hawaiian Islands, which was answered in the negative, and a direct inquiry as to the size of the population, in answer to which Dr. Mori stated that "there seemed to be precautionary measures taken."

Dr. Mori also advised of the reported arrival and departure of the Russian Ambassador to the United States Litvinoff. A further inquiry of the person in Japan was as to the type of flowers in bloom in Hawaii, to which the answer was that hibiscus and poinsettia were in bloom.

On Saturday evening, December 6, the Special Agent in Charge of the Honolulu Field Division of the Federal Bureau of Investigation transmitted the contents of the Dr. Mori conversation to Army and Navy authorities. The FBI official insisted the message was peculiar, in view of the fact that no one would talk from Japan to Hawaii eighteen minutes about flowers and the climate. The FBI official insisted the reference to flowers pertained to identification of islands. The Office of Naval Intelligence scoffed at the significance

Justice Department memorandum dated December 12 about the Japanese plans for Pearl Harbor (National Archives).

Neither one was aware of any communication from G-2 in Washington that contained any narrative of a complete Japanese plan to attack Pearl Harbor, nor any code words that would indicate that the Japanese task force was to attack. Hoover subsequently wrote a letter to Stephen Early, Secretary to the President detailing Ladd's intelligence.

> FEDERAL BUREAU OF INVESTIGATION
>
> DML:CSH
>
> Date 12/11/41
>
> Mr. Clegg
> Mr. Foxworth
> Mr. Glavin
> Mr. Ladd
> Mr. Nichols
> Mr. Rosen
> Mr. Carson
> Mr. Drayton
> Mr. Quinn Tamm
> Mr. Rendon
> Mr. Coffey
> Mr. Harbo
> Tele. Room
> Your Room
> Mr. Kleinkauf
> Mr. Tracy
> Miss Beahm
> Miss Gandy
>
> MEMORANDUM FOR THE DIRECTOR
>
> ▓▓▓▓▓ today informed ▓▓▓▓▓ in the strictest of confidence (and with the statement that if it ever got out that he had disclosed this information he would be fired), that about ten days before the attack on Pearl Harbor a number of Japanese radio intercepts had been obtained in Hawaii. When they were unable to break the code in these intercepts in Hawaii they sent them in to Washington where G2 broke them. It was found that these radio messages contained substantially the complete plans for the attack on Pearl Harbor, as it was actually carried out. The messages also contained a code Japanese word which would be sent out by radio to the Japanese fleet as the signal for the attack, when this word was repeated three times in succession. A message was sent by Army radio to the Hawaiian Islands, setting forth this entire plan for the information of the authorities in Hawaii.
>
> On Friday morning, December 5th, the code words referred to in the previous messages as the signal for the attack were intercepted, which should have indicated that the attack was to be on either Saturday or Sunday, and this information was sent by military radio to the Hawaiian Islands.
>
> ▓▓▓▓▓ stated there was a great deal of inquiry going on at the present time for the purpose of determining the reason for the fiasco at Hawaii, the inquiry being directed along two lines, first whether there was a breakdown in the military radio and a failure of the message to get across, or second whether the message was delivered and not acted upon by the military authorities. ▓▓▓▓▓ stated it was his understanding that when this all came out they would clean house in the Navy.
>
> ▓▓▓▓▓ stated with reference to the danger to the naval vessels, it was his understanding that one battleship, the West Virginia, was sunk; another one, believed to be the Oklahoma, is on its side, but can be salvaged; a third exploded but is in shallow water and the anti-aircraft guns can still be utilized; and 3 others were damaged. ▓▓▓▓▓ stated the reason this matter is being kept so quiet is that it is the hope of the Navy that they can get the Oklahoma afloat and repair it and the other ships enough so that they can be taken to Bremerton, Washington for repairs under their own power; that the Navy is afraid if word gets out that all six have not been sunk the Japanese will come back and again attack these ships.
>
> Respectfully,
>
> D. M. Ladd
>
> (INFORMATIVE MEMORANDUM - NOT TO BE SENT TO FILES SECTION)

Memorandum dated December 11 from D.M. Ladd, assistant director of the FBI Intelligence Unit, to the FBI director about the complete Japanese plans to attack Pearl Harbor (National Archives).

Ladd's memo to Hoover dated December 11, 1941, included the following information:

1. The name of the informant on the author's copy of the memorandum is redacted and that he was concerned about being fired if the information he disclosed to Ladd ever got out.

2. The Ladd memorandum says that ten days before the attack on Pearl

11. Connecting the Dots 191

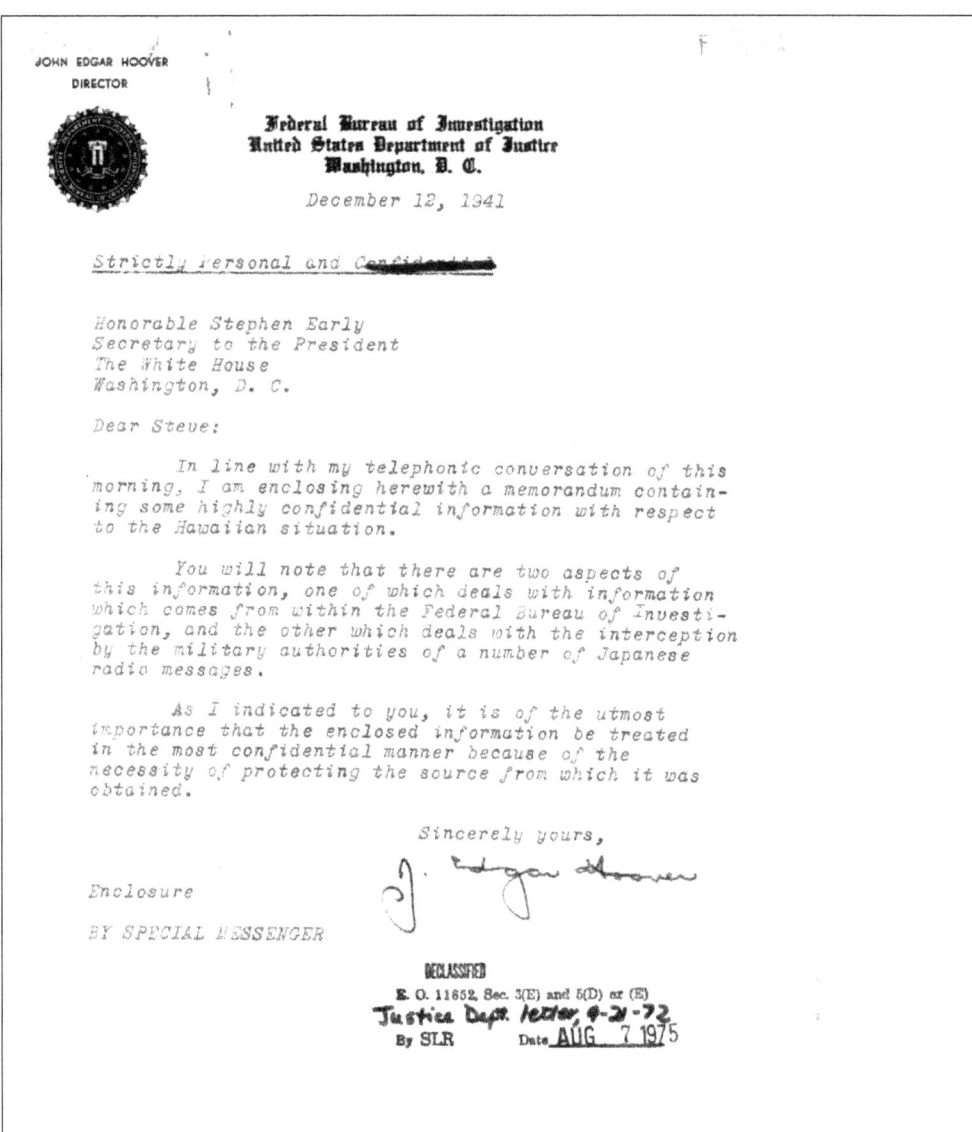

Letter dated December 12, 1941, from FBI Director J. Edgar Hoover to Stephen Early, secretary to the president, regarding a number of Japanese radio messages and information that comes from within the FBI (National Archives).

Harbor, a number of Japanese radio intercepts had been obtained in Hawaii and subsequently sent to G2 in Washington.

3. The decrypted intercept revealed the complete plans for the attack on Pearl Harbor as it was carried out.

4. The informant's choice of words "setting forth" in this context would be defined as the "forecasting of a future event" and clearly indicate that the messages were deciphered prior to the attack on Pearl Harbor.

Certainly the informant would be concerned about being fired if the Japanese intercepts were deciphered before the Pearl Harbor attack for the information would have far reaching consequences. Also of interest, as stated in the prior chapter, is that Colonel Verkuyl and his Dutch intelligence group in Java deciphered a J-19 consular-coded radio message in late November 1941 which revealed that Japan was going to attack Hawaii. In addition, the same message stated that attacks would also be made on the Philippines, Malaya, and Thailand and would be signaled by a weather broadcast (the "winds" message). [This message is very similar to the message reported in the Ladd memo to J. Edgar Hoover. The name on the memorandum was revealed in 2002 to be Colonel John T. Bissell, who at that time Chief of Counter Intelligence at Army G-2.]

HYPO, on one hand, could decipher PA-K2 and LA coded messages, but on the other lacked the capability to decipher J-19 consular messages.[4] Thus, the unencrypted message was sent to Army intelligence in Washington for decryption.

Therefore, both the HYPO and the Verkuyl messages were in the J-19 consular code and both messages were very similar in content, thus validating each other. This was particularly important for Verkuyl's decryption, the proof of the existence of which was destroyed when Japan invaded Java. Thus, another dot is connected. This further supports the position that the U.S. government had advance knowledge of the attack on Pearl Harbor.

In the 1946 Joint Congressional Committee hearings, upon questioning from Senator Homer Ferguson (MI), Justice Roberts, head of the Roberts Commission on Pearl Harbor, revealed that he made no serious attempt to find the real origin of a memorandum he received from J. Edgar Hoover. Once Roberts found out there was no connection in the memorandum to Kimmel and Short, the Roberts commission investigation came to a halt. Nor was Hoover ever asked to testify at any of the Pearl Harbor hearings.[5]

We now turn to a question that has been asked many times over the years by historians: "To what extent could Navy intelligence read the JN-25B Japanese naval code?" The general consensus has been that OP-20-G (Washington intelligence) could read about ten percent of the JN-25B code prior to the Japanese attack on Pearl Harbor.

A Navy report, declassified on March 6, 1982, revealed that 85 percent of its efforts in intelligence communications in November and early December 1941 were devoted to Japanese naval traffic. This revelation indicated that naval intelligence spent the majority of its time reading Japanese naval messages in the weeks preceding the attack.[6] SRH-149, *Communications Intelligence in the United States* by Captain L. Safford, head of Naval Security Group; *Listening to the Enemy* by Ronald Spector, DE 1988, Chapter 1.

In 1997, the Navy's official position on its capability to read the main Japanese fleet code (JN-25B) was declassified. National Archives RG457, SRH-355, p. 398. It stated: "By December 1, we had it solved to a readable extent." *Naval Security Group History to World War II* by Captain J.S. Holtwick, Jr., USN, Chief of Staff, National Security Agency. Until it was admitted in 1997, naval intelligence denied it could substantially read JN-25B.

On December 10, 1941, Captain Safford gave authority to HYPO to work on the JN-25B code. On December 22, 1941, only 15 days after the Pearl Harbor attack, U.S. intelligence in Hawaii was able to determine that *Tone, Chikuma, Hiryu,* and *Soryu* had become part of the 24th Flotilla of Japan's Fourth Fleet at Wake Island. Rochefort reported that the intelligence derived from the Japanese radio communications was the result of the data-processing of traffic analysis, call-sign analysis, and direction findings.[7]

The preceding discussion brings us to the very important role that radio traffic analysis played in helping connect the dots regarding advance knowledge of the Pearl Harbor attack. On November 25 (U.S. date), there was intensive radio communications between Admiral Nagumo, Japan's Central Pacific Commander Vice Admiral Inouye, and Vice Admiral Shimizu Mitsumi, commander of the Advanced Submarine Force. Nagumo broke radio silence as his task force sailed east toward Hawaii. The three-way conversations were detected by HYPO's RDF operators at Heeia. At mid-morning on this date, Japanese aircraft carriers were heard transmitting on 4,963 kilocycles by Homer Kisner's (Pacific Fleet's radio intercept chief) operators at HYPO. Harry Hood, one of the Navy intercept operators stationed at KING at Dutch Harbor, reported to author Stinnett that the RDF position of the Japanese warships near the Kurile Islands was not only detected but reported directly to Rochefort in Pearl Harbor by priority radio dispatch from Dutch Harbor. Hood was never asked to testify before any of the post–Pearl Harbor hearings.[8]

On November 30, 1941, directional finders at Station KING and many other U.S. listening stations covering the Pacific detected intensive radio communications emanating from the northwest Pacific. The radio intercept operators at Dutch Harbor placed Japanese warships near the Kurile Islands and indicated that the ships were sailing eastward.[9] Japanese radio traffic continued through December 4 and was also picked up by San Francisco's Twelfth Naval District: Stations ITEM, CAST, H, KING, SAIL, and Matson liner SS *Lurline*, all placing Japanese warships in the north Pacific. Station CAST actually identified that the warships included carriers and that Admiral Yamamoto was involved in the transmissions. All of this intelligence was logged in official Navy reports and forwarded through the intelligence pipeline intended for the White House. Incredibly, none of the foregoing detailed information was given to Admiral Kimmel. However, according to Elliot Carlson in his book *Joe Rochefort's War*, as of December 2, 1941, Rochefort and most of the HYPO analysts believed the carriers were still in Japan waiting to sail. In the hearings that followed, Rochefort testified, "The task to detect the location of the Japanese ships was impossible because they were not transmitting. They were on radio silence."[10]

This explanation by Rochefort hinges on the untruth that the Japanese task force maintained complete radio silence on its way to attack Pearl Harbor. Stinnett, in his book *Day of Deceit*, unequivocally refutes this premise, presenting definitive documentary evidence that radio silence was broken by the Japanese leadership.

In particular, Stinnett states that on December 5, 1941, at 1300 Kisner delivered ten messages from Yamamoto to Rochefort's office in Pearl Harbor. Sent from Station CAST, these were crucial messages from Japanese carriers which included the names of most of these carriers. Rochefort ignored the CAST reports and never passed this intelligence on to Layton or even admitted to their existence. In his Daily Communication Summaries of December 1–5, he wrote, "Not one carrier has been identified."[11] On December 6, 1941, Rochefort did inform Admiral Kimmel of the intercepts he received on December 5. In six words, he informed Kimmel that Admiral Yamamoto had "originated several [not the ten messages that were sent] messages to the carriers."[12] The messages revealed by Stinnett are still classified and not available to the public, but Stinnett clearly documents that the Kido Butai did break radio silence and that Rochefort was part of the Navy cover up. Until the publication of Stinnett's book, the strongest argument of those who believe that the U.S. government had no prior knowledge of the attack on Pearl Harbor was that the Japanese task force maintained complete radio silence during en route to Hawaii. The question is not, "Did the U.S. have foreknowledge of the attack on Pearl Harbor?" but rather, "Why was the available intelligence not acted upon by the many people who had access to it?"

Carlson states in his book *Joe Rochefort's War* that as of December 22, 1941, "It would be many weeks before JN-25B would be readable."[13] Many weeks is a relatively short period of time compared to the fact that CAST (Philippine intelligence) and OP-20-G were working unsuccessfully on breaking the JN-25B code for the entire year preceding the attack on Pearl Harbor. Even if it were true that U.S. naval intelligence could only decipher ten percent of the JN-25B code as of December 7, 1941, there clearly was enough evidence even without this source of information to conclude that Japan was going to attack Pearl Harbor.

There is additional evidence in support of the prior statement, namely that the bomb plot message previously described is intimately connected to the intelligence given by Popov to the FBI that Pearl Harbor was going to be attacked. Japanese spy Morimura Tadashi arrived in Hawaii on March 27, 1941. The day before his arrival, Navy intelligence, with the FBI's approval, was given primary responsibility for the spy's surveillance. However, the FBI still continued to follow the Japanese spy. On August 21, 1941, Morimura had been working on a secret grid outlining the U.S. ships' anchorages in Pearl Harbor, which paralleled and reinforced the intelligence given by Popov to the FBI (see Chapter 10). Using the J-19 consular code, Morimura sent his bomb plot grid from Honolulu to Tokyo intelligence and to the Japanese embassy in Washington. At this time (August 1941), Frederick Tillman of the FBI was still leading the agency's surveillance of the Japanese spy. The J-19 coded bomb plot message sent by Morimura to Tokyo and Washington was decoded by Washington intelligence. However, the decrypted bomb plot message was never sent to Tillman. On August 27, 1941, Tillman sent the first bomb plot map of Pearl Harbor to Hoover at the FBI and to Adolf Berle, Jr., FDR's personal representative to the Joint Intelligence Committee, at the State Department.[14] On August 21, 1941, after the bomb plot message was decrypted by Washington intelligence, Captain Kirk of Naval Intelligence and Captain Bode of Foreign Intelligence insisted that Admiral Turner of the War Plans Division inform Admiral Kimmel. Their strong position on the matter resulted in their being removed from their jobs in Washington and sent elsewhere. What reason could Admiral Turner have for not informing Kimmel about intelligence that a spy in Hawaii had made a grid of the locations of the ships in Pearl Harbor? It makes no sense that intelligence of such high importance was not passed on to Kimmel, unless there was another reason, such as concern that the readiness of the Army and Navy in Hawaii might prevent Japan from striking the first blow. As stated earlier, Roosevelt was emphatic that Japan must strike the first blow in order for America to fully support a war in the Pacific.[15]

The FBI knew that spy Morimura was traveling in Hawaii and surveying the disposition and location of U.S. ships in Pearl Harbor in August 1941. In addition, it can now it can now be shown with the release of declassified files that there was a meeting between Popov and the FBI, and possibly one with J. Edgar Hoover, in August 1941. There is also evidence that Popov's intelligence was passed on to the FBI. The FBI files released in 1983 reveal that Popov's questionnaire contained two critical questions: What was the depth of the water in Pearl Harbor? Were there torpedo nets in place?[16] Popov's intelligence and the bomb plot message both clearly indicate that Japan was seriously considering an attack on Pearl Harbor.

Obfuscation Along the Way

Over the past 75 years, it has been difficult to obtain the answers to critical questions about the Japanese attack on Pearl Harbor. On November 30, 1941, Robert Orr, stationed with the Twelfth Naval District Intelligence Office in San Francisco, obtained Japanese radio direction readings that placed Japanese warships in the Pacific, north of Hawaii, from November 30 to December 4, 1941. Records of the events Orr observed were not retained by him because Navy intelligence personnel were forbidden to remove classified documents from the office. Subsequently, in 1984, he recommended to Stinnett that he investigate the records at Station King in Dutch Harbor which also had picked up the Japanese radio signals.

In 1984, all original intercept records of the Pacific Theater were classified and were held in the custody of the National Security Group Command (NSGC) in Washington. Stinnett went to NSGC and was told by Navy historians George W. Henriksen and Commander Irwin Newman that there were no such records in the NSGC files. Undaunted, in October 1985 Stinnett turned to RDF Station KING's files in Seattle where he found definitive proof of Orr's assertions. In addition, Stinnett also found there the records of HYPO in Hawaii that revealed that they too had picked up an *Akagi* broadcast on November 26, 1941.[17]

As for the SS *Lurline*, that story has already been told (pages 179–180), but now the reader understands why *Lurline*'s records were illegally removed from the National Archives in San Bruno, California, most likely by the Navy.[18] The reason for their removal, this author submits, is to hide the evidence that reveals that Japanese war ships were detected in the northwest Pacific in late November 1941, which would prove radio silence was broken by the Japanese on their way to Hawaii.

The foregoing documentation is substantial evidence that the U.S. government at the highest levels knew in advance of the Japanese plan to attack Pearl Harbor and, indeed, knew that the Japanese task force had left the Kurile Islands in late November and was steaming toward Pearl Harbor. Was the lack of the U.S. response to this intelligence a result of negligence, or a deliberate attempt by the United States to allow Japan to strike the first blow against the United States in the war in the Pacific?

It is difficult to understand why senior officials of the Navy, Army, and FBI and the president of the United States did not inform Admiral Kimmel and Hawaii intelligence of the bomb plot information, Popov's report to the FBI, and the radio directional findings of November 29 to December 4, 1941; not grant HYPO permission to work on the JN-25B code; deprive Hawaii of Purple intelligence from mid–July to mid–October 1941; and, perhaps most important of all, not give Hawaii intelligence a Purple machine, while giving three machines to Britain without a substantial explanation.

The reason for this inexplicable behavior can very easily be attributed to this plausible explanation: politically the American populace would not support a war in the Pacific in which the United States struck the first blow. Indeed, the United States did not declare war on Germany until Germany declared war on America five days after Pearl Harbor. This also explains the strange behavior, as previously described, of General Marshall on the night of December 6 and the morning of December 7, 1941. It also explains the disappearance of evidence from San Bruno, the decision of the FBI not to arrest the Japanese spy Yoshikawa Takeo in Hawaii, the FBI denial that Popov ever met with Hoover until that agency released the truth in 1983, and the ineptness of Associate Justice Roberts in his hearing of 1941. Lastly, it is a rational explanation of why only four days after Japan's attack on Pearl Harbor, Rear Admiral Noyes, the Navy's director of communications, instituted a 54 year censorship policy that confined all pre–Pearl Harbor Japanese military and diplomatic intercepts to Navy vaults where they would be free from public scrutiny. In addition, he ordered the following: "Destroy all notes or anything in writing."[19] His actions allowed for the exclusion of Japanese military intercepts pre–Pearl Harbor from the presidential-appointed Roberts Commission and subsequent investigations. First, Noyes denied giving the order to his subordinates. Later, he said, "I may have instructed my subordinates to destroy personal memoranda. Nothing was said to destroy official records." However, personal memoranda written by Navy officials in Navy offices rightly belong to the people of the United States if the files concern naval matters. They cannot be destroyed, except by the authority of Congress.

One more piece of evidence that supports the fact that Churchill knew of Japanese intentions to attack Pearl Harbor came to light in May 1994, when the British government declassified the intelligence that it could freely read the Japanese fleet code (JN-25B) during October and November 1941. This was possible because the Japanese Navy made an incredible blunder when, in October 1941, they introduced a new version of the Japanese fleet code book (JN-25B) by retaining the former reciphering table and indicating system which the Allies had already solved. This meant that not only the dictionary was exposed, but also that JN-25B was readable throughout until June 1942.[20]

This mistake was extremely important because it meant in effect that Britain, and most likely the United States, had free access to the deciphering of the JN-25B fleet code in the critical months of October and November leading up to the Japanese attack on Pearl Harbor. It is important to note that the preceding British declassification stated that the code books were already solved by the Allies. It is also to be noted that as of December 10, 1941, Britain knew of a coming attack by the Japanese on the *Prince of Wales* and *Repulse*. This clearly supports the fact that Britain had the ability to decipher the JN-25B.[21]

As stated above, the best argument against the premise that the U.S. government had prior knowledge of the Japanese attack on Pearl Harbor is that all the Japanese ships maintained radio silence on their way to Hawaii. However, this position has proven to be untrue. There is an old saying that if a given answer is not consistent with the facts, then one must look elsewhere for the answer. The answer, I submit, is that:

1. The U.S. government did know of the attack on Pearl Harbor.
2. The U.S. government deliberately withheld critical intelligence from Kimmel and Short in Hawaii to ensure that Japan would strike the first blow.[21]

3. In so doing, they gained the support of the U.S. public, the majority of which in 1941 were opposed to going to war with either Japan or Germany.

Not only did the U.S. government at its highest levels know of the impending attack on Pearl Harbor, but reacted in such a way as to keep this intelligence a secret. On November 25, 1941, the day the Japanese carrier force sailed for Pearl Harbor, the Vacant Sea directive was issued by Rear Admiral Turner. The directive clearly ordered all U.S. and allied military and commercial shipping out of the northern route to Hawaii. This action was taken even though War Plan 46 from the War Plans Division stated that a Japanese attack on Oahu would likely arise not from the northwest but from the southwest, emanating from the Marshall Islands southwest of Hawaii. Thus, the Vacant Sea directive clearly indicates that the United States was aware that the Japanese were sailing on a northerly route to Hawaii. In addition, the United States wanted to be sure the Japanese task force remained undetected so that the task force would not turn around. This position was taken because FDR had made it clear that he wanted Japan to strike the first blow. Again, the political climate in the Unites States at that time would not support a war in the Pacific if the U.S. again were the aggressor. Independent of the Churchill/FDR scrambler phone issue, it can be reasonably concluded that the U.S. government at its highest levels had foreknowledge of the Japanese attack on Pearl Harbor and deliberately failed to act on this intelligence for political reasons. In closing, I have presented the truth as I see it. It is now up to the reader to decide if my conclusion is warranted by the facts presented in this book.

CHAPTER 12

Epilogue

The story told in this book leads to the aftermath and consequences of the decision-making by all senior leaders involved in the attack on Pearl Harbor. On the Navy side, Admiral Husband E. Kimmel was named by ranking government officials as one of the two individuals who were held totally responsible for the U.S. disaster. The other was Army Lieutenant General Walter C. Short. They would suffer the brunt of the blame resulting from the failure of high-ranking officials in the Navy, Army, FBI, Naval and Army intelligence and President Roosevelt to inform them of critical intelligence regarding the upcoming attack on Pearl Harbor. Kimmel's Navy career and reputation were destroyed on December 16, 1941, when his rank was reduced to two stars, and he was relieved of his Pacific command. Lieutenant General Short was also relieved of his command. All others escaped with little or no real consequences for the role they played in the attack.

To the uninitiated, the story begins with a flashback in order to appreciate what really happened and how it ties into the narrative presented in the previous chapters. The account begins on board Rear Admiral Turner's fast battleship/flagship *South Dakota*. The ship was present at the signing of the Japanese surrender ceremony in Tokyo Bay on board USS *Missouri* on August 15, 1945. Present that evening in the ship's wardroom was Admiral Turner, a personal guest of Admiral Chester W. Nimitz, Commander-in-Chief of the Pacific Fleet. Also present in the war room was Captain Edwin T. Layton, fleet intelligence officer for Nimitz throughout most of the war and for Kimmel during his time as Commander-in Chief, Pacific Fleet. In his capacity as chief of war plans, Turner had been a forceful junior member of the triumvirate who virtually ran the office of the Chief of Naval Operations throughout 1941. He had assumed responsibility for many of the traditional functions of the Office of Navy Intelligence. In order to protect himself and other senior officers, he led the charge to have a policy to discredit Kimmel in public. Turner remarked to Layton that Kimmel had all the intelligence necessary to protect Pearl Harbor. "Admiral," Layton said, "I'm sorry but Kimmel did not have that information. You say he did. I know he did not and I was there." This brings us full circle to the events as they unfolded during the days and months preceding the attack on Pearl Harbor.[1]

The keys to the guilt or innocence of Admiral Kimmel were (1) whether or not he had received the critical intelligence that Washington had in its possession and (2) were the warnings to him from CNO Stark about a possible Japanese attack on Pearl Harbor specific enough for Kimmel to place the fleet on high alert. One cannot act responsibly without the critical intelligence to do so. Thus, we will now examine the communications sent to Kimmel from Stark in the months preceding the attack and the intelligence that he was deprived of which Washington had in its possession. One must not forget the Vacant Sea order, which prohibited Kimmel and his fleet and all commercial ships from sailing into the northwest Pacific waters. This directive alone took away one avenue left to Kimmel in that the Japanese ships could have been spotted early and may have alerted him early in the game as to an impending Japanese attack.

On October 17, 1941, a personal letter from the CNO came to Kimmel. It stated, "Personally I do not believe the Japs are going to sail into us. And the message I sent you merely stated that possibility."[2] The contents of the letter came as a surprise to Kimmel since a week earlier Stark had sent an official message to Kimmel warning about the "grave situation" of a possible Japanese attack. (Stark's letter was written a day after the alert.) This is one example of the ambiguous and cryptic nature of the communications being sent to Kimmel.

Another fact not well appreciated in the historical literature is that on the morning of November 26, 1941, Secretary of the Navy Frank Knox, Army Chief of War Plans Brigadier General Leonard T. Gerow, and CNO Admiral Harold R. Stark met and agreed upon a memorandum for the president that what the United States needed was more time. In the memorandum, Roosevelt was advised against presenting Japan with an ultimatum and that military response was only to be considered if Japan attacked the United States first. After receiving the memorandum, Roosevelt telephoned his approval. General Marshall and Admiral Stark ordered that warnings of imminent attack be sent to their respective Pacific commanders, General MacArthur, Admiral Hart, and Admiral Kimmel. Rear Admiral Turner drafted the Navy's message as a "war warning." Marshall's message to MacArthur included an order to begin air reconnaissance and not to alarm the civilian population. It added that while he should be ready for an attack, Japan must be allowed to strike the first blow.

For Admiral Hart's benefit, Turner listed the anticipated targets in the Western Pacific but did not even mention the possibility that Japan could strike Pearl Harbor, to Admiral Kimmel's great detriment. The communications sent to these commanders mentioned no fewer than three times in each letter that Japan must commit the first overt act before any offensive action was to be taken. The fact that the Navy message drafted by Turner failed to specify any likely targets where the Japanese might strike concerned Admiral Stark. In response, Turner revised the message, used the phrase "war warning" then proceeded to list targets—inexplicably—on the other side of the Pacific. The communication impressed Admiral Hart but not Pacific Fleet headquarters, 4,000 miles away from the proposed scene of the attack.[3]

On November 27, 1941, Kimmel received another message from Admiral Stark, directing that *Enterprise* and *Lexington* were to transfer half of the Army's P-40s to Wake and Midway Islands. This directive was a clear sign to Kimmel that an attack on Pearl Harbor was neither imminent or probable. Also on November 27, Kimmel received the following message from Stark that had been drafted by Turner. It stated:

> This dispatch is to be considered a war warning. Negotiations with Japan looking toward stabilization of conditions in the Pacific have ceased and an aggressive move by Japan is expected within the next few days. The number and equipment of Japanese troops and the organization of naval task forces indicate an amphibious expedition against either the Philippines, Thai or Kra peninsula or possibly Borneo. Execute an appropriate defensive

deployment preparatory to carrying out our tasks assigned in WPPAC-46.* Inform District and Army authorities. A similar warning is being sent by the War Department SPENAV [Special Naval Observer in London] inform British. Continental districts Guam, Samoa directed to take appropriate measures against sabotage.[4]

In February 1941, Kimmel and his chief planner, Captain Charles McMorris, developed a plan called WPPAC-46. It anticipated a Japanese attack throughout the Western Pacific, Philippines, Malaya, Borneo, and Indonesia (the Greater Co-Prosperity Sphere). It assumed that the United States would have some warning of Japanese intentions. Raids on U.S. bases such as Wake Island, and even Pearl Harbor itself, were considered, but deemed unlikely in view of the lack of Japanese resources needed to execute attacks over such a wide geographic area. Any direct attempt to relieve the Philippines was rejected because of the lack of U.S. resources, lack of adequate and secure bases, and strong Japanese air power. The United States would launch immediate raids against the Marshall Islands. All U.S. pre-war plans underestimated the strength and quality of Japanese airpower.[5]

The Army warning sent to General Short included the following words: "Undertake no offensive action until Japan has committed an overt act."[6] There was no mention at all that Pearl Harbor might be a target of the Japanese Navy. The focus was on defensive action and specific areas in the Far East were mentioned as targets of Japan's offensive to begin the war. Washington sent a second dispatch, approved by Marshall, that was addressed only to General Short. It stated that Short was "not to alarm the civil population."[7]

As for Admiral Kimmel, it is clear that he never received critical intelligence known to OP-G-20, by either deciphered Purple intercepts or JN 25B radio intelligence. Nor was Kimmel made aware of the intelligence in the hands of the FBI that was pivotal in discerning that Pearl Harbor was a target of the Japanese Navy. In addition, the Vacant Sea policy issued to Kimmel on November 25, 1941, the day the Kita Butai sailed from the Kuriles to Pearl Harbor, prevented him from sending ships into sea area north and northwest of Oahu.

The following is a list of the intelligence, in chronological order, that was not passed on to Admiral Kimmel:

1. January 27, 1941: U.S. Ambassador to Japan Grew presents his rumored report that in case of war, Pearl Harbor will be attacked.[8]

2. March 27, 1941: Morimura Takeo arrives in Honolulu. His activities of providing significant operational intelligence to Japan on Pearl Harbor were known to the FBI and the Navy. He was permitted to operate freely in his espionage activities throughout the entire year of 1941. His investigation was approvingly turned over to the Navy by the FBI from the inception of Morimura's arrival on Oahu, until his departure on December 6, 1941.[9]

3. April 1941: Rear Admiral Ingersoll, Assistant Chief of Naval Operations, orders CAST to supply Purple intercepts to Admiral Hart and General MacArthur without passing the same intercepts to Admiral Kimmel. General Marshall, Captain Alan Kirk, director of Naval Intelligence, Joseph Redman, assistant to Rear Admiral Leigh Noyes, director of Naval Communications, and Commander Laurence Safford, head of Station U.S., all knew of this arrangement.[10]

4. August 11, 1941: Dusko Popov informs the FBI that the Japanese were

interested to learn if Pearl Harbor had any torpedo nets or whether barrage balloons had been installed.[11]

5. September 24, 1941: Lieutenant Tachibana Itaru issues a dispatch to the consul general in Honolulu requesting the location of the anchorage of U.S. warships and aircraft carriers in Pearl Harbor. Morimura is told to plot an invisible grid over the harbor; thus it became known as the bomb plot message. The message was encoded in the J-19 consular code and deciphered by OP-20-G on October 9, 1941.[12]

6. November 15–December 6, 1941: As the Japanese are sailing to Pearl Harbor, they transmit over 129 radio messages, which are intercepted by Stations H and CAST. Stinnett reports that for the 21-day period, both stations averaged 6.3 intercepts a day from all categories of Japanese carriers and carrier commands. This data is derived from an analysis of the intercepts performed by Captain Duane Whitlock of Station Cast and Homer Kisner of Station H.[13]

Kisner, Pacific Fleet's radio intercept chief, told Stinnett in 1988 that the bearing locations derived from the radio direction finder operators were part of the daily complete intelligence delivered to HYPO. Until the end of October, these reports were sent to both Kimmel and the White House. Beginning on November 1, 1941, the RDF reports were no longer delivered to Kimmel. Kisner was shocked when presented with the information that Kimmel had not received the intelligence and exclaimed, "Who held them back? They should have gone to the admiral!"[14]

On June 4, 1983, Lieutenant Commander Thomas Dyer, second in command to Rochefort and chief cryptographer at HYPO, wrote a letter to Stinnett stating that at HYPO, "There was not the slightest reason to believe that JN-25 or any other Navy system contained anything that would have forecast the attack."[15]

However, there were numerous indicators found, to the contrary, in the form of intercepted Japanese broadcasts in Station H records. The narrative speaks for itself. The important fact is that Kimmel was deprived of the RDF transmission interceptions of the Japanese carrier fleet as it was sailing toward the Oahu. Rochefort's original Communication Summaries were found by Stinnett in the Navy Records at the National Archives, but all the RDF reports were cut from each copy that had been prepared for Kimmel. Richard A. von Doenhoff, a specialist in the Pearl Harbor section of the National Archives, confirmed that more than 65 of Rochefort's November and December summaries intended for Kimmel had been altered. The Japanese warship locations had been removed prior to the start of the 1945 congressional hearings.[16]

As stated earlier, in December 1941, President Roosevelt appointed Associate Justice Roberts of the U.S. Supreme Court to preside over a commission to investigate the Pearl Harbor disaster. On December 18, 1941, the investigation hearings opened and ended on January 23, 1942. The Roberts Commission issued its report the very next day, on Saturday, January 24, 1942. It concluded that the attack was successful because of failures and errors of judgment by Admiral Kimmel and General Short. They were charged with dereliction of duty. At the same time, General Marshall and Admiral Stark were cleared of any wrong doing, saying they fulfilled their command obligations.[17]

To ensure secrecy, on December 11, 1941, four days after the attack, Rear Admiral

Noyes issued a 54-year censorship policy that resulted in all pre–Pearl Harbor Japanese military and diplomatic intercepts and the relevant directives being secluded in Navy vaults. Noyes told his subordinates that day, "Destroy all notes or anything in writing."[18]

We will now address the issue of dereliction of duty as charged by Roberts in his 1942 report. The charge is based on Kimmel not having the Pacific fleet on high alert and not maintaining adequate air patrol areas north and northwest of Oahu.

The issues will be addressed one at a time.

Lack of Adequate Long Range Air Reconnaissance

1. According to John Lambert and Norman's Polmar's *Defenseless: Command Failure at Pearl Harbor* (2003), 18 operational PBYs could conduct a search pattern 5 degrees apart to a distance of 700 miles. To cover an entire 360-degree arc, it would have required all 81 of the Oahu–based PBYs. However, some of these aircraft in the first week of December were operating out of Midway; others were patrolling ahead of the two task forces at sea; other PBYs were searching an arc from Wake to Johnston to Midway Islands. There were eight B-17s, 21 B-18s, and 6 A-20s that could have been utilized in the search, which could have included the area south southwest to due north.[19]

Layton's *And I Was There* (1985) contends that there were only 6 B-17s available. The Navy had 81 PBYs, but crew and plane fatigue and a weary 16-hour 700-mile search cut the patrol wing by one third of its strength. Fifty-four of the 81 planes were new arrivals with inadequate training and no spare parts for their aircraft. It would have taken at least 250 PBYs to complete a full 360-degree search on a continuing basis. Layton also points out that on Thursday, December 5, 1941, the PBYs on Midway departed for Wake Island and conducted a 500 mile search. Still, in the week before December 7, the Navy aircraft searched over two million square miles of the Pacific without finding a single Japanese warship. Yet Kimmel was censored for not conducting adequate long range air patrols.[20]

Not on High Alert

2. Nine U.S. military commanders are on record as receiving the war warning of impending Japanese action against the United States. Seven of the nine commanders immediately placed their units on high alert. The Army and Navy commanders at Pearl Harbor did not. However, the war warning sent on November 27 to Admiral Hart, General MacArthur, and Kimmel listed Japanese targets such as the Philippines, Thai, the Kra peninsula, and possibly Borneo, but not Pearl Harbor. On December 8, 1941, MacArthur's fighter aircraft alerted by radar took off to challenge incoming bombers but could not find them. According to Japanese accounts, no aircraft had left Formosa to attack the Philippines, due to inclement weather. MacArthur learned of the news of the Pearl Harbor attack on at 3:15 a.m. (Philippine time) on December 8. At first, he declined to attack Formosa, where Japan's air attack would originate. His basis for the decision was that he wanted Japan to make the first overt

act against the Philippines. Finally, at 11:30 a.m., MacArthur decided to approve the attack against Formosa. With the weather improving over Formosa, Japan's bombers finally were able to take off. At 12:15 p.m., the Japanese aircrews over Clark Air Base discovered all of MacArthur's B-17s on the ground, being serviced for an attack against Formosa. Most of the B-17s were lost in the ensuing attack. There never has been an official investigation of these events, nor was MacArthur or anyone else ever held accountable.

On November 25, Admiral Hart received permission from Washington to sail ten of his warships from the Philippines south to join up with the Dutch fleet. Eight of the ships were eventually destroyed by Japanese forces in the opening salvos of the war in the Philippines. Hart did have about 24 submarines which were not placed on high alert but kept in port. In Panama, General Frank Andrews of the Panama Command and General John Dewitt of the Western Defense Command placed their troops on an instant war footing. Everyone was on continuous watch, and Navy vessels patrolled the sea lanes leading to the Panama Canal. Army radar operations worked around the clock to detect enemy aircraft, but that was not the case on Oahu.[21]

Looking back nearly 80 years, it is striking how strong are the feelings of many citizens about the events of 1941 when the United States willingly or unwillingly entered World War II. Starting at the outset of the war were investigations, hearings, and inquires, extending into 1946.

Although accusations of blame for being taken by surprise were widely spread, in the end the two Pacific commanders, General Walter Short and Admiral Husband Kimmel, bore the brunt and suffered the humiliation of being reduced several steps in rank to pre-war status. After that, journalists and historians plunged into the morass of documentation that had been generated to discover answers to questions that had arisen but were generally ignored by U.S. Congress and the Pentagon. These often controversial colloquies continue even now.

Major General Short died in 1949 at the age of 69. Rear Admiral Kimmel died in 1968 at age 86, but his sons and grandsons continued their mission to attempt to clear the admiral's good name and restore his four-star active duty rank.

Until the 1990s, they accomplished little. But in 1991, a bipartisan coalition of five senators asked then President George Herbert Walker Bush to review the matter of restoring the rank of these officers. In support, a group of 36 high ranking naval officers, nearly all World War II veterans, signed a letter to the president, arguing that Husband Kimmel, at long last, should be restored to his four-star rank. Among them were two former Chiefs of Naval Operations Admirals Thomas B. Hayward and James L. Holloway, III; Admirals Wesley L. McDonald and Horacio Rivera, Jr.; and Admiral William J. Crowe, Jr., former chief of the Joint Chiefs of Staff.[22]

Unfortunately, the president took no action, probably for political reasons. In 1994–95, the Kimmel family mounted another attempt that persuaded the Secretary of Defense William Perry to conduct a review to determine whether the dismissal and demotion of Kimmel and Short had been excessively harsh. Under Secretary of Defense Edwin Dorn chaired the study, concluding that although many people shared in flawed actions and omissions to act, the ultimate responsibility still lay in the errors in judgment committed by Kimmel and Short, even though they were denied some of the information that would have aided them in their decisions. Finally, in May 1999, the U.S. Congress tried again, and without debate included a non-binding resolution to restore their ranks as part of a National Defense Authorization bill, but President Bill Clinton refused to sign it. This reluctance to forgive on the part of the civil-military establishment has given rise to the charge that Kimmel and Short were made scapegoats for the egregious acts of others who were their superiors but who refused to accept responsibility for their own actions.

In closing, the consequences of not informing Kimmel of vital intelligence and in being vague and misleading in the messages sent to him during the year 1941 cost not only 2,403 men, women, and children's lives and 1,143 wounded but also the careers and reputations of a four star navy admiral and a three star army general.

Appendix A

General George Marshall's Actions on the Morning of December 7, 1941

1. 0930: Bratton was unable to reach Marshall because he was horseback riding along the Potomac.
2. 1030: Marshall calls Bratton at the War Department. Marshall testifies at the subsequent hearings that he never spoke to Bratton.
3. 1130: Marshall arrives at the War Department.
4. 1135–12:00: Marshall reads all 14 parts of the Japanese diplomatic message to its envoys. Marshall rejects the use of the scrambler phone, and instead he chooses to write a joint dispatch longhand to be signed by CNO Admiral Harold Stark and him. Marshall calls Stark. Telegram sent. The communication was to be sent to Army Command first and then forwarded by them to Navy Command. 0803 (Hawaii time), 1303 (Washington time) telegram reaches the RCA Honolulu office and is scheduled for routine delivery to Fort Shafter (Army base). The Pearl Harbor attack had already begun at 0748. [Rear Admiral Elmer T. Layton, *And I Was There* (New York: William Morrow, 1985), p. 306.]

Appendix B

The Pearl Harbor Attack: December 7, 1941

Japanese Forces

Japanese Task Force

Carriers	Battleships	Light Cruisers	Heavy Cruisers	Destroyers
Akagi	*Haruna*	*Abukuma*	*Chikuma*	*Urakaze*
Kaga	*Kirishima*	*Tone*	*Isokaze*	
Soryu			*Tanikaze*	
Hiryu				*Hamakaze*
Zuikaku				*Shiranui*
Shokaku				*Akigumo*
				Kasumi
				Arare
				Kagero

Tankers	Submarines	Destroyers at Midway
Kenyo Maru	*I-19*	*Akabono*
Kyokuto Maru	*I-21*	*Ushio*
Kokuyo Maru	*I-23*	*Shinkoku Maru*
		Toho Maru
		Toei Maru
		Nippon Maru

Total: 22 ships + 3 submarines = 25 vessels + 8 tankers
Aircraft on:

Akagi: Its water displacement was 30,074 tons (standard). It was 857 feet in length with a 100 feet flight deck. Its speed was 32.5 knots. Its crew was composed of 1600 men. It could carry up to 60 aircraft.

Kaga: Its water displacement was 30,074 tons (standard). It was 812 feet in length with a 100 feet flight deck. Its speed was 27.5 knots. It had a crew of 1340 men. It could carry up to 90 aircraft.

Soryu: Its water displacement was 16,154 tons (standard) It was 746 feet in length with a flight deck of 85.5 feet. Its speed was 34.5 knots. It had a crew of 1100 men. It could carry up to 70 aircraft.

Hiryu: Its water displacement was 16,154 tons (standard). It was 746 feet in length with a flight deck of 85 feet. Its speed was 34.5 knots. It had a crew of 1100 men. It could carry up to 70 aircraft.

Zuikaku: Its water displacement was 25,675 tons (standard). It was 844 feet in length with a flight deck of 95 feet. Its speed was 34.25 knots. It had a crew of 1660 men. It could carry up to 80 aircraft.

Shokaku: Its water displacement was 25,675 tons (standard) It was 844 feet in length with a flight deck of 95 feet. Its speed was 32.25 knots. It had a crew of 1660 men. It could carry up to 84 aircraft.

Total aircraft on board all six carriers was 399 with 353 planes operational for the attack. The first wave consisted of 183 aircraft:

Forty-nine Nakajima B5N2 Type-97 Carrier Attack Bombers
Fifty-one Aichi D3A1 Type 99 Carrier Bombers
Forty Nakajima B5N2 Carrier Attack Torpedo Bombers
Forty-three Mitsubishi A6M2 Type 00 fighters

The second wave consisted of 170 aircraft:

Fifty-four Nakajima B5N2 Type 97 Carrier Attack Bombers
Eighty Aichi D3A1 Type 99 Carrier Bombers
Thirty-six Mitsubishi A6M2 Type 00 fighters

U.S. Naval and Army Air Forces on Oahu on December 7, 1941

Ships anchored on the northwest side of Ford Island (Numbers represent ships from NW to SW in location on the west side of Ford Island):

1. USS *Detroit* (**CL-8**): an Omaha-class light cruiser, launched on June 29, 1922.
2. USS *Raleigh* (**CL-7**): an Omaha-class light cruiser, launched on October 25, 1922.
3. USS *Utah* (**AG-16**): a Florida class battleship built in August 1911. The battleship was hit by Japanese aerial torpedoes, leading to roll over and sank.*
4. USS *Tangier* (**AV-8**): a cargo ship, converted to a seaplane tender, launched on September 15, 1940.

Ships located on the northeast side of Ford Island. (Numbers represent ships from NE to SE in location on the east side of Ford Island):

5. USS *Nevada* (**BB-36**): a Nevada-class battleship, launched on July 11, 1914. She was the only battleship to get underway during the attack and grounded herself on Hospital Point to avoid sinking in the channel. The ship was hit by one torpedo and six bombs during the attack and eventually sank to the harbor floor. The battleship was subsequently salvaged and modernized to see action in both the Atlantic and Pacific.
6. USS *Arizona* (**BB-39**): a Pennsylvania class "super-dreadnought"

---

*Ships sunk or totally disabled.

battleship. The battleship was launched on June 19, 1915. *Arizona* received eight bomb hits, one of which landed on the forecastle (the upper deck of a ship forward of the foremast) and penetrated the flight deck to explode below and ignite the black powder magazine which set off explosions in the adjacent magazines. Subsequently, the battleship sank. Of the men on board, 1,400 of the 1,777 crew died.*

    7. USS *Vestal* (AR-4): a repair ship that was anchored outboard the USS *Arizona* to port. The ship was launched on May 19, 1908. During the attack, the ship sustained two bomb hits which ultimately permitted the ship to be grounded as *Vestal* was sailing away from the Arizona. Seven men were killed in the bombings and numerous causalities occurred.

    8. USS *Tennessee* (BB-43): the lead class of a new series of battleships. The ship was launched on April 30, 1919. In the Pearl Harbor attack, the ship was struck by two armor-piercing bombs. The bombs did not detonate completely but did serious damage to the center gun of turret two and disabled the gun entirely. The second bomb crashed through turret three, sending debris over to the outboard anchored USS *West Virginia*, killing its commanding officer. The battle ship was trapped for 10 days in her berth due to the sinking of the nearby USS *West Virginia* in the attack.

    9. USS *West Virginia* (BB-48): a Colorado-class battleship. The ship was launched on November 19, 1921. The battleship was sunk by six aerial torpedoes and two bombs in the attack on Pearl Harbor. The ship was outboard of the USS *Tennessee* and its sinking prevented any chance of escape for the USS *Tennessee*. After the attack, the ship was repaired with an extensive refit and saw action in the latter years of the Pacific war.*

    10. USS *Maryland* (BB-46): a Colorado-class battleship. The ship was launched on March 20, 1921. The ship sustained mild damage during the attack. Two armor-piercing bombs struck the ship but detonated low on her hull. The ship was moored inboard of the USS *Oklahoma*. The first bomb made a hole 12 by 20 feet in the forecastle awning and the second exploded after entering the hull at the 22 feet water level at Frame 10 causing flooding. She was repaired at Puget Sound and went back into action in June 1942. The first damaged ship to return to action in the Pacific.

    11. USS *Oklahoma* (BB-37): a Nevada-class battleship. The ship was launched on March 23, 1914. The ship was anchored outboard of the USS *Maryland*. She was hit by a great number of Japanese Type 91 aerial torpedoes. With her port side torn open over almost the length of the ship, the battleship flooded and rolled over on its side and sank to the bottom. Although attempts were made to salvage the ship, the battleship was too old and badly damaged and was decommissioned in September 1944. While on her way from Hawaii to California to be scrapped, the battleship sank while under tow.*

    12. USS *Neosho* (AO-23): a Cimarron-class fleet oiler tanker. The ship was launched on April 29, 1939. The ship survived the Pearl Harbor attack only to be severely damaged by Japanese aircraft and subsequently sunk by an American destroyer in the Battle of the Coral Sea in May 1942.

    13. USS *California* (BB-44): a Tennessee–class battleship. The ship was launched on November 20, 1919. The ship was moored at the southernmost berth

of Battleship Row. In the attack, the ship was struck twice on the port side from aerial Japanese torpedoes. Subsequently, there were two bombs dropped on the battleship: one was a direct hit, the other was a near miss. The attacks resulted in the *California* sinking to the bottom of the harbor.*

14. USS *Avocet* (AVP-4) (AVP): a Lapwing-class minesweeper. The ship was launched on March 9, 1918. Five bombs were dropped in the nearby berth, but none exploded. The minesweeper was responsible for shooting down a Nakajima B5N2 carrier attack plane from *Kaga*.

Ships in the dry dock which was located southwest of Ford Island:

1. USS *Pennsylvania* (BB-38): the lead ship in the Pennsylvania-class of super-dreadnaught battleships built in the 1910s. The battle ship was in dry dock No. 1 in Pearl harbor at the time of the attack. The ship was launched on March 16, 1915. Japanese torpedo planes made a number of attempts to have their torpedoes hit their mark but were unsuccessful as the ship was protected by the dry dock. The planes then decided to strafe *Pennsylvania*. One of the bombers that then attacked the ship was able to penetrate the deck and explode in casemate No. 9. The adjacent destroyers were on fire, so the dry dock was flooded to help contain the fires. With marginal damage during the attack, the battleship was refloated and taken out to sea on December 12, 1941. At Hunter's Point, in San Francisco, she went underwent final repairs which were completed on January 12, 1942.

2. USS *Downes* (DD-375): a Mahan-class destroyer which was launched on April 22, 1936. The ship came under attack on December 7, 1941, with a bomb falling between the destroyer and USS *Cassin* which was alongside USS *Downes*. The attack resulted in raging fires on both destroyers. This resulted in explosions from stored torpedo warheads and ammunition and abandonment of the two ships. The destroyer caused *Cassin* to slip from her keel blocks and rest against the USS *Downes*. The ship was decommissioned on June 20, 1942.*

3. USS *Cassin* (DD-372): a Mahan-class stationed in dry dock with *Downes* and *Pennsylvania* during the Pearl Harbor attack on December 7, 1941. The ship was launched on October 28, 1935. As cited above, a bomb landed between *Downes* and *Cassin*, igniting uncontrollable fires on both destroyers. So much damage occurred to the *Cassin* that she was decommissioned on the same day as the attack.*

4. USS *Oglala* (CM-4): a mine sweeper which was the flagship of the minecraft for the Battle Force of the Pacific Fleet. The ship was acquired on October 31, 1917. On December 7, 1941, a Nakajima B5N2 carrier torpedo bomber released its torpedo that detonated near *Oglala's* port side. As a result, the mine sweeper began to immediately take on water. Five minutes later, a bomb fell between *Oglala* and the light cruiser *Helena* and detonated near the mine sweeper's fireroom. About two hours later, the mine sweeper rolled over and sank. On December 23, 1942, after many months of salvage and repair, the ship was seaworthy.*

5. USS *Helena* (CL-50): a Baltimore-class light cruiser. The ship was launched on August 27, 1938. The light cruiser was moored at 1010 Dock Navy Yard. During the battle one Nakajima torpedo bomber launched its torpedo and struck *Helena* on the starboard side. The cruiser immediately took on water and listed to about five degrees. The list was corrected by counter-flooding. The ship

was kept afloat. The ship was moved after the attack to dry dock the next day, but would not be fully repaired until June 1942.

6. **USS *Shaw* (DD-373):** a Mahan-class destroyer which was moored in dry floating dock (YFD-2, Yard, Floating, Dry-dock). The ship was launched October 28, 1935. The destroyer sustained three bomb hits during the attack, resulting in a spectacular explosion of her forward magazine. The ship was abandoned, repaired in San Francisco, and returned to Pearl Harbor on August 31, 1942.*

Airfields Attacked During the Pearl Harbor Attack

Army Air Force

Hickam Field—On December 7, 1941, there were 12 B-17s, 33 obsolete B-18s, and 12 A-20 attack bombers neatly lined up, wingtip to wingtip on the field. Japanese dive bombers in the first wave attacked Hickam Air Field, resulting, ultimately, in the loss or damage of the 55 aircraft on the base.

Wheeler Field—The airfield was attacked by Japanese dive bombers in the first wave. Present on the air field were P-36 Hawk and P-40 aircraft on the ground. Of the 233 aircraft assigned to the base, 146 were in commission before the attack. After the attack, 83 were in commission, and 76 aircraft were totally destroyed.

Bellows Field—The airfield was attacked by only one Japanese Zero fighter.

Navy and Marines

Ewa Marine Corps Air Station—There were 48 aircraft on Ewa Marine Air Field on December 7, 1941, including 23 new SBD-3s and F4F fighters. The air station and its runway were strafed by 6 Zeros which had been escorting the Japanese torpedo bombers in the first wave on their way to Pearl Harbor. After the air attack, 33 of its 48 aircraft, which included 18 dive bombers and 9 fighters, were either destroyed or damaged.

Ford Naval Station—There were 26 PBYs on Ford Island that were destroyed by Japanese dive bombers.

Kaneohe Nava Air Station—The naval air base was the home of 36 PBY Catalina flying boats. Twenty-six of the aircraft were destroyed with six additional PBYs damaged.

Aircraft Lost in the Pearl Harbor Attack

U.S. Navy:	90 lost	33 damaged
U.S. Army:	77 lost	128 damaged
Japan:	29 lost (9 fighters, 15 dive bombers and 5 torpedo bombers)	

Killed at Pearl Harbor

U.S.	2,390
Japan	62

Chapter Notes

Preface

1. Robert B. Stinnett, *Day of Deceit* (New York: The Free Press 2000), 208–209.

Chapter 1

1. William Durant, *The Story of Civilization* (Norwalk: The Easton Press, 1935), 914.
2. *Ibid.*, 833.
3. *Ibid.*, 835.
4. *Ibid.*
5. *Ibid.*, 836.
6. *Ibid.*, 837.
7. Marius B. Jansen, *The Making of Modern* Japan (Cambridge: The Belknap Press, 2000), 283.
8. *Ibid.*, 294.
9. Durant, *The Story of Civilization*, 916.
10. *Ibid.*
11. *The World of 1898: The Spanish American War*, Researched on October 13, 2019, Annexation *Hawaii, 1898*, State Government, 2008. https://2001-2009.state.gov/r/pa/ho/time/gp/17661.htm.
12. *Russo-Japanese War: The Battle of Tsushima*, Military History, 2013 Researched on July 2006. https://www.history.com/topics/korea/russo-japanese-war.
13. Bradley and Dice, *The West Point*, 2.
14. *Ibid.*
15. *Ibid.*
16. Jansen, *The Making of Modern Japan*, 521.
17. *Nine Power Treaty*, U.S. State Department, Office of, 2013. Researched on August 2007. https://history.state.gov/milestones/1921–1936/naval-conference.
18. *Ibid.*
19. *Ibid.*
20. *A Tribute to Herbert Yardley*, National Cryptologic Museum, sscnet.ucla.edu/geog/gessler/borland/cryptology.htm, 4. Researched on October 2019. https://www.nsa.gov/about/cryptologic-heritage/historical-figures-publications/hall-of-honor/Article/1623030/herbert-o-yardley/.
21. *Ibid.*

Chapter 2

1. *A Tribute to Herbert O. Yardley*, National Cryptologic Museum, scnet.ucla.edu/geog/geog/gesslarptology.htm, 2008, 4. Researched on October 2019. https://www.nsa.gov/about/cryptologic-heritage/historical-figures-publications/hall-of-honor/Article/1623030/herbert-o-yardley/.
2. Kahn, *The Code Breakers*, 355.
3. *Ibid.*
4. *Ibid.*
5. *Ibid.*
6. *Ibid.*
7. *Ibid.*
8. *Ibid.*
9. *Ibid.*
10. *Ibid.*
11. *Ibid.*, 357.
12. *Ibid.*, 357–358.
13. *Ibid.*, 359.
14. *Ibid.*
15. *Ibid.*
16. *Ibid.*, 360.
17. *Ibid.*
18. *Ibid.*
19. *Ibid.*
20. *Ibid.*
21. *Ibid.*
22. *Ibid.*
23. *Ibid.*
24. *Ibid.*, 385.
25. *Ibid.*
26. *Ibid.*
27. *Ibid.*, 386.
28. *Ibid.*
29. *Ibid.*
30. Rear Admiral Layton, Edwin, USN (Ret.), Captain Roger Pineau USNR (Ret.) and John Costello, *And I Was There* (New York: William Morrow & Co., 1985), 29.
31. *Ibid.*, 31.
32. *Ibid.*, 32.
33. *Ibid.*, 31.
34. *Ibid.*, 32.
35. Robert Stinnett, *Day of Deceit* (New York: The Free Press, 2000), 68.
36. *Ibid.*, 68.
37. Layton, *And I Was There*, 57.
38. Kahn, *The Code Breakers*, 1.
39. *Ibid.*
40. *Ibid.*
41. Larry Riddle, *Agnes Meyer Driscoll, Biographies of Women Mathematicians*, 2008, 1. Researched on May 2005. https://www.agnesscott.edu/lriddle/women/driscoll.htm.
42. *Ibid.*
43. *Ibid.*
44. *Ibid.*
45. *Ibid.*
46. *Ibid.*
47. Layton, *And I Was There*, 33.
48. *Joseph J. Rochefort*, Captain, USN, Hall of Honor, National Security Agency, 2008, 1 Researched in April 2007. https://www.nsa.gov/about/cryptologic-heritage/

historical-figures-publications/hall-of-honor.
49. Layton, *And I Was There*, 33–34.
50. *Ibid.*
51. *Ibid.*
52. *Ibid.*, 32.
53. *Ibid.*, 34.
54. *Ibid.*, 35.
55. *Ibid.*, 36.
56. *Ibid.*
57. *Ibid.*

Chapter 3

1. Marius B. Jansen, *The Making of Modern Japan* (Cambridge: The Belknap Press, 2002), 512.
2. Scott Reilly, "Inside the Archives: Hector Bywater and William Honan in the Naval Historical Collection, U.S. Naval War College," *International Journal of Naval History*, December 2015, vol. 12, Issue 3.
3. William H. Honan, *Visions of Infamy: The Untold Story of How Journalist Hector C. Bywater Devised Plans That Led to Pearl Harbor* (New York: St. Martin's Press, 1991).
4. *Ibid.*
5. Jansen, *The Making of Modern Japan*, 523–524.
6. *Ibid.*, 533.
7. *Ibid.*, 516.
8. *Ibid.*, 580.
9. *Ibid.*, 583.
10. *Ibid.*
11. John Toland, *The Rising Sun* (New York: The Modern Library, 2003), 38.
12. *Ibid.*
13. John Toland, *The Rising Sun*, 41.
14. Jansen, *The Making of Japan*, 619.
15. John Tolland, *The Rising Sun*, 49.
16. Chang, *The Rape of Nanking*, np.
17. Rear Admiral Edwin T. Layton, USN (Ret.), Captain Roger Pineau, USNR (Ret.) and John Costello, *And I Was There* (New York: William Morrow & Co., 1995), 35.
18. *Ibid.*, 45.
19. *Ibid.*, 80–81.
20. Personal conversion with Rear Admiral Donald "Max" Showers, USN (Ret.), assigned to the Hypo Unit in Hawaii.
21. *London Naval Treaty*, U.S. Department of State, Office of the Historian, 2013. Researched April 2008. https://2001–2009.state.gov/r/pa/ho/time/id/87716.htm.
22. Personal conversion with Rear Admiral Donald "Max" Showers, USN (Ret.) assigned to the HYPO Unit in February 1942.
23. *Ibid.*
24. *London Naval Treaty*, U.S. Department of State Office of the History, 2013.

Chapter 4

1. John H. Bradley, Jack W. Dice and Thomas E. Greiss, *The Second World War: Asia and the Pacific* (Wayne: Avery Publishing Group Inc. 1984), 5.
2. John Toland, *Infamy* (New York: Doubleday, 1982), 112–116.
3. Gordon W. Prange, *At Dawn We Slept* (New York: McGraw-Hill & Co., 1981), 39.
4. *Ibid.*, 37–39.
5. Rear Admiral Edwin T. Layton, USN (Ret.), Captain Roger Pineau, USNR (Ret.) and John Costello, *And I Was There* (New York: William Morrow & Co., 1985), 71.
6. *Ibid.*
7. Prange, *At Dawn We Slept*, 31.
8. Layton, *And I Was There*, 77.
9. *Ibid.*
10. *Ibid.*, 86.
11. *Ibid.*, 77.
12. *Ibid.*, 78–79.
13. David Kahn, *The Code Breakers* (New York: Scribner, 1967), 23.
14. Prange, *At Dawn We Slept*, 66.
15. *Ibid.*, 70.
16. *Ibid.*, 148.
17. Layton, *And I Was There*, 94.
18. Toland, *Infamy*, 261.
19. Robert Stinnett, B., *Day of Deceit* (New York: The Free Press 2000), 144–145.
20. Prange, *At Dawn We Slept*, 145.
21. Stinnett, *Day of Deceit*, 145, 349.
22. Layton, *And I Was There*, 224.
23. Prange, *At Dawn We Slept*, 131, 153.
24. *Ibid.*, 110.
25. *Ibid.*, 117.
26. *Ibid.*, 118.
27. *Ibid.*, 120.
28. *Ibid.*, 128.
29. Layton, *And I Was There*, 92.
30. *Ibid.*, 94.
31. *Ibid.*
32. *Ibid.*, 113.
33. Prange, *At Dawn We Slept*, 150.
34. *Ibid.*, 152.
35. *Ibid.*, 159.
36. *Ibid.*, 160.
37. *Ibid.*, 139.
38. *Ibid.*, 143.
39. *Ibid.* 144.
40. Layton, *And I Was There*, 114.
41. *Ibid.*, 130.
42. *Ibid.*, 128.
43. *Ibid.*, 127.
44. *Ibid.*
45. Prange, *At Dawn We Slept*, 145.
46. Layton, *And I Was There*, 130.
47. *Ibid.* 130.
48. *Ibid.*, 132.
49. *Ibid.*, 133–134.
50. *Ibid.*, 138.
51. Layton, *And I Was There*, 144–145.
52. *Ibid.* The Four Principles of Freedoms are: freedom of speech and expression; freedom of religion; freedom from want; and freedom from fear, p. 165.
53. *Ibid.*, 141.
54. *Ibid.*, 142.
55. Hervie Haufler, *The Spies Who Never Were* (New York: New American Library, 2003), 110–120.
56. *Ibid.*
57. *Ibid.*
58. *Ibid.*
59. Prange, *At Dawn We Slept*, 176.
60. *Ibid.*, 181–182.
61. *Ibid.*, 184.
62. *Ibid.*, 185–186.
63. *Ibid.*, 190.
64. *Ibid.*, 192.
65. *Ibid.*, 197–198.

66. *Ibid.*, 204.
67. *Ibid.*, 206.
68. *Ibid.*, 219.
69. *Ibid.*, 223.
70. *Ibid.*, 225.
71. *Ibid.*, 225–229.
72. *Ibid.*, 234.
73. *Ibid.*, 238.
74. Layton, *And I Was There*, 155.
75. *Ibid.*, 151.
76. *Ibid.*, 152.
77. *Ibid.*, 153.
78. *Ibid.*, 154.
79. Prange, *At Dawn We Slept*, 239.
80. *Ibid.*, 242.
81. *Ibid.*, 243.
82. *Ibid.*, 147.
83. *Ibid.*, 162–163.
84. Prange, *At Dawn We Slept*, 239.
85. Layton, *And I Was There*, 164–165.
86. Toland, *Infamy*, 261.
87. *Ibid.*, 289.
88. Prange, *At Dawn We Slept*, 255–256.

Chapter 5

1. Gordon W. Prange, *At Dawn We Slept* (New York: McGraw-Hill Book Co., 1981), 259.
2. *Ibid.*, 261.
3. *Ibid.*, 263.
4. *Ibid.*, 268.
5. *Ibid.*, 275.
6. *Ibid.*, 278.
7. Rear Admiral Edwin T. Layton, USN (Ret.), Captain Roger Pineau, USNR (Ret.) and John Costello, *And I Was There* (New York: William Morrow & Co., 1985), 160.
8. *Ibid.*, 166.
9. Prange, *At Dawn We Slept*, 282.
10. *Ibid.*, 285.
11. *Ibid.*, 315.
12. *Ibid.*, 316.
13. *Ibid.*, 317.
14. *Ibid.*, 318–319.
15. *Ibid.*, 324.
16. *Ibid.*
17. *Ibid.*, 287–288.
18. *Ibid.*, 289.
19. *Ibid.*, 296.
20. *Ibid.*, 308.
21. *Ibid.*, 335.
22. *Ibid.*
23. Layton, *And I Was There*, 196.
24. *Ibid.*, 194.
25. Prange, *At Dawn We Slept*, 355.
26. *Ibid.*, 356.
27. *Ibid.*, 357.
28. *Ibid.*, 343.
29. *Ibid.*, 346.
30. *Ibid.*, 359.
31. Layton, *And I Was There*, 205.
32. *Ibid.*, 206.
33. *Ibid.*
34. Stinnett, *Day of Deceit* (New York: The Free Press, 2000), 49.
35. Layton, *And I Was There*, 194.
36. *Ibid.*, 366.
37. *Ibid.*, 377.
38. *Ibid.*, 199–200.
39. *Ibid.*
40. *Ibid.*
41. *Ibid.*
42. *Ibid.*
43. *Ibid.*
44. *Ibid.*
45. *Ibid.*, 202.
46. *Ibid.*
47. *Ibid.*, 202–203.
48. *Ibid.*, 202.
49. *Ibid.*
50. *Ibid.*
51. *Ibid.*, 202–203.
52. *Ibid.*, 203–204.
53. Ralph Briggs, *Lost Wind Execute Message Controversy* (Eugene: NCVA Cryptology, Fall 1986), 1–4. Researched, February 2008. http://www.patriot.dk/pearlharbour.html.
54. Layton, *And I Was There*, 219.
55. Prange, *At Dawn We Slept*, 458.
56. Ralph Briggs, *Lost Wind Execute Message Controversy* (Eugene: NCVA Cryptology, Fall 1986), 1–4. Researched February 2008. http://www.patriot.dk/pearlharbour.html.
57. *Ibid.*
58. *Ibid.*
59. *Ibid.*
60. Prange, *At Dawn We Slept*, 417.
61. *Ibid.*, 426.
62. Layton, *And I Was There*, 221, 261.
63. Stinnett, *Day of Deceit*, 160.
64. Robert J. Cressman, *A Magnificent Fight* (Annapolis, MD: U.S. Naval Institute, 1995), 63.
65. Stinnett, *Day of Deceit*, 152.
66. Layton, *And I Was There*, 504.
67. *Ibid.*, 227.
68. Mitsuo Fuchida and Masatake Okumiya, *Midway* (New York: Ballantine Books, 1955), 117.
69. Stinnett, *Day of Deceit*, 189–194.
70. *Ibid.*, 194.
71. *Ibid.*, 195, 205.
72. *Ibid.*, 197.
73. *Ibid.*, 198.
74. *Ibid.*
75. *Ibid.*, 203–205.
76. *Ibid.*, 205.
77. *Ibid.*, 206–207.
78. *Ibid.*, 207–208.
79. *Ibid.*, 209.
80. *Ibid.*
81. *Ibid.*, 211.
82. *Ibid.*, 215.
83. Rear Admiral Edwin T. Layton, USN (Ret.), Captain Roger Pineau, USNR (Ret.) and John Costello, *And I Was There* (New York: William Morrow & Co., 1985), 236.
84. *Ibid.*, 240.
85. *Ibid.*, 239.
86. *Ibid.*, 241.
87. Robert B. Stinnett, *Day of Deceit* (New York: The Free Press, 2000), 219.
88. *Ibid.*, 194.
89. Layton, *And I Was There*, 240–241.
90. Stinnett, *Day of Deceit*, 43–44.
91. Layton, *And I Was There*, 249.
92. *Ibid.*, 250.
93. *Ibid.*, 252.
94. *Ibid.*
95. Stinnett, *Day of Deceit*, 209.

Chapter 6

1. Rear Admiral Edwin T. Layton, USN (Ret.), Captain Roger Pineau, USNR (Ret.), and John Costello, *And I Was There* (New York: William Morrow & Co., 1985), 246.
2. *Ibid.*, 258.
3. *Ibid.*
4. *Ibid.*, 259.

5. *Ibid.*, 261–262.
6. Robert B. Stinnett, *Day of Deceit* (New York: The Free Press, 2000), 160–161.
7. Captain Robert C. Gillette, USN (Ret.), *With A Little Bit Luck* (Manuscript 2008), 49–56; Captain Peter B. Weed, USNR, Navy Combat Documentation Detachment 206, March–May 1997, 6–7.
8. Layton, *And I Was There*, 264.
9. *Ibid.*, 269.
10. *Ibid.*, 273.
11. *Ibid.*
12. *Ibid.*, 276.
13. Gordon W. Prange, *At Dawn We Slept* (New York: McGraw-Hill Book Co., 1981), 81–82.
14. Layton, *And I Was There*, 277.
15. *Ibid.*, 278–279.
16. *Ibid.*, 280.
17. *Ibid.*
18. *Ibid.*, 282.
19. *Ibid.*
20. *Ibid.*, 283.
21. *Ibid.*, 286.
22. *Ibid.*
23. *Ibid.*
24. *Ibid.*, 289.
25. *Ibid.*
26. *Ibid.*
27. *Ibid.*, 292.
28. *Ibid.*
29. *Ibid.*
30. *Ibid.*, 295.
31. *Ibid.*, 298.
32. *Ibid.*, 299–300.
33. *Ibid.*, 300.
34. *Ibid.*
35. *Ibid.*, 301.
36. *Ibid.*, 302.
37. *Ibid.*, 303.
38. *Ibid.*
39. *Ibid.*, 304.
40. *Ibid.*, 305.
41. *Ibid.*
42. *Ibid.*, 304–309.
43. *Ibid.*, 307.
44. *Ibid.*, 308.
45. *Ibid.*, 310.
46. Prange, *At Dawn We Slept*, 31.
47. Hervie Haufler, *Codebreakers' Victory* (New York: Penguin Books, 2003), 106.
48. *Ibid.*, 107.
49. *Ibid.*, 108.
50. *Ibid.*
51. *Ibid.*

52. Hiroyuki Agawa, *The Reluctant Admiral* (Tokyo: Kodansha, International, 1979), 251.
53. *Ibid.*
54. *Ibid.*
55. Ian Pfennigwerth, A Man of Intelligence: *The Life of Captain Eric Nave, Australian Codebreaker Extraordinary* (Australia: Rosenberg Publishers, 2006), 304.
56. Layton, *And I Was There*, 259.
57. *Ibid.*, 206.
58. *Ibid.*, 206–207.
59. Pfennigwerth, *A Man of Intelligence*, 180.
60. James J. Martin, *Beyond Pearl Harbor: Essays on Some Historic Consequences of the Crisis in the Pacific in 1941* (Ontario: Plowshare Press, 1983), 121.
61. *Ibid.*
62. *Ibid.*
63. *Ibid.*
64. Layton, *And I Was There*, 305.
65. Stinnett, *Day of Deceit*, 351–352.
66. *Ibid.*
67. *Ibid.*
68. *Ibid.*, 134.
69. Layton, *And I Was There*, 514.
70. *Ibid.*, 208.
71. *Ibid.*, 162–163.
72. Stinnett, *Day of Deceit*, 49.
73. *Ibid.*
74. *Ibid.*
75. *Ibid.*
76. *Ibid.*, 48.
77. *Ibid.*, 209.
78. Fuchida, *Midway*, 117.
79. Layton, *And I Was There*, 206.
80. *Ibid.*, 339.
81. *Ibid.*, 382–383.
82. Stinnett, *Day of Deceit*, 145.

Chapter 7

1. Gordon W. Prange, *At Dawn We Slept* (New York: McGraw-Hill Book Co., 1981), 501.
2. *Ibid.*, 503.
3. Dan Van Der Vat, *Pearl Harbor* (Toronto: Madison Press Books, 2001, 64–65.

4. *Ibid.*, 95.
5. Prange, *At Dawn We Slept*, 506.
6. *Ibid.*, 508.
7. *Ibid.*, 509.
8. *Ibid.*, 510–511.
9. Van Der Vat, *Pearl Harbor*, 101.
10. *Ibid.*, 513.
11. *Ibid.*, 514.
12. *Ibid.*, 69.
13. *Ibid.*, 91.
14. Prange, *At Dawn We Slept*, 524.
15. *Ibid.*
16. *Ibid.*
17. *Ibid.*, 534.
18. *Ibid.*, 527.
19. *Ibid.*, 530.
20. *Ibid.*, 532.
21. *Ibid.*, 536.
22. *Ibid.*, 537.
23. *Ibid.*, 536–537.
24. *Ibid.*, 538.
25. *Ibid.*, 539.
26. *Ibid.*, 554.
27. *Ibid.*, 558.
28. *Ibid.*, 564.
29. *Ibid.*, 568.
30. *Ibid.*, 541.
31. *Ibid.*, 542–543.
32. *Ibid.*, 543.
33. *Ibid.*, 550.
34. *Ibid.*, 573–574.
35. Robert Cressman, et al., *A Glorious Page in Our History* (Missoula: Pictorial Histories Publishing Co., 1990), 19–20.
36. Prange, *And I Was There*, 575.
37. *Ibid.*, 576.
38. *Ibid.*, 578.
39. *Ibid.*, 576.
40. Layton, *And I was There*, 512–513.
41. *Ibid.*, 515.

Chapter 8

1. *Pan Am Clipper Flying Boats, Pan Am Across the Pacific*, 1–6. Researched on May 2008. https://www.clipperflyingboats.com/transpacific-airline-service.
2. Robert J. Cressman, *A Magnificent Fight* (Annapolis, U.S. Naval Institute, 1995), 88–89.
3. *Ibid.*, 121.
4. *Ibid.*, 158.
5. John B. Lundstrom, *Black Shoe Carrier Admiral*

(Annapolis, MD: Naval Institute Press, 2006), 16.
 6. John B. Lundstrom, *The First Team* (Annapolis, MD: Naval Institute Press, 1984), 33.
 7. Cressman, *A Magnificent Fight*, 152.
 8. *Ibid.*, 156.
 9. *Ibid.*, 166.
 10. *Ibid.*, 160.
 11. *Ibid.*, 158.
 12. Lundstrom, *The First Team*, 38.
 13. Cressman, *A Magnificent Fight*, 179.
 14. *Ibid.*, 185.
 15. Lundstrom, *The First Team*, 41.
 16. Lundstrom, *Black Shoe Carrier Admiral*, 54.
 17. Cressman, *A Magnificent Fight*, 223.
 18. *USS SARATOGA, World War II Data Base*, 2004–2011. Researched on May 2008. https://ww2db.com/ship_spec.php?ship_id=315.
 19. *Appearance and Performance, New Orleans Class Cruisers*, 2011. Researched on June 2008. https://en.wikipedia.org/wiki/New_Orleans-class_cruiser.
 20. Cressman, *A Magnificent Fight*, 190.
 21. *Ibid.*, 204.
 22. *Ibid.*, 208.
 23. Lundstrom, *Black Shoe Carrier Admiral*, 45–46.
 24. Cressman, *A Magnificent Fight*, 214.
 25. *Ibid.*, 225.
 26. *Ibid.*, 254.
 27. International Midway Memorial Foundation, *Against All Odds* (Bethesda, Public Interest Video Network 2000).

Chapter 9

 1. John H. Bradley, Jack W. Dice and Thomas E. Griess, *The Second World War: Asia and the Pacific* (Wayne: Avery Publishing Group, Inc., 1984), 72.
 2. *Ibid.*, 73.
 3. *Ibid.*, 74.
 4. *Ibid.*
 5. Michael Gough, *Failure and Destruction, Clark Field, the Philippines, December 8, 1941, Military History Online*, November 11, 2007. Researched on August 2008. https://www.militaryhistoryonline.com/?aspxerrorpath=/wwii/articles/failureanddestruction.
 6. *Ibid.*
 7. Bradley, *The Second World War*, 75.
 8. *Ibid.*, 76.
 9. *Ibid.*, 77.
 10. *Ibid.*, 81.
 11. *Ibid.*, 83.
 12. *Ibid.*
 13. *Ibid.*, 84.
 14. Mitsuo Fuchida and Masatake Okumiya, *Midway* (New York: Ballantine Books 1958), 45–46.
 15. *Ibid.*, 46.
 16. *Ibid.* 47–48.
 17. Paul S. Dull, *A Battle History of the Imperial Japanese Navy* (Annapolis, MD: Naval Institute Press 1978), 53.
 18. Fuchida, *Midway*, 48.
 19. *Ibid.*, 49.
 20. *Ibid.*, 50.
 21. *Ibid.*, 51.
 22. *Ibid.*
 23. *Ibid.*, 52.
 24. *Ibid.*
 25. John B. Lundstrom, *The First Team* (Annapolis, MD: Naval Institute Press 1984), 24.
 26. *Ibid.*, 25.
 27. *Ibid.*, 30.
 28. *Ibid.*, 45.
 29. *Ibid.*, 49.
 30. *Ibid.*, 51.
 31. *Ibid.*, 51–52.
 32. *Ibid.*, 52–53.
 33. *Ibid.*, 53–54.
 34. *Ibid.*, 55.
 35. *Ibid.*, 56.
 36. *Ibid.*, 59.
 37. *Ibid.*
 38. *Ibid.*, 60.
 39. *Ibid.*, 61.
 40. *Ibid.*, 66.
 41. *Ibid.*
 42. *Ibid.*, 67–68.
 43. *Ibid.*, 70.
 44. *Ibid.*, 72.
 45. *Ibid.*, 73–74.
 46. *Ibid.*, 78–79.
 47. *Ibid.*, 84.
 48. *Ibid.*, 85.
 49. *Ibid.*, 87.
 50. *Ibid.*, 91.
 51. *Ibid.*, 97.
 52. *Ibid.*, 102.
 53. *Ibid.*, 111.
 54. *Ibid.*, 113–115.
 55. *Ibid.*, 114.
 56. *Ibid.*, 117–121.
 57. *Ibid.*, 122.
 58. *Ibid.*, 123.
 59. *Ibid.*, 124.
 60. *Ibid.*, 125.
 61. *Ibid.*, 126.
 62. *Ibid.*, 129.
 63. *Ibid.*, 131.
 64. *Ibid.*, 134.

Chapter 10

 1. Robert B. Stinnett, *Day of Deceit* (New York: The Free Press, 2000), 144.
 2. *Ibid.*, Pearl Harbor Part Transcript (PHPT444) 1942.
 3. *Ibid.*, 145.
 4. *Ibid.*, 98–99.
 5. Rear Admiral Edwin T. Layton, USN (Ret.), Captain Roger Pineau, USNR (Ret.), and John Costello, *And I Was There* (New York: William Morrow & Co., 1985), 166.
 6. Stinnett, *Day of Deceit*, 47–51.
 7. *Ibid.*
 8. *Ibid.*
 9. *Ibid.*
 10. John Toland, *Infamy* (New York: Doubleday, 1982), 279, 285.
 11. Stinnett, *Day of Deceit*, 197.
 12. *Ibid.*, 197–198.
 13. *Ibid.*, 197.
 14. *Ibid.*, 198.
 15. *Ibid.*, 194.
 16. *Ibid.*, 209.
 17. *Ibid.*, 98–102.
 18. Frederick Parker, *Pearl Harbor Revisited* (National Security Agency, 2013), 43.
 19. Layton, *And I Was There*, 215.
 20. *Investigations*, National Security Agency/Central Security Service. Researched on April 2008 https://www.nsa.gov/news-features/declassified-documents/ig-reports/.
 21. Prange, *At Dawn We Slept*, 31.
 22. Layton, *And I Was There*, 73.
 23. Prange, *At Dawn We Slept*, 33.
 24. Stinnett, *Day of Deceit*, 6–8.
 25. Layton, *And I Was There*, 73.

26. *Ibid.*, 139.
27. *Ibid.*, 142.
28. Layton, *And I Was There*, 142–144.
29. *Ibid.*
30. Hervie Haufler, *The Spies Who Never Were* (New York: Open Road, 2006), 112–113.
31. *Ibid.*
32. Toland, *Infamy*, 259.
33. Haufler, *The Spies Who Never Were*, 117.
34. *Ibid.*, 122.
35. Toland, *Infamy*, 260.
36. George Larder, Jr., "Memos Amplify Hoover's Prewar Actions," *Washington Post*, April 2, 1983. https://www.washingtonpost.com/archive/politics/1983/04/02/memos-amplify-hoovers-prewar-actions/7fac66a9-a446-4e1e-b04c-7ab3800c9092/.
37. John Bratzel and Leslie B. Rout, *The American Historical Review*, Vol. 87, No. 5, December 1982, 1342–1351. Research date October 10, 2019. https://www.jstor.org/stable/305051.
38. George Lander, Jr., "Memos Amplify Hoover's Prewar Actions," *Washington Post*, April 2, 1983.
39. *Ibid.*
40. Toland, *Infamy*, 260–261.
41. *Ibid.*, 289–290.
42. *Ibid.*
43. *Ibid.*, 281–282.
44. *Ibid.*, 290–291.
45. Layton, *And I Was There*, 111.
46. *Ibid.* 292.
47. *Ibid.*, 293.
48. *Ibid.*, 295.
49. *Ibid.*
50. *Ibid.*, 295.
51. *Ibid.*, 305.
52. *Ibid.*
53. *Ibid.*, 306.
54. Proceedings of Clark's Investigation, p. 141 Researched October 9, 2019. http://www.ibiblio.org/pha/myths/Missing_Carriers.html.
55. Stinnett, *Day of Deceit*, 162–163.
56. Mark Weber, *Roosevelt's Secret Map Speech, Journal of Historic Review*, Spring 1985 Vol. 6, No. 1, 125–127 and in April 2016. https://ihr.org/jhr/v06p125_Weber/html.
57. *Ibid.*
58. *Ibid.*
59. Layton, *And I Was There*, 121.
60. Edward S. Miller, *Bankrupting the Enemy* (Annapolis, MD: Naval Institute Press, 2007), 245–247.
61. Layton, *And I Was There*, 54.
62. U.S. Holocaust Memorial Museum, *How Did Public Opinion About Entering World War II Change between 1939 and 1941?*, April 23, 2018. https://exhibitions.ushmm.org.
63. Thomas K. Kimmel, Jr., J.A. Williams and Paul Glyn Williams, *The FBI's Role in the Pearl Harbor Attack, Journal of American Intelligence*, Fall 2009, 41–42.
64. *Ibid.*, Pearl Harbor Army. 29PHA137.
65. *Ibid.*
66. Layton, *And I Was There*, 203.
67. *Ibid.*
68. *Ibid.*, 204.
69. *Ibid.*
70. John Costello, *Days of Infamy* (New York: Pocket Books, 1995), 322.
71. Stinnett, *Day of Deceit*, 194.
72. *Ibid.*, 208.
73. National Archives: GR 450, SRH 406, 000110.
74. *Ibid.*, 0000115.
75. Layton, *And I Was There*, 231.
76. Churchill, Winston S., The last volume of his multi-volume history of World War II, *The Grand Alliance* (Cambridge: The Riverside Press, 1950), 598.
77. Costello, *Days of Infamy*, 318–322.
78. *Ibid.*, 322.
79. Michael Smith, *The Emperor's Codes* (New York: Arcade Publishing, 2000, 2011), 5.
80. Mark Willey, *Final Secret of Pearl Harbor Declassified* (Editorial), 12/8/97. Researched on May 2018. http://www.fepow-community.org.uk/arthur_lane/html/pearl_harbor.htm.
81. Warren F. Kimball, *Churchill & Roosevelt* (Princeton, NJ: Princeton University Press 1984), 280.
82. Gregory Douglas, *Gestapo Chief* (San Jose R. James Bender Publishing, 1995), 42.
83. *Ibid.*
84. *Ibid.*, 45.
85. Ruth Ive, *Listening in on Churchill* (London: November 14, 2014), http://wwr/bbc.eo.uk/London/content/articles/2008/09/01/ruth_ive_feature.sntml.
86. David Kahn, *The Code Breakers* (New York: Scribner, 1967), 555.
87. David Kahn, *Hitler's Spies* (Da Capo Press, 2000), 173.
88. Thomas K. Kimmel, et al, "A Diplomatic Analysis of a Document Purported to Prove Prior Knowledge of the Attack on Pearl Harbor," *The Journal of Intelligence and National Security*, 2009, 587.
89. Personal correspondence with Thomas K. Kimmel in November 2020.
90. Mitsuo Fuchida and Masatake Okumiya, *Midway* (New York: Ballantine, 1955), 37.
91. *Ibid.*
92. Stinnett, Robert, *Day of Deceit* (New York: The Free Press, 2000), 195.
93. Layton, *And I Was There*, 203.
94. William Casey, *The Secret War Against Hitler* (Washington, D.C.: Regnery Gateway, 1988), 7.
95. Layton, *And I Was There*, 198.
96. *Ibid.*, 214–215.
97. FDR Library: Project of the Pare Lorentz Center, Transcripts of November 28, 1941.
98. *Ibid.*
99. Kimmel, "A Diplomatic Analysis of a Document Purported to Prove Prior Knowledge of the Attack on Pearl Harbor," *Journal of Intelligence and National Security*, August 2009, 590.
100. *Ibid.*, 590–591.

Chapter 11

1. John Toland, *Infamy* (New York: Doubleday,1982), 260–261, 289–290.
2. Dusko Popov's Questionnaire Annotated. Researched July 2017. https://www.historyonthenet.com/dusko-popov-the-triple-agent-real-life-james-bond-who-warned-the-u-s-about-pearl-harbor.
3. D.M.Ladd,*Memorandum for the Director*, December 11, 1941.
4. Rear Admiral Edwin T. Layton, USN (Ret.), Captain Roger Pineau, USNR (Ret.), and John Costello, *And I Was There* (New York: William Morrow & Co., 1985), 94.
5. Thomas, K. Kimmel, Jr., et al, *The FBI's Role in the Pearl Harbor Attack*, 43–44.
6. (SRH-149) *Communications Intelligence in the United States* by Captain L. Safford, head of Naval Security Group; *Listening to the Enemy* by Ronald Spector, DE 1988, Chapter 1.
7. Elliot Carlson,*Joe Rochefort's War* (Annapolis, MD: The Naval Institute, 2011), 208. (Naval Security Group; *Listening to the Enemy* by Ronald Spector, DE 1988, Chapter 1).
8. Robert B. Stinnett, *Day of Deceit* (New York: The Free Press, 2000), 164.
9. *Ibid.*, 195.
10. Elliot Carlson,*Joe Rochefort's War* (Annapolis, MD: The Naval Institute, 2011), 182.
11. Stinnett, *Day of Deceit*, 183–184.
12. *Ibid.*
13. Carlson, *Joe Rochefort's War*, 208.
14. Stinnett, *Day of Deceit*, 98–107.
15. Layton,*And I Was There*, 162–168.
16. J. Edgar Hoover, Letter to the Secretary of the President Stephen Early, December 12, 1941.
17. Dusko Popov's Questionnaire Annotated.
18. Stinnett, *Day of Deceit*, 198.
19. *Ibid.*, 255.
20. John Costello, *Days of Infamy* (New York: Pocket Books, 1995), 322.
21. I have deliberately not further elaborated on the transatlantic telephone conversation between FDR and Churchill other than what I have already written until the original document now in the hands of Admiral Husband Kimmel's grandson Thomas Kimmel, Jr., has been tested for its authenticity. To date, the German and United States governments have not seen fit to do so. Thus, we will approach the FBI and others to determine the transcript's authenticity. An addendum to this book will follow when the test results are completed.

Chapter 12

1. Rear Admiral Edwin T. Layton, USN (Ret.) USN, Captain Roger Pineau, USNR (Ret.) with John Costello, *And I Was There* (New York: William Morrow & Co.), 21.
2. *Ibid.*, 169.
3. *Ibid.*, 210–211.
4. *Ibid.*, 215.
5. Christopher Califiero, *Kimmel's War Plan* (Avalanche Press, 2014), 1.
6. Layton,*And I Was There*, 211.
7. *Ibid.*
8. Gordon W. Prange, *At Dawn We Slept* (New York: McGraw-Hill Book Company, 1981), 31.
9. Robert B. Stinnett, *Day of Deceit* (New York: The Free Press 2000), 85.
10. *Ibid.*, 80.
11. Thomas K. Kimmel, Jr., J.A. Williams and Paul Glyn Williams, "The FBI's Role in the Pearl Harbor Attack," *American Intelligence Journal*, Fall 2009, 43.
12. Stinnett, *Day of Deceit*, 102–103.
13. *Ibid.*, 218.
14. *Ibid.*, 207.
15. *Ibid.*, 204.
16. *Ibid.*, 207–08.
17.
18.
19. John Lambert and Norman Polmar, *Defenseless: Command Failure at Pearl Harbor* 2003.
20. Layton,*And I Was There*, 204.
21. Stinnett, *Day of Deceit*, 173–174.
22. Anthony Summers, and Robbyn Swan, *A Matter of Honor: Pearl Harbor: Betrayal, Blame, and a Family's Quest for Justice* (New York: Harper Collins, 2016), 361–362.

Bibliography

Bradley, John H., Thomas E. Griess, and Jack W. Dice. *The Second World War: Asia and the Pacific*. West Point: Avery Publishing Group, 1984.

Carlson, Elliot. *Joe Rochefort's War*. Annapolis, MD: Naval Institute Press, 2011.

Casey, William. *The Secret War Against Hitler*. Washington, D.C., Regnery Gateway, 1988.

Chang, Iris. *The Rape of Nanking: The Forgotten Holocaust of World War II*. New York: Basic Books, 1997.

Charmley, John. *Churchill's Grand Alliance*. New York: Harcourt Brace, 1995.

Churchill, Winston S. *The Grand Alliance*, vol. 3 of *The Second World War*, 6 vols. Boston: Houghton Mifflin, 1950.

Costello, John. *Days of Infamy: MacArthur, Roosevelt, Churchill: The Shocking Truth Revealed How Their Secret Deals and Strategic Blunders Caused Disasters at Pearl Harbor and the Philippines*. New York: Pocket Books, 1994.

Cowley, Robert. *What If? Eminent Historians Imagine What Might Have Been*. New York: G.P. Putnam's Sons, 1999.

Cressman, Robert J. *A Magnificent Fight: The Battle for Wake Island*. Annapolis, MD: U.S. Naval Institute, 1995.

Cressman, Robert J., et al. *A Glorious Page in our History*. Missoula: Pictorial Histories, 1990.

Douglas, Gregory. *Gestapo Chief: The 1948 Interrogation of Heinrich Muller*. San Jose: R. James Bender Publishing, 1999.

Dull, Paul S. *A Battle History of the Imperial Japanese Navy*. Annapolis, MD: Naval Institute Press, 1998.

Durant, Will and Ariel. "The Story of Civilization," vols. 1–11, *Our Oriental Heritage*. Easton Press, 1935.

Dyer, George C. *On the Treadmill to Pearl Harbor: The Memoirs of Admiral James O. Richardson as Told to George Dyer*. 2 vols., United Kingdom 1973.

Fuchida, Mitsuo, and Masatake Okumiya. *Midway: The Battle That Doomed Japan*. New York: Ballantine Books, 1955.

Glines, Carroll. *The Doolittle Raid. America's First Strike Against Japan*. Atglen: Schiffer Military Aviation History, 1991.

Hanson, Baldwin. *Great Mistakes of the War*. New York: Harper & Brothers, 1950.

Haufler, Hervie. *The Spies Who Never Were, The True Story of the Nazi Spies Who Were Actually Allied Double Agents*. New York: New American Library, 2003.

Jansen, Marius. *The Making of Modern Japan*. Cambridge: Belknap Press, 2000.

Jenkins, Robert. *World War 2: Pearl Harbor Through Japanese Eyes*. New York: Center for International Training and Education, Kindle Edition, 2015.

Kahn, David. *Hitler's Spies, German Military Intelligence in World War II*. Da Capo Press, 1978.

Kimmel, Husband, E., Admiral. *Admiral Kimmel's Story*. Henry Regnery, 1954.

Landis, LCDR Kenneth, USNR (Ret.), et al. *Deceit at Pearl Harbor, From Pearl Harbor to Midway*. First Books Library, 2001.

Layton, Rear Admiral Edwin T., Captain Pineau Roger, and John Costello. *And I Was There*. New York: William Morrow, 1985.

Lee, Bruce. *Marching Orders*. New York: Crown, 1995.

Loewenheim, Francis et al. (Editors). *Roosevelt and Churchill: Their Secret Wartime Correspondence*. New York: Saturday Review Press/E.P. Dutton & Co, 1975.

Lord, Walter. *Day of Infamy*. New York: Macmillan, 1957.

Lundstrom, John B. *Black Shoe Carrier Admiral, Frank Jack Fletcher at Coral Sea, Midway, and Guadalcanal*. Annapolis, MD: U.S. Naval Institute, 2006.

Lundstrom, John B. *The First Team: Pacific Naval Air Combat from Pearl Harbor to Midway*. Annapolis, MD: U.S. Naval Institute. 1984.

Martin, James J. *Beyond Pearl Harbor: Essays on Some Historic Consequences of the Crisis in the Pacific in 1941*. Ontario: Planshare Press, 1983.

Miller, Edward S. *Bankrupting the Enemy: The U.S. Financial Siege of Japan Before Pearl Harbor*. Annapolis, MD: Naval Institute Press, 2007.

Moore, Steven L. *Pacific Payback: The Carrier Aviators Who Avenged Pearl Harbor at the Battle of Midway*. New York: Penguin Publishing Group,. 2015.

Morrison, Samuel Eliot. *Coral Sea, Midway and Submarine Actions*. Boston: Little, Brown, 1985.

Parshall, Jonathan, and Anthony Tully. *Shattered Sword*. Washington, D.C.: Potomac Press, 2005.

Perry, Commodore M.C. *Narrative of the Expedition to the China Seas and Japan*. Mineola: Dover Publications, 2000.

Pfennigwerth, Ian. *A Man of Intelligence: The Life of Captain Eric Nave, Australian Codebreaker*. Australia: Rosenberg Publishers, 2000.

Polmar, Norman. *Aircraft Carriers: A History of Carrier Operations and Its Influence on World Events*. Dulles: Potomac Books, 2008.

Prange, Gordon W. *At Dawn We Slept*. New York: McGraw & Hill, 1981.

Russell, Henry Dozier General, *Pearl Harbor Story*. Macon: Mercer University Press, 2001.

Smith, Michael. *Emperor's Codes: The Breaking of Japan's Secret Cipher*. London: Bantam Press, 2000.

Smith, Page. *The History of America*. Norwalk: Easton Press, 1982.

Stile, Mark. *The Coral Sea 1942, The First Carrier Battle*. Great Britain: Osprey Publishing, 2000.

Stinnett, Robert B. *Day of Deceit*. New York: Free Press, 2000.

Summers, Anthony and Robbyn Swan. *A Matter of Honor, Pearl Harbor: Betrayal, Blame and a Family's Quest for Justice*. New York: Harper-Collins, 2017.

Symonds, Craig L. *The Battle of Midway*. New York: Oxford University Press, 2011.

Toland, John. *Infamy*. New York: Doubleday, 1982.

Toland, John. *The Rising Sun*. New York: Modern Library, 2005.

Ugaki, Admiral Matome. *Fading Victory*. Pittsburg, PA: University of Pittsburg Press, 1991.

United States Navy. *Aerology and Naval Warfare*. Create Space Independent, 2012.

Van Der Vat, Dan. *Pearl Harbor: An Illustrated History*. Toronto: Madison Press, 2001.

Walsh, George. *The Battle of Midway: Searching for the Truth*. Create Space Independent, 2015.

Index

ABCD Powers 41, 46
ABDA 140
Abe, Rear Adm. Hiroaki 129
Abe, Adm. Kobe 40, 162
Abukuma 67, 140
Abwehr 62
AD Code 27, 33, 99
Agawa, Hiroyuki 68, 91, 92
Akagi 32, 44, 50, 58, 61, 67, 68, 70, 71, 72, 76, 80, 105, 106, 112, 117, 139, 140, 142, 175, 184, 195
Allen, LCDR Preston 71, 157
American Black Chamber 12, 13
And I Was There 65
Anderson, Capt. Walter S. 122
Andrews, Gen. Frank 203
Antares 89
ANZAC 148
Arizona 106, 107, 114, 115, 120, 121, 130
Army Court of Inquiry 177
Army Signal Corps 14, 28
Arnold, Maj. Gen. H.H. "Hap" 42, 136
Asanagi 152
Asplund, Rudy 157
Astoria 128, 130, 131, 151, 153
AT & T 178, 182, 183
Atake, Petty Officer 3rd Class Tomita 147
Augusta 38, 172
Aylwin 127

Bagley 148
Baldwin, Hanson 97
Barbers Point 105, 112
Barkley, Sen. Alben 69
Bataan Peninsula 138, 139
Battle of Nomonhan 22
Beardall, Capt. John R. 84, 116
Beatty, Frank 85, 169
Bellinger, Rear Adm. Patrick N.L. 30, 161
Bellows Field 113
Berkley, Elizabeth 173
Berle, Adolf, Jr. 194
Berndtson, Commodore C.A. 157
Bicknell, Col. George 188

Bissell, Col. John T. 192
Black Chamber 14, 22
Bloch, Rear Adm. Claude C. 127
Blue Book 23, 27
Bode, Capt. Howard D. 52, 155, 194
Bomb Plot Message 48, 76, 98, 99, 194, 201
Bond, James 41
Bratton, Col. Rufus 48, 85, 87, 88, 89, 95, 96, 97, 168, 169
Bratzel, John F. 164
Brereton, Maj. Gen. Lewis 135, 136, 137
Briggs, Ralph 66, 67
Brown, LCDR Cedric 67
Brown, Vice Adm. Wilson 127, 128, 129, 130, 132, 143, 145, 148, 152, 153
Bryant, Harold L. 83
Bush, Pres. Herbert Walker 203

California 105, 106, 114, 120, 129
Camp O'Donnell 138
Cannon, Lt. George 1, 121
Canton Island 151
Carlson, Elliot 193, 194
Caroline Islands 121, 139
Carter, Pres. Jimmy 156
Casey, William 184
Cassin 114
Chambers, Whitaker 173
Chang Tso-lin 19
Cherry Blossom Coup 19
Chester 146, 147
Chiang Kai-shek 18, 20, 21, 43, 57, 63, 160, 173, 174
Chicago 127
Chikuma 55, 61, 67, 104, 121, 129, 140, 192
China Incident 68
Churchill, Winston 2, 28, 38, 39, 41, 60, 64, 65, 74, 93, 163, 172, 173, 174, 175, 176, 177, 178, 182, 183, 184, 185, 196, 197
CINCPAC 130
Clark 148
Clark Field 136, 137, 203

Clausen, Henry 98
Clear, Maj. Warren J. 30
Climb Mount Niitaka 74
Clinton, Pres. William 124, 204
Coddington, Capt. L.C. 42
Coe, CDR Charles 117
Coleman, LCDR Herbert 76
Collins, Virginia 61
Condor 86, 87
Coral Sea 102, 103, 119
Cornwall 141
Corregidor 72, 138, 139
Crace, Rear Adm. John G. 148
Creighton, Capt. John 78
Creighton, John M. 137
Cressman, Robert L. 131
Crocker, Edward 27
Crowe, Adm. William J. 203
Cunningham, CDR Winfield Scott 126, 130, 132, 134

Dale 127
D'Amato, Anthony 185
Del Carmen 137
Devereux, Maj. James 126, 132, 134
Dewey 127
Dewitt, Gen. John 203
Dies, Sen. Martin 49
Dillon, John 112
Distinguished Gentleman 110
Dixon, Lt. H.C. 67
Doenhoff, Richard A. 72, 201
Donovan, William 171
Doorman, Rear Adm. Karel 140
Dorn, Under Secretary of Defense Edwin 203
Dorsetshire 140
Double-Cross System 41
Douglas, Gregory 177, 178, 183, 185
Downes 114
Driscoll Meyer, Agnes 16, 22, 28
Drought, Father James 32
Dutch Harbor 70, 71, 101, 158, 175, 193, 195
Dyer, LCDR Thomas H., USN 22, 23, 27, 72, 73, 201

Index

Early, Stephen 188
East Field 145
East Wind Rain Message 66, 67
Edgars, Dorothy 82, 83
Egusa, LCDR Takeshige 43, 114
Elliott, Private George F. 90
Ellis, Dick 163
Enigma 17
Enterprise 69, 89, 107, 108, 117, 118, 119, 120, 122, 126, 129, 130, 132, 133, 143, 144, 146, 147, 150, 151, 158, 170, 199
Era of Meiji 10
Etorofu 52
Europe First Policy 33
Ewa Marine Corp Air Station 49, 105, 110, 111, 144

Far East Combined Bureau (FECB) 59, 176
Farragut 127
Farrier, George 31
Farthing, Col. William F. 42
FBI 62, 63, 163, 164, 168, 188, 194, 195, 200
Fellers, Col. Bonner 78, 93
Fengtien Army 19
Ferguson, Sen. Homer 192
Fielder, Col. Kendall 188
Fitch, Rear Adm. Aubrey Wray 143
Five Power Treaty 11
Fleming, Ian 41
Fletcher, Rear Adm. Jack Frank 128, 129, 130, 131, 132, 145, 147, 153
Flusser 129
Flynn, John T. 123
Foote, Dr. Walter 75, 166
Ford Island 61, 86, 104, 105, 110, 111, 112, 128, 146
Forrestal, James 123
Fort Shafter 89, 170
Four Power Treaty 4
Four Principles of Freedom 38, 56, 57
Fourteen Part Message 84, 85, 87
Fourteenth Naval District 89, 90
Fox, Robert 71
Foxworth, Percy Sam 40, 41, 91, 92, 163
French, Col. Edward 89
Friedman, William 23, 28
Fuchida, LCDR Mitsuo 43, 50, 51, 54, 55, 61, 70, 94, 101, 104, 105, 106, 112, 117, 118, 184
Fujita, Sub Lt. Iyozo 112
Fukudome, Vice Adm. Shigeru 56, 121

Genda, CDR Minoru 32, 3, 43, 44, 50, 51, 52, 54, 55, 68, 70, 117, 118, 119, 120, 121

Gerow, Brig. Gen. Leonard 48, 85, 137, 168, 199
Gilbert Islands 44, 129, 139, 145, 146, 151
Gillette, Sen. Guy 49, 165, 188
Goepner, Lt. O.W. 89
Goto, Lt. Jinichi 106, 146
Grand Alliance 176
Grannis, CDR Lawrence 89
Gray, Lt. James 146
Gray Code 84, 88
Greer 46, 171
Grew, Joseph Clark 27, 88, 91, 160–162, 187, 200
Grogan, Leslie 71, 75, 156
Guadalupe 151
Guam 17, 30, 44, 49, 125, 127, 160, 165, 200

Haan, Kilsoo 48, 49, 165, 188
Haleiwa Air Field 110, 111, 112
Halifax, Lord Edward F. 74, 76, 174
Halsey, Vice Adm. William F. 129, 132, 144, 145, 146, 147, 148, 150, 151
Hamilton, Maxwell 49, 165
Hanna, Lt. Robert 132
Harding, Warren 14
Harper, Capt. John S. 67
Harrison, Landreth 62
Hart, Adm. Thomas C. 33, 48, 78, 135, 136, 138, 199, 200, 202, 203
Hasegawa, Capt. Kiichi 117
Hashimoto, Col. Kingoro 24
Hashirajima Bay 139, 142
Haufler, Hervie 92, 93
Hawaii Sakusen Senshi Sosho 68
Haworth, Dr. Emerson 14
Hayate 127
Hayward, Adm. Thomas 75, 203
Hebern, Edward 16
Helena 105
Henriksen, George W. 175, 195
Henning, Capt. J.W. 60, 67
Hermes 142
Hewitt, Adm. Kent W. 123
Hickam Air Field 42, 49, 61, 86, 105, 110, 111, 112, 113, 117, 162, 163
Hiei 55, 59, 67, 140
High Frequency Direction Finder (HFDF) 12, 28, 124, 127, 128
Himmler, Heinrich 178
Hirata, Shinsaku 26
Hirohito, Michinomiya 43, 45, 51, 56, 90
Hiroshima Bay 31, 121
Hiryu 37, 58, 67, 105, 112, 121, 127, 129, 130, 131, 133, 134, 138, 139, 140, 192
Hitler, Adolf 75

Hitokappu Bay 52, 55, 58, 60, 66, 68, 69, 100, 101, 155, 156, 174
Holloway, Adm. James L. 203
Holtwick, Capt. J.S., Jr. 192
Homma, Lt. Gen. Masaharu 138
Honolulu 115
Hood, Harry 193
Hoover, J. Edgar 13, 23, 34, 40, 41, 91, 92, 93, 163, 164, 188, 189, 190, 192, 194, 195
Hopkins, Harry 85
Hornbeck, Dr. Stanley 62, 63
Hosho 32
Hosmer, Ellsworth 70, 71, 101, 175
Hospital Point 114
Hotta, Masayoshi 10
Houston 140
Howard, Joseph 74
Hughes, Adm. Charles, USN 17
Hull 127
Hull, Secretary of State Cordell 32, 42, 46, 49, 51, 53, 55, 57, 61, 62, 63, 78, 84, 88, 90, 112, 116, 123, 173, 185
HYPO Unit 27, 29, 30, 33, 34, 35, 36, 39, 66, 69, 70, 72, 73, 81, 89, 97, 98, 99, 102, 103, 162, 192, 193, 195, 201

Iba Airfield 136, 137
Idaho 47
Indianapolis 127, 148
Infamy 124
Ingersoll, Rear Adm. Royal 31, 40, 84, 154, 161, 200
Inouye, Vice Adm. Shigeyoshi 153, 193
Ishiwara, Lt. Col. Kanji 19
Itagaki, Col. Seishiro 19
Itaya, LCDR Shigeru 43, 61
Ito, Rear Adm. Seiichi 95
Ive, Ruth 182

J-19 Code 30, 34, 39, 52, 58, 59, 60, 81, 82, 94, 99, 176, 192, 194, 201
Jaluit 37, 128, 129, 130, 146, 147
Japanese Naval Gen. Staff 36, 41, 42
Japanese Surprise Attack Fleet 79
Jarvis 145
Jebsen Johnny 40, 91, 162
JN-25A Code 28, 33, 34, 176
JN-25B 28, 33, 34, 59, 74, 93, 94, 98, 99, 102, 176, 192, 194, 196, 200
Johnston Islands 121, 127, 129, 143, 144

Kaena Point 105
Kaga 32, 55, 58, 67, 105, 108, 112, 139, 140, 141, 176, 177

Kagoshima 91
Kahn, David 23, 183
Kahuka Point 90, 104, 111, 112
Kajioka, Rear Adm. Sadamichi 127, 130
Kanai, Noboru 121
Kanji, Lt. Col. Ishiwara 19, 168
Kanoehe Naval Air Station 49, 61, 105, 108, 112, 113, 162, 163
Karsthoff, Ludovico 162
Kavieng 139
Kearny 171
Kellogg-Briand Pact 21
Kent, Tyler 25
KGMB Radio Station 86, 87, 90
Kido, Marquis Koichi 90
Kido Butai 55, 59, 60, 68, 69, 70, 71, 72, 73, 75, 76, 78, 79, 80, 86, 87, 88, 92, 94, 98,100, 101, 102, 103, 104, 117, 119, 120, 143, 174, 194, 200
Kimball, Warren F. 177
Kimmel, Adm. Husband E. 27, 29, 31, 33, 35, 36, 37, 39, 43, 44, 47, 48, 51, 52, 55, 58, 59, 64, 69, 72, 73, 76, 78, 86, 88, 90, 96, 103, 117, 122, 123, 127, 128, 129, 143, 154, 155, 156, 158, 159, 160, 161, 162, 170, 171, 194, 195, 198, 199, 200, 201, 202, 203, 204
Kimmel, Thomas K., Jr. 183, 185, 193
King, Adm. Earnest J. 144, 152
King, Maj. Gen. Edward 138
KIngoro, Col. Hashimoto 21
Kinoaki, Matsuo 49
Kirk, Capt. Alan C. 36, 52, 155, 161, 194, 200
Kiroshima 55, 67, 71, 140
Kisaragi 127
Kisner, Homer 72, 73, 193, 201
Kita, Consul Gen. Nagao 29, 48, 53, 54, 59, 82, 168
KItajima, Ichiro 105
Kiyokawa 152
Knox, Capt. Dudley W. 122
Knox, Secretary of the Navy Frank 26, 41, 48, 55, 84, 85, 88, 112, 116, 133, 169, 199
Kobe, Rear Adm. Abe 91, 93
Koki, Maru 152
Komote, Col. Daisaku 19
Kondo, Adm. Nobutake 140
Konoye, Fumimaro 41, 42, 45, 46, 51, 55
Kotoshirodo, Richard 159
Kramer, Capt. Alwin 48, 66, 67, 80, 82, 83, 84, 86, 87
Kuehn, Fritz 81, 82
Kurakane, Yoshio 147
Kuomintang–Communist Agreement 22

Kurile Islands 58, 59, 60, 61, 69, 76, 94, 98, 100, 103, 119, 155, 156, 158, 171, 184, 193, 195, 200
Kuroshima, Capt. Kameto 41
Kuroshima, Capt. Osami 50, 56
Kurusu, Saburo 57, 73, 116
Kusaka, Rear Adm. Ryunosuke 31, 44, 50, 52, 55, 56, 61, 117, 118
Kusumi, Lt. Tadashi 130
Kwajalein 146, 147
Kwantung Army 20
Kyushu 58

LA cipher 81
Ladd, D.M. 164, 189, 190, 192
Ladybird 21
Lae 153
Lahaina Bay 61
Lahaina Heights 26, 29, 80, 104, 172
Lambert, John 202
Lamson 129
Langfang 23
Langley 24
Lardner, George, Jr. 164
Layton, LCDR Edwin T. 30, 33, 36, 65, 66, 68, 72, 74, 75, 80, 81, 161, 173, 193, 198, 202
League of Nations 20, 21
Lee, Clark 97
Lexington 24, 69, 79, 107, 118, 119, 120, 122, 127, 128, 130, 132, 133, 143, 144, 145, 148, 149, 152, 153, 158, 170, 199
Lockard, Private Joseph L. 90
London Naval Treaty 24
Longmore, Air Marshall Arthur 78, 93
Loudon, Alexander 75
Louisville 145, 147, 151
Lundstrom, John 130, 131
SS *Lurline* 71, 75, 101, 156, 157, 158, 193
Luzon Peninsula 135, 136, 137, 138

MacArthur, Maj. Gen. Douglas 44, 78, 85, 135, 136, 137, 138, 169, 199, 200, 202, 203
MacDonald, Adm. Wesley L. 127
MacKay Radio 99
Maeda, Rear Adm. Minora 120, 121
Maejima, Toshihide 53, 59
Magellan, Ferdinand 135
Magic 17, 37, 39, 57, 63, 66, 82, 85, 155, 159, 161, 169, 185
Mahan 129
Malinta Tunnel 139
Manila 136, 137, 138
Mao Tse-Tung 20
Marblehead 135, 140

Marco Polo Bridge 20
Marcus Island 151
Marshall, Gen. Army Chief of Staff George 39, 55, 57, 61, 64, 69, 85, 86, 87, 88, 89, 94, 96, 97, 98, 117, 122, 136, 137, 138, 158, 160, 168, 169, 170, 171, 182, 196, 199, 200, 201
Marshall Islands 44, 56, 69, 117, 126, 127, 128, 129, 130, 131, 132, 139, 143, 144, 145, 146, 148, 161, 197, 200
Martin, Maj. Gen. Frederick L. 30, 47, 161
Martin-Bellinger Report 30, 161
Maryland 106, 114, 120
Masterman, John Sir 41, 163, 164
Matsumura, Heita 105
Matsuo, Sub Lt. Keiu 53, 59
Mayfield, Irving 58, 80
McClusky, LCDR Wade 146
McCollum, Arthur H. 27, 30, 73, 86, 87, 91, 122, 160, 161
McCrea, John 85, 169
McCullough, Capt. Richard 70, 101
McDonald, Adm. Wesley 203
McMorris, Charles 200
Meiji Mutsuhito 46
Menzies, Stewart 91, 163
MI-6 40, 41, 162, 163, 188
MI-8 12
Mid-Pacific Radio Direction Finder 70, 71, 73
Midway 10, 46, 49, 55, 61, 69, 70, 79, 101, 102, 103, 108, 119, 121, 122, 125, 127, 129, 130,134, 143, 144, 145, 158, 165, 184, 199, 202
Miles, Gen. Sherman 48, 84, 85, 87, 88, 166, 168
Mindanao 138
Minneapolis 128, 130, 131, 143, 148
Mississippi 33
Modus Vivendi 57, 61, 62, 64, 95, 173, 174, 184
Moffett, W.A. 24
Monaghan 127
Moore, Maj. Gen. George 135
Morgenstern, Capt. George 123
Morgenthau, Henry 171
Mori, Mrs. 80
Morison, Rear Adm. Samuel Eliot 130, 131
Most Secret 112
Mugford 128
Muller, Heinrich 184
Murata, Lt. Shigeharu 43, 61, 105, 108
Musashi 55
Mutsuhito, Emperor Meiji 2

224　Index

Nagano, Adm. Osami 45, 51, 56, 73, 97
Nagato 86
Nagi Tsuyoshi 105
Nagumo, Vice Adm. Chuichi 31, 32, 43, 44, 45, 50, 52, 53, 59, 61, 68, 70, 71, 72, 76, 77, 98, 101, 117, 118, 119, 120, 121, 127, 129, 139, 140, 141, 142, 171, 174, 193
Naito, LCDR Takeshi 54
Nakai, Lt. Kazuo 147
Nanking 21
National Security Agency 14
Naval Court of Inquiry 123, 161
Naval Gen. Staff 45, 56, 59, 140, 142
Nave, Eric 93
Neches 128, 129, 130, 131, 132, 145
Negato 52, 121
Negotiations Off 62, 158
Neosho 127, 143, 148
Nevada 108, 114, 120
New Mexico 33
Newman, CDR Irving 157, 175, 195
Newton, Rear Adm. John 79, 143
Nichols Field 70, 137
Nielson Field 135, 137
Nimitz, Adm. Chester W. 120, 144, 145, 146, 151, 152, 153, 198
Nine Power Treaty (Washington Conference Treaty) 19
Nomura, Adm. Kichisaburo 32, 36, 37, 41, 42, 43, 53, 56, 57, 66, 73, 83, 84, 85, 90, 95, 116, 155, 168
North Carolina 55
Northern Expedition 18
Northhampton 150
Noyes, Rear Adm. Leigh 39, 48, 52, 66, 83, 84, 122, 196, 200, 202

Oahu 58, 61, 72, 75, 76, 80, 86, 87, 88, 90, 103, 104, 105, 107, 108, 111, 112, 119, 131, 133, 143, 151, 155, 161, 163, 164, 184, 197, 200, 201, 202, 203
O'Donnell, Lt. Jerry 79
Office of Naval Communications 14, 15, 16, 17, 27, 48, 83, 122, 176, 196, 200
Office of Naval Intelligence 14, 16, 17, 27, 30, 31, 33, 36, 40, 48, 57, 74, 75, 84, 91, 122, 155, 160, 161, 165, 176, 194, 198
Ogg, Robert 6, 70, 71, 101, 175
Oggi 165
Oglala 105, 115
O'Hare, LCDR Edward 149
Ohnesorge, Dr. Wilhelm 178

Oil Embargo 47, 57
Oishi, CDR Tomatsu 44, 117
Oklahoma 105, 107, 114, 120
Okumura, Katsuzo 90
Onishi, Takijiru 50
Ono, LCDR Kenjiro 44
OP-20-G 17, 34, 36, 37, 57, 66, 67, 81, 82, 83, 86, 98, 99, 101, 102, 176, 192, 200, 201
Opana Mobile Radar Unit 90, 117
Open Door Policy 11
Orange 23
Orin, Adm. Murfin 122
Orr, Col. Raymond 85
Orr, Robert 157, 158, 169, 195
Oshima, Hiroshi 37, 173
Outerbridge, Capt. William W. 86, 89

PA-K2 code 81, 82, 99, 192
Pan-AM 125, 162
Panay 21
Parker, Frederick 159
Parker, Maj. George 135
Patterson 128
Peacock Point 132, 133
Peale Island 125, 150
Pearl Harbor 25, 26, 27, 29, 30, 31, 32, 33, 34, 35, 36, 37, 38, 40, 41, 42, 43, 44, 45, 48, 49, 50, 51, 52, 53, 54, 55, 56, 58, 59, 60, 61, 65, 66, 67, 68, 69, 70, 72, 73, 74, 75, 76, 79, 80, 81, 82, 85, 86, 87, 88, 89, 90, 91, 92, 93, 95, 96, 98, 99, 101, 103, 104, 105, 107, 108, 110, 112, 113, 114, 117, 118, 119, 120, 121, 122, 123, 124, 127, 128, 129, 131, 132, 133, 135, 136, 137, 139, 142, 143, 145, 147, 148, 149, 151, 153, 154, 155, 156, 157, 158, 159, 160, 161, 162, 163, 164, 165, 166, 168, 169, 170, 171, 172, 174, 175, 176, 177, 182, 183, 184, 185, 187, 188, 189, 190, 192, 193, 194, 195, 196, 197, 198, 200, 201, 202
Pease, LCDR George 71, 157
Pennsylvania 33, 11, 12
Pensacola 148
Perry, Commodore Matthew C. 9, 10, 24
Perry, Secretary of Defense William 203
Pfennigwerth, Ian 93
Phelps 127
Philippine Islands 135, 136, 138, 139, 140, 160, 165, 166, 192, 200, 202, 203
Phillips, Tom Sir 78
Polk, Frank L. 7
Polmar, Norman 202

Poorten, Gen. Heinter 60, 75, 94, 156, 166
Popov, Dusko 40, 41, 91, 98, 162, 163, 164, 165, 188, 194, 195, 200
Port Darwin 140
Port Moresby 102, 153
Porter 129
Portland 127, 153
Potomac 38
Prange, Gordon W. 66, 68, 70
Prince of Wales 78, 135, 139, 177, 196
Purple 23, 27, 29, 30, 32, 33, 35, 37, 38, 39, 46, 48, 51, 52, 57, 62, 73, 76, 81, 82, 83, 99, 155, 159, 161, 162, 168, 176, 200
Putnam, Maj. Paul 132
Pye, Vice Adm. William 129, 130, 131, 132, 133
Pyle, Ernie 97

Rabaul 139, 148, 149, 152, 153
Radio Direction Finders (RDF) 201
Rainbow Five 136
Raleigh 105, 114
Ralph Talbot 128
Ranger 144
Ranneft, Capt. Johan E.M. 74, 75
Rawie, Lt. Wilmer 147
RCA Radio and Globe Wireless 123
Red Book 15, 16, 17
Red Code 14, 22
Redman, Capt. Joseph J. 83, 200
Reichpost 178, 183
Repulse 78, 135, 139, 177, 196
Richardson, Adm. James O. 26, 27, 29, 123, 172
Rivera, Adm. Horacio, Jr. 203
Roberts, Justice Owen J. 122, 123, 201
Roberts Commission 98, 188
Rochefort, LCDR Joseph J., USN 16, 33, 52, 58, 59, 69, 70, 71, 72, 81, 97, 98, 102, 156, 175, 193, 194, 201
Rockwell, Rear Adm. Francis 138
Roger's Airport 162
Roi-Namur 147
Room 1649 15
Roosevelt, Pres. Franklin D. 1, 2, 3, 28, 32, 36, 37, 38, 41, 42, 45, 46, 47, 49, 51, 55, 57, 60, 61, 62, 63, 64, 65, 74, 76, 78, 84, 85, 86, 91, 92, 93, 98, 99, 116, 117, 122, 123, 133, 138, 158, 161, 163, 164, 165, 171, 172, 173, 174, 177, 178, 182, 183, 184, 185, 194, 197, 198, 201
Roosevelt, Col. James 64, 173
Roosevelt, Theodore 28

Index

Rose, Maj. Elmer 65
Rout, Leslie B. 164

Safford, Lt. Laurence F., USN 15, 16, 27, 52, 59, 66, 67, 76, 83, 84, 96, 102, 176, 192, 200
Saint Louis 115, 145, 147, 199
Sakagami, Commander Goro 44
Sakaibara, Shigemitsu 134
Salamaua 153
San Francisco 128, 130, 131
San Francisco's Twelve District 44
Saratoga 24, 120, 122, 127, 128, 130, 131, 132, 143, 144, 148
Sarnoff, David 58
Sasbe, LCDR Otojiro 44
Sasebo Bay 58
Sazanami 120
Schivers, Robert L. 50
Schmitt, Father Aloysius 107
Schofield Barracks 49, 86
Schreiber, Ricardo Rivera 27, 91
Schultz, Lt. Lester 84
Second London Naval Treaty 30
Section 8 (MI-8) 7
Seki, Kohichi 29
Selective Service Act 26
Selfridge 80, 128
Sellstrom, Ensign Edward R. 149
Sevareid, Eric 48, 165, 188
Sharp, Brig. Gen. William 135
Shaw 114
Sherman, Capt. F.C. 79
Sherrod, Robert 97
Shidehara, Kijuro 19
Shimada, Keiichi 73
Shimada, Shigetaro 51
Shimazaki, LCDR Shigekazu 51, 61, 112
Shimizu, Vice Adm. Mitsumi 43, 193
Shindo, Saburo 61
Shivers, Robert L. 34
Shokaku 55, 58, 67, 110, 111, 112, 139, 140, 141, 153
Short, Lt. Gen. Walter C. 31, 42, 48, 58, 86, 96, 98, 111, 117, 122, 123, 155, 158, 162, 170, 198, 200, 201, 203, 204
SIGABA 17
Signal Intelligence Service (SIS) 17, 28, 83
Slawson, CDR Paul Sidney 75
Smith, Col. Bedell 85, 168
Smith, Michael 177
Sorge, Richard 65
Soryu 58, 67, 105, 112, 121, 127, 129, 130, 131, 133, 134, 139, 140, 192
South Dakota 198
South Manchurian Railroad 20
Southern Cross 68

SPENAVO 159, 200
Spence, Congressman Floyd 31, 155
Stahlman, James G. 85, 169
Stalin 22
Stark, Adm. Harold R. 29, 30, 35, 38, 39, 40, 48, 51, 52, 55, 57, 61, 64, 69, 73, 84, 85, 86, 87, 88, 89, 98, 101, 112, 122, 129, 133, 144, 154, 155, 158, 159, 161, 169, 170, 171, 172, 185, 198, 199, 200, 201
Station AE 15
Station Baker 15
Station CAST 15, 27, 29, 33, 35, 36, 72, 73, 81, 101, 156, 157, 158, 176, 193, 194, 200, 201
Station FRUMEL 15
Station George 34, 35, 36
Station H 15, 60, 71, 72, 73, 74, 77, 97, 100, 101, 156, 157, 158, 171, 174, 175, 184, 193, 201
Station ITEM 15, 157, 193
Station King 15, 71, 157, 175, 184, 193, 195
Station P 15
Station Sail 71, 157, 193
Station US 97
Stephenson, Sir William 41, 64, 163, 164, 173
Stimson, Secretary of War Henry L. 13, 41, 45, 48, 51, 55, 63, 64, 84, 85, 88, 95, 98, 99, 112, 117, 123, 169, 170, 185
Stinnett, Robert B. 69, 71, 72, 73, 77, 79, 97, 100, 101, 156, 175, 193, 194, 195, 201
Straits of Tsushima 3
Suganami, Lt. Masaharu 104
Sugiyama, Gen. Hajime 45
Sun Yat-sen, Dr. 20
Sung Chi-yuen, Gen. 20
Surabaya 140
Sutherland, Brig. Gen. Richard 136
Suzuki, LCDR Suguru 53, 59, 100, 156

Tachibani, LCDR Itaru 34, 47, 201
Tadeo 117
Taiyo Maru 53, 54, 59
Takahashi, LCDR Kakuichi 104
Tangier 127, 128, 129, 130, 132, 133
Tanikaze 121
Taranto Bay 27, 40, 91, 93, 162, 163, 188
Tarawa 139
Taroa 146, 147
Tatekawa, Yoshitsugu 19
Tatsuta Maru 29
Taussig, Rear Adm. J.K. 24

Taylor, Lt. Kenneth 112
Tennessee 107, 120
Thayer, Dr. Frank 185
Thorpe, Gen. Elliot 75, 166
Thurmond, Sen. Strom 31, 155, 156
Tillman, John 177, 194
Timor 140
Togo, Shigenori 56, 57, 74
Tojo, Gen. Hideki 51
Toland, John 70, 71, 156, 157, 162, 165, 166, 175
Tomioka, Rear Adm. Sadatoshi 42, 56, 59, 121
Tone 55, 61, 67, 71, 104, 121, 129, 140, 192
Tora, Tora, Tora 105, 112
Torres Strait 31, 44, 154
Treaty of Paris 10, 125
Tricycle 40, 162
Trincomalee 141, 142
Tripartite Pact 25, 37, 45, 56
Truk 139, 148
Turner, Rear Adm. Richmond Kelly 30, 31, 33, 34, 35, 39, 40, 48, 55, 73, 76, 84, 103, 112, 154, 155, 161, 170, 187, 194, 197, 198, 199
Twelfth Naval District 157, 175, 195

Ultra 83
U.S. Army Forces Far East 135, 137
Urakaze 121
Uritsky 68, 69, 78, 79
Ushio 120
Utah 105, 108, 120

Vacant Sea Order 31, 68, 79, 154, 155, 197, 199, 200
Verkuyl, Col. J.A. 60, 75, 94, 166, 192
Verona 173
Vestal 106, 107, 115
Vetterlein, Kurt 178, 183
Visayas 135

Wainwright, Maj. Gen. Jonathan 138
Wake Island 44, 46, 49, 55, 61, 69, 83, 84, 89, 107, 121, 125, 126, 127, 128, 130, 131, 132, 133, 134, 139, 140, 143, 144, 145, 148, 150, 151, 158, 165, 193, 199, 200, 202
Walsh, Bishop James E. 32
War Plan 46, 197
Ward 86
Washington 55
Washington Naval Conference 11
Washington Naval Treaty 30

Watson, Maj. Gen. Edwin 63
WE WE Code 34, 36
Welch, Lt. George S. 23, 112
Wenger, Lt. Joseph 27
West Virginia 105, 107, 120
Wheeler Field 49, 61, 105, 111, 112, 113, 162, 163
White, Harry Dexter 173
Whitlock, Capt. Duane 101, 156, 201
Wilkes Island 125, 132, 133, 134
Wilkinson, Rear Adm. Theodore 48, 74, 84
Williams Ward Burroughs 127

Winds Message 192
Woodrough, Fred 82, 192
Woodward, Farnsley C. 81, 82
Worden 127
Wotje 146, 147

Yamaguchi, Capt. Bunjiro 120, 121
Yamaguchi, Rear Adm. Tamon 32, 52, 129
Yamamoto, Adm. Isoroku 26, 41, 42, 43, 44, 45, 50, 52, 56, 92, 97, 119, 121, 193
Yamato 55

Yardley, Herbert O. 12, 13, 14, 22
Yokohama 156
Yorktown 33, 122, 144, 145, 146, 151, 153
Yoshikawa, Ensign Takeo (Morimura Tadashi) 29, 30, 44, 48, 49, 53, 54, 58, 81, 99, 155, 159, 166, 168, 194, 196, 200, 201
Young, Robert S. 164
Yubari 127, 152
Yunagi 152

Zuikaku 55, 58, 67, 111, 112, 139, 140, 141, 153

www.ingramcontent.com/pod-product-compliance
Lightning Source LLC
Chambersburg PA
CBHW060342010526
44117CB00017B/2925